AF213638

ONTOLOGY IN INFORMATION SCIENCE

Edited by **Ciza Thomas**

Ontology in Information Science
http://dx.doi.org/10.5772/65599
Edited by Ciza Thomas

Contributors

Farzad Sanati, Patricia Bertin, Ivo Pierozzi Junior, Claudia Regina Delaia Machado, Alessandra Rodrigues Da Silva, Mauricio Almeida, Christiano Pessanha, Renata Barcelos, Bohdan Hejna, Boris Fomin, Tamara Kachanova, Oleg Fomin, Larysa Globa, Rina Novogrudska, Alexander Koval, Vyacheslav Senchenko, Fethi Ghazouani, Imed Riadh Farah, Basal Solaiman, Kingsley Okoye, Syed Islam, Usman Naeem, Wulystan Mtega, Mpho Ngoepe, Stein E. Johansen, Frank Stumpe

Published by InTech
Janeza Trdine 9, 51000 Rijeka, Croatia

Publishing Process Manager Martina Usljebrka
Technical Editor SPi Global
Cover InTech Design team

First published March, 2018
Printed in Croatia
Legal deposit, Croatia: National and University Library in Zagreb

Additional hard copies can be obtained from orders@intechopen.com

Ontology in Information Science, Edited by Ciza Thomas
p. cm.
Print ISBN 978-953-51-3887-7
Online ISBN 978-953-51-3888-4

For EU product safety concerns:
IN TECH d.o.o., Prolaz Marije Krucifikse Kozulić 3, 51000 Rijeka, Croatia,
info@intechopen.com or visit our website at intechopen.com.

Meet the editor

Dr. Ciza Thomas is currently working as professor and head of Electronics and Communication Department of College of Engineering, Trivandrum, India. Her area of expertise is network security with research interest in the fields of information security, data mining, sensor fusion, pattern recognition, information retrieval, digital signal processing, and image processing. She has publications in more than 40 international journals and international conference proceedings. She has edited many books in the field of sensor fusion, data mining, complexity, sustainability, and innovation and also published six book chapters in the field of network security and pattern recognition. She is a reviewer of more than 10 reputed international journals including IEEE transactions on signal processing, IEEE transactions on neural networks, International Journal of Network Security, International Journal of Network Management, and IEEE-John Wiley International Journal on Security and Communications Network. She is a recipient of achievement award in 2010 and the e-learning IT award in 2014 from the government of Kerala.

Contents

Preface

In recent years, with the fast development of the Internet, the available information online has increased exponentially. Information systems involve many fields like computer science, psychology, political science, linguistics, operation research, sociology, and organizational theory. Information systems provide the required information for decision-making by creating, processing, and storing information to help humans make meaningful and rational decisions. Information science provides many of the vital foundations to manage the huge quantity of information for supporting knowledge management. This was through catalogues and bibliographic information in the beginning, extending to text documents and now to multimedia databases available on the Internet. The developments in documentation methods and practices support in classifying the vast spread of human knowledge for access by end users. The advances in computations of information science, mainly the rigorous processing and search using computers, have simplified the information retrieval. Yet, many significant challenges remain.

Standardization and universal terminology for information exchange and communication are the need of the hour. Hence, there is a growing interest in the application of ontologies that use the semantics of information from various sources and provide a standardized and concise description. This helps to solve modeling and classification problems in different areas of information retrieval, knowledge management, and artificial intelligence. Ontology in information systems aims to facilitate better human decision-making with inferences based on domain knowledge by retrieving context-sensitive information, which could be reused. Ontology formalizes the relationships among the concepts, which makes computers and humans interpret the semantic relationships among the concepts and infer the implicit knowledge. Thus, ontologies aid a higher level of applicability with the ability to define relations, strong semantics, and better clarity over the conventional techniques used in information science.

Ontology is a cross-disciplinary field concerning the precise specifications of the terms in a particular domain and the relations among them that support the building of shared conceptualizations of particular domains. It is mainly used among those sharing information in a particular domain as ontology defines a universal vocabulary in the domain. In order to create an effective representation, it is necessary to know about the involved objects and properties and relations in general. This provides robust taxonomies of the types of entities used in given application domains. This helps in better analysis of domain knowledge, separating it well from the operational knowledge. It also enables different application systems to reuse the same program elements over and over again and in a way simplifying the application systems.

Ontology can find a large number of applications in the field of information science. This book on *Ontology in Information Science* provides researchers and practitioners working in the field of ontology and information science an opportunity to share their theories, methodologies, experiences, and experimental results related to ontology development and application in various areas. It also includes the design aspects of domain ontologies considering the architecture, development strategy, and selection of tools.

The book spans the entire spectrum of information science with applications of ontology. This book constitutes 12 chapters, selected after a thorough review. Each chapter gives an explicit conceptualization of the semantics and pragmatics of a particular domain. The authors are mainly researchers and academicians with diverse domain interests from the fields of computer science, library science, information science, knowledge management, e-commerce, and artificial intelligence. In this book, through the various chapters, the authors investigate different areas for their specific research problems with a deep knowledge of existing literature and available ontology design methodologies to design, develop, and build domain ontologies for each of the identified problems. Chapter I discusses an ontological approach of information architecture for organizations. Chapter II includes details of ontology for application development. Chapter III includes some examples of ontology model usage in engineering fields. Chapter IV proposes the semantic knowledge maps that include application modeling of the ontological nature of data and information governance. Chapter V proposes e-service composition ontology. Chapter VI discusses the ontology in IT projects based on OSM. Chapter VII presents ontology as a core process mining and query-enabling tool. Chapter VIII is on generating scientifically proven knowledge about ontology of open systems. Chapter IX is on semantic remote sensing scenes and its interpretation and change interpretation. Chapter X is the systematic unfolding of differential ontology from qualitative concept of information. Chapter XI is on strengthening the flow of agricultural knowledge among agricultural stakeholders. Chapter XII discusses the information transfer and thermodynamics point of view on Goedel proof.

The targeted beneficiaries of this book are the information system designers, developers, managers, decision-makers, and consumers for potential applications. The book aims to narrow the gap between theoretical and practical research and the marketable use of ontology in information system.

I thank the InTech publishing house, especially Publishing Process Manager, Ms. Martina Usljebrka, for their commitment to the success of the proposed book, the authors for their informative submissions, and the publishing team for their dedicated and hard work.

Prof. Ciza Thomas
Professor and Head, College of Engineering
Trivandrum, India

Chapter 1

Information Architecture for Organizations: An Ontological Approach

Maurício B. Almeida, Christiano P. Pessanha and Renata Barcelos

Additional information is available at the end of the chapter

http://dx.doi.org/10.5772/intechopen.69161

Abstract

In the scope of corporations, information and knowledge management are essential practices that are carried out through information systems. In this chapter, we discuss the foundations of an ontological-based architecture for organizing information and knowledge within corporations. Our research focus on three main efforts: (i) to shed some light on the ontological status of corporations, (ii) to understand the relations between corporate units, and (iii) to approach the duties that corporations have to manage. After presenting background theories, we analyze the corporation through two dimensions, namely, a descriptive and a normative. While the former approaches the structure of the corporation from the point of view of its units, the latter approaches it from the point of view of duties and obligations. The descriptive side of our investigation is conducted through principles of top-level formal ontologies; the normative side is addressed through the so-called social ontology. The relevance of developing such analysis rests on the need of a better understanding of corporations, its structures, and its activities. Such insight can provide a formal framework suitable to be applied in information systems, working in the context of modern technologies like the Semantic Web.

Keywords: corporation, ontology, theory of corporation, knowledge management

1. Introduction

In recent years, corporations have made significant investments in information and knowledge management initiatives mainly through the development of information systems. Among the many techniques utilized for this end, ontologies are an alternative that have received an increased amount of attention [1–3].

Ontology is a term originated in Philosophy also employed to describe a hierarchical structure composed by entities and relations for purposes of representation. The issue of defining ontologies lies on the fact that different research communities have adopted different perspectives: Computer Science, for example, Artificial Intelligence, Databases, and Software Engineering; Library and Information Science; and Logic and Philosophy, to mention but a few [4].

A diversity of initiatives for using ontologies in corporations can be found in the literature since the 1990s [5–8]. However, the research on ontologies lacks an applied ontology approach for corporations that mirror two main applications of ontologies: ontology as an inventory of entities for information systems modeling and ontology as a formal theory for purposes of automatic reasoning. This chapter presents an ongoing research that seeks to cover this gap. At this point of our ongoing research, we focus on three efforts: (i) to shed some light on the ontological status of corporations, (ii) to understand the relations between corporative units, and (iii) to approach the duties that a corporation has to manage.

In order to reach our purposes, we first present a background of formal theories and doctrines of the nature of corporation. Subsequently, we provide an analysis of the corporation through two dimensions, namely, a *descriptive* and a *normative*. In the *descriptive dimension*, we approach the structure of the corporation from the point of view of units and subunits; in the *normative dimension*, we approach the structure of the corporation from the point of view of its rights, duties, and obligations. In the descriptive side of our investigation, we employ principles and notions of top-level formal ontologies; in the normative side, we make use the so-called social ontology approach, including theories of social acts, speech acts, and document acts.

We believe in the relevance of developing this kind of analysis in order to improve the understanding of both corporations and the activities that take place within them. We also can provide a formal framework to be applied in the context of modern technologies like the Semantic Web. In addition, an ontological theory for corporations can be the basis for architecture for organizing information and knowledge within corporations, allowing the integration and coordination of the extensive variety of information systems in charge of corporate procedures.

The remaining part of the chapter is organized as follows: Section 2 provides some introductory background; Section 3 presents an overview of the main doctrines, legal and economic, about the nature of corporations; Section 4 addresses corporations through an ontological analysis; Section 5 discusses our findings; and finally, Section 6 presents our final remarks and prospects for future research.

2. Background

In order to properly understand our organization of entities that compose a corporation from an ontological point of view, we need to explain essentials of some subjects. This section brings those explanations organized as follows: Section 2.1 explains the basic of the discipline of ontology; Section 2.2 explains formal ontology and top-level ontology; Section 2.3 briefly presents ontological theories related with whole and parts; and finally, Section 2.4 deals with essentials of the social ontology.

2.1. Essentials of ontology

Ontology is a term that assumes diverse connotations in different scientific fields like Philosophy, Computer Science, and Library and Information Science.

In *Philosophy*, ontology is a branch of Metaphysics, which includes notions of being, identity, change over time, dependency, quality, and so forth. Systems of categories structured in hierarchical levels are the most important topic to be studied in any ontological approach. There are several philosophical systems of categories developed since ancient times, but new systems have been introduced in the last 50 years, for example, see [9–12].

It is worth mentioning a relevant distinction about ontology within Philosophy, which is not always apparent, but is important for our purposes here. The term ontology, in general, refers to which one could call "natural ontology." Such a natural ontology corresponds to an exhaustive classification of natural types and relations by which entities are tied together. When one says "natural types," she should not consider the realm of artifacts created by humans [13]. In contrast, there is another philosophical approach one can call the ontology of the social reality, or "social ontology," which deals with the full range of human artifacts and social devices, for example, money, property, governments, nations, marriages, and so forth [14].

In *Computer and Information Science*, two senses for the term ontology are considered the most important: (i) the use of ontological principles to understand and represent reality, as support to modeling activities [15] and (ii) the representation of a domain of knowledge through a formal language to be processed by automatic reasoners [16]. In the former application, ontology is aligned with its original role of providing an account of reality; in the latter application, it corresponds to a software engineering artifact.

As a result of the current widespread prevalence of digital resources, new category systems for knowledge representational have been developed to meet specific goals of modeling, automatic reasoning, and information retrieval. The most currently referenced systems are DOLCE, which stands for *Descriptive Ontology for Linguistic and Cognitive Engineering* [17], and BFO, which stands for Basic Formal Ontology [18]. This kind of category system, in general is called as top-level ontology, conveys the two senses of the term ontology: they are computational artifacts founded in philosophical theories specified in a formal language.

In the context of the research conducted under the label applied ontology, a well-known approach is the so-called ontological realism [19]. The main instrument of ontological realism, largely applied in the information systems realm, is BFO. As a top-level ontology, BFO intends to define the most generic categories and provides means of categorizing entities in a domain to be represented. BFO has a large acceptance in medicine, biology, bioinformatics, and related fields.

2.2. Formal ontology and levels of BFO

Defining "formal ontology" is not a simple endeavor. Ref. [20], for example, dedicates a full chapter in trying to accomplish such a task. There are, certainly, several good definitions in the literature, but we do not discuss the merits of each one here. For the sake of simplicity, we adopt the notion of formal ontology as the set of terms specified in logical statements and applied to represent the reality in a domain. In this sense, BFO can be called a top-level formal ontology. In the remaining part of the section, we describe the BFO's levels.

BFO is comprised by some levels of well-characterized kinds of entities. We do not describe all levels here, but just that one required to understand the essentials of BFO, which is adopted as the starting point of our investigation. A full account of BFO can be found in Ref. [21]. Several examples presented here are due to Ref. [22]. All levels and categories mentioned are depicted in **Figure 1**.

BFO's first level has the general designation of "entity." The second level (below) acknowledges two distinct groups of entities. On the one hand, it considers substantial entities called *continuants*; on the other hand, it considers processual entities called *occurrents*. Continuants endure over time while maintaining their identity. Examples of continuants are a person, a fruit, an orchestra, and a law. Occurrents happen, unfold, and develop through time. Examples of occurrents are the respiration and the functioning of a body organ, a part of your life.

Listed under continuants, BFO's third level contains three categories: (i) *independent continuants*, (ii) *specifically dependent continuants*, and (iii) *generically dependent continuants*. Independent continuants are bearers of qualities, that is, there are qualities that inhere in them, for example, the red color that inheres in a tomato. Specifically dependent continuants are entities that depend on one or more specific independent continuants for their existence, for example, the pain in my

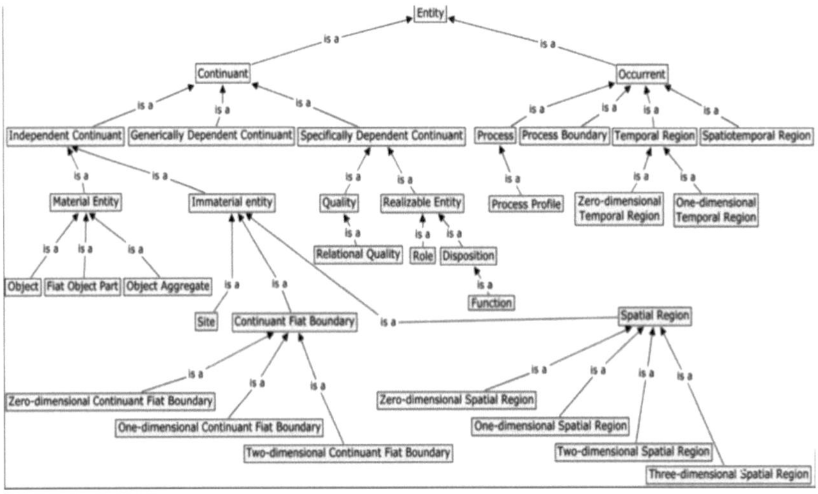

Figure 1. BFO top-level ontology, its levels, and its categories. Source: [21].

head depends on me, the disposition of fruits to decay depends on fruits, and the role of a professor in a university depends on a person. Generically dependent continuants are entities that also depend on independent continuants, but in contrast to specifically dependent continuants, the instance that works as bearer can undergo changes over time. One example is the Odyssey by Homers that has many bound copies.

Under occurrents, BFO's third level contains four categories: (i) *processes*, (ii) *process boundaries*, (iii) *temporal regions*, and (iv) *spatial temporal regions*. Processes are entities that unfold in time, have temporal parts, and always maintain a relationship of participation with independent continuants. Examples are the process of digestion, the course of a disease, and the flight of a plane. Process boundaries, temporal regions, and spatiotemporal regions are not described since they are not important for our purposes.

BFO's fourth level of continuants contains important categories, such as (i) *material entities*, for example, *objects* and *aggregates*; examples of objects are an apple and a mountain; examples of aggregates are an orchestra and a pile of stones; (ii) *qualities* are properties of entities, for example, the color or the smell of something; and (iii) *realizable entities* are entities whose instances contain periods of actualization in the course of their existence, for example, the role of antibiotics in healing a disease and the disposition of people to grow. The fourth level of occurrents also contains categories for representing the world, such as *processes profile* and *temporal regions*.

2.3. Essentials of mereology and granular partitions

A variety of formal frameworks is available for creating and testing ontological developments. Indeed, one can count with a range of theories deriving from the advances of formal logic and set theory in terms of which ontologies can be formulated. These theories allow ontologists to both express intuitive principles in a rigorous way and test ontologies developed for consistency and completeness [13].

One can argue why it would be required to resort to theories that deal with parts and wholes to explain corporations. As we will see later in this chapter (Section 4), one can benefit from employing these aforementioned theories in describing the descriptive dimension of corporations, which involves units, subunits, and members. Two well-known of these theories—*mereology* and *Theory of Granular Partitions*—are explained in the remaining part of this section (respectively, in Sections 2.3.1 and 2.3.2).

2.3.1. Mereological principles

Mereology is a theory that deals with the relations of parts to the whole and the relations of part to part within a whole, from a formal point of view. There are two main groups of principles one can use to explain these relations between parts and wholes: *principles of decomposition*, which take one from a whole to its parts, and *principles of composition*, which take one from the parts to the whole. These principles, in addition to some basic notions, give rise to the core of mereological theories. All introductory notions presented in this section are based mainly on Refs. [23, 24].

A single part of relation between two elements—*x is part of y*—has the mathematical properties of *reflexivity*, *transitivity*, and *asymmetry* [25]. An example of *reflexivity* is John resembles himself; an example of *transitivity* is if John is in front of Harry and Harry is in front of Bill, then John is also in front of Bill; an example of *symmetry* is if John is married to Mary, Mary is married to John.

These properties capture some intuitions what people have regarding the aforementioned properties and the part-whole relation. The reflexivity property means that everything is part of itself; the transitivity property means that any part of any part of a thing is itself part of that thing; the asymmetry property means two distinct things cannot be part of each other. These notions compose what is usually called *basic mereology*. It is the common basis for any part-whole theory, but other properties can be added to this basic framework, like *equality*, *proper part*, *overlap*, and *underlap*.

The first extension to the *basic mereology* is called *extensional mereology*. It involves the so-called decomposition principles: principles that take one from a whole to its parts. The intuitive notion behind decomposition is that whenever something has a proper part (a part that does not correspond to the whole), it actually has more than one. In other words, nothing can have a single proper part, which implies the existence of a remainder between a whole and its proper parts (*mereological difference*) in any process of the decomposition.

There is more than one possibility to capture the intuition behind the mereological difference. One possibility is called *supplementation*, a principle holding that every proper part of a whole must be supplemented by another part, which is disjointed from the first one. There is a slightly different version of this principle known as *strong supplementation*, which corresponds to the idea that if an object fails to include another one among its parts, then there must be a remainder. The strong principle of supplementation gives rise to a property named *extensionality*, which ensures that entities are completely defined by their parts and that no composite objects with the same proper parts can be distinguished.

Finally, the so-called classical mereology involves *composition principles*, which are principles that take one from the parts to the whole. The notion behind composition is that whenever there are things, there exists a whole that is formed exactly by those things. This means that there is a unique sum for arbitrary entities. The uniqueness is guaranteed by the property of extensionality, implied by the principle of supplementation in the scope of the extensional mereology. The existence of this sum implies that there is always a fusion between two or more parts, called *mereological sum*.

There is more than one possibility to capture the notion behind the mereological sum, namely, the *upper bound* and the *sum*. The *upper bound* of two objects is another object of which both the original ones are parts. The *sum* is a mereological upper bound of which any part overlaps one of the two individuals summed [26]. In other words, a mereological sum between two objects must be something composed exactly of their parts and nothing else.

2.3.2. Granular Partition Theory principles

Granular partitions are a name for cognitive devices that people can employ to label, list, sort, or catalog activities performed by other people. Examples of granular partitions are lists, hierarchies, classifications, and so forth. Ref. [27] introduced the notion of granular partitions corresponding to a generalization of the concept of classes as mereological sums originated in set theory. All principles presented in this section are based on Ref. [25].

As mentioned, there are several kinds of partitions, and all of them consider the existence of objects. In the context of granular partitions, an object is everything existent that can be recognized by some units of partition. Objects can be either *bona fide objects* or *fiat objects*: while the former exists independently of human partitioning or demarcating activities, the latter exists only because of the very same activities. Indeed, partition units can recognize fiat objects from limits based on human cognition, and fiat objects are created through the projection of partitions in a portion of reality [28]. This distinction is very relevant for the purposes of this chapter, as we will make clear ahead (Section 4).

A formal Theory of Granular Partitions is composed by two different theories: Theory A reflects that partition units can recognize fiat objects based on human cognition and Theory B explains how fiat objects are created through the projection of partitions in reality. These two theories (**Figure 2**) are the mereological counterparts of set theory: Theory A is the counterpart of the relations between sets and subsets; Theory B is the counterpart of relations between a set and its member.

Theory A is a theory for formation of partitions. A partition can have *units* and *subunits*, also called, respectively, *cells* or *subcells*. A unit is defined by its position within a partition and by its relations to other units, for example, the relation between the class of fruits and the class of food. Conversely, Theory B is the theory between partitions and reality, for example, the relation between the fruit partition and fruits in reality.

Units in partitions can be nested one inside another constituting what is called *subunit*. The *unit-subunit relation* has several mathematical properties that are not important for our purposes here. Relevant, nonetheless, is its property of transitivity, which allows the formation of chains of units structured in a way that a *maximal unit* encompasses all the other

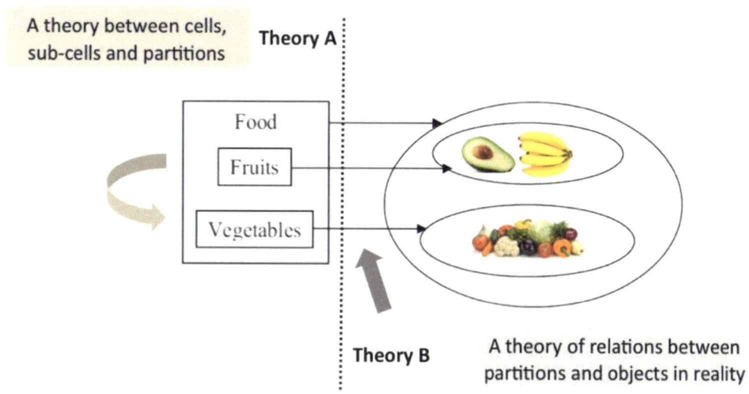

Figure 2. Theory of Granular Partitions. Source: adapted from Ref. [25].

existent subunits until to reach a *minimal unit*. So, if two units of a partition overlap, then one is subunit of the other.

Theory B involves the projection of partitions in reality and location of objects in the partition. Projection is then a relation, which is successful if an object on which a unit is projected is located in that unit. So, the result of a successful projection has a location as a result in two directions: from the mind to the world and from the world to the mind. Ref. [25] makes this point clear through an example:

> *"Projection is like the relation which holds between your shopping list and the items which, if your shopping trip is successful, you will actually buy. Location is like the relation which obtains between the items you have bought and the new list your mother makes after your return, as she checks off those items which you have in fact succeeded in bringing back with you."*

2.4. Essentials of s-acts, d-acts, mental states, and intentionality

In order to reach the aforementioned descriptive and normative analysis, we need to approach notions of some relevant related subjects, namely, *social acts*, based on the work of Reinach[1]; *mental acts*, *speech acts*, *intentionality*, and *document acts*, mainly based on Searle [29–34].

The theories that try to explain people's acts—spoken or written—as well as results of these acts were first advanced by Reinach. Reinach's theory, based on ideas of Husserl's[2] phenomenology, suggested the existence of an a priori law containing juridical concepts free of human interpretation and intellectually self-evident. In this effort of establishing the grounds of a theory independent of the positive law, the *spontaneous acts* were an important concept defined as the set of experiences a person could have in which the very same person has an active participation.

Some experiences require the existence of a subject for reference. Reinach called them non-self-directable. Such experiences involve acts that, in addition to refer to another subject, have to be perceived by the very same subject. Acts that need to be perceived are then called *social acts*, actually acts with intentional roots. Speech acts and document acts, which are relevant for the goals of this chapter, were developed from the social acts theory.

Mental states are another fundamental concept that needs some clarifications, since it contributes to the understanding of speech acts and intentionality (explained later in this section). Mental states are phenomena approached in Neuroscience and Philosophy of Mind.

In Philosophy of Mind, for example, Ref. [32] furnishes a view that avoids the mind-body dualism. In such view, one can realize an attempt to harmonize the mechanistic and the materialist accounts of the functioning of mind. In addition, this attempt includes an explanation of both subjective and intentional aspects of the human consciousness without to ignore the *qualia*—what constitutes the experience of to be conscious—of the mental experiences possessed and known by people.

[1] Adolf Bernhard Philipp Reinach, 1883–1917, German philosopher, jurist and law theorist
[2] Edmund Gustav Albrecht Husserl, 1859–1938, German philosopher and mathematician

Such approach to mental phenomena guides one to an account of Philosophy of Language regarded as a branch of Philosophy of Mind [32]. The structural similarity between mind and language impacts in Searle's approach to speech acts, one of the most known and well-founded contemporary theories.

> *"It should not seem at all surprising to us that the structure of linguistic acts and the structure of mental states should be similar, because one of the chief functions of language is to express our thoughts and feelings, and even when we are performing speech acts […]."* [32]

The *Theory of Speech Acts* was originally proposed by Austin[3] and conceived as a method to analyze philosophical questions. The analysis departed from the examination of language as a way to perform acts through words. Speech Acts Theory proposes that the elementary units to use and to understand natural language are speech acts. A speech act is the basic unit of meaning, constituted by three connected dimensions: *locutionary acts, illocutionary acts,* and *perlocutionary acts*.

The locutionary act corresponds to the linguistic dimension, which considers sentences endowed with both meaning and reference and employed according to grammatical rules. The illocutionary act, which is the core of the speech act, keeps as a fundamental aspect called *illocutionary force*. This force, which consists of the performative acts itself, represents the kind of act performed. For example, in the proposition "I promise to pay you tomorrow," there is an utterance (verb "promise") that constitutes the own act of promising and does not represent any description of intentions or of mental states. When a person utters the sentence, the promise is concretized, that is, the force that characterizes the act is the promise.

Searle [30] develops a classification of speech acts, in substitution of the initial proposal of Austin, which presents the following kinds of acts: *assertive, commissive, directive, declarative,* and *expressive*. In addition, seven components of illocutionary force are defined. Then, the result of a speech act is the combination three factors: (i) a proposition, which can be true or false; (ii) the semantic content related to the facts of the world; and (iii) the illocutionary force added to the proposition.

One issue regarding the speech acts is its evanescence, a result of its inherent orality. This makes the range of acting of a speech act temporally constrained. Smith [34] tries to approach this issue through the *Theory of Document Acts*. Indeed, a speech act exists only in the moment of its performance; documents, on the other hand, are continuant entities able to persist in time while absorbing modifications through its history.

In small communities, promises and obligations can be established through speech acts, but such compromises cannot be maintained in large and multi-faceted societies. Promises and obligations transcend the local character of personal contacts, since the psychological facts that could guarantee the fulfillment of a promise, mainly based on human memories, are not enough in large communities. On the other hand, documents maintain its identity through the time, and one can manipulate it in archiving, destroying, signing, registering, inspecting, or transferring it. Then, documents made possible new and persistent kinds of relations and

[3]John Langshaw Austin, 1911–1960, British philosopher of language

social entities that work as extensions of our memories. Documents do not only register information, but they can also be used to create a variety of social and institutional powers, which in turn allow the establishment of ways of life in society.

The last concept to be introduced here, which is relevant for the purposes of our goals in this chapter, is *intentionality*. It is a philosophical concept that traces back the medieval scholastics and was retrieved by Brentano,[4] employed to define a statute for the fact that human conscience is directed to something or is about something. The term was also later employed by Husserl, who advocated the idea that consciousness is always intentional. Indeed, the intentionality distinguishes a property of mental phenomena, namely, the property of being directed to an object, real or imaginary.

Nowadays, a very accepted account of intentionality is due to Ref. [31]. In such account statements can be bearers of meaning. The performance of an illocutionary act necessarily specifies a mental state of who utters it, since illocutionary acts exhibit satisfaction conditions identical to the respective mental states. The performance of illocutionary acts depends on the ability of the human cognition in specify intentional mental states associated to the very same illocutionary acts and in assigning to latter the same satisfaction conditions of the former.

3. The nature of corporations

There are several theories and doctrines about the nature of corporations in scientific fields like History, Politics, Moral and Ethics, Philosophy, Metaphysics, and Theology, to mention but a few. This section focuses on doctrines originated in two scientific fields—law and economics—which, in general, have been taken as authoritative in defining and explaining the nature of corporations.

3.1. The nature of organization in law theories

In the scope of law, there has been a lot of discussion about the nature of corporations since the ninth century. Indeed, the corporation is a product of Roman civil law, and Ancient Rome had already perfected the notion of corporation to include all legal attributes one can see in modern corporations today [35].

Pope Innocent IV[5] promulgated a theory about "corporate bodies." The idea that corporations are personae citae (fictitious persons) was firstly directed to ecclesiastical institutions. Indeed, since these kind of institution did not have body of soul, they could not be punished or excommunicated. The doctrine suggested that being a person was denied to civil groups because of the dominant conception of a person. Such conception was due to St. Thomas Aquinas and took one back to metaphysical discussions of Aristotle about the nature of substance [36].

[4]Franz Clemens Honoratus Hermann Brentano, 1838–1917, German philosopher
[5]Innocent IV, 1195–1254, Pope from 1243 to 1254

A substantial understanding of the legal nature of corporation had already existed when the English Crown began to charter the first business corporations in the fifteenth century. The first jurists to formally establish what a corporation is and what are its legal attributes were Sir Edward Coke, author of the treatise *The Law of Corporation*, from 1702, and later both Sir Willian Blackstone—author of *Commentaries on the Law*, from 1765—and Steward Kyd, author of *Corporation*, from 1793 [37].

These pioneering jurists, although bearing in mind ecclesiastical bodies, described the corporation in a form that also applies to current business corporations. A corporation would be a legal unit with its own legal rights and responsibilities; it is distinct from the individuals who are members constituting it over time; it is a creation of law and could achieve legal status by an act of the state.

These core attributes assigned to corporations in England were borrowed by American jurists and applied in America, where a corporation possessed some legal attributes: it could contract, sue, and be sued; it could acquire and dispose property; it has its own seal by which it could act as a body distinct from its members; its shares are transferable; its membership may change without affecting its perpetual existence; it cannot commit assault or treason; and it cannot serve as a trustee [38].

The classical formulation of these attributes has come to known as the "artificial person" doctrine of the corporation. This is one of the several doctrines and theories that arose trying to understand the notion of "corporate personality." Such a notion was needed to explain what would be the essence of this soulless and bodiless person. The orthodox doctrine of corporate personality considered that corporations are intangible legal entities. Thus, as a legal person, a corporation has a personality separated from the personality of the members that compose the very corporation.

In Anglo-American world, the orthodox statement was widespread. For example, law in United States[6] maintains that a corporation must be treated as a person. This extension of rights and obligations from a natural person to a corporation comes from the interpretation of the word "person" in the Fourteenth Amendment. However, in countries like France, Germany, and Italy, there was a great debate and different theories arose [39]: *Fiction Theory, Concession Theory, Group Personality Theory* or *Realist Sociological Theory, The Bracket Theory* or *Symbolist Theory, Purpose Theory* or *Theory of Zweck Vermogen, Hohfeld's Theory,* and *Kelsen's Theory.*

The so-called Fiction Theory—first advanced by *Savigny*[7]—debated who would be the real owner of a property considering that property, in law, can belong to a corporation. The solution was the creation of a sort of *fictitious person*, which is the owner of the corporate property. The corporation would be a creation of law having no existence apart from its individual members, who form the corporate group and whose acts are attributed to the corporate entity. In this context, the personality of a corporation would be different from that one of its members, and any change in membership does not affect the existence of the corporation.

[6]US Code: Title 1,1. Words denoting number, gender, and so forth. Legal Information Institute (LII)

[7]*Friedrich Carl von Savigny*, 1779–1861, German jurist and historian

The property of a corporation is not the same property of its members, since a corporation can go bankrupt, while its members remain rich.

Concession Theory—advanced by *Savigny*, *Dicey*[8], and *Salmond*[9]—is often mentioned as being part of Fiction Theory, but it has a different origin and rests on different interests. Actually, it is a product of a centralized model of national state that started to compete with the power of religious congregations and feudal organizations. Concession and Fiction Theories assert that corporations have no legal personality. However, while Fiction Theory is ultimately a Philosophical Theory suggesting that a corporation is a thing of the intellect, the concession theory focuses on the source of its legal power. Indeed, Concession Theory is indifferent to questions of reality and states that a juridical person is merely a concession of a national state.

Real Entity Theory, also called *Group Theory* and *Realist Sociological Theory*, was advanced mainly by *Althusius*[10] and *Gierke*.[11] This group of theorists focused on sociological facts and in the belief that collective groups (as corporations) have a real mind, a real will, and a real ability to action. Thus, a corporation would have a real existence even though it does not receive recognition from the state. According to this theory, the existence of a corporation is not based on any fiction, because it is a psychological reality. A corporation is a social organism, whose law has no power to create, but only to recognize.

Associational Theory, also called *Bracket Theory* or *Symbolist Theory*, was propounded by *von Jhering*[12] and others, suggesting that the juristic corporate personality is only a symbol employed to facilitate the working of corporate bodies. On the one hand, this theory follows fictitious theory in maintaining the existence of a corporation as a fiction metaphor; on the other hand, it states that the corporate personality is not created by the state because actually it does not exist; it is solely an abbreviated form to represent several people that are members of the corporation. Only members of the corporation are real persons, and the corporation is a merely economic device by which one can simplify the task of coordinating legal relations.

Purpose Theory, also called *the Theory of Zweck Vermogen*, is a variant of the Fiction Theory created by *Bekker*[13] and *von Brinz*[14] to explain the ownership in charitable corporations. It also considers a corporation as a fictitious entity but is focusing on the purpose of those who manage the property, instead of focusing on the ownership of property by an object. This theory asserts that only human beings could be subject matter of rights and duties. Thus, a juristic person is not a real person, but merely a property destined for particular purposes. As in the context the legal relations involving corporations, there is ownership, but no owner; a juristic person could not be equivalent to a group of persons. Rather, it would be based on objects and purposes.

[8]Albert Venn Dicey, 1835–1922, British jurist and constitutional theorist
[9]John William Salmond, 1862–1924, legal scholar, public servant and judge in New Zealand
[10]Johannes Althusius, 1563–1638, German jurist and Calvinist political philosopher
[11]Otto Friedrich von Gierke, 1841–1921, German legal scholar and historian
[12]Caspar Rudolph Ritter von Jhering, 1818–1892, German jurist
[13]Ernst Immanuel Bekker, 1827–1916, German jurist and professor
[14]Alois Ritter von Brinz, 1820–1887, German jurist and politician

There are also complementary theories of legal personality, like *Hohfeld's*[15] *Theory* and *Kelsen's*[16] *Theory*. The former declares that juristic persons are creations of arbitrary procedures. Human beings alone are capable of having both rights and duties, and when the law ascribes juristic personality to any group, it makes this merely as a procedure for dealing with legal rights. The latter said that there is no difference between the legal corporate personality and the individual personality. Indeed, the corporate personality would be only a technical personification of a set of norms that assign rights and duties to people.

3.2. The nature of the organization in economic theories

Economics and Management are research fields that maintain a special interest in de ning corporations insofar as they involve many aspects of the society and play a central role in economic analysis.

The context for evaluating the nature of corporations involves two basic entities: persons and ownership. In general, if people are subjects of property rights and things are objects of property rights, then people own things and things are owned by people. In the traditional sole-proprietorship corporation, the individual capitalist is the subject of the property right, and the corporate assets are the object of property right. In the partnership corporation, a group of individuals owns the assets jointly. In order to perform activities and reach goals, corporations enter in several contractual relations with other parties, like employees, suppliers, customers, etc. Within this scenario, whenever there is a withdrawal or an admission of a new partner, each contract has to be rewritten. In addition, when the corporation grows and numerous outside relations take place, the transaction costs can be prohibitively high.

The corporation is then a solution for the existence of multiple transactions, insofar as a group of individuals in creating a corporation also create an additional person who has the same legal capacity to own real assets as the partners themselves have. Outside parties enter into a contract with this additional person, independently of the number of shareholders.

Considering that to evaluate the nature of corporations, one has to understand both persons and ownership relations, she can realize that corporations play a dual role: they can be a person and they can be a thing. The corporation (as person) owns its assets, and it is owned (as thing) by shareholders. In the former case, it acts legally as a person; in the latter, it acts legally as a thing. This duality gives rise to discussions about the origin of the corporate personality, since a corporation is in reality neither a person nor a thing, but an entity endowed with both personality and thingness. The fact that a corporation can be owned by persons means that it is not a person, unless we consider that slavery exists; the fact that it can own other things does not allow it to be a thing, since things cannot own other things. This can be considered a sort of indeterminacy, in which law is unable to determine the legal nature of a corporation within its own system [40].

[15]Wesley Newcomb Hohfeld, 1879–1918, American jurist
[16]Hans Kelsen, 1881–1973, Austrian jurist, legal philosopher and political philosopher

Despite controversies, these theories bear a resemblance to aforementioned legal theories of corporate personality. Differently from legal theories, the modern theories in Economics and Management fields aim to explain the economic behavior.

Some theories consider two different mechanisms within the economy: the price system, which could not explain all the economic behavior, let alone the decisions taken within a corporation, and the hierarchy employed in corporations to allocate and reallocate resources. So, to delimit a corporation within the market, one should consider two kinds of relations: those internal to the corporation, namely, authority relations, and those external, namely, contract relations [41]. This theory, known as the *Evolutionary Theory*, has several representatives, for example, Refs. [42–44]. There are evidences that these theories are descendants of the already mentioned *Real Entity Theory*. Winter Sidney and Nelson [43] say that organizations know how to do things, and individuals can come and go. This seems very close to the premises of *Real Entity Theory*, in which corporations exist as real persons, as social organisms have a real will that enable them to decide how to do things.

Other theories propose that there is only one mechanism at work in modern economy, namely, the price mechanism. A theory like this is the so-called Contractual Theory of the Firm [45], which also has different considerations about the form of delimiting the corporation within the market. It considers that the limits of a corporation are more permeable than one can think and that the distinction between the corporation and the market is not so clear. According to this kind of theory, corporations are really another type of market: they are legal fictions that serve as links between contracting relationships representing individuals. Several authors represent this slant, for example, Refs. [46–48]. There are evidences that these theories are descendants of the already mentioned *Associational Theory*. Ref. [45], for example, says that corporations are legal fictions which serve as a connection for contracting relations among individuals. This seems similar to the premises of the Associational Theory, in which there is no corporation, but just legal relations among groups of individuals.

3.3. Issues in Law and Economic Theories

After presenting a diversity of theories about the nature of corporation and about a so-called corporate personality, one can ask why additional analysis would be required. The answer is that all corporate theories presented so far, despite their historical and social importance, contain issues that do not make them eligible as the best candidates to an account for representing corporations.

Fiction Theory, for example, lies on the notion that corporations can own property, but corporations do not have will, and then the solution is to create a fictitious person. Likewise, a corporation is distinct from the sum of its members, that is, the corporate ownership is a non-summative collection. Indeed, for example, a school can preserve its identity independently of the different generations of students that left it behind.

We can organize the issues of Fiction Theory in three main contradictions [49]: (i) if one accepts that corporate ownership is non-summative and accepts that ownership involves the possession of will by the owner, then she is committed to the fact that corporations have will, which contradicts one of the main statements of the theory; (ii) if one accepts that corporate ownership is non-summative and accepts that a corporation does not possess will, she must deny that ownership involves the possession of will by the owner; and (iii) if one accepts that ownership involves the possession of will by the owner and accepts that a corporation does not possess a will, then she must reject even the idea that the corporate ownership exists.

Real Entity Theory, as described before, suggests that corporations are organisms that possess real will and senses as natural persons. Naturally, it would be difficult to prove that a corporation is a real person. For example, a corporation can neither marry nor be given in marriage as a natural person. Actually, a corporation is not a rational being, it is not capable of understanding commands of law, and it has no will. In expressing commands to a corporation, law is speaking to the human beings that compose it [39].

Associational Theory, basically, advocates that the corporation is just a group of individuals, not an entity. This does not seem to be true: a company that has 100 years is not identical to its members. IBM, for example, is not a succession of entities in which every change in membership results in a cessation of one corporate entity and the creation of a new one. Also, "the Ford Motor Company today is very different from the same company of 1970, yet many essential characteristics remain so that Ford is still Ford, for better or worse" [50].

Finally, Economic Theories already presented just seek to describe and explain the economic behavior. There is no ontological debate about the kinds of entities that could exist in social reality.

4. Ontological analysis of the corporations

Despite the issues of Law and Economic Theories in explaining the nature of corporations, they gather several characteristics of a corporation as we currently know it. From what we have presented so far about such theories, one can sketch some hypothetical features to the corporation: (i) corporations maintain their identity over time; (ii) corporations have real existence separated from their members; (iii) corporations are artificial (or *fiat*) entities; (iv) corporations are non-summative aggregates; and (v) corporations are long-lasting entities.

In this section, we check these hypotheses by providing an ontological analysis, which reveals the multitude of entities, both natural and social, that compose a corporation: the corporation itself and its parts; entities that correspond to the several roles that a corporation can play, for example, plaintiff, property owner, taxpayer, etc.; and entities that correspond to the several events in which a corporation can participate, for example, paying taxes, selling or buying, auditing, etc.

We make use of the formal ontology machinery—mainly Basic Formal Ontology (BFO) and some theories presented before as background—in trying to describe the structure of a corporation according to two dimensions, namely, a descriptive and a normative. On one hand, a descriptive (or scientific) statement is true or false; it is not a command; on the other hand, a prescriptive (or normative) statement is concerned to which has to be done or not; it is about how to comply

[51]. In our approach, the descriptive dimension accounts the way in which a corporation is organized in units and subunits (Section 4.2); and the normative dimension accounts the way in which social entities—duties and obligations—can be handled within a corporation (Section 4.3).

4.1. The structure of the organization I: units and subunits

As BFO conveys transcategorial entities to be represented in information systems, we try to check which of its entities can account corporations or parts of corporations. In doing this, we try to answer the question (in the ontological sense): what kind of entity is a corporation? In this section, we discuss the descriptive dimension of the corporation, namely, that one which describes units and subunits, as well as the roles that compose them. The strategy is assuming the corporation and its entities as entities of BFO and then verifies the correctness of that assumption.

Considering the second level of BFO, our first verification is as follows: are corporations independent continuants? According to BFO, independent continuants are entities which change over time while retaining something of their identity [18]. Independent continuants are BFO's representatives of Aristotelian substances, which are characterized by the following: (i) substances exist on their own and do not require a support from other substances in order to exist; (ii) substances remain numerically one and the same, as well as can admit accidents at different times; (iii) substances are able to stand in causal relations; (iv) substances are "one by a process of nature"; and (v) substances have no proper parts which are themselves substances [52].

What about corporations? What of such features they possess? So, corporations do not depend on other entities unless constitutive entities; they remain numerically one and the same; corporations can only indirectly stand in causal relations through their members; they do not exist by a natural process; they are composed by substances, which are their members. As one can notice, corporations have in common with Aristotelian substances only the two first characteristics just mentioned. Thus, corporations are not exactly Aristotelian substances, but they have the marks of independent continuants insofar as at any given time, all of its parts are present, and its existence does not depend on any other discrete entities.

What kind of whole a corporation would be? We can divide this question in three parts: (i) are corporations summative wholes? (ii) Are corporations integral wholes? or (iii) Are corporations aggregate wholes?

Summative wholes are exhaustively defined by their constituent parts, and according to the principle of mereological extensionality, objects with the same parts are equal. However, this notion does not conform to the intuitive notion we have in which corporations can preserve identity even undergoing changes in membership. So, corporations are not summative wholes. Integral wholes, on the other hand, have strong structural connections among their parts, differently of corporations, which are not maximally connected, for example, organisms. Finally, in opposite of sums, aggregates are not defined in terms of their own elements. Otherwise, they have detached parts that integral wholes do not have. As corporations have members linked together (persons, units, for example), one can acknowledge that corporations are kinds of aggregates: they are material entities consisting exactly of a plurality of objects, and these objects are member parts of it all times at which it exists.

To start a way of representing the corporation and entities that compose it as BFO's entities, we seek inspiration in Popper's Theory of Three Worlds [53]. In this kind of representation based on levels, we can correspond corporations (and other entities) in reality to BFO's aggregates, as depicted in **Figure 3**. The first level is the reality level; the second level (above the first one) corresponds to people's cognition, in which people perceive and model reality; and the third level is the level of representations concretized from the cognitive models. In **Figure 3**, examples of entities in reality—Ford, IBM, John, NYC, etc.—are modeled and then concretized as representations in the third level, in this case, in BFO. Then, for example, Ford Motor Company is an instance of object aggregate, which is a BFO's transcategorial entity.

One can argue why it would be useful to represent Ford Motor Company as an aggregate. In the subsequent analysis, we hope the usefulness of this procedure becomes clear. For now, we inquire: how to divide the corporation in units and subunits? In order to answer, we make use of background theories presented in Section 2: mereology and granular partitions.

Mereology, despite to contain several relevant principles, deals with material entities and does not seem to be the best framework to explain corporations and its units because of several issues. It is hard to believe that the relation between a corporation and its members is a part-whole relation; insofar as in mereology, the part-whole relation is transitive. Accordingly, one might say inconsistent statements, for example, if John is part of a corporation, any part of John, as his eyes or his mouth, is also part of the corporation. In addition, mereology cannot account the fact that a corporation preserves its identity over time even when it loses or gains members [49].

The Granular Partitions Theory, on the contrary, uses cognitive devices to show how people divide the world. It relies on the distinction between bona fide objects and fiat objects, as mentioned before: bona fide objects exist independently of human subdividing activity; and fiat objects exist only because of the very same subdividing activity. Using the Granular Partitions Theory—namely, Theory A—one can define units, subunits (or cells and subcells), as well as the relation between unit and subunit (or cell and subcell). The application of Theory A to corporations is illustrated in **Figure 4**: there is a certain car company partitioned into two subcells, "the human resources department" and "the board of directors."

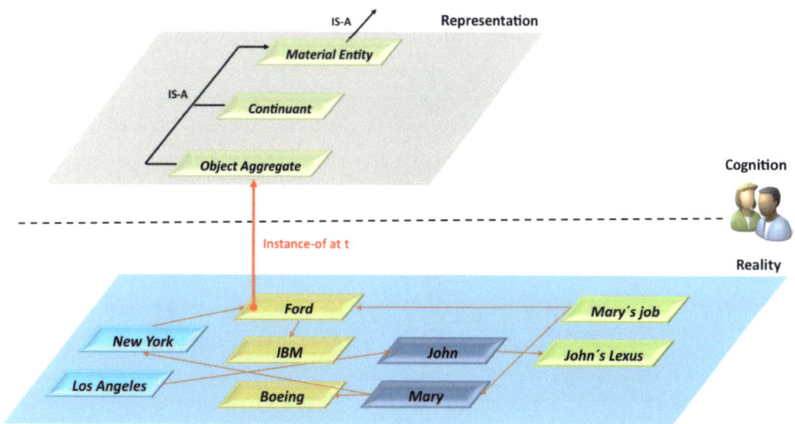

Figure 3. Levels from reality to BFO. Source: [49].

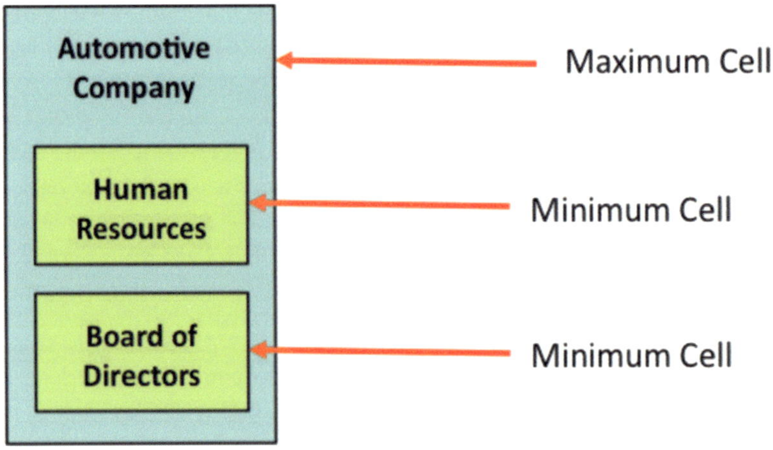

Figure 4. Theory A representing the structure of a corporation. Source: [49].

Likewise, using the Granular Partitions Theory—namely, Theory B—one can define the projection relation, which holds from a cell to the reality, and the location relation, which holds from an object to a cell. The application of Theory B to corporations is illustrated in **Figure 5**: there is a certain car company partitioned into two subcells, "the human resources department" and "the board of directors." In addition, "John" in reality projects onto the "John cell" within the corporation, as well as "John cell" is located in "John" in reality. We also can say that "the human resources department" is a cell within the corporation, but the minimum cell is "John cell." The same relations hold for "Mary."

After applying the Granular Partitions Theory to the corporation, we are ready to make another attempt following our proposal of characterizing corporate entities. If the corporation can be considered a maximal cell, a cell which every other cell is subcell, then corporate units are cells and subcells. Thus, one can consider that units and subunits can be considered fiat object parts. A fiat object is another BFO's transcategorial entity. **Figure 6**, similarly to **Figure 3**, presents three levels: the first level is the reality; and above the second level (of cognition), we draw two other representation levels—a level concretized in a Granular Partition Model and a level concretized in BFO.

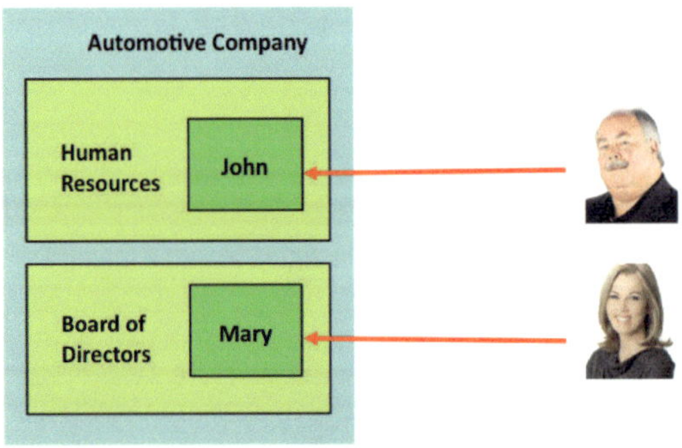

Figure 5. Theory B representing the structure of a corporation. Source: [49].

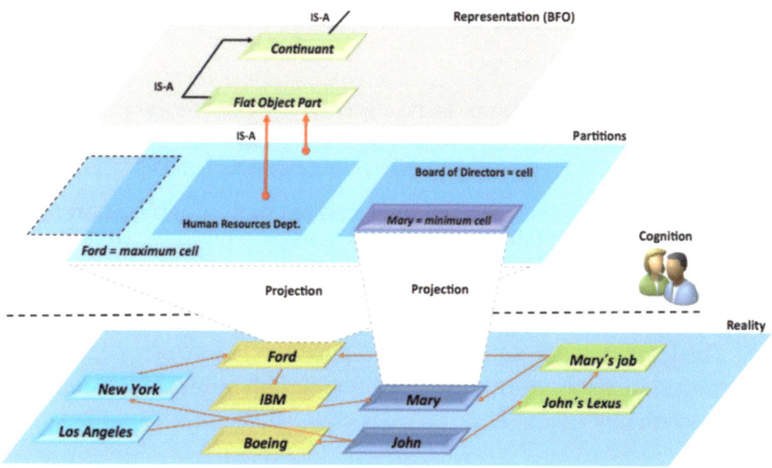

Figure 6. Levels from reality to partitions and partitions to BFO. Source: [49].

So, finally, as we suggested before, the corporation is a kind of aggregate. However, either a colony of ants or a swarm of bees also are aggregates. What is the difference between an "aggregate corporation" and other kinds of aggregates? What distinguishes a corporation from a colony of ants? To answer this question, we need to approach the normative dimension of the corporation.

4.2. The structure of the organization: duties, obligations, and responsibilities

As mentioned before, a corporation can be analyzed from two main dimensions. In the prior section (Section 4.1), we tried to approach the descriptive dimension of the corporation. At the present section, we cover the normative dimension in seeking to explain what distinguishes a corporation from other aggregates. As one can realize, unlike colonies of ants and other aggregates, corporations have normative partitions.

We begin by explaining how units and subunits are assigned with duties and obligations. So, according to Granular Partitions Theory, a successful projection lies on the side of the reality. For example, considering an architectural blueprint, the reality should match the blueprint by constructing something. Likewise, a corporation should match, for example, a statute of the company and its strategic plan, as well as other documents related to its creation and functioning.

If corporate units may be fiat objects, as stated in Section 4.1, one can argue: how a fiat object comes to existence? In this case, the answer is simple: a fiat object comes to existence through the cognition. A person can create a mental partition, which, for example, delimits a corporate unit. After all, more important is asking how a fiat object is sustained in existence, because corporations are long-lasting entities. So, a fiat object is sustained when the verbal form of corporate norms is translated to a written form. Here, we are approaching the realm of the social ontology: to explain the verbal form, we use the *Theory of Speech Acts* [14, 54]; to explain the written form, which records the speech acts, we use the *Theory of Document Acts* [34]. In addition, we use the notion of *social acts* [55].

A social act is a kind of act that needs to be perceived by someone [55]. A special type of social act, which is relevant for our purposes here, is the *declaration*. Declarations express what ought to be, for example, a promise is a declaration of how things ought to be. Declarations can either create or demolish reality: a promise creates both an obligation to a person and a claim to another person; but a declaration can also revoke some order or obligation. We use the document acts theory to record the cause of claims and obligations. Indeed, documentation of the cause for claims and obligations is one of the driving forces in the creation of documents. Then, we reach a kind of "social partition" in which people perform social acts in filling appropriate paperwork and approving it with appropriate authorities. Ref. [34] explains the connection among the three theories:

> *"[...] a theory of document acts supplementing the traditional Reinach-Austin-Searle theory of speech acts with an account of the ways in which, by doing things with documents [...] we are able to change the world by bringing into being new types of ownership relations, of legal accountability, of business organizations, and [...]"*

The document acts theory, which is crucial to represent long-lasting duties, obligations, and responsibilities within a corporation, can be related to BFO through the *Document Acts (d-acts) Ontology* [56]. *D-acts Ontology* contains *Social Generically Dependent Continuants* (SGDCs). D-acts are kinds of SGDCs. SGDCs are kinds of *Generically Dependent Continuants* (GDCs), which are representative of social entities. GDCs, as we know, are kinds of BFO's transcategorial entity.

D-acts Ontology incorporates the aforementioned kinds of acts presented in the Document Acts Theory: *social acts, declarations,* and *document acts*. A *social act*, as Reinach's definition posed, is a process carried out by someone and directed toward another one, who perceives it; a *declaration* is a social act that brings about, transfers, or revokes a SGDCs; and a *document act* is a declaration made using a document in order to temporally extend the effects of the declaration.

Examples of the relation between document acts and SGDCs in d-acts ontology are as follows: (i) a document act can *create* a SGDC, for example, when John claims a piece of land; a document act can *transfer* a SGDC, for example, when John transfers his claim to Mary; and a document act can *revoke* a SGDC, for example, when a judge signs divorce papers filled in by a couple. In addition, d-acts ontology maintains specific roles and bearers: the creator of the document is called *document act template creator role*; the user of the document is called *declaration performer role*, and the target bearer of the SGDC is called *declaration target*. **Figure 7** presents the scheme of d-acts ontology and its relations to BFO.

A full example illustrates the operation of d-acts ontology: a fictitious case of recruitment in a corporation. A director signing and stamping an official memorandum to recruit a janitor is a *document act*; the official memorandum from the board of directors legally enables the recruitment process; a memorandum is the specified input of the document act of the director's order to recruit the janitor; the human resources manager responsible for the recruitment process is the bearer of the *document act template creator role*; the director is the bearer of the *declaration performer role*; a human resources employee responsible for the recruitment procedures is the *declaration target*, which becomes endowed with the right to perform procedures enabling the recruitment.

Finally, we present **Figure 8**, which is similar prior to **Figures 3** and **6**, containing the representation levels: the first level continues to represent the reality; the second level is now concretized in a d-acts Ontology model; the third level is a representation also concretized in BFO.

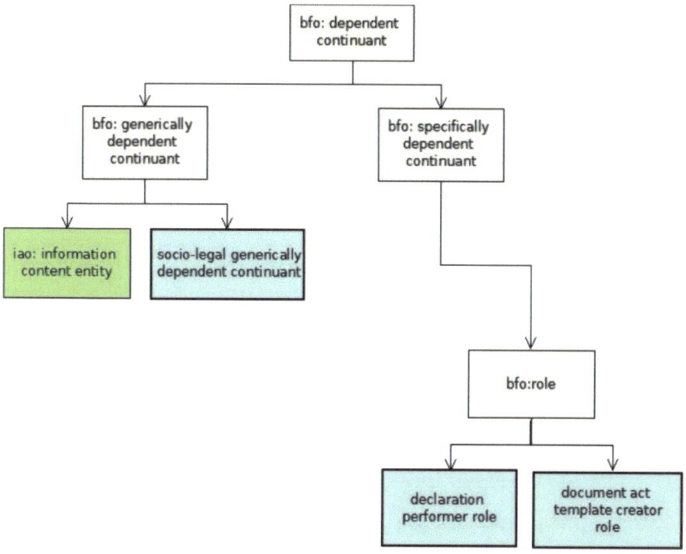

Figure 7. Classes of BFO (prefix :bfo), classes of IAO (prefix: iao) and classes of d-acts (without prefix) connected. Source: adapted from [57].

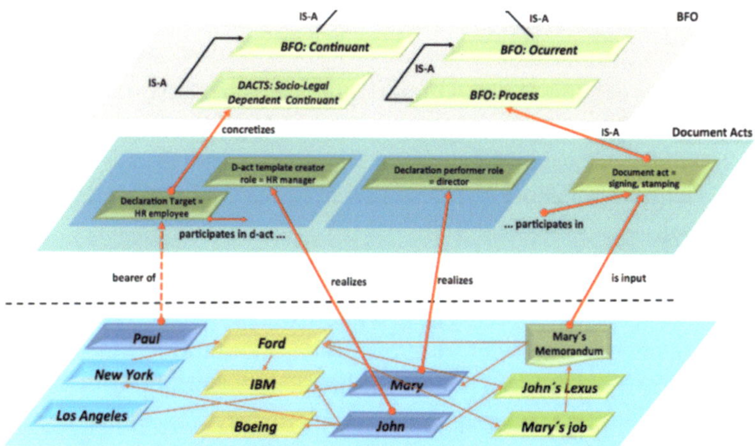

Figure 8. Levels from reality to d-acts and from d-acts to BFO. Source: [49].

5. Discussion

The normative dimension of analysis presented before (Section 4) seems to allow interesting possibilities for discussion, since processes, orders, tasks, nominations, obligations, recruitment and dismiss, as well as several other corporate-related activities occur through formal acts conveyed first, in the form of speech acts, and then recorded in the form of document acts. As our research is under way, at this moment we raise some speculations that admittedly need to be scientifically proved in future works. One speculation regards the relevance of corporative documents and respective document acts for charactering corporations and kinds of corporations.

We believe one can characterize the kind of corporation through both the documents that serve as inputs to document acts and the kinds of the very same document acts. We survey some theoretical evidences, coming from philosophers and researchers, for our premise that corporations are distinguished by documents they produce and use.

Brochhausen et al. [57] say that practices and resources regarded to both record production and record keeping reveal how one does organization within a corporation. The way one structure records imposes certain kinds of administration to workers and eventually creates indexes of how the corporation is managed. Indeed, "records are the information base of the modern state and of the modern organization" [57], since they are both the means and the results of a continuous process of notation, summarization, and information dissemination that aims to construct a depiction of what happens in the corporate environment.

Ledema [58] conjectures about the ubiquity of documents in our society through an ambitious theory called *documentality*, according to which "there is nothing social outside the text" [58]. Undoubtedly, a marriage or a contract that was not recorded would not exist as an (social) object, but a mountain can easily exist without being mapped. Since nothing social exists outside the text, society would be based on registration in documents, and this very act of registering is the condition for creating social objects. Thus, documents constitute the fundamental ingredient of the social world.

Ferraris [59] also places documents in an important position to explain society and social relations, for example, those ones produced and manipulated within a corporation. As the society became more and more complex, "the mnemonic powers of individuals have been extended prosthetically through documents in ways which have given rise to a variety of novel artifacts of social reality" [34].

So, we also say that one could identify the kind of corporation through the kinds of document acts performed. Consider a very typical document of a specific kind of corporation, for example, the *medical record* in the context of medical and healthcare units. A medical record can serve [59] to support patient care in the coordination of clinical processes, to allow better decision-making and for the creation of demographic surveys; to fulfill external obligations regarding health insurance plans, reimbursements, auditing, and accreditation; to support administration in planning, controlling, and quality management; and to allow scientific research and clinical education. Our speculation is that identifying the kinds of d-acts that a medical record contains or generates may provide clues to formally distinguish the medical corporation from other ones. As we mention before, such idea has to be proved, what we expect to do in future works.

6. Final remarks

In this chapter, we proposed the preliminary foundations of an ontological-based architecture for organizing information and knowledge within corporations. We sought to clarify the ontological status of corporations, to understand the relations between corporate units, and to approach the duties within a corporation. We presented a background of formal theories required to understand the research and some of the main doctrines about the nature of corporations. Then, we analyzed the corporation through two dimensions we called descriptive and normative. The descriptive dimension deals with the structure of the corporation from the point of view of units and subunits, while the normative dimension deals with duties and obligations. We conducted our research using well-founded theories, for example, formal ontology, speech acts, and document acts. Finally, we offered a brief discussion focused on the normative aspects related to document and document acts.

As our final remarks, we would like to emphasize the connection among the levels of representation existing throughout our ontological analysis (Section 4). In **Figure 9**, we again display the level of reality along with two representation levels, namely, a level for partitions and the level for document acts. As one can realize, these two representation levels, additionally to describe the dimensions of analysis proposed, maintain co-relations that, once gathered, can offer a view of which would be an ontological-based information architecture to corporations. For purposes of formalization and application in the modern information systems, it is worth remembering that all representation levels described throughout the chapter can be mapped to BFO, a transcategorial formal top-level ontology.

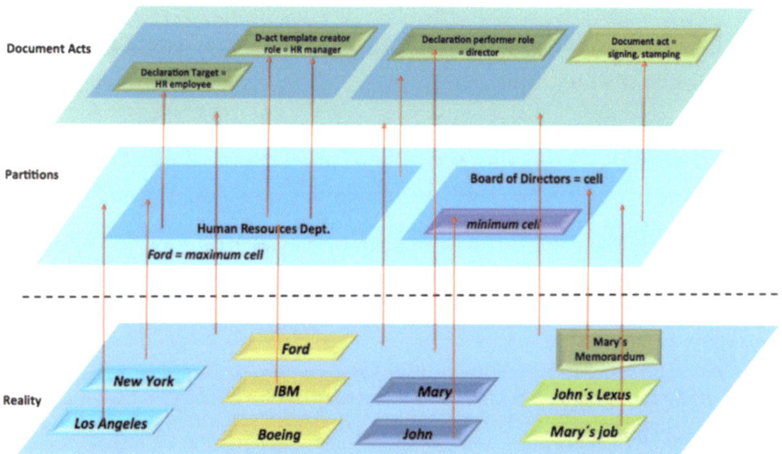

Figure 9. Descriptive and normative dimensions of the corporation. Source: [49].

As we have already mentioned, the relevance of such analysis rests on the need of a better understanding of corporations, as well as the advantages of a formal framework to be applied in information systems working in the context of Semantic Web. In future works, we intend to advance the discussion offered here and sketch an ontology-based model for medical organizations, along with semiformal definitions and hierarchy.

Author details

Maurício B. Almeida*, Christiano P. Pessanha and Renata Barcelos

*Address all correspondence to: priv.mba@gmail.com

Federal University of Minas Gerais, Belo Horizonte, Brazil

References

[1] Almeida MB, Barbosa RR. Ontologies in knowledge management support: A case study. Journal of the American Society for Information Science and Technology. 2009;**60**(10):2032-2047

[2] Fonseca F. The double role of ontologies in information science research. Journal of the American Society for Information Science and Technology. 2007;**58**(6):786-793

[3] Guizzardi G. Ontological foundations for structural conceptual models [thesis]. Twente: University of Twente; 2005

[4] Obrst L, Hughes T, Ray S. Prospects and possibilities for ontology evaluation: The view from NCOR. In: 15th International World Wide Web Conference; 2006; Edinburgh, UK. 2006

[5] Bernus P, Nemes L, Williams TJ, editors. Architectures for Enterprise Integration. London: Chapman & Hall; 1996

[6] Fillion E, Menzel C, Blinn T, Mayer R. An ontology-based environment for enterprise model integration. In: Proceedings of the Workshop on Basic Ontological Issues in Knowledge Sharing at IJCAI95; 1995; Menlo Park, CA: AAAI Press; 1995. pp. 33-45

[7] Fox MS. The TOVE Project: Towards a common-sense model of the enterprise. In: Belli F, Radermacher FJ, editor. Proceedings of Fifth International Conference Industrial and Engineering Applications of Artificial Intelligence and Expert Systems; London: Springer; 1992. pp. 25-34

[8] Uschold M, King M, Moralee S, Zorgios Y. Enterprise ontology. Knowledge Engineering Review. 1998;**13**(1):31-89

[9] Chisholm R. A realistic Theory of Categories. Cambridge: Cambridge University Press; 1996

[10] Grossman R. The Categorial Structure of the World. Blommington: Indiana University Press; 1983

[11] Lowe EJ. The Four-Category Ontology: A Metaphysical Foundation for Natural Science. New York: Oxford University Press; 2007

[12] Armstrong DM. Universals: An Opinionated Introduction. London: Westview Press; 1989

[13] Smith B. Ontology and Information Systems [Internet]. 2003. Available from: http://www.ontology.buffalo.edu/ontology(PIC).pdf [Accessed: April 16, 2009]

[14] Searle J. Making the Social World: The Structure of Human Civilization. Oxford: Oxford University Press; 2010

[15] Wand Y, Weber R. Mario Bunge's ontology as a formal foundation for information systems concepts. In: Weingartner P, Dorn JWG, editors. Studies on Mario Bunge's Treatise. Amsterdam: Rodopi; 1990

[16] Staab S, Studer R. Handbook on Ontologies. Berlin: Springer; 2004

[17] Gangemi A, et al. Sweetening Ontologies with DOLCE [Internet]. 2002. Available from: http://www.loa.istc.cnr.it/Papers/DOLCE-EKAW.pdf [Accessed: January 10, 2010]

[18] Grenon P, Smith B, Goldberg LJ. Biodynamic ontology: Applying BFO in the biomedical domain. In: Pisanelli DM, editor. Ontologies in Medicine. Amsterdam: IOS Press; 2004

[19] Smith B, Ceusters W. Ontological realism: A methodology for coordinated evolution of scientific ontologies. Applied Ontology. 2010;**5**:139-188

[20] Hening B. What is formal ontology. In: Munn, Smith, editors. Introduction to Applied Ontology. Berlin: Ontos-Verlag; 2008. pp. 39-56

[21] Arp R, Smith B, Spear AD. Building Ontologies with Basic Formal Ontology. Cambrigde: MIT Press; 2015

[22] Spear AD. Ontology for the Twenty First Century: An Introduction with Recommendations [Internet]. 2006. Available from: http://ifomis.uni-saarland.de/bfo/documents/manual.pdf [Accessed: January 10, 2013]

[23] Simons P. Parts: A Study in Ontology. Oxford: Oxford University Press; 1987

[24] Varzi A. Parts, wholes, and part-whole relations: The prospects of mereotopology. Data and Knowledge Engineering. 1996;**20**:259-286

[25] Bittner T, Smith B. The theory of granular partitions. In: Munn, Smith, editors. Introduction to Applied Ontology. Berlin: Ontos-Verlag; 2008. pp. 125-158

[26] Gotts, NM, Cohn AG. A mereological approach to representing spatial vagueness. In: Principles of Knowledge Representation and Reasoning, Proc. 5th Intl. Conf. KR'96; Amsterdan: Morgan Kaufmann; 1995. pp. 230-241

[27] Smith B, Brogaard B. Quantum mereotopology. Annals of Mathematics and Artificial Intelligence. 2000;**35**(1-2):153-175

[28] Smith B. Fiat objects. Topoi. 2001;**20**(2):131-148

[29] Searle JR. Speech Acts: An Essay in the Philosophy of Language. Cambridge University Press; 1969

[30] Searle JR. A classification of illocutionary acts. Language in Society. 1976;**5**(01):1-23

[31] Searle JR. Intentionality: An Essay in the Philosophy of Mind. Cambridge: Cambridge University Press; 1983

[32] Searle JR. Minds, Brains and Science. Harvard: Harvard University Press; 1984

[33] Searle JR. Speech acts, mind, and social reality. In: Grewendorf G, Meggle G, editors. Speech Acts, Mind, and Social Reality: Discussions with John R. Searle. Amsterdan: Springer Science & Business Media; 2002. pp. 3-16

[34] Smith B. How to do things with documents. Rivista di Estetica. 2012;**50**(2):179-198

[35] Williston S. History of the Law of Business Corporations before 1800. II. (Concluded). Harvard Law Review. 1888;**2**(4):149-66. DOI: 10.2307/1321930

[36] Dewey J. The historic background of corporate legal personality. The Yale Law Journal. 1926;**35**(6):655-73. DOI: 10.2307/788782

[37] Blumberg PI, Georgakopoulos NL, Strasser KA, Gouvin EJ. Blumberg on Corporate Groups. New York: Aspen Publishers Online; 2004

[38] Blumberg PI. The Multinational Challenge to Corporation Law: The Search for a New Corporate Personality. Oxford: Oxford University Press; 1993

[39] Machen AW. Corporate Personality. Harvard Law Review. 1911;**24**(4):253-267. DOI: 10.2307/1324056

[40] Iwai K. What Is Corporation? The Corporate Personality Controversy and Comparative Corporate Governance [Internet]. 2001. Available from: https://www.researchgate.net/publication/24135014_What_is_Corporation_---The_Corporate_Personality_Controversy_and_Comparative_Corporate_Governance

[41] Coase RH. The nature of the firm. Economica. 1937;**4**(16):386-405. DOI: 10.1111/j.1468-0335.1937.tb00002.x

[42] Penrose E. The Theory of the Growth of the Firm. Oxford: Oxford University Press; 1959

[43] Winter Sidney G, Nelson RR. An Evolutionary Theory of Economic Change. Rochester, NY: Social Science Research Network; 1982

[44] Prahalad CK, Hamel G. The Core Competence of the Corporation [Internet]. 1990. Available from: http://globex.coe.pku.edu.cn/file/upload/201606/27/1756365219.pdf

[45] Jenson MC, Meckling WH. Theory of the firm: Managerial behavior, agency costs and ownership structure. Journal of Financial Economics. 1976;**3**:305-360

[46] Easterbrook F, Fischel DR. The Economic Structure of Corporate Law. Cambrigde: Harvard University Press; 1991

[47] Williamson OE. The Economic Institutions of Capitalism. New York, NY: The Free Press; 1985

[48] Grossman SJ, Hart OD. The costs and benefits of ownership: A theory of vertical and lateral integration. Journal of Political Economy. 1986;**94**(4):691-719

[49] Almeida MB. An ontological study of healthcare corporations and their social entities. In: ICBO Workshop; Buffalo. 2016

[50] Vizenor L. Corporate Being: A Study in Realist Ontology [dissertation]. Buffallo: University at Buffalo; 2006

[51] Stein E.W. Organizational Memory: Review of concepts and recommendations for management. International Journal of Information Management. 1995;**15**(1):17-32

[52] Sparks AW. Talking Philosophy: A Wordbook. London: Routledge; 1991

[53] Smith B. On Substances, Accidents and Universals: In Defence of a Constituent Ontology. Philosophical Papers. 1997;**26**:105-127

[54] Popper K. Three Worlds [Internet]. 1978.Available from: http://tannerlectures.utah.edu/_documents/a-to-z/p/popper80.pdf

[55] Austin JL. How to Do Things with Words. 2nd ed. Cambridge, MA: Harvard University Press; 1975

[56] Crosby JF, editor. The Apriori Foundations of the Civil Law. Frankfurt: Ontos-Verlag; 2012

[57] Brochhausen M, Almeida MA, Slaughter L. Towards a formal representation of document acts and the resulting legal entities. In: Johanssonian Investigations. Frankfurt: Ontos; 2013. pp. 120-39

[58] Ledema R. Discoursers of Post-Bureaucratic Organization. Amsterdam: John Benjamins Publishing Company; 2003

[59] Ferraris M. Documentality: Why It Is Necessary to Leave Traces. 1st ed. Fordham University Press; 2012

Chapter 2

Ontology for Application Development

Larysa Globa, Rina Novogrudska,
Alexander Koval and Vyacheslav Senchenko

Additional information is available at the end of the chapter

http://dx.doi.org/10.5772/intechopen.74042

Abstract

The chapter describes the process of ontology development for different subject domains for application designing. The analysis of existing approaches to ontology development for software platform realization in some subject domains is depicted. The example of ontology model development for telecom operator billing system based on descriptive logic is shown. For ontology model designing, it is proposed to use two formal theories: descriptive logic and set theory, which allow to systematize data and knowledge, to organize search and navigation, and to describe informational and computational recourses according to the meta-notion standards.

Keywords: ontology, descriptive logic, semantic information processing

1. Analysis of approaches to ontology designing

One of the existing approaches to the subject domain (SD) identification, based on the idea of conceptual modeling is ontological modeling. A conceptual domain model (CDM) describes the SD as a collection of concepts (terms) and relations between them. The entities from the real world correspond with the term of ontology and relations between such terms. This corresponds to the classical representation of the ontological model in which the ontology is defined by three finite subsets: concepts, connections, and interpretation functions. When a subject domain is modeling as a sphere of activity, the connections between concepts are also the terms that describe these relations. Concepts referred to a class of relations are used to describe the processes and phenomena of the real world. The conceptual model of the subject domain is defined as the totality of concepts (terms) and relations between them, which correspond to entities from the real world, realized as an oriented labeled graph. The content model of the subject domain for the conceptual model is given by an oriented labeled graph whose vertices are interpreted as information elements corresponding to the real objects of the domain. Accordingly, two types of relations are defined in the models union: informative—to define the information element relation to another and conceptual—to define the relations of the element to the subject domain.

For a rapidly developing subject domain, the conceptual model is a constantly changing and developing structure. At the same time, the content model accumulates changes which over time lead to a modification of the conceptual model. The use of dynamic ontologies that are changeable in time will guarantee the actuality and adequacy of ontological models and, thereby, make them practically applicable to a wide range of tasks.

Ontologies are new intellectual tools for resources like Internet searching, new methods of knowledge, and queries presenting and processing. They can accurately and effectively describe the data semantics for a certain subject domain and solve the problem of concepts: incompatibility and inconsistency. Ontologies have their own processing facility (logical inference), corresponding to the tasks of semantic information processing. So, using ontologies, to execute searching request, the user will be able to receive in response resources that are semantically relevant to the query.

There are several approaches to the ontology concept definition, but there is no generally accepted definition. Depending on each specific task, it is convenient to interpret this term in different ways: from informal definitions to descriptions of ontologies in concepts and constructions of logic and mathematics.

Ontology is an attempt at a comprehensive and detailed formalization of a certain subject domain with the help of a conceptual scheme. Usually, such a scheme consists of a structure containing all relevant classes of objects, their relations, and rules (theorems, constraints) accepted in this field.

Ontology model advantages:

- Organization of semantic search
- Structuring of subject domain information.

For the systematization of information and computing resources, the ontological model can be used for such resources linking and description.

1.1. Advantages of using Semantic Web technologies

Nowadays, the search for advanced methods of information access, processing, presentation, and systematization is an important issue. The usage of ontologies reduces the time of computation and information retrieval, improves the efficiency of existing knowledge usage, performs logical deductions based on existing knowledge and integrates data from different sources using common semantics [1].

The sharing of information and semantics by people or program agents is one of the most common goals of developing ontologies.

Providing the possibility of SD knowledge reusing is an essential advantage of ontologies. To develop large ontology, it is in need to integrate several existing ontologies that describe parts of a complex subject domain. It is also possible to reuse the basic ontology and extend it to describe SD.

The analysis of knowledge in the subject domain is possible when there is a declarative specification of terms (that represent such knowledge). Formal analysis of terms is extremely valuable both when trying to reuse existing ontologies and when expanding them.

Thus, the usage of ontologies has several significant advantages. There is still a problem concerning searching the most complete method for ontologies development, with a view to their further usage. Based on large-scale projects, several approaches to ontology designing have been developed, but a single standardized method has not yet been selected.

1.2. Ontology development method

Several research groups offer methods for ontology development that were developed during the execution of their projects. However, these methods are different and none of them are standardized. Method of ontology development is an essential element in ontology designing to bring the process of development to the common, standard stages.

1.2.1. Approach Cyc

Cyc is the artificial intelligence project attempting to assemble ontology and knowledge base spanning the basic concepts and "rules of thumb" about how the world works [2]. The Cyc approach was formed during the execution of the project to develop a large base of general knowledge, which was executed in 1980s of the last century under the direction of D. Lenat. Within the framework of the Cyc project, the first tools of knowledge engineering were developed, and the knowledge representation language CycL, which was based, on the one hand, on the calculation of higher order predicates, and on the other hand, based at that time the language of the artificial intelligence systems Lisp. Within the framework of this project, the task of forming large knowledge bases, validation, and verification of such databases, as well as the task of knowledge-based deduction, was first posed and solved. In the framework of the Cyc-project, the idea of KB structuring in the form of microtheories was proposed, including knowledge from different areas, presented from different points of view.

Ontology development using Cyc project assumes the following phases [3]:

- "Manual" coding of explicit and implicit knowledge contained in knowledge sources.
- "Manual" knowledge encoding by means of programmatic facilities, using the knowledge that already exists in the Cyc.
- Semiautomatic phase, when the developer "recommends" the software tools for the source of knowledge for processing and "explains" to them the most complex places of processed texts.

At the same time, as a rule, two main tasks are solved at each phase:

- Development of a knowledge representation system and a top-level ontology that contains the most abstract concepts.
- Knowledge representation that was remained outside the formalization after the first task was solved on the basis of primitives, which was developed and implemented in the process of solving the first problem.

Currently, the Cyc KB already contains several hundred thousand terms and basic statements and millions of general knowledge statements derived from them. The Cyc KB fragment was recently released into open access called Open Cyc (one version of Open Cyc 2006 contains about 50,000 concepts and 300,000 facts), which is available to researchers in the field of artificial intelligence under the research Cyc license.

As Cyc approach applications, we can distinguish:

- System integration of heterogeneous databases, in which Cyc dictionary appears in the database schema, the resulting data from the database are interpreted in accordance with the terms of Cyc-ontology.
- An intelligent mechanism for searching images based on information contained in signatures to them.
- Module for the integration of structured terminology, which provides complex dictionary import, their integration and supports the corresponding management processes.
- The module for searching information on the Internet for the Cyc expansion.

1.2.2. Uschold and King's method

Uschold and King's method was proposed based on the results of the business process ontology modeling development that used enterprise ontology [4]. It was offered the methodology of designing that propose following stages:

1. Definition of purpose. Specification on why an ontology is developed, and how it will be used.
2. The ontology development. This stage is carried out in the following phases:

   2.1. Ontology fixation, where occurs:

   - detection (identification) of key concepts and relations,
   - the development of precise textual definitions for each concept and relation,
   - the identification of terms pertaining to each concept and relation,
   - matching of all knowledge obtained in the process of developed ontology fixing.

   2.2. The ontology coding. At this stage, the formal representation in the chosen language of knowledge representation is carried out.

   2.3. At this phase, the possibilities of existing ontologies using and their integration into new ontology are realized.

3. The ontology evaluation. The stage is used for the developed ontology evaluation according to criteria such as:

    3.1. The ontology correspondence to the original goals and objectives

    3.2. Used software efficiency.

4. Documentation description.

The most important project using the method and methodology developed by Uschold and King was the Enterprise Project, which was carried out by the Artificial Intelligence Applications Institute of Edinburgh University with partners such as IBM, Lloyd's Register, Logic UK Limited, and Unilever, and the most important application of the method is the Enterprise Ontology development that is a collection of terms and definitions related to business enterprises.

With the use of Enterprise Ontology, the enterprise toolset toolkit was created that used the agent's architecture to integrate standard software products, serially produced in the plug-and-play style.

1.2.3. Gruninger and Fox methodology

Gruninger and Fox methodology was formed using the experience of specific ontology developing (using TOVE [5]) and focused on the subject domain of business processes modeling. This methodology provides the ontology development as a logical knowledge model and includes the following stages:

- Fixation of the motivational scenario. Within the framework of this methodology, it is postulated that the creation of any ontology is motivated by certain scenarios that arise in a particular subject domain, which specify a number of intuitively possible solutions for the problems indicated in the scenario.
- Formation of competence testing informal issues. The questions of ontology competence evaluation based on motivational scenarios are considered as requirements to the subject domain representation and the ability to solve problems specified in motivational scenarios with its help.
- Specification of the ontology terminology in the formal language, which is based on the following phases:
- Obtaining an informal ontology. As the result of ontology competence testing, a lot of terms are singled out that should be the basis for specification in the formal language.
- Specification of formal terminology. The terms identified in the previous phase are described in the formal language.
- Formulating questions of competence assessment using ontology terminology. At this stage, a specification of queries in the formal language to assess the competence of the ontology occurs.

- The specification of axioms for ontology terms in the formal language. Here, the semantics of ontology terms and restrictions on their interpretation are defined in the form of statements of first-order logic.
- Specifying the conditions for ontology completeness. At this stage, the conditions are set. Issues in solution implementation related to the competence of the ontology will be complete.

The most significant applied programs of Gruninger's and Fox's methodology are [3]:

- Enterprise Design Workbench is a designed environment that allows the user to analyze enterprise projects. An important functional feature of Enterprise Design Workbench is the support of an enterprises alternative projects comparative analysis.
- Integrated Supply Chain Management Project agent is the organization of the chain supply as a network of interacting intellectual agents. Every one of them performs one or more functions in the supply chain and coordinates its activities with other agents.

1.2.4. Methodology named "METHONTOLOGY"*

Methodology named "METHONTOLOGY" [6] was developed in the Madrid Polytechnic University laboratory. A distinctive feature of it is that METHONTOLOGY is formed on the basis of main activity analysis and rethinking for the activities inherent in the processes of software development and knowledge engineering. Thus, METHONTOLOGY integrates the experience of designing complex objects from two areas of knowledge.

This methodology includes the identification of the ontologies development process, the life cycle based on the prototypes evolution and individual techniques for performing each activity. The life cycle includes such stages as specification, conceptualization, formalization, implementation, and maintenance, as well as basic processes such as management, quality control, knowledge acquisition, integration, evaluation, documentation, and configuration management.

Examples of ontologies developed using METHONTOLOGY are [3]:

- CHEMICALS (contains knowledge in the field of chemical elements and crystalline structures).
- Monatomic Ions (collects information about monatomic ions).
- Environmental pollutant ontologies (represent methods to identify various polluting components in water, air, ground, and the maximum permissible concentrations of these substances, considering existing laws).
- The reference ontology (basic ontology for describing ontologies of "yellow pages" type directories).
- Silicate ontology (simulates the properties of minerals and silicates in particular).
- Ontologies developed in the IST-1999-2010,589 MKBEEM project (travel, textile catalogs, housing, used in the multilanguage e-commerce platform).
- OntoRoadMap (meta-ontology, ontology development methodologies, ontology development tools, ontology-related events (conferences, seminars, etc.)).

Examples of applications that use some of the above ontologies:

- (Onto) Agent (an ontology broker that uses reference ontology as a source of knowledge and finds a description of the ontologies that satisfy the given constraint).
- OntoRoadMap application developed as (Onto) Agent. This is an ontology-based web application that allows the community to register, view, and find ontologies, methodologies, software tools and languages for ontologies development, programs in Semantic Web, e-commerce, NLP, etc., as well as major conferences, seminars, and events in these fields).
- Ontogeneration (a system using the ontology CHEMICALS and the linguistic ontology of GUM to generate texts in Spanish in response to a query in the field of chemistry).

1.3. Comparative characteristics of methods for ontology development

The methods of ontology development described above were comparable in the following parameters:

- Terms of use. Shows the necessary conditions of use for ontology designing proposed in the ontology development method.
- Development process. It shows the method's specific features for ontology development and its stages.
- The implementation process.
- Preservation and use. This stage shows whether the proposed method further preserves and uses the developed ontology.
- Knowledge obtaining. This stage shows whether the method described the possible knowledge ontology acquisition.
- Ontology control and confirmation.
- Ontology configuration management. This stage shows whether the method described controlling the ontology configuration.
- Ontology documentation.

The comparison results of considered ontology development methods by these parameters are given in **Table 1**. The sign (+) means "described in detail," (+/−) means "interrupted," and (−) means "not parsed."

1.4. Methods of semantic web usage for data warehouses development

Data storage (DS) provides multidimensional view of a huge amount of historical data from operational sources; thus, they provide useful information that allows decision makers to improve business processes in an organization. Multidimensional models allow you to structure information into facts and measurements. The fact contains the necessary dimensions (attributes of the fact) of the business process (sales, deliveries, etc.), while the dimension is a context for the analysis of facts (product, client, time, etc.)

	Cyc	Uschold and King's	Gruninger and Fox	METHONTOLOGY
Terms of use	—	—	+	+
Development process	—	—	+/—	+
The implementation process	+/—	+/—	—	+
Preservation and usage	—	—	—	+/—
Knowledge obtaining	+/—	+/—	+/—	+
Control and confirmation	—	+/—	+/—	+/—
Ontology configuration management	—	—	—	+/—
Documentation	+/—	+/—	+/—	+

Table 1. Comparative characteristics of ontology development methods.

Data storage contains information that is specified for data analysis. This information is obtained from existing OLTP databases and is preprocessed to synchronize syntax and semantics. Thus, one of the main goals of data warehouses is the integration of information obtained from different sources. After that, OLAP systems can be used for efficient use of stored information. Both types of systems use multidimensional data models [7].

Integration of information coming from different sources is one of the main goals of data storages. The Semantic Web technology can be used to develop data storages since data structures depend on the context to determine the actual data semantics and to provide context-sensitive knowledge [8].

Semantic Web is a source of knowledge, the exploitation of which will open new opportunities for academic and business tasks. One such feature is the analysis of information resources to support decision-making, such as the trends identification and the discovery of new influence factors. Semantic annotations are a formal information resource description that is usually based on common ontologies of SD [9]. The main reason for using domain ontologies is to develop common terminology and logic concepts that are available in a specific SD.

The topic of ontologies used for the data storage development was partially covered by other authors in some aspects such as ETL processes [10] or data sources [11].

Data storage designing and development uses ontologies in the following cases.

1.4.1. Requirements analysis

In order to reach the understanding of designing requirements by all project participants, ontology implementation is very important. Participants may have incompatible needs; thus, it is especially useful [12]. It is convenient to manage business models in the form of ontologies because they represent a descriptive abstraction of the environment in which the software (including data storage) should work. They also contain semantics that have already been agreed upon with the stakeholders in the process. In addition, ontology can be used as an auxiliary tool for information requirement analyses [13].

1.4.2. Needs and data source matching

One approach to reconciling the needs and sources of data is closely related to the idear of ontology using to obtain multidimensional data [11]. It is a method for detecting a multidimensional structure from ontologies. This method consists of:

- identifying facts and measurements by matching and categorizing,
- selecting the view and determining the measurements for the facts,
- determining the basis for the search and filtering,
- and determining the aggregation hierarchy by identifying the relations between entities. Elements of measurement are determined using heuristic procedures based on structural aspects (such as cardinality and selectivity). Another approach to use heuristics is given in [14]. The scientific community should work on providing both semantic rules and (public) repository of multidimensional annotated ontologies. At the end, the ontology of Cyc, or its open source version of OpenCyc, is interesting.

1.4.3. Data types in dimensions

Defining data types at the ontology level in systems with multidimensional models allows data storage designers to correctly describe model sample with the necessary data types in dimensions. Many existing subject domain ontologies can help developers to design OLAP systems in accordance with generally accepted requirements.

1.4.4. Incomplete input data

The data sources used in the SD may contain not all the necessary information. An additional set of data can be obtained from other publicly available sources of information. For example, commonly used ontologies, such as WordNet (lexical base), can be used to fill elements that are not supported in data sources. Another example is the Computing Classification System Taxonomy, which can be used for computer classification and obtaining more detailed aggregation of measurements in data repositories [15].

1.4.5. Logical output when querying OLAP systems

Requests to OLAP systems are based on manipulations with aggregation data. However, the algebra of OLAP systems is based on computations instead of logic. Any statement to the account of a multidimensional model cannot be proved, but only calculated.

The main advantage using ontologies in data repositories is the extension of OLAP requests with the possibility of logical output.

Requests for OLAP systems are based on manipulations with aggregation data. However, the OLAP systems algebra is based on computations instead of logic. Any statement to the account of a multidimensional model cannot be proved, only calculated.

The main advantage of ontologies using in data storages or data repositories is the extension of OLAP requests with the possibility of logical output.

2. Ontology model of the billing system

2.1. Descriptive logic for ontology development

One of the main tasks of the ontology development is the definition of the descriptive logic that will be used. It is necessary to determine the solvability and computational complexity of the logic used, characterizing the possibility and speed of obtaining logical inferences from an ontology. Based on the chosen logic, the ontology definition language (OWL-DL, OWL-Lite, OWL-FULL) and the corresponding tools for implementation are selected.

Descriptive logic (DL) is a family of logics with different capabilities. Accordingly, for different tasks depending on the purposes, different DL logics are chosen. For example, the OWL Lite language is based on a DL called SHIF (D), and OWL-DL is based on SHOIN (D) (the explanations of the abbreviations will be explained below).

Any DL is a subset of FOL (first-order logic). This means that any statement on DL can be represented as an FOL formula (but not vice versa). At the same time, they are semantically compatible, that is, if you turn the knowledge base of DL into a knowledge base of FOL, then it will be possible to draw the same logical conclusions from it as to the transformation.

DL syntax does not explicitly use variables and quantifiers. For example, the statement $A \subset B$ in DL is the same as the FOL-formula $\forall x\ A\ (x) \rightarrow B\ (x)$, but without variables.

Most DL logic is usually solvable that is achieved by cutting some FOL capabilities (in particular, variables). It should be noted that OWL DL is solvable and there are logical processors for it, and OWL Full, which is not based on DL, does not exist and there are no logical processors for it [15].

DL logic combines rich expressive possibilities and good computational properties such as solvability and relatively low computational complexity of the main logical problems that make their application possible in practice.

ALC logic is one of the main descriptive logics, which is basic to many others. For many real ontologies, ALC logic is enough.

The ALC language contains the alphabet (that is, the set of base characters) that consists of three components:

- A set of base-class names (NC) and two special classes (top or universal class and bottom-empty class)
- A set of relations names (NR)
- A set of instance names (NI).

http://dx.doi.org/10.5772/intechopen.74042

The central feature of ALC, as many DLs, is the ability to describe complex classes (concepts). This is done with the help of the following statements called class constructors [16]:

- Class crossing or conjunction ($C \cap D$)
- The union of classes or the disjunction ($C \cap D$)
- Addition of class or negation ($\neg C$)
- Universal constraint ratio ($\forall$ *RC)*
- Existential restriction ratio ($\exists$ *RC*)
- Logical formulas in ALC are called axioms. There are three types of axioms:
- Relations of the "class-subclass" type. These axioms have the form "$C \subset D$," where *C* and *D* are arbitrary (possibly complex) classes.
- Relations of the type "class individual" They have the form "*a: C*," where "*a*" denotes an object and *C* is an arbitrary class.
- Relationships of the type "relationship individual" type. They have the form "(*a*, *b*): *P*," where "*a, b*" denote two objects and *P* is an arbitrary relation.

A set of axioms of type 1 is called TBox (abbreviation of terminological box). A set of axioms of types 2 and 3 is called *ABox* (assertional box).

The knowledge base (or ontology) in the ALC is a collection of *TBox* and *ABox. TBox* is actually a description of the class hierarchy (domain concepts). *ABox* is a collection of facts about specific objects, to which classes they relate to and what relations they have.

At the heart of the ALC semantics, there are two key components: domain Dom and the interpretive function *I*. Dom is a limited set of elements (sometimes called "real world" elements) and is defined as follows:

- Each base class in NC is linked to a subset of *Dom*, with *I* (*top*) = *Dom* and *I* (*bottom*) = *empty set*
- Each relation in NR is linked by some relation to *Dom*.

(the subset of *Dom x Dom*)

- I maps each object in the NI per element in *Dom*.
- In other words, *I (C)* = *X* means the following: "The symbol *C* denotes the set of elements *X* of the real world."
- Interpretation of complex classes [16]:
- Interpretation $C \cup D$ (or $I\ (C \cap D))$ is equivalent to $I\ (C) \cap I\ (D)$
- $I\ (C \cup D) = I\ (C) \cup I\ (D)$
- $I\ (\neg\ C) = Dom \neg I\ (C)$

- $I\,(\forall\, R.C)$ = all such $x \in Dom$ that for any $y \in Dom$ it is true that

$(x, y) \in I\,(R) \rightarrow y \in I\,(C)$

- $I\,(\exists\, RC)$ = all such $x \in Dom$, that there exists $y \in I\,(C)$ such that $(x, y) \in I\,(R)$

Explanation: For example, the precedence formula defines the following simple meaning for the constructor: *RC*: "If class *X* is defined as ∀ *RC*, then *X* denotes the set of all objects *x* such that all objects associated with them for the relation R are elements of class *C*."

- Axioms of logic:
- Interpretation *I* satisfies the axiom $C \supset D$ if $I\,(C) \subset I\,(D)$.
- *I* satisfies the axiom A: $C \in D$ if $I\,(a) \in I\,(C)$.
- *I* satisfies the axiom (x, y): P if $(I\,(x), I\,(y)) \in I\,(P)$.

If interpretation *I* satisfies some axiom *A*, then it is called the model *A*. Interpretation *I* satisfies the *TBox* (or is a *TBox* model) if it is a model of all the axioms of the *TBox*. The *ABox* model is similarly defined. An interpretation is a model of ontology if it is a model of its *TBox* and *ABox*.

Using the domain and the interpretive function, "formally" defines the meaning of classes, objects, relations, and logical formulas (axioms).

Let us describe logical output in ALC. Knowledge bases are formulated in the language of descriptive logics, they are used not only to represent knowledge of the SD, but also for the logical analysis of knowledge, that is to check the absence of contradictions in them, the withdrawal of new knowledge from existing ones, and the ability to make inquiries to knowledge bases. Due to the fact that knowledge bases of DL are written in formalized form, it is possible to make a strict logical conclusion. As the syntax and semantics of the descriptive logics are developed in such a way that the basic logical problems are solvable, the derivation of new knowledge can be developed by computer means—output machines.

For an ALC, you can see the basic tasks of the logbook [16]:

- Consistency (or noncontradiction) ontology. An ontology is coherent if it has at least one model. In other words, if there is such a way of interpreting (i.e., assigning meaning) classes, objects, and relations that do not conflict with any of the given axioms (TBox or ABox).
- Class feasibility. *A* class *C* is called coherent in the ontology of *O* if at least one model O interprets it as a nonempty set.
- The conclusion of the axioms. From the ontology *O*, an axiom is derived, and each model of *O* is also a model of *A*. In other words, if the interpretation does not contradict the axioms in *O*, it does not contradict the *A*.

Important is the fact that the two last tasks are reduced to the task of coherence in the following way:

- Class *C* is coherent in the ontology of *O* if and only if the addition of a new axiom *A*: *C* (where the object "*a*" has not previously met in *O*) does not lead to a loss of consistency. That is, the issue of coherence *C* is solved by adding a new axiom to *O* and checking consistency.

- Axiom A is derived from the ontology of O if and only if adding the "negation" of axiom A to the ontology of O leads to a loss of consistency.

Here, it is necessary to determine what denial of the axioms is. For the axiom "$C \supset D$," the axiom $A: (C \cup \neg D)$ will be denied, and for $A: C$, the denial will be a: $\neg C$.

This is a classic method of proof "from the opposite." If the addition of the negation of the statement leads to contradiction, then the statement is true (that is, it logically follows from the ontology).

Practical importances are nonstandard algorithmic problems, in particular [17]:

- Classification of terminology: for this terminology (i.e., TBox) to develop a taxonomy or hierarchy of concepts needs to arrange all atomic concepts concerning meaning (relative to a given TBox).
- Extraction of concept copies: find all instances of a given concept based on a given knowledge base.
- The narrowest concept for an individual (instances): find the smallest (by attachment) concept, an example of which is a given individual with respect to a given knowledge base.
- Response to knowledge base query: give out all sets of individuals that satisfy a given query to a given knowledge base. Conjunctive queries to knowledge bases (and also their disjunctions), which are similar to queries from the field of databases, have been extensively studied.

2.1.1. Extension of ALC logic

There are numerous extensions of ALC logic to additional constructors for concepts, roles, and additional axioms in *TBox* description.

The most famous extensions are [18]:

F: Functional roles: concepts of the form ($\leq 1\ R$) that means: there is no more than one R follower

- *N*: limitations of cardinal roles: concepts of the view ($R \leq n$) that means: there are no more R followers.
- *Q*: qualitative limits of cardinal roles: concepts of the form ($\leq n\ R.C$) that means: there are no more R followers in C.
- *I*: reversal roles: if R is a role then R^{-} also has a role that means the treatment of a binary relation O.

Nominees: if b is the name of an individual, then $\{b\}$ is a concept that means a single-element set.

- *H*: hierarchy of roles: in the *TBox*, the axioms of the nesting of the roles $R \subseteq S$ are allowed.
- *S*: transitional roles: in the *TBox*, the axioms of transitivity of the form $Tr\ (R)$.
- *R*: The axioms components of the role nesting in the *TBox* $(R \bigcirc S \subseteq R, R \bigcirc S \subseteq S)$ with the condition of acyclicity where $R \bigcirc S$ represents the composition operation for roles Language Extensions by specific domains (data types).

2.2. Stages of ontology development

On the basis of the methods discussed in the first section for ontology development, the following steps were selected:

- Defining goals, scope of application of ontology, and set of terms. Ontology of billing is developed as an integral part of the general ontology of OSS/BSS systems for the integration of information from various sources.
- Define classes and develop a hierarchy.
- Definition of relations.
- Limitations and relations of properties. In determining the constraints and properties, available ontology ratio is also determined by the descriptive logic that is required for this ontology.
- Creating instances of classes.

Below is a detailed description of each stage on an example of the ontology development of one of OSS/BSS components—the billing system.

2.2.1. Definition of goals, scope, and set of terms

To determine the goals and scope of application of ontology, it is necessary to answer the following questions [19]:

- What is the SD that the ontology reflects? What will be used? What types of questions, the information presented in the ontology, must be answered and who will use this ontology?
- Billing is an automated system of accounting for the services rendered, their billing and invoicing for payment. Billing system is an important element of software for any operator activity. Ontology of billing system was developed as an integral part of the general ontology for OSS/BSS systems.

At an early stage, it is important to develop a complete list of terms, including concepts that overlap and duplicate.

2.2.2. Define classes and develop a hierarchy

Classes in the developed ontology should be close to physical or logical objects, and their relations to the relations of these objects.

There are several approaches to creating a hierarchy of classes [20]:

- From up to down. It starts with defining the most general concepts of the domain and further detailing the objects in the hierarchy.
- From bottom to the top. It starts with defining detailed and specific classes (the end of the hierarchy tree) with further grouping into more general concepts.

- Combination of the first two methods. It consists in the creation of objects that are completely understandable and then group them into groups and develop more specific objects.

There are six main classes: "Provider," "Service," "Tariff plan," "Account," "User," and "Account." There are also three subclasses for the "Service" category: "Telephony," "Internet," and "Television" and three subclasses for the "Account" class: "Receipt," "Balance," and "Bill of Invoice."

- Class "Provider" contains information about the service provider.
- Class "Service" contains information about the services provided by the provider and their description. It is a parent for subclasses of Internet, Television, and Telephony services.
- Class "Tariff plan" contains information about the tariff plans of the provider.
- The "Account" class is a user account (person).
- The "User" class is direct information about a person who has an account (his/her name, address, etc.).

The "Account" class contains information about the cash accounts associated with this user account. This class is a parent for the "Received" (Receipt), Balance, and "Invoice" classes.

2.2.3. Relations definition

There are two types of relations: the relations between classes and the relations between data types. You can also classify the relations by the following types:

- Internal relations: these are the relations that are inextricably linked with the object.
- External relations are those relations that describe the connection of objects with external objects.
- Relations between instances of this class.
- The relations between instances of different classes from different parts of the hierarchy.

The class "Provider" is associated with the "Service" class with the "has a Service" relation, with the Tariff Plan class relation "has a Tariff Plan", and with the "User" class the relation "has a relation." The class has data-type relations:

- "has a name" with the data type string (the name of the "Provider");
- "has a date of creation" with a data type dateTime (the date of "Provider creation");
- "Has a description" with the data type string (additional description of "Provider").

The "Service" class has the following data type relations:

- "named" with string data type (name "Services")
- "has a description" with the data type string (description of "Services").

The "Tariff Plan" class is related to the "Service" class with the "has Service" relation. It has the following data type relations:

- "named" with string data type (name "Tariff Plan");
- "has a description" with the data type string (description of "Tariff Plan");
- "has value" with the data type integer (the value of "Tariff Plan").

The "Account" class is related to the "Account" and "Tariff Plan" classes in relation to "Has a Bill" and "Uses the Tariff Plan," respectively. It also contains the following data type relations:

- "has login" with data type string (Login "Account");
- "has a password" with the data type string (Account password);
- "has an email" with the data type string (registered e-mail "Account").

The class "User" is associated with the "Account" class with the relation "has an Account," with the class "Service" with respect to "using the Service" and with the "Provider" class, the relation "has a relation." In the class description, there are following relations of data types:

- "has a full name" with string data type (username "User");
- "has passport data" with string data type (Passport data of "User");
- "has address" with data type string (address of "User").

The "Account" class is associated with the "Tariff Plan" class for the "has a Tariff Plan."

The "Payed Invoice (Receipt)" class has the following data type relations:

- "has a paid amount" with the data type integer (paid amount)
- "has a payment date" with the dateTime (date of payment for this account).

The "Balance" class has the following data type relations:

- "has a sum" with the type of data integer (amount of money on the balance sheet)
- "has a balance date" with the dateTime (date for which the balance information is viewed).

The main classes of ontology and the basic relations between them are depicted in **Figure 1**.

2.2.4. Relation limitations and relation properties

Restrictions on relations allow you to describe the valid values, type, number of values, and other features that a property of this class can possess. Relations can be symmetrical, reflexive, traceable, reversible, may have functional limitations, or be hierarchical.

A detailed description of the constraints and relation properties available on this ontology is given in section "Definition of descriptive logic."

2.2.5. Creating class instances

The validation of the developed ontology and the creation of specific instances of classes are performed at this stage.

The important question is: "Whether to develop a new subclass or make a new value an instance of an existing class?"

There are several rules that can be used to answer this question [21]:

The subclass of an existing class is usually:

- Has a relations that a superclass does not have.
- Has other restrictions on the ratio, unlike the restrictions in the superclass.
- Participates in other interactions between classes, unlike the superclass.

2.3. Definition of descriptive logic

To determine descriptive logic and, the writing language of ontology, which is necessary to describe this ontology, it is necessary to determine which types of relations and constraints are present in this ontology:

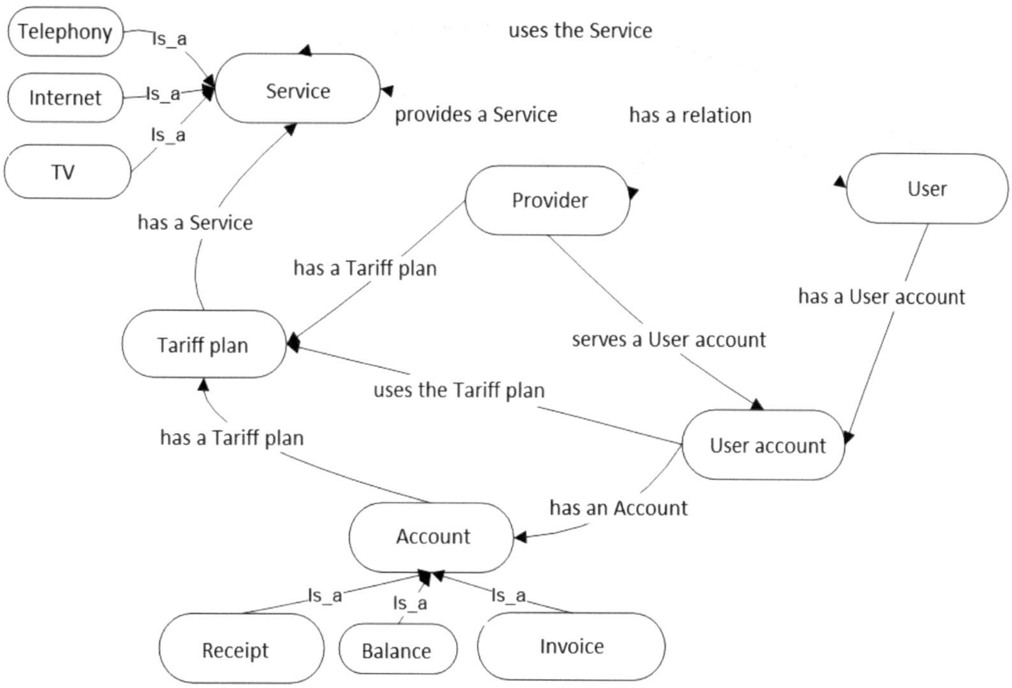

Figure 1. Billing system ontology.

- Inversion of the relations $R \equiv S-$. Many relations in ontology have explicitly defined reciprocal relations. This relation has a "Bill" and "is a Bill," "has an Account" and "is an Account," "has Service" and "is a Service," and "has a Tariff Plan" and "is a Tariff Plan." Reverse relations are convenient to avoid errors when filling in information. If one of them is present in ontology, inverse relations will be listed automatically with the output machine. It is also possible to use implicitly given inverse relations. For example, to describe the relations "has a relation," an inverse "serving account" was used.
- Relations of hierarchy $R \subseteq S$. In general, these relationships correspond to the hierarchy of classes. The relationship "has an Internet service," "has a Service Telephony," and "has a TV service" is a subsidiary of the "has Service" relationship. The ratio is "Balance," "Has a Bill of Account," and "Has a Paid Account", a subsidiary of the "Has Account." As a result of the deduction, if there is a child relationship in the ontology, the output machine will be added to the relation for the parental relation.
- The symmetry of relations $R \subseteq (R^{-})$ and the asymmetry of the relations $R \subseteq$ not (R^{-}).

The relation "has relations" between the classes "User" and "Provider" is symmetric. Most of relations are asymmetric, for example, the ratio "has a Tariff Plan," "serves the Account," etc. For symmetric relations, the relation for the inverse pair is automatically added during derivation. For preventing errors when filling in information in an ontology asymmetry for relations is indicated.

- Functionality of relations (≤ 1 R). Most typified relations are functional, for example, the "has a password" relations for the "Account" class or "has a creation date" for the "Provider" class.
- Irreflexivity of relations. In the absence of reflexive relations, all relations of this ontology are irreflexive. This attribute property is added to prevent errors that may occur when filling in information in an ontology.
- Composition of relations R o S. It is used to determine relations "has a relation" defined as the composition of relations "has an Account" and "inverse servicing Account," and to determine the relation "uses the Service," defined as the composition of relations "has an Account," "Uses the Tariff Plan," and "has a Service." These ratios are added by the output machine if the ontology has the necessary chain of relations.
- Data type relations

For this ontology, the expression of the SRIF (D) is very clear, where the letters SR mean transitivity, composition, and characteristics (symmetry, reflexivity, etc.) roles, I—inversion, F —functionality, and (D)—the ratio of data types. Since the ontology uses the composition of the relations and they were added only in the version of the language describing the ontology OWL 2, this language was chosen for the further ontology development.

2.4. Managing metadata in data storage

Data vault implementation is a complex task that requires developers and architects to have sufficient knowledge in the SD and appropriate expertise. The use of ontology can be useful in many aspects of designing data storage.

Semantic Web allows companies and organizations to store and process a huge amount of valuable semantically annotated data. To date, many applications attach metadata and semantic annotations to the generated information (using domain and application ontologies ontology).

Consider, for example, a customer relationship management (CRM) system in which customer addresses are stored, and a billing system in which we can find information on account receipts, debts, etc. Transferring this information to the data vault, the ontology can set up the necessary links to provide combined customer information, as well as for further analysis (for example, the most risky and unreliable locations).

In order to be able to manage complex processes and large volumes of data, data warehouse system (DWH) should be supplemented with additional information. The framework for managing metadata, using the metadata repository as the basis, allows you to effectively develop and store such metadata. **Figure 2** depicts the general architecture of the data store. Data come from heterogeneous internal and external data sources and integrate into data storage for further analysis.

Since different data sources have heterogeneous data models that are different from the data storage model, data transformation needs to be implemented to ensure structural and semantic compliance. The ETL process between the levels of data sources and data management ensures appropriate extraction, clearing, transformation, and downloading of data from sources to the SD. The upper level of architecture is analysis level that provides various analytical tools [22].

All levels of architecture are connected to the metadata repository, which stores metadata for all four levels. The metadata store contains information that is needed to support the administration, development, and use of the data storage.

Data storage metadata can be used for different purposes and include different types of information. The two main areas of application are tracking the origin of the data and analyzing the data interconnections. Tracking the origin of the data allows the business user to track the data elements within data storage or other systems that are data sources. The data impact analysis is used to identify the potential impact of planned changes on some data elements in the DWH or the source system before they are actually implemented. Requests for this type are usually processed in graphs that show how data elements are converted to different levels of data storage. In order to analyze these graphs, using relational database tools and SQL queries, complex algorithms are required. Regarding this, some commercially available metadata management tools (such as ASG Rochade) do not open access to their mechanisms.

Semantic Web technologies, the Resource Description Framework, OWL (Web Ontology Language), OWL (Web Ontology Language), program logic modules, rules for adding rules, such as SWRL (Semantic Web Rule Language), as well as SPARQL query language, provide proven, standardized management tools structures of graphs. In addition, mapping using ontologies can be used to manage, store, and integrate metadata in heterogeneous data storage systems.

Data storage is used to support users in achieving more efficient and fast business decisions or to open business trends. Data are extracted from various sources of internal and external data

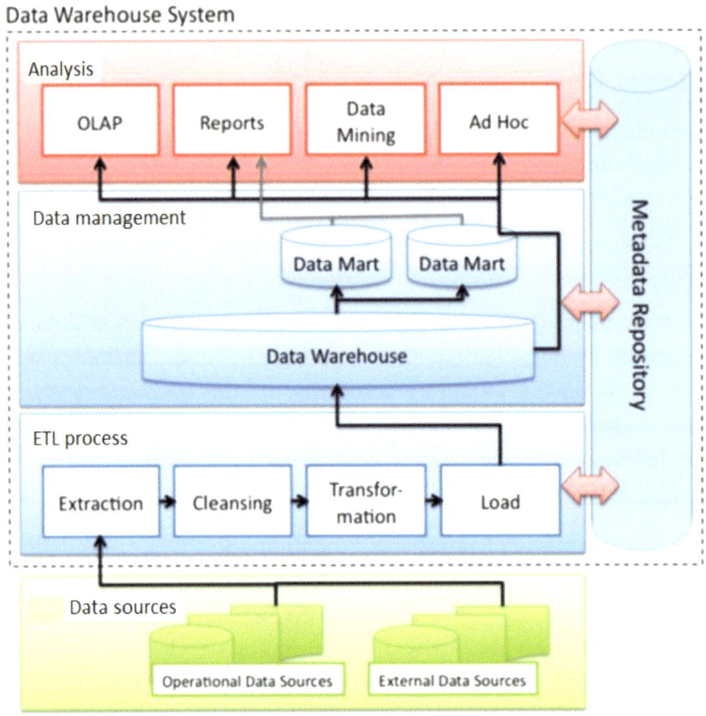

Figure 2. The data store general architecture of the billing system.

and historically integrated into the data storage, serving as the basis for analytic queries. Since different data sources have heterogeneous patterns and structures that are different from the data storage data model, transformation is required in order to eliminate structural and semantic differences.

In **Figure 3**, the ETL process is depicted as the level between data sources and the level of data management. It covers copying, clearing, converting, and downloading data to data storage. The level of data analysis that reflects various analytical systems, such as OLAP and data mining, is placed above the data management level. All data storage levels are connected to a metadata repository, which stores the metadata of each component. The metadata contains information that supports the operation, development, and administration of data storage.

Comprehensive, manageable metadata storage improves the extraction of information, reduces efforts to develop and administer [23]. The metadata include the logical and physical models of the data of individual components and their relations. With this information, two of the main metadata management tasks—the origin of data and impact analysis—can be addressed. Data origin requests are used to trace the path of certain data elements through various DWH components, for example, a user who has requested a certain metric and wants to know which system the attribute starts with [24]. Impact analysis is aimed at identifying the possible effects of modifications of data elements, showing which other data elements will also be affected by this change.

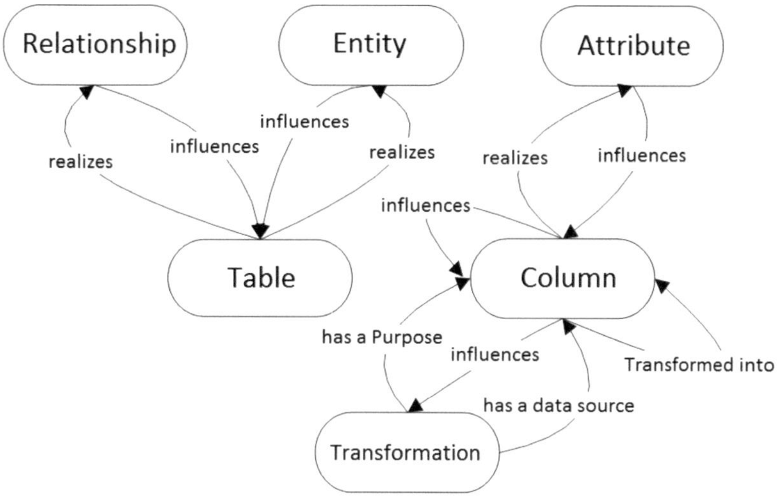

Figure 3. The data storage metamodel.

Most ETL software has a metadata management system (e.g., Informatica PowerCenter, IBM DataStage, Microsoft SQL Server Integration Services). Also, these vendors provide tools for importing and exporting metadata.

There are also decisions that relate directly to subject domain and do not relate to individual ETL programs. In this case, you need to look for a way to download them to the system. However, the mechanisms used in these cases are commercial secrets (for example, in ASG Rochade use the internal procedural language Rochade Procedural Language (RPL)) or based on a relational database.

Since elements of different levels of data vault are connected through transformation, these connections can be described as a graph. The main task of the metadata management system in this case is an effective analysis of queries in these graphs. For these purposes, it is proposed to use Semantic Web technologies: RDF, OWL, software for logical output to improve the efficiency of queries.

The DWH metadata model should be displayed as an OWL ontology, in which the metadata itself will be stored as an ontology instance. Using OWL language features and using language to create rules for SWRL, logical output can be obtained by a more complete ontology. Requests for these data can be done using the SPARQL language.

Let us describe the example of a metadata model (**Figure 3**). In the model, the following logical elements are present: *Relations, Entity, Attribute*, physical elements: *"Table," "Column,"* as well as a separate *"Transformation"* element that reflects the transformation of some columns of tables into others. There is a detailed description of the items below:

Class *"Relations"* is used to store information about the relations between entities in the data model. As the connections example, it is possible to use the external key. This class can be used with the attitudes *"influences"* and *"realizes"* with the class *"Table."*

Class "*Entity*" is used to represent objects of the subject domain. The "*Table*" class implements physically this class. This class may have relations "*realizes*" and the relations "*influences*" with the class "*Table.*"

Class "*Attribute*" logically reflects the objects attributes of the subject domain. The class "*Column* implements physically this class, but it can relate to relations "*realizes*" and "*influences*" with this class.

Class "*Column*" is a physical implementation of the "*Attribute*" class. It is a base for the "*Transformation*" class and may have such relations as "*influences,*" "*realizes,*" and "*transforms.*"

Class "*Table*" is a physical realization of the classes "*Entity*" and "*Relations*" and is a domain class for the ratio "*realizes*" for these two classes.

Class "*Transformation*" is additional for the metadata model and is designed to display the relations between the columns of data sources and data storage columns. It may have relations "*has_a goal*" and "*has a data source.*"

The logical element implementation in physical level is displayed using the ratio "*realizes.*" This model is implemented as OWL ontology. Also, in the model, there are relations between the columns "*transforms_into,*" which is defined by the "*has_a_goal*" and "*has_a data_source*" data.

The ratio of "*influences*" is defined by the ratio "*realizes*":

- has a data source (? *t*.? *a*) ∧ has a goal (? *t*.? *b*) → transforms (? *a*?, *b*)
- realizes (? *a*?, *b*) → influences (? *a*.? *b*)
- realizes (? *b*.? *a*) → influences (? *A*.? *B*)
- has a data source (? *T*.? *A*) → influences (? *A*.? *T*)
- has a goal (? *T*.? *A*) → influences (? *T*.? *A*).

The used Turtle code to describe the properties of relations data is given in **Figure 4**.

```
#########################################################################
#  Object Properties
#########################################################################
:influence rdf:type owl:ObjectProperty ;
      owl:propertyChainAxiom ( [ owl:inverseOf :has a data source] ) , ( :realizes) ,
(:has a goal) , ( [ owl:inverseOf :realizes]) .
:has a data source rdf:type owl:ObjectProperty ;
:has a goal rdf:type owl:ObjectProperty ;
:realizes rdf:type owl:ObjectProperty .
:transforms_в rdf:type owl:ObjectProperty ,
                  owl:TransitiveProperty ;
          owl:propertyChainAxiom ( [ owl:inverseOf :has a data source]:has a goal)
```

Figure 4. Example of the Turtle code.

It becomes possible to obtain new data due to logical deduction using the proposed model. By specifying, for the data source columns, additional metadata that will indicate in which transformations these speakers are involved, it will be possible to trace the data path from the sources to the data storage. Also, the use of this model makes it possible to detect the impact on the system of changing certain components of the data vault.

3. Summary

1. An analysis of the feasibility of ontology development is conducted, and the main advantages of using Semantic Web technologies in information systems are given.
2. A detailed review of existing methods of ontology development is carried out, and features, priorities, and drawbacks of each of them are given, and a comparative description of methods of ontology development is given.
3. Examples of applications of Semantic Web technologies at different stages of development and use of data warehouses, namely, for requirements analysis, reconciliation of needs and data chains, determination of types of data in measurements, and incompleteness of input data are considered.
4. The semantics and syntax of the main descriptive logic ALC was described, and the basic axioms, extensions, problems of logical conclusion, and nonstandard algorithmic problems were defined.
5. The stages of the ontology of the billing system were defined and described, the basic classes were defined, the hierarchy and relations between classes were described, and class instances were created for checking ontology for incompatibility and obtaining output.
6. The method of metadata management with the use of Semantic Web technologies is proposed, the metadata ontology is described, the logical and physical classes are described, and the relations between them are determined.
7. For the proposed metadata ontology, the properties of the relationships between classes were described, which in the future would allow new data to be extracted as a result of logical output, as well as in listing the Turtle code to describe these relationships.

Author details

Larysa Globa[1]*, Rina Novogrudska[1], Alexander Koval[1] and Vyacheslav Senchenko[2]

*Address all correspondence to: lgloba@its.kpi.ua

1 National Technical University of Ukraine, Kyiv Polytechnic Institute, Kyiv, Ukraine

2 Institute for Information Recording, Kyiv, Ukraine

References

[1] Голиков НВ. Применение онтологий/Н.В. Голиков//Институт вычислительных технологий СО РАН, Новосибирск [Електроний ресурс] Електрон. текстові дані. Режим доступу: http://www.ict.nsc.ru/ws/YM2006/10628/golikov.html Середа. 15 квітня 2014

[2] Cyc, access address: https://ru.wikipedia.org/wiki/Cyc, access data: 5.12.2017

[3] Ефименко ИВ. Онтологическое моделирование: подходы, модели, методы, средства, решения. И.В. Ефименко, В.Ф. Хорошевский [Електроний ресурс] Електрон. текстові дані. Режим доступу: http://www.hse.ru/data/2011/12/22/1261631357/WP7_2011_08_1.pdf Понеділок. 17 березня 2014

[4] Dietz J. Enterprise Engineering Enterprise Ontology [Електроний ресурс] Електрон. текстові дані. Режим доступу: http://www.siks.nl/map_IO_Archi_2006/J.Dietz.pdf Вівторок. 6 травня 2014

[5] TOVE Ontology Project [Електроний ресурс] Електрон. текстові дані. Режим доступу: http://www.eil.utoronto.ca/enterprise-modelling/tove/Неділя травня; 2014

[6] Ferndndez M. METHONTOLOGY: From Ontological Art Towards Ontological Engineering./ M. Ferndndez, A. Gomez-Perez, N. Juristo [Електроний ресурс]. Електрон. текстові дані. [Режим доступу: http://oa.upm.es/5484/1/METHONTOLOGY_.pdf Субота. 3 травня 2014

[7] Rizzi S, Abelló A, Lechtenbörger J, Trujillo J. Research in data warehouse modeling and 20 design: Dead or alive. In: Song I-Y, Vassiliadis P, editors. DOLAP '06: Proceedings of the 9th ACM International Workshop on Data Warehousing and OLAP. New York, USA: 2006. pp. 3-10

[8] Santini S. Ontology: Use and abuse. In: N. Boujemaa, M. Detyniecki, A. Nu rnberger, editors. Adaptive Multimedia Retrieval, Vol. 4918 of Lecture Notes in Computer Science. Spring; 2007. pp. 17-31

[9] Oren E, Moller K. What are Semantic Annotations/Digital Enterprise Research Institute, National University of Ireland, Galway [Електроний ресурс] Електрон. текстові дані. Режим доступу: http://www.siegfriedhandschuh.net/pub/2006/whatissemannot2006.pdf Неділя, 11 травня; 2014

[10] Skoutas D, Simitsis A. Ontology-based conceptual design of ETL processes for both structured and semi-structured data. International Journal on Semantic Web and Information Systems. 2007;**3**(4):1-24

[11] Romero O, Abelló A. Automating multidimensional design from ontologies. In: DOLAP. 2007:1-8

[12] Nuseibeh B, Easterbrook S. Requirements engineering: A roadmap. In: Proceedings of the Conference on the Future of Software Engineering. New York, USA: ACM; 2000. pp. 35-46

[13] Jureta I, Mylopoulos J, Faulkner S. Revisiting the Core Ontology and Problem in Requirements Engineering. RE. 2008:71-80

[14] Mazón J-N, Trujillo J. A model driven modernization approach for automatically deriving multidimensional models in data warehouses. ER. 2007:56-71

[15] The ACM Computing Classification Systems [Електроний ресурс] Електрон. текстові дані. Режим доступу: http://portal.acm.org/ccs.cfm?part=author&coll=portal&dl=GUIDE Неділя. 18 травня, 2014

[16] Клинов П. О формальных основах OWL [Електроний ресурс]. Електрон. текстові дані. Режим доступу: http://semanticfuture.net/index.php/ О_формальных_основах_OWL Четвер. 4 квітня, 2013

[17] Glimm B, Horrocks I, Lutz C, Sattler U. Conjunctive query answering for the description logic SHIQ. In: Proceedings of the Twentieth International Joint Conference on Artificial Intelligence (IJCAI 2007). 2007;**31**:c. 151-198

[18] Бочаров ВА. Основы логики: підруч. В.А. Бочаров, В.И. Маркин — М.: ИНФРА-М; 2001. 296 с

[19] Noy N, McGuinness D. Ontology Development 101: A Guide to Creating Your First Ontology. Access address: https://protege.stanford.edu/publications/ontology_development/ontology101.pdf, access data: 10.12.2017

[20] Uschold M, Gruninger M. Ontologies: Principles, methods and applications. Knowledge Engineering Review. 1996;**11**(2):93-155

[21] Koval S. Automatic text processing based on the object predicate system, Structural and applied linguistics. St. Petersburg; 1998;(5):199-207

[22] Reisser A, Priebe T. Utilizing semantic web technologies for efficient data lineage and impact analyses in data warehouse environments. In: Proceedings of 20th International Workshop on Database and Expert Systems Application DEXA'09. IEEE; 2009. pp. 59-63

[23] Do HH, Rahm E. On metadata interoperability in data warehouses, technical report. Department of Computer Science, University of Leipzig, Tech. Rep.; 2000. http://doi.uni-leipzig.de/pub/2000-13/

[24] Cui Y, Widom J. Practical lineage tracing in data warehouses. In: ICDE; 2000. pp. 367-378

Chapter 3

Examples of Ontology Model Usage in Engineering Fields

Larysa Globa, Rina Novogrudska,
Alexander Koval and Vyacheslav Senchenko

Additional information is available at the end of the chapter

http://dx.doi.org/10.5772/intechopen.74369

Abstract

The proposed research deals with the improvement of engineering knowledge classification and recognition by means of ontology usage. Ontology model allows structure information as well as to raises the effectiveness of search. Research describes the development of ontology models for engineering knowledge in Internet portal and modeling system for the classification and recognition of marine objects. The ontology model usage for the engineering knowledge portal development allows to systematize data and knowledge, to organize search and navigation, to describe informational and computational recourses according to the meta-notion standards. The description of modeling system subject domain is based on ontology that allows to realize the recognition of marine objects based on their parameters.

Keywords: ontology, knowledge portals, marine object, the marine objects classification and recognition

1. Ontology model of engineering knowledge portals

There exists a great number of engineering equipment and software to solve specialized tasks of different types. However, they are either very expensive or much closed. The important theoretical and practical results obtained by the researches are mostly limited to specific scientific institutions. Thus, the process of knowledge concentration is going on and knowledge becomes being accessed only by limited groups of people. That is why the most urgent task is to give the possibility of using this knowledge by wider groups of investigators for whom this knowledge is intended to and is in need of. Besides access to knowledge, such shortcomings are characterized as poorly structured and insufficiently systematized information on the Internet. In addition, the information is widely distributed through various Internet sites, numerous electronic archives and libraries. From the preceding, it is evident that the necessity of new method is urgent to develop specialized Internet knowledge portal using vast amounts of various informational and computational resources in definite sphere. Ontology model takes into the account specifics of Internet portals. Suggested model gives the possibility to systematize and structure Internet portals information as well as to organize informational search.

The aim of this research is to improve access to engineering knowledge by means of designing specialized Internet portal of engineering knowledge (e.g., the portal in the field of strength of materials). The following tasks are to be solved:

- qualitative knowledge presentation on the portal;
- to systematize and structure information;
- to formalize the engineering knowledge and
- to organize an effective and purposeful search.

It is necessary to design the model of knowledge representation at the portal of engineering knowledge. It is clear that the model of high-quality designing to represent knowledge at the portal may allow realizing all the abovementioned requirements. Ontology was used as a model knowledge representation at the portal [1].

Formally, the ontology may be specified as

$$O = \{C, A, R, T, F, D\}$$

where

- C is the set of classes that describes the notions of a subject domain;
- A is the set of attributes that describes the features of notions and relations;
- R is the set of relations specified for classes:

$$R = \{R_{AS}, R_{IA}, R_n, R_{CD}\},$$

where

R_{AS} is the associative relation $R_{AS}(O_2) = \{C_i(O_2) \times C_j(O_2), M(R_{AS}) = \{str\}$, where M is the type of relation meaning,

R_{IA} is the relation "is-are" $R_{IA}(O) = C_k(O) \subset C_m(O)$,

R_n is the relation of "heredity" $R_n(O) = a_i, r_i \,|A_{C_m}(O) \to a_i, r_i|\, A_{C_k}(O)$,

R_{CD} is the relation "class-data" $R_{CD}(O) = C_j(O) \subseteq D_i(O)$;

- T is the set of standard types of attribute values;
- F is the set of limits for values of attribute notions and relations;
- D is the set of class exemplar.

Ontology described here may serve to present notions that are necessary for describing knowledge in the field of strength of materials as well as for engineering activities performed in this context.

1.1. Elements of portal ontology

The ontology of the portal in the field of strength of materials includes four ontologies such as engineering activity ontology, engineering knowledge ontology, engineering computations ontology and subject domain ontology [2]: $O_{portal} = \{O_1(O_2, O_3, O_4), O_5\}$ (**Figure 1**).

Engineering ontology consists of engineering activity ontology, engineering knowledge ontology and engineering computations ontology:

$$O_2 \supset O_2, O_3, O_4$$

Engineering activity ontology includes general classes of notions related to the organization of engineering activities such as *Person, Organization, Activity, Event, Literature, Documents, Teaching materials, Publication* and *Location*:

$$O_2 = \{C_{O_2}, A_{O_2}, R_{O_2}, T_{O_2}, F_{O_2}, D_{O_2}\}$$

Engineering knowledge ontology includes the meta-notions that specify structures to describe the problem. The classes of this ontology correspond to *Research method, Research object, Research result, Research purpose* and *Research equipment*:

$$O_3 = \{C_{O_3}, A_{O_3}, R_{O_3}, T_{O_3}, F_{O_3}, D_{O_3}\}$$

Engineering computations ontology unites classes that describe calculation abilities realized at the portal. Engineering computations ontology includes classes such as *Calculation, Service, Service Parameters, Results* and *Interface*:

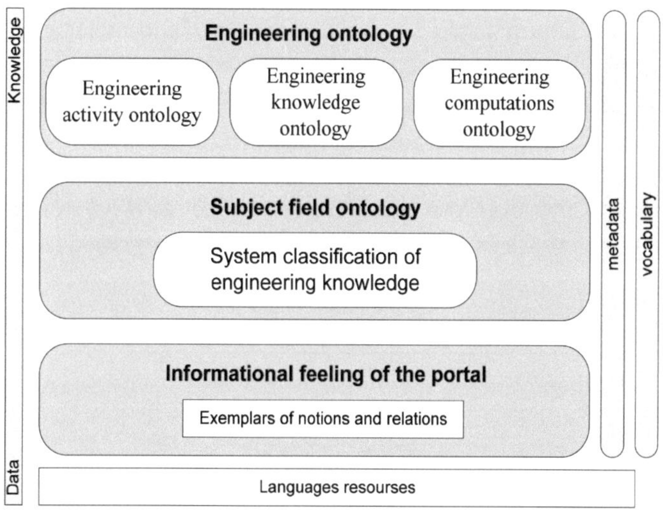

Figure 1. Ontologies of the portal.

$$O_4 = \{C_{O_4}, A_{O_4}, R_{O_4}, T_{O_4}, F_{O_4}, D_{O_4}\}$$

The classes enumerated are related to each other with classes of one ontology and to the classes of other ontologies by means of associative relations. For example, classes of engineering activity ontology "*Person*" and "*Organization*" are related through associative relations "*Be a member of*". It means that in real life, a person may be a member of some organization. Associative relations may correlate not only with classes of one ontology, but also with classes that belong to different ontologies. For example, class "*Literature*" being a class of engineering activity ontology is associatively correlated by relation "*Describe*" with the engineering computations ontology class "*Research result*". In addition to associative relations in working up the portal ontologies, the relations of the type "is-are" to relations of subclasses with their parent classes are used. For example, class "*Literature*" is related by means of "is-are" with classes "*Documents*", "*Training materials*" and "*Published materials*". It means that class "*Literature*" is parent class for its subclasses "*Documents*", "*Training materials*" and "*Published materials*".

Subject domain ontology represents general knowledge of subject domain such as hierarchy of notion classes and their semantic relations. Ontology of subject domain describes the strength of materials as a whole as science and its parts, notions and their connections. These notions are realizations of meta-notions of engineering knowledge ontology and may be put in the order into hierarchy "is-are". For example, "*Research methods*" (class of engineering knowledge ontology) correspond to such methods as methods of strain, defluction, stress distribution, and so on in the field of strength of materials [3]. "*Research objects*" are materials, material groups or specific material properties. Main class of engineering computations ontology "*Calculation*" corresponds to such notions from the field of strength of materials as limit state design, deformation analysis, stress calculation, and so on.

1.2. Searching process based on ontology

The search for information is also based on ontology model. Due to this fact, user can set the search request not only with the help of keywords, but also with the help of terms of subject domain, which are well-known to the user. The main elements of such search request are basic notions of ontology: its classes, attributes and relations of various kinds. Search request that is formed by means of ontology is simple for user and is full from a perspective of information found. For example, the search request: "*To find the results of research, that was held with steel, received by Gain V.A. in 2008 and that are described in the book "Steel behavior,"* published by the German Institute of Material Science" in a formal way can be presented as:

Class: "Research result"

Relation: "Was held with"

Class: "Research object"

Attribute: "Name"

Class exemplar: "Steel"

Relation: "Received"

Class: "Person"

Attribute: "First name, Last name, Surname"

Class exemplar: "Gain V.A."

&

Class: "Research result"

Attribute: "Year"

Class exemplar: "2008"

Relation: "Described"

Class: "Literature"

Relation: "is-are"

Class: "Teaching materials"

Attribute: "Name"

Class exemplar: "Steel behavior"

Relation: "Published"

Class: "Organization"

Attribute: "Name"

Class exemplar: "German Institute of Material Science"

After presentation of search request in the terms of ontology model, let us make the formalized presentation of them:

C_1= {*research result*}, R_{AS_1} = {*was held with*},

C_2= {*research object*}, A_{C_2}= {*name*},

D_{C_2}= {*steel*}, R_{AS_2}= {*received*},

C_3= {*person*}, $A_{C_{3_1}}$ = {*First name, Last name, Surname*},

$D_{C_{3_1}}$ = {*Gain V.A.*}, C_1= {*research result*},

$A_{C_{3_2}}$= {*year*}, $D_{C_{3_2}}$ = {*2008*},

R_{AS_3}= {*Described*}, C_4 = {*literature*},

$R_{IA_{45}}$={*is-are*}, C_5 = {*teaching materials*},

A_{C_5}= {*name*}, D_{C_5} = {*steel behavior*},

R_{AS_4}= {*published*}, C_6 = {*organization*},

A_{C_6}= {*name*}, D_{C_6} = {*German Institute of Material Science*}.

For search request realization such description of classes and relations are actual:

- classes: $C_2(A_{C_2}, D_{C_2}, R_{C_2})$, $C_3(A_{C_3}, D_{C_3}, R_{C_3})$, $C_4(A_{C_4}, D_{C_4}, R_{C_4})$, $C_5(A_{C_5}, D_{C_5}, R_{C_5})$, $C_6(A_{C_6}, D_{C_6}, R_{C_6})$,
- relation of "is-are" type: $R_{IA_{45}} \leftarrow C_4 \subset C_5$,
- associative relations: $R_{AS_1} = \{ C_1 \times C_2\}$, $R_{AS_2} = \{ C_1 \times C_3\}$,
- $R_{AS_3} = \{ C_1 \times C_4\}$, $R_{AS_4} = \{ C_5 \times C_6\}$.

With the help of formal description given earlier, search request could be given as shown in **Table 1**. **Figure 2** shows the process of search through the elements of portal ontology. Class and relations exemplars, set by user in the terms of search request, are marked with bold text and bold line. Class "*Research result*" is connected by appropriate associative relations with classes "*Research object*," "*Literature*," "*Person*" and "*Organization*." In these classes, the exemplars set by the user are found: Steel, Gain, Steel behavior, German Institute of Material Science. In such a way, exemplar of class "*Research result*" that corresponds to these exemplars could be found. Therefore, this exemplar is the theory of strength.

From the practical point of view, implementation of the method will make it possible to give the most optimal result for search request. As the search process is held according to the tree of terms determined in the ontology model, the search query implementation makes all of its terms associated with the relationship of the ontological model. Thus, the result of a search query will be the most appropriate term assignments to the terms in the search query.

1.3. Ontology model integration into knowledge portals

Most of the portals use relationship databases to organize and to process data. To provide information on the existing knowledge portal in the form of ontological models, it is possible to use a relational database to get data for ontological model designing.

This module should give API to represent ontological model for knowledge portal. This model is based on data from the database. Ontological model that is accessible via modules API is in RDF format. **Figure 3** presents the portal with ontology integration schema of used relational database. The schema includes:

- Relational database;
- Knowledge portal component;

Search request	Description
$C_1 \vdash$	Research result
$\xrightarrow{R_{AS_1}} D_{C_2}$	Held with steel
$\xrightarrow{R_{AS_2}} D_{C_{3_1}} \ \& \ D_{C_{3_2}}$	Received by Gain V.A. in 2008
$\xrightarrow{R_{AS_3}} D_{C_5} \xrightarrow{R_{AS_4}} D_{C_6}$	Described in the book "Steel behavior", published by the German Institute of Material Science"

Table 1. Search request formalization.

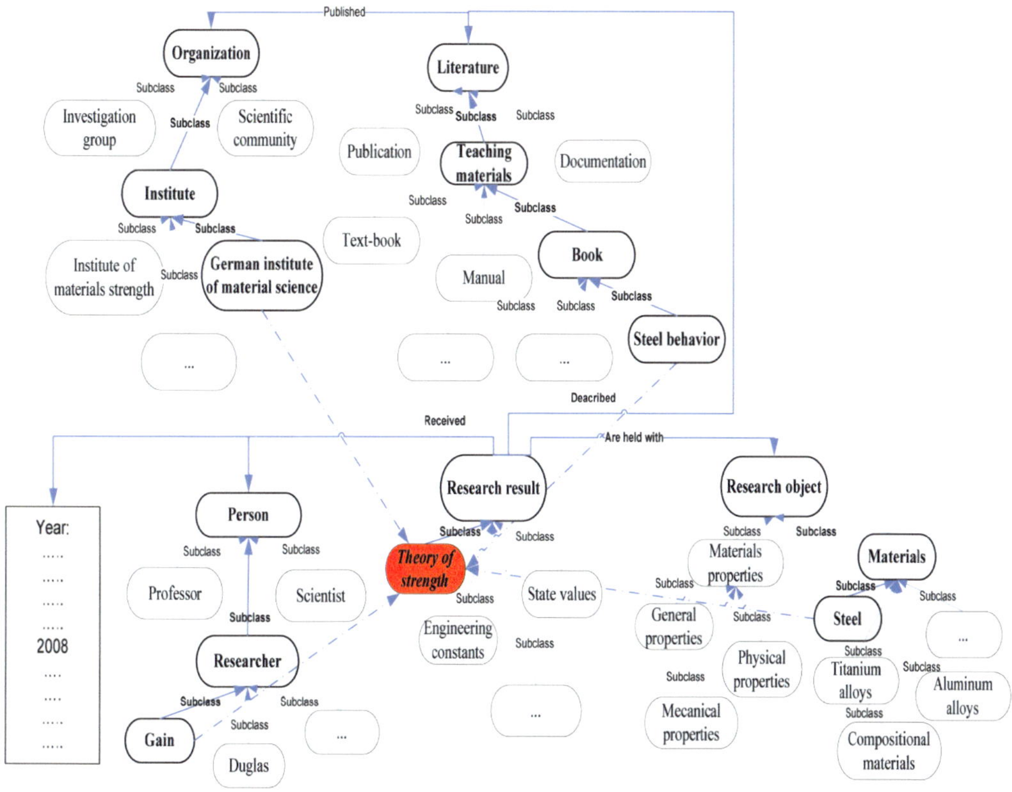

Figure 2. Search request realization process.

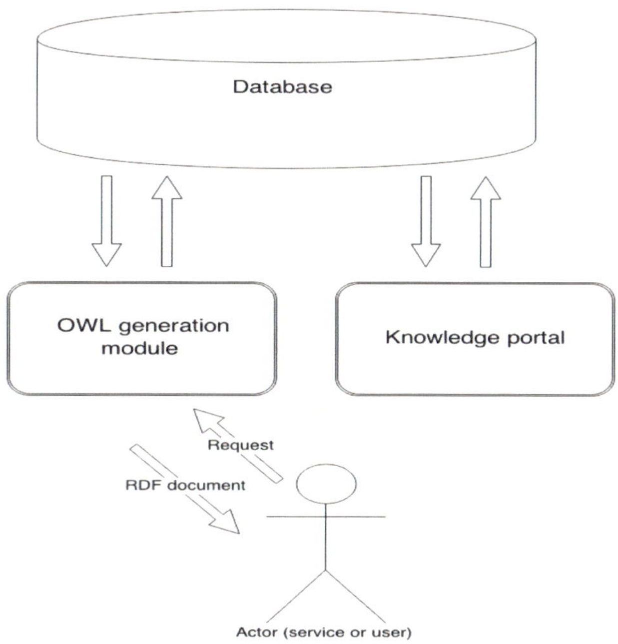

Figure 3. Schema of the portal with ontology integration.

- Generator of Web Ontology Language (OWL) representation and
- Actor (service or user).

To get ontological representation, actor makes requests to OWL generator, OWL generator uses portal database to generate RDF document that corresponds to the ontological model. The main advantage of this approach is that it is not necessary to modify existing knowledge portal.

Let us consider the process of generating RDF document (**Figure 4**). To generate RDF document using specific program module it is in need to link ontology classes with SQL query. Module gets query using the class name and execute SQL request to database of portal. When database returns appropriate data, the module generates this data in RDF view. After all processing, the module returns RDF document to the client.

Knowledge portals have complex structure. It should be possible to visualize the ontological model on the portal. The end user should have tools for the knowledge portal structure modification using its functionality. Basic requirements for visualization module are as follows:

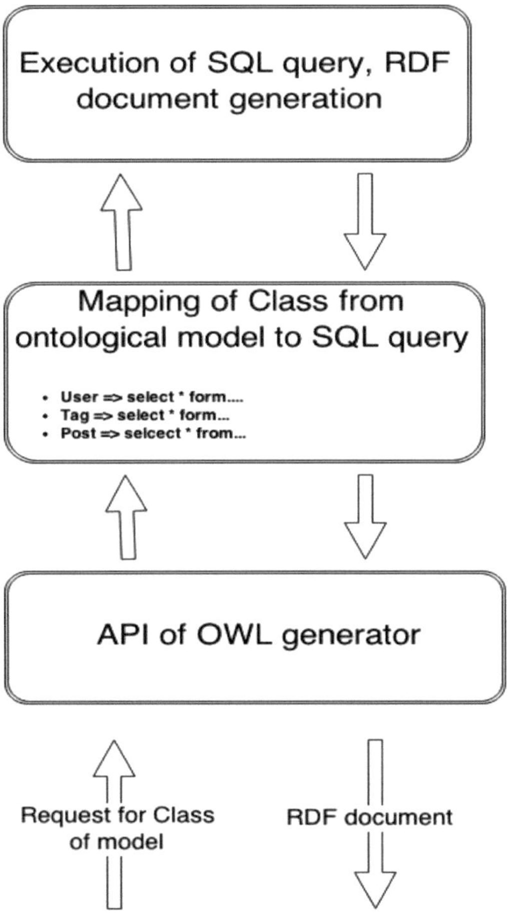

Figure 4. The process of RDF document generation.

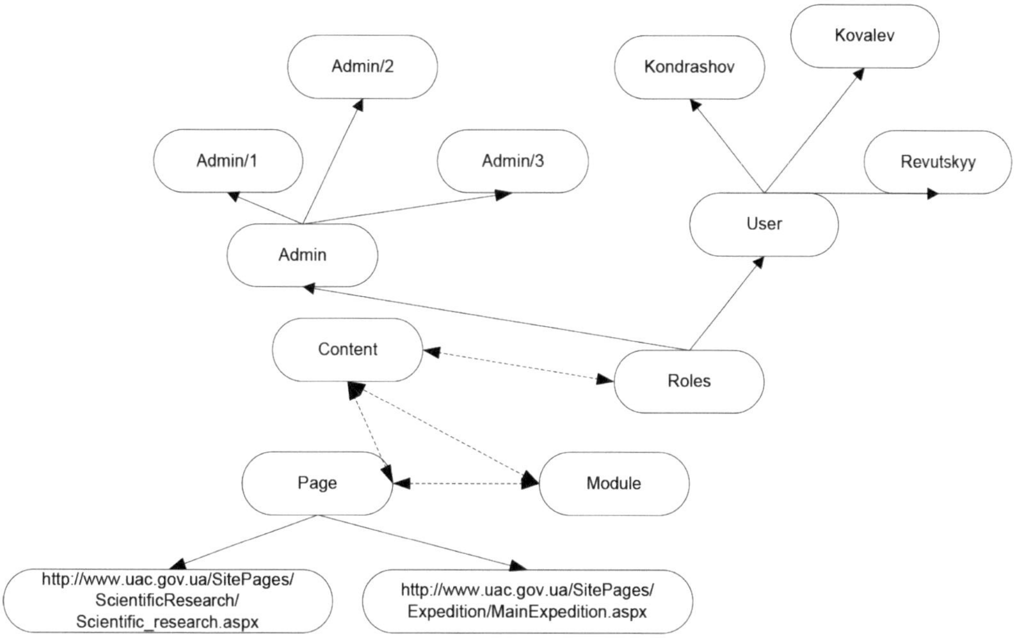

Figure 5. Visualization of classes.

- ability to integrate with portal interface,
- visualize ontological model as a graph,
- each class of models should have unique color and
- visualization should be able to adapt to complex models

Proposed solution developed as a JavaScript module that can be integrated easily with portal interface. Examples of visualization are shown in **Figure 5**.

The classes have different colors. Class "*User*" (user of a portal) has five fields. Class *Post*, which represent note on portal, has nine fields. Also, there are six instances of class *Post*.

2. The ontology model for classification and recognition of marine objects

2.1. Features of semantic modeling technology

The main feature of semantic technology is to store and maintain the integrity of semantics (meaning of knowledge) separately from the contents of data files and from the code of the programs that implement them [4]. Semantic simulation technology differs from traditional methods that combine the meaning of data and the processing procedures directly in the program code. This often leads to the need for a radical manual redevelopment of data structures and total revision of programs during their development or migrate to another platform.

Semantic technologies allow obtaining logical conclusions based on the rules of conceptual models and perform automatic redesign of data structures. Experience the semantic modeling of intelligent systems using ontologies indicates that any subject domain (SD) can be described considerable number of ontologies. From the methodological point of view, it is quite understandable—each ontology reflects a person's perception of the developer of the functioning model of ontology (the main entities, classes, subclasses and their relationships within the general idea about the subject domain). Therefore, it is advisable for the developer to apply such methodology and tools, which allow not only to develop an ontology model, but also to correct it in the process of mastering it, and understanding the features of its functioning, been aimed at the most correct model development.

Under the term ontology, we understood a system of concepts domain, which is represented by a set of entities and their properties, interconnected relations, in order to develop knowledge bases on their basis. Consequently, the main purpose of ontological modeling is to develop a formalized knowledge model of the domain, which is stored electronically and may further improved through a more in-depth understanding of the features of the subject domain.

For the implementation of knowledge-based systems, it is expedient to use common language for describing ontologies such as OWL Lite, OWL DL and OWL 2 [5] that use discriminatory logic for knowledge work. In this case, the semantic modeling process has been performed using the open knowledge base connectivity (OKBC) [6]. This model is based on the theory of frames and uses concepts such as "conceptualization of classes," "objects," "slots," "facets" and "inheritance" for representing knowledge about the subject domain, which allows to develop various knowledge-based applications with a high level of interoperability.

The formal semantics of the subject domain on the OWL describes how to obtain logical investigations, having the ontology of SD, which is to obtain facts that are not represented literally in the ontology, but logically follow from its semantics.

2.2. Methodological aspects of semantic modeling using web ontology language

An applied ontology should describe concepts that depend both on the ontology of tasks and on the ontology of the subject domain. The purpose of the applied ontology is to develop an electronic model of knowledge that allows:

- creation of general terminology of a subject domain, for common use and understanding by all users—system developers;
- give an exact and consistent definition of the meaning of each term and
- provide semantic tasks using axioms that automatically allow you to answer the main questions about the subject domain.

One of the most common languages for representing ontology is the Web Ontology Language (OWL). The OWL language contains elements such as classes, properties and individuals [7]. All concepts of the subject domain are divided into classes, subclasses and instances (copies). The tag describes classes as:

<owl:Class rdf:about = "http://untitled-ontology-9#APM_MK">

Thus, the process of semantic modeling using the unified OKBC model consists of the following steps:

- Definition of the concepts of the subject domain, that is, the basic concepts such as classes, entities, categories (Active Ontology, Entities and Classes) that describe the SD;
- Determination of the set of properties, which describes the properties of the concepts of SD and allow in the final sense to develop a knowledge base of the domain. Formation of concept properties in AKVS is performed using the mechanisms of definition, attributes and roles (Data Properties);
- Establishing relations between concepts of the subject domain and their properties using the mechanisms of forming predicates (Object Properties), which should be taken into account the functional orientation of relations, for example, "solves problems", or "is part of", and so on;
- Setting numerical or logical constraints, which are used to describe the properties of instances (Individuals) of the knowledge base. This is realized through the mechanisms of axiom definition (Axiom) or facet (Value). For example, the maximum speed for terrestrial objects is limited to the value;
- Formation of knowledge base using the mechanism of description of instances of the knowledge base and its filling (Individual by class);
- Development of typical query patterns for the knowledge base using the query language, DL Query and the output machine, Reasoner;
- Checking the correctness of the functioning of the ontological model of SD from the point of view of its correspondence to the initial goals and the task and finding gaps in the ontology using the OntoGraf research mechanism. The evaluation is based on the analysis of the results of testing by various output machines (Reasoner) and the compilation of various types of requests;
- Development of a strategy for improving the ontological model of SD and carrying out the relevant work.

Taking into account the complexity and ambiguity that arises in the process of describing the subject domain, modern science offers several approaches to the creation of ontology:

- Top-down. The use of this method requires the definition of the most general concepts of the domain, with further detail of objects in the class hierarchy and the concepts of the subject domain.
- Down to the top. This approach begins with the definition of detailed and specific classes (the end of the tree of the hierarchy), followed by grouping into more general concepts.
- Combination of the first two methods. First, a description of the concepts that are fully understood, then associate them into groups and develop more complex concepts of subject domain.

2.3. Definition of the depth and scope of the subject domain

It is advisable to start developing an ontology with the purpose of determining its scope and scale. That is, the answer to a few basic questions:

- Which SD will cover the ontology?
- What types of questions should answer information in ontology be?
- Who will use and maintain an ontology?

Of course, the answers to these questions change during the process of designing ontology software, but at any time, they allow you to limit the scale of the ontology if it becomes too complicated.

Consider the methodology for creating an ontology in an example of An Intelligent System For Studying Hydroacoustical Processes.

The main quality of such systems is the accumulation of two types of information:

- real data—hydroacoustic as a result the marine area scanning,
- data modeling—obtained as a result of mathematical modeling, the behavior of the object.

Modeling of hydroacoustical processes requires the development of component models, including the information model of the water area, the database of the parameters of the marine environment (sea noise, ground, coastline, water temperature, deep, salinity) and the parameters of hydroacoustic devices and their interaction with the modeling medium.

Hydroacoustic processes allow to take into account both problems of direct modeling (for the purpose of obtaining objective data-knowledge about the marine facilities under study), and combine the obtained data with expert knowledge (represented as a characteristic set of parameters of real objects and their assessments based on the expert's experience).

Generalized structure of the knowledge-based modeling system for the identification, classification and definition of parameters of movement of marine facilities is shown in **Figure 6**. The conceptual model consists of such structural components [8]:

- Simulation of marine environment performs the functions of creating a simulation scene (parameters of depths, temperatures and salinity, type of bottom, coastline, etc.) and location and specification of the parameters of marine objects (type, size, direction, speed, etc.);
- Modeling of hydroacoustic device sets the scene of the location of fixing devices and their parameters (type, dimensions, sensitivity);
- Hydroacoustic signal analysis is a set of tools for creating models for generating sonar signals and working out methods for their analysis (fast Fourier transforms, digital filtering, spectral, frequency, correlation analysis, etc.);
- Knowledge base maintenance contains a set of tools for testing models of object recognition, their identification, classification and definition of the parameters of the movement of objects, including methods of fuzzy logic;

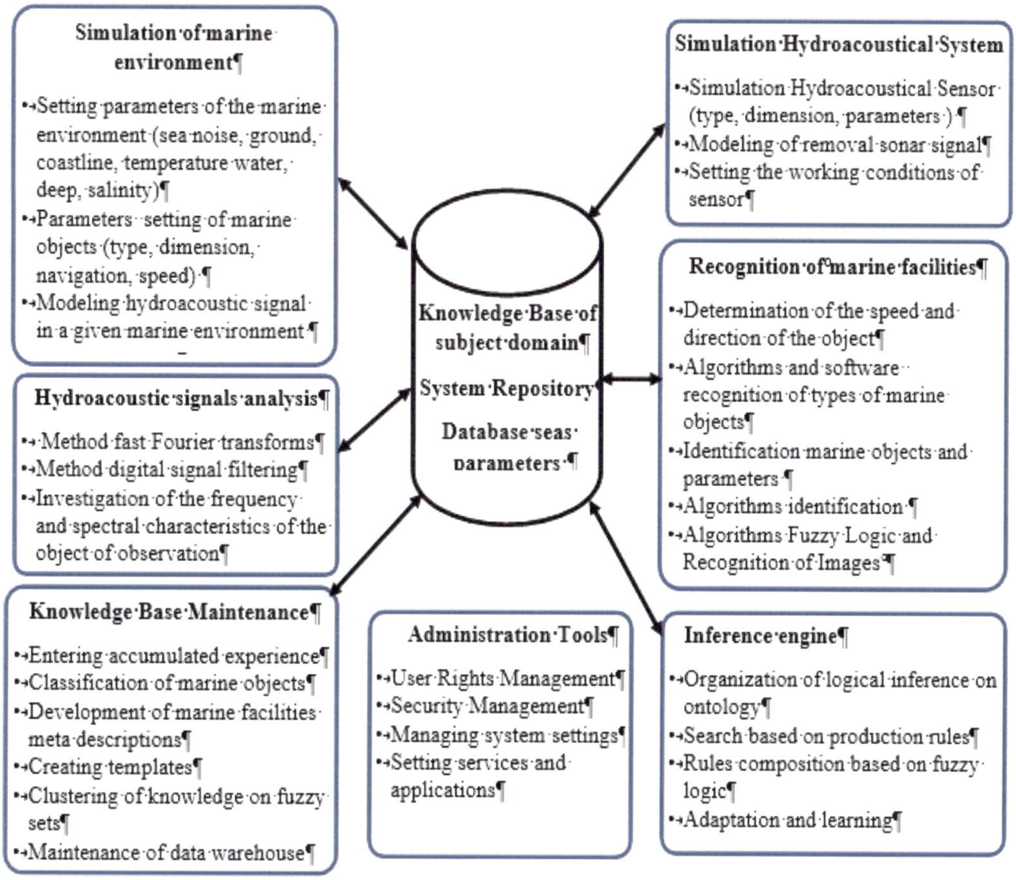

Figure 6. Modeling system structure.

- Knowledge base maintenance is intended for the organization of tools for forming a knowledge base for solving problems of identification and classification of marine objects;
- Inference engine designed to organize logical inference based on accumulated knowledge, including means of composition of product rules, self-learning and adaptation;
- Information storage is the core of the system and provides information to all the structural components of the modeling system, and also contains information with expert assessments of the experiments conducted;
- Administration and management tools provide settings for services and applications to manage user access rights to information resources, manage security and performance of the modeling system.

The proposed system provides opportunities for end-to-end documentation of the processes of hydroacoustic experiments, which gives additional advantages in the formation and accumulation of knowledge about the studied processes, including the formation of scenes and modeling scenarios. Simulation involves the following steps:

1 Creation and maintenance of library of hydroacoustic models, including signal generation models, signal extraction models, signal analysis models, implementation of algorithms for classification and identification of objects.

2 Creation and maintenance tools for entering both types of data such as model and real data (scanning water areas) into the knowledge base;

3 Development of subject domain ontology;

4 Development of algorithms and software for recognition and identification types of marine objects

5 Organization of logical inference on ontology

6 Creation of learning system (scripts and learning algorithms considering SD).

7 Maintenance tools for rules setting based on fuzzy inference;

8 Development of algorithm identification based on logical inference on the ontology and production rules.

9 Development of algorithms for knowledge classification and clustering;

10 Formation of classifiers of the system (noise-emitting objects, hydroacoustic systems, water areas).

11 Scene formation and creating an experiment scenario

12 Fixing the experiment results in DB

13 Evaluation of simulation results

2.4. Conceptual model of the subject domain ontology

Ontology model Ont(SD) of the intellectual system contains the basic concepts (entities—basic concepts of the subject domain), their attributes and describes the relations between them and can be represented as:

$$Ont(SD)_{IS} =< C^{(Ax)}, Ex^{(C)}, Rel^{(H)}, T^{(Q)}, Ax^{(s)}, Rul^{(S)} >$$

where $C^{(Ax)}$-classes (Classes) are a finite set of basic concepts of hydroacoustic processes;

$Ex^{(C)}$-set exemplars classes of ontology;

$Rel^{(H)}$-relations between classes and their types:

$T^{(Q)}$-attributes of each class, their data types and value fields;

$Ax^{(s)}$-axioms that define the basic concepts of SD, which are always true for it and

$Rul^{(S)}$-rules of logical conclusion.

Detailed consideration of the concepts of the subject domain and functional problems leads to the allocation of the following main classes:

1 Experiment class $C^{(Exp)}$: defining characteristics of the conducted experiment—identification number, date of conduct, researcher identifier, service data.

2 Models_Hydroacoustic_processes class $C^{(Mod)}$: describing various models, methods and algorithms for generation, selection and analysis of signals as well as methods and algorithms for classification and identification of marine objects.

3 Hydroacoustic_objects class $C^{(Obj)}$: consisting of some subclasses (marine objects, underwater objects and air objects) and describing properties objects/

4 Aquatorium class $C^{(Sea)}$: describing the maritime area chosen for the experiment: the type of aquatorium, the name and refinement parameters for the type modeling algorithms (coordinates, depths, temperatures, salinity).

5 Experiment_scene class $C^{(Sn)}$: describing the simulation scene, taking into account the characteristics of the marine region as well as the characteristics of the objects that participate in the experiment.

6 Hydroacoustic_System class $C^{(Div)}$: describing the coordinates, composition and types of hydroacoustic devices.

7 Modeling_Scenario class $C^{(Sig)}$: specifying the sequence of individual stages of the simulation. Each step is a set of procedures "start-run-fix the result."

8 Model_estimation class $C^{(Val)}$: for fixing the results of modeling and estimating the correctness of models.

9 Acoustic signal class $C^{(Sig)}$: defining the signal characteristics, including the date of the signal detection and the parameters of the locking device.

10 Waveguide class $C^{(Noise)}$: describing the hydroacoustic interference affecting the propagation and distortion of the hydroacoustic signal as well as the means of neutralizing interference.

In the ontology model, in addition to the main classes, subclasses representing instances of the corresponding classes are also included.

In accordance with the basic rules of the OWL language, a triplet called the RDF graph describes the class. In this graph, vertices are objects and objects, and as arcs are predicates [9]. From a mathematical point of view, the triplet is an instance of an element of a certain binary relation. The expression of the triplet asserts that certain relations indicated by the predicate connect objects marked as the subject and object in particular in the triplet [10].

One of the tools for semantic modeling is the well-known ontology visual editor Protégé 5—Designed by the University of Stanford [11]. Visual methods of designing ontologies help quickly and fully understand the structure of knowledge of the subject domain, which is especially valuable for researchers working in the new subject domain. The Protégé 5 supports all phases of the ontology life cycle in accordance with ISO/IEC 15288: 2002 [7] requirements—from the development of a semantic network and the creation of a knowledge base on its basis, to the formation of user requests to these bases in order to obtain knowledge.

The main window of the Protégé 5 editor consists of tabs that represent the various tools to develop model of knowledge such as <*Active Ontology*>, <*Entities*>, <*Classes*>, <*Data properties*>, <*Object properties*>, <*Individuals by class*>, <*DL Query*>, <*SPARDL Query*>, <*OntoGraf*> and so on (**Figure 7**).

2.5. Formation of the hierarchy of the main classes: Taxonomy of the subject domain

Defining classes and creating their hierarchy (taxonomy) are keys in the development of ontology SD. The taxonomy of classes is a tree of descriptive terms that have a hierarchical structure.

In Protégé 5 editor, creating classes $C^{(Ax)}$ occurs in the bookmark <*Classes*>. In the OWL, classes are interpreted as a subset of individuals that are part of a defined class.

The peculiarity of designing in the environment Protégé is that classes are considered as subclasses of the general ontology THING. According to the CamelCase notation for OWL [12], all class names must begin with a capitalization and should not contain spaces. For securing the classifications, simply press the <*Add subclass*> button, in the window that opens, you must enter the name of the class. (**Figure 8**).

By default, classes in OWL can intersect. In order to divide the classes, they need to be disjointed. This ensures that an individual cannot be an instance of more than one class. To do this, in the <*Classes*> tab you need to define a class that should not intersect, then in the <*Description*> field, you need to click on the + side of the Disjoint With function and in the <*Class hierarchy*> window, open the class that should not overlap with the specified class (**Figure 9**).

OWL allows you to develop annotations with various information (comments, creation date, author, links to resources, etc.) and metadata classes, properties, individuals and ontologies.

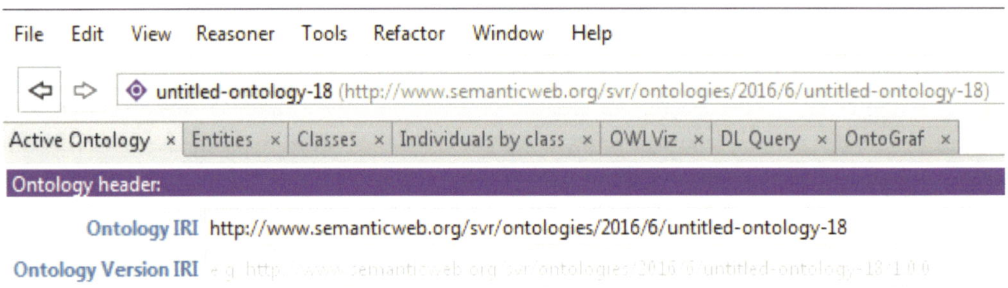

Figure 7. Main functional toolbar of the Protégé 5 editor.

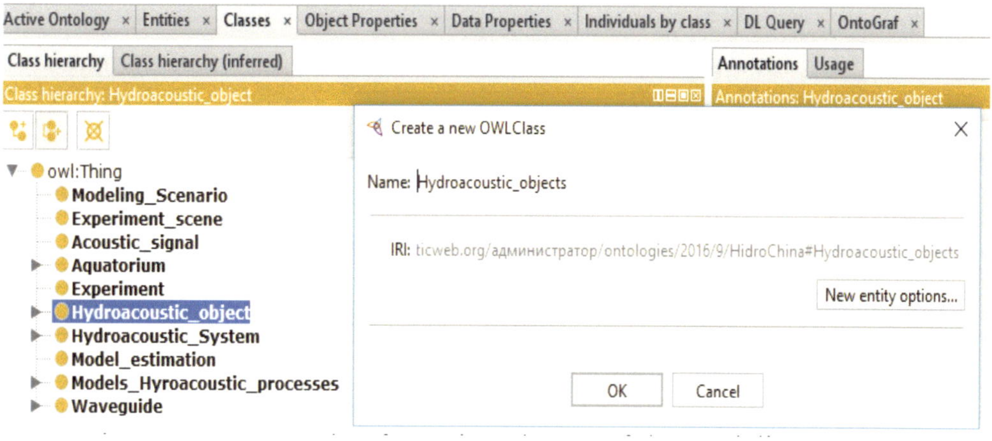

Figure 8. An example of creating classes of the modeling system.

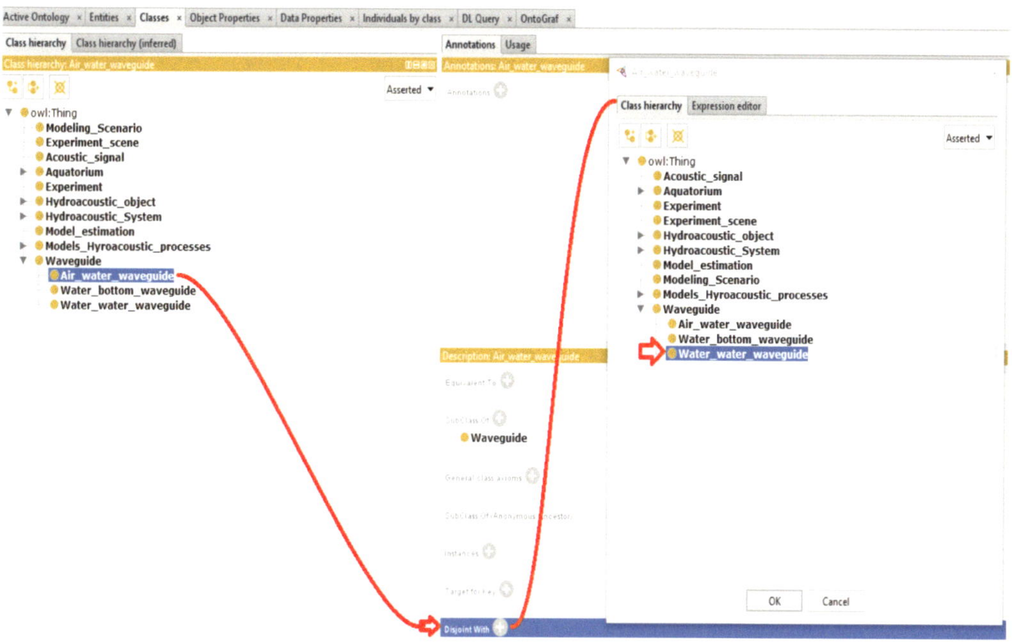

Figure 9. Separation of classes into disjointed ones.

Tabs <*Classes*>, <*Object Properties*> and <*Data Properties*> are used to develop annotations. Next, in the <*Annotations*> tab, click on the "+" and in the opened window, enter the desired comment (**Figure 10**).

In the Protégé editor, each class defined by properties that describe the relations between classes are divided into two types [13]:

- <*ObjectProperty*> —describes relations $Rel^{(H)}$ (types of relations) that are established between particular classes of ontology.

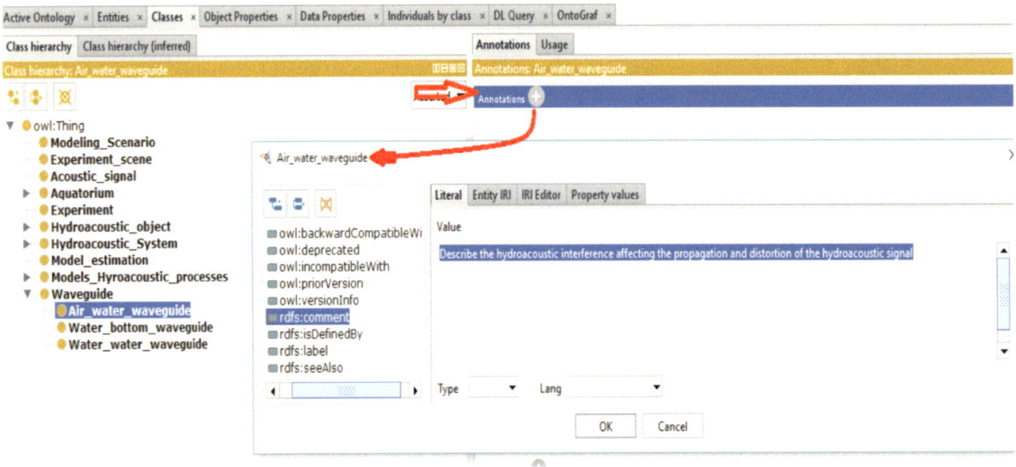

Figure 10. Adding comments to the selected class.

- *<DatatypeProperty>* —describes the specific attributes $T^{(Q)}$ (characteristics) that define the class. For example, the speed of the marine objects, their dimensions, technical parameters, and so on

2.6. Formation of a subset of the domain attributes

A subset of attributes $T^{(A)}$ describes the properties of classes $C^{(Ax)}$ and is used to enter specific values of instances in classes - $Ex^{(C)}$.

The creation of attributes subset by the Protégé editor has been performed by using the *<Datatype Properties>*tab on toolbar of the Protégé editor 5. Next, the window containing the *<OWL: DataProperty>*tab is displayed. When you click a button  in toolbar, opens the window *<Create a new OWLDataProperty>*, in which you can enter a name property such as *<Cruising Speed>* and click OK (**Figure 11**). After performing the corresponding actions provided by the process, a new type of property appears in the left frame.

Repeating this procedure can form a whole set of attributes for a SD. For a complex domain, *<OWL: DataProperty>* can be represent as a hierarchy structure. A set of properties for different instances of classes can be completely individual.

The predefined attributes has been specified in the XML schema dictionary and can be represented in a variety of data formats such as integers, floating point, lines, logical values, and so on.

An example of the owl tag: *DatatypeProperty*<URI> in XML, which describes the class *<Underwater_object>*:

<owl: DatatypeProperty rdf: about = "http://www.semanticweb.org/svr/ontologies/ -9# = "#Underwater_ object_dimensions"/>

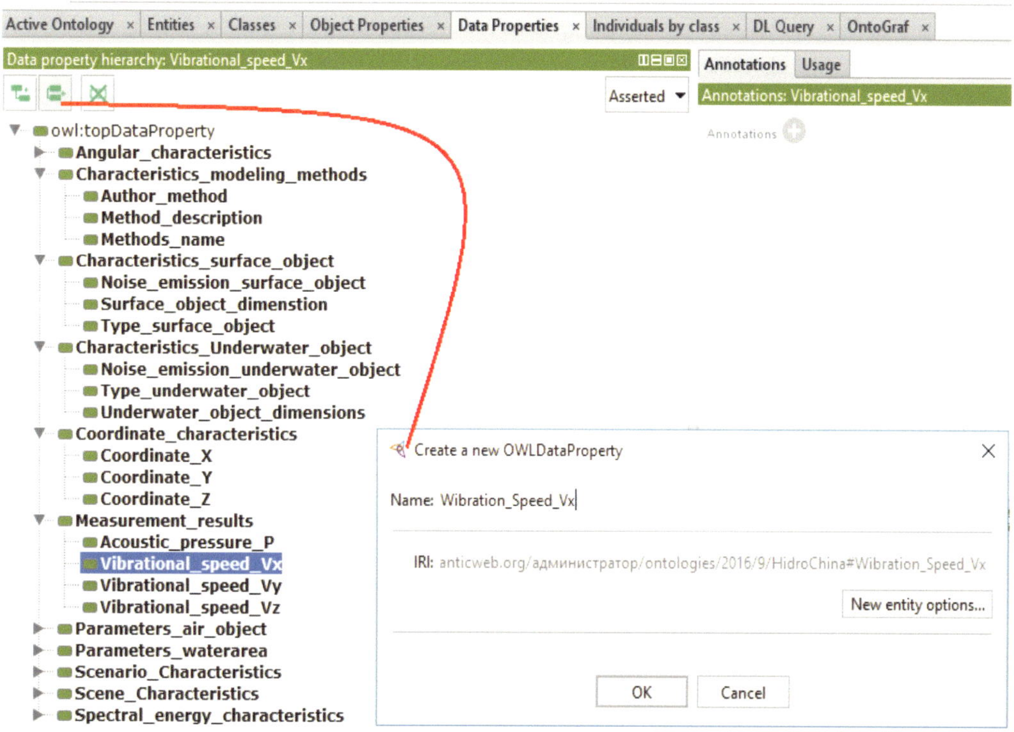

Figure 11. Creation of a new attribute in the Protégé editor.

2.7. Formation of instances of classes for filling the knowledge base

Examples of classes $Ex^{(C)}$ are specific objects of SD (instance) that belongs to a certain class $C_i^{(Ax)}$. Every class $C_i^{(Ax)}$ describes a subset of attributes $T_i^{(A)}$.

Instance creating process is executed through the tab <*Individuals by class*>, which is written by the type tag.

<owl: *NamedIndividual rdf: about* = "…..">

Process of creating a new instance consists of the following steps:

1 Select a class by using the <*Classes*> or <*Entities*> tab. For example,

2 Select tab <*Individuals by class*> in a toolbar of the Protégé editor. New window is activated. In this window, it is possible to develop an ontology instance.

3 To create a new instance of the selected class (*Southern seas*), you should click on the button , as shown in **Figure 12**. This opens a new window <*Create a new OWLNamedIndividual*>, which is intended to input the name of an instance. After performing the corresponding actions provided by the process, a new instance of the selected class appears in the left frame, for example, <*Taiwan Strait*>.

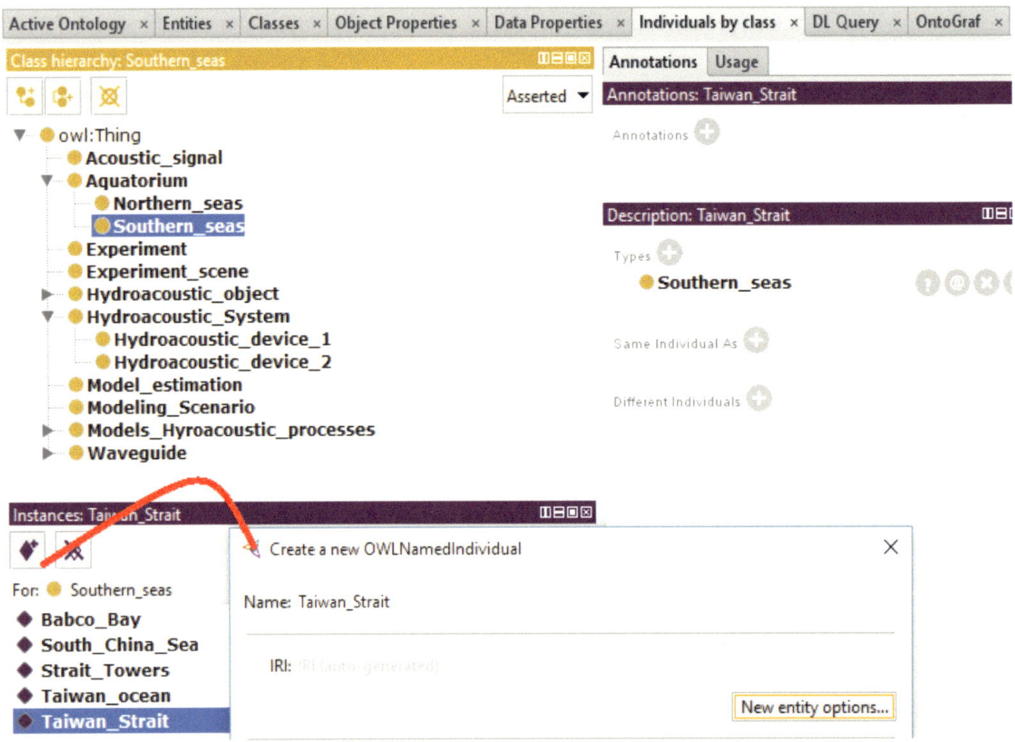

Figure 12. Example of adding a new instance.

The procedure <*Create a new OWL Named Individual*> can also be used to fill the knowledge base with test samples. To do this, select the desired instance of the specified class (*Southern_Seas*) and in the field <*Property assertions*> with the instance name (*Babco Bay*), click on the icon <+> next to the function <Data Property assertions>. When clicked the icon, a new <*Data Property*> window appears where, required in entity, <Owl:*TopDataProperty*> the user selects the appropriate attribute, for example, <*Maximum_depth*> and enters its value in the field <*Value*> of right window (**Figure 13**). After clicking the OK button in the ontology database, its value is written.

Since an instance of the class is described by some subset of attributes, this value-adding procedure must be repeated for each attribute.

A set of properties for different instances of classes can be completely individual.

2.8. Defining and forming a relation subset and linking classes

In the Protégé editor, each class is defined by properties that describe the relationship between classes. In the Protégé editor, the object properties describing [14] by tab <*ObjectProperty*> are relations between two classes and individuals.

With the help of the <*ObjectProperty*> tab, the following actions are performed:

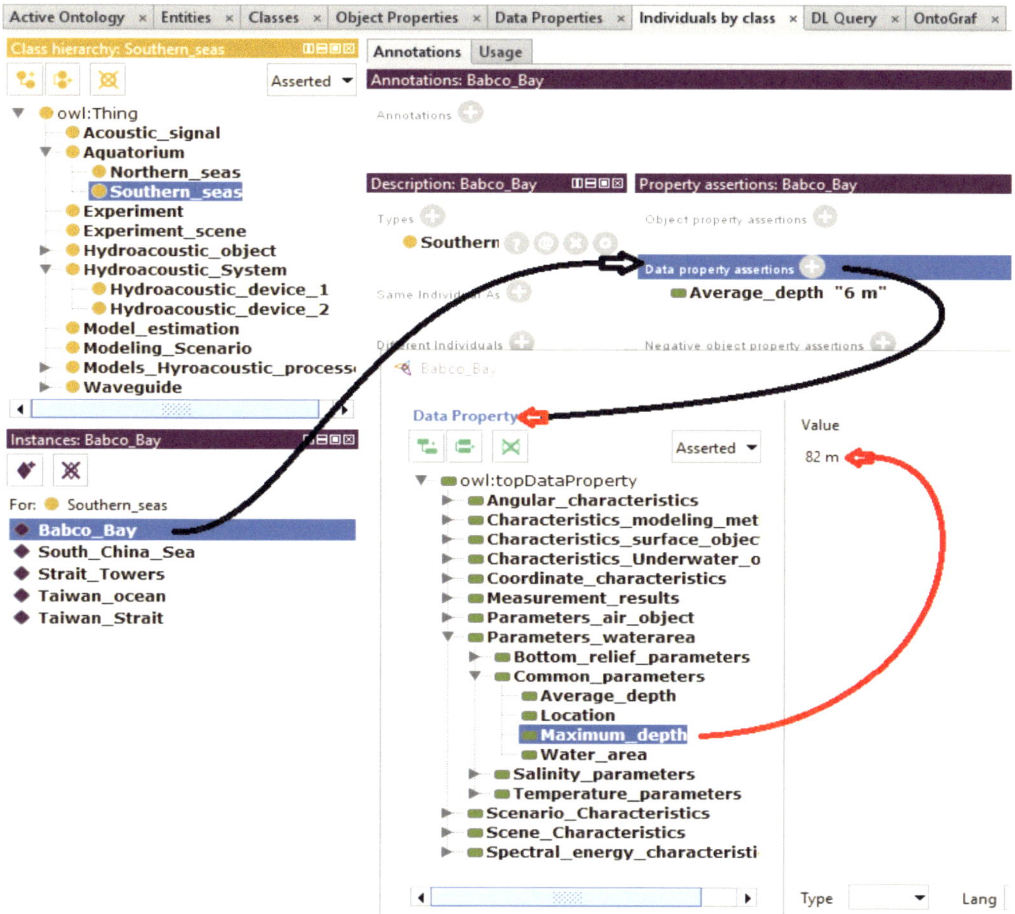

Figure 13. Example of entering the value of a particular attribute.

1 Formation of a subset of the relationship $Rel^{(H)}$ between classes $C^{(Ax)}$ in a defined subject domain by adding types of relationships to the list <owl: *topObjectProperty*>.

2 Formation of a subset of axioms $Ax^{(s)}$ in a defined subject domain by binding certain class ontology relations using the predicates from <owl: *topObjectProperty*>.

3 Formation of relationships between individuals using the predicates contained in <owl: *topObjectProperty*>

Forming a relationship subset in a defined subject domain.

To create a subset of relationships and adding it to *owl: topObjectProperty*, you must select the <*ObjectProperty*> tab in the Protégé 5 and go to the *owl: topObjectProperty* line. The toolbar opens the tools to describe relationships. To add a new type of relationship, you need to click a button. In the window named <*Create a new OWLObjectPropertty*>, you must enter a name for the type of relation, for example, <*has_communication_*>(**Figure 14**) and press OK.

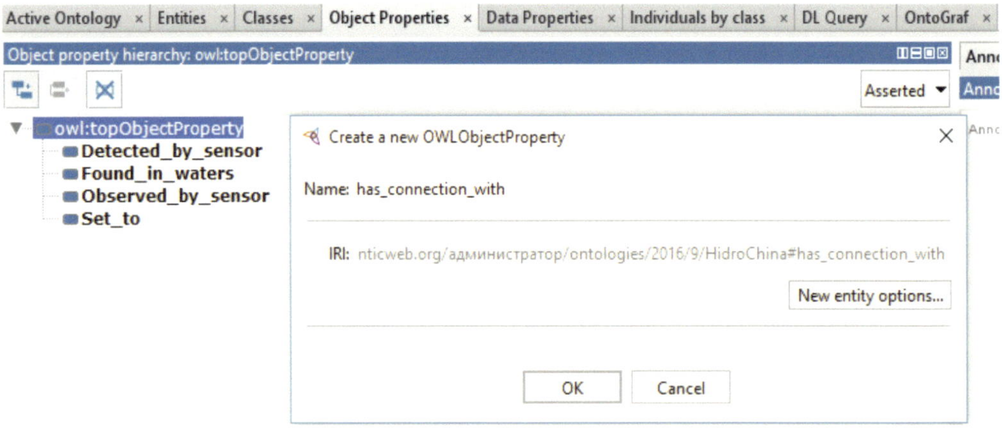

Figure 14. An example of formation of a new type of relationship.

After performing the appropriate actions provided by the process, a new type of connection appears in the *<owl: topObjectProperty>* subset. Repeating this process for SD, it is possible to form the whole subset of the types of zips for the selected SD.

3. Formation of a subset of axioms

Under the axiom are assertions that introduced into the ontology in the finished form, from which other statements can be deduced. Axioms bind two classes (the concept) with certain relations.

The link between classes is described by the RDF graph.

The created relationship between classes (axioms) is described by the RDF graph: *<subject-predicate-object>*:

Subject $C_{si}^{(Ax)}$ - is the class of ontology;

$Rel_{ij}^{(H)}$-is the predicate binding of two classes;

Object $C_{oj}^{(Ax)}$ - is the class of ontology.

In the editor Protégé 5, two functions used to define the axiom of subject domain:

- Domains (intersection)—asserts that the subjects of such property statements must belong to the class extension of the indicated class description.
- Ranges (intersection)—asserts that the values of this property must belong to the class extension of the class description or to data values in the specified data range.

To create a subset of axioms, you must select the *<ObjectProperty>* tab in toolbar of the Protégé 5 and go to the *owl: topObjectProperty* line. In the <owl: *topObjectProperty*> subset, select the

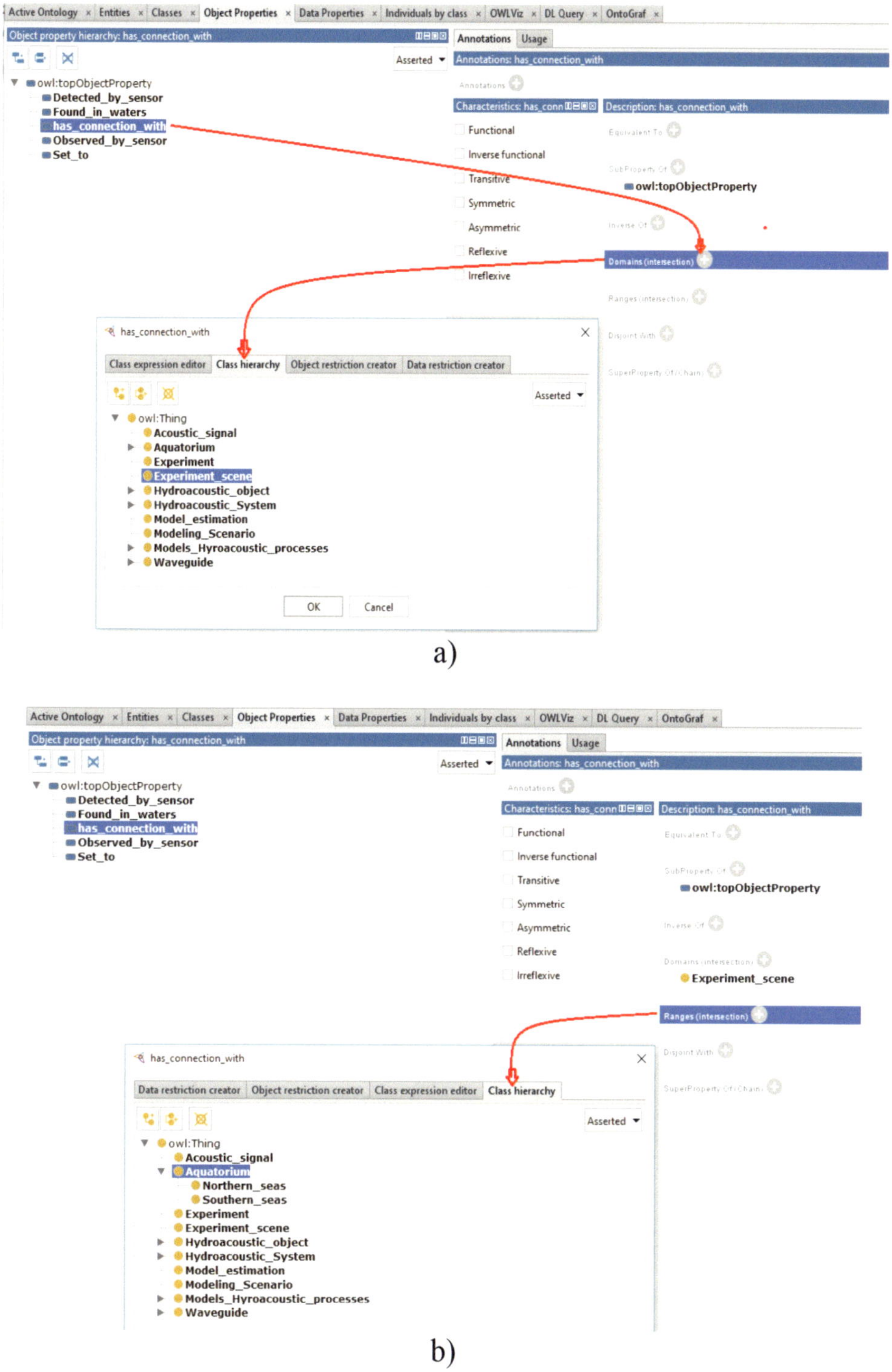

Figure 15. Example of created relationship between classes.

desired relationship type, which binds two classes, for example, class <*Experiment_scene*> connected with class <*Aquatorium*> relationship <*has_connection_with*>.

To do this, on the <*ObjectProperty*> tab in the <*Description*> window, you need to click on the "+" next to the function <*Domains (intersection)*>. When you click "+", a separate window opens where you want to select the <*Class hierarchy*> tab (**Figure 15a**) and define the class (<*Experiment_scene*>) in which the selected property is given.

When selecting second class, you need to click on the "+" next to the function <*Ranges (intersection)*> in the <*Description*> window. Further, in the opened window, you must select the class (<*Aquatorium*>) and click OK (**Figure 15b**). After completing the corresponding actions, a new relationship between the classes has created and stored in the model ontology of Subject Domain.

4. Formation of relationships between individuals

For formation of relationships between two individuals in the Protégé 5, you need to click in the <*Entities*> tab of toolbar. In the opened window <*Individuals by type*>, there is a class hierarchy that has instances. Next, in the class hierarchy (e.g., <*Helicopter*>), you must select an instance (subject) and open it (<*BoeigCH-47*>). Then, two windows open, that is, <*Description*> and <*Property Assertions*>. For formation of relationships between selected individual, you need to click on the "+" next to the function <*Object Property Assertions*>. Then, a new form to enter two fields <*Object property name*> and <*Individual name*> opens (**Figure 16**).

For example, individual <*BoeigCH-47*> characterized by a high level of acoustic noise, the limiting values of which are recorded in the individual <*Big_acoustic_noce*>. In the field <*Object property name*>, you need to enter the relationship <*Has_acoustic_noce*> and in the field <*Individual name*>, register individual <*Big_acoustic_noce*> and then click OK.

After completing the corresponding actions, a new relationship between the individuals has created and stored in the model ontology of Subject Domain.

Figure 17 presents The hierarchy of classes developed by means of the Protégé.

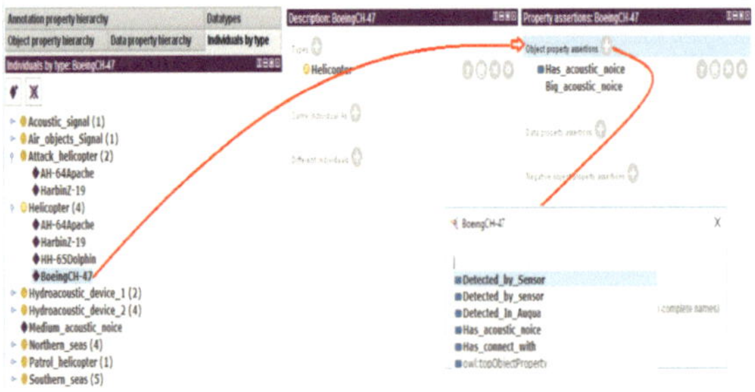

Figure 16. Process of creation of relationship between individuals.

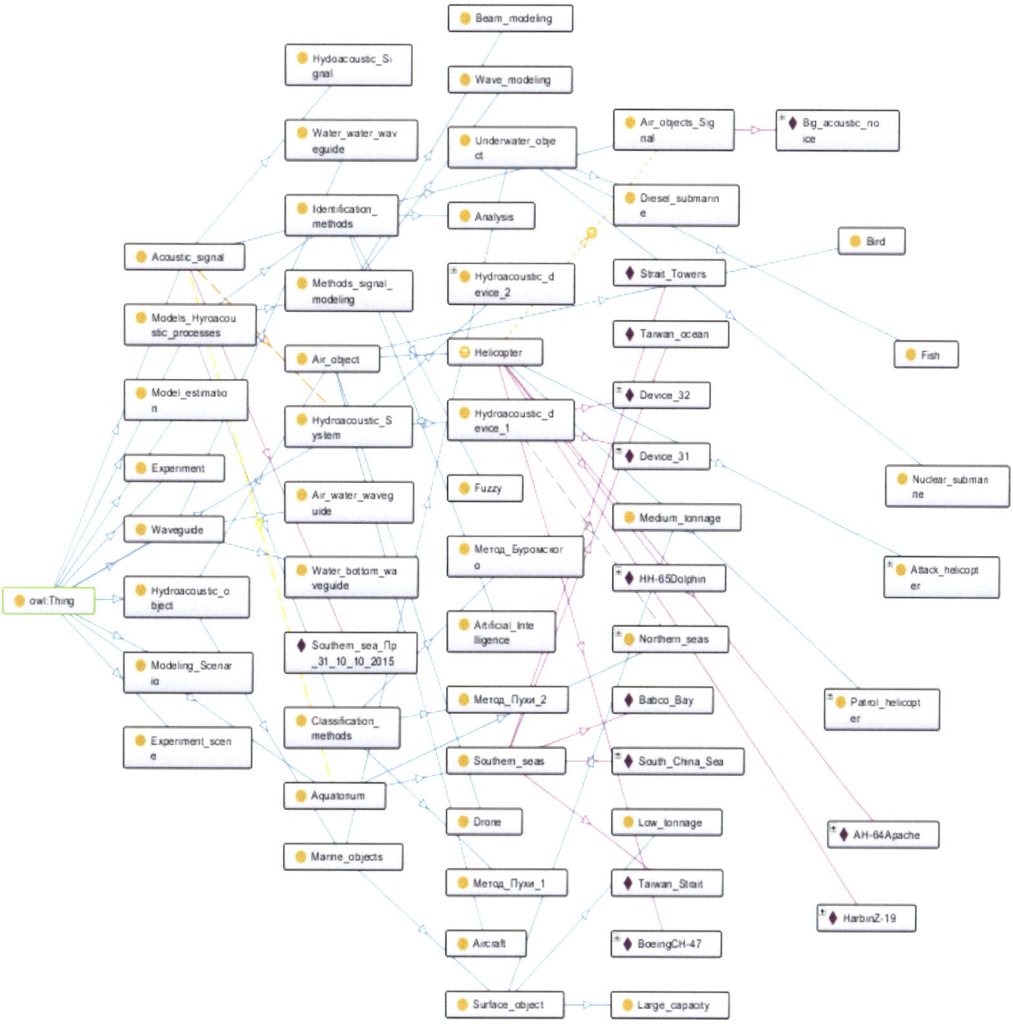

Figure 17. Graph of ontology model using the Protégé.

Subject domain ontology includes 34 classes, each of them has 5–15 attributes, nearly 30 axioms, 23 associative relations, 15 "is-are" relations, nearly 70 heredity relations and 50 "class-data" relations are described; standard types of attributes values and limits for values of attributes are highlighted.

For example, acoustic signal—class $C^{(Sig)}$ has the following attributes:

- Frequency of the signal
- Phase
- Amplitude
- Interference level

- Spectral-energy characteristics
- Vector-phase characteristics to identify the object
- Coefficient of total attenuation (pressure signals, speed along the axes: V_x, V_y and V_z)
- Location coordinates
- Distance to the object,
- Speed of propagation,
- Position of the object relative to the receiver,
- Pressure at the depth of the receiver,
- The results of modulation of the noise spectra of objects
- Coefficient of noise emission.

Thus, ontology represents the description of subject domain notions in terms of knowledge processing theory. It allows to describe the subject domain notions in terms of ontology classes, subclasses and classes exemplars as well as to define relations between them. After all ontology elements are described, it is possible to use algorithms of descriptive logic for ontology information processing.

5. Summary

The approach to the Internet portal in the field of materials' strength is presented. The usage of ontology model for portal knowledge representation allows to structure and systematize portal data and knowledge as well as to organize meaningful search through portal informational space.

The ontology model for the classification of marine objects was proposed, and elements of such ontology was described. The process of ontology development using the Protégé is depicted. The usage of ontology gives the possibility to execute the recognition of marine objects within the developed modeling system.

Author details

Larysa Globa[1*], Rina Novogrudska[1], Alexander Koval[1] and Vyacheslav Senchenko[2]

*Address all correspondence to: lgloba@its.kpi.ua

1 National Technical University of Ukraine "Kyiv Polytechnic Institute", Kyiv, Ukraine

2 Institute for Information Recording, Kyiv, Ukraine

References

[1] Zagogulko YA, Borovikova OI. The technology of ontologies constructing for the portals of scientific knowledge. Gornal of NGU. 2007;**5**:12-15

[2] Globa LS, Novogrudskaya RL. Engineering knowledge portal designing approach. Workshop Intellectual analysis of information 2010. Kyiv: KPI; 2010. pp. 53-62

[3] Fridman YB. Mechanical properties of metal. M: Mechanical engineering. 1974

[4] Semantic Technology. Available at: https://en.wikipedia.org/wiki/Semantic_technology

[5] Knowledge Representation Languages: Available at: http://www.cs.man.ac.uk/~stevensr/onto/node14.html

[6] Open Knowledge Base Connectivity: Available at http://www.ai.sri.com/~okbc/

[7] Web Ontology Language: Available at: http://www.w3.org/TR/owl-features/

[8] Senchenko VR, Koval OV, Globa LS, Novogrudska RL. Intelligent modeling system based on cloud-technology. Proceedings of International Conference Radio Electronics & Info Communications (UkrMiCo). DOI:10.1109/UkrMiC.2016.7739646. IEEE Digital Library, 2016

[9] RDF Model Theory: Available at: https://www.w3.org/TR/2002/WD-rdf-mt-20020429/

[10] Semantic Web Technologies. 2013: Available at: https://open.hpi.de/course/semanticweb

[11] Protégé - Free, open-source ontology editor and framework for building intelligent systems: Available at http://protege.stanford.edu

[12] Camel Case Notation: Available at https://en.wikipedia.org/wiki/Camel_case

[13] OWL 2 Web Ontology Language Document Overview (Second Edition) W3C Recommendation 11 December 2012: Available at: http://www.w3.org/TR/owl2-overview/

[14] Jureta I, Mylopoulos J, Faulkner S. Revisiting the Core Ontology and Problem in Requirements Engineering, In: RE; 2008. pp. 71-80

Chapter 4

Towards Semantic Knowledge Maps Applications: Modelling the Ontological Nature of Data and Information Governance in a R&D Organization

Ivo Pierozzi Junior, Patrícia Rocha Bello Bertin,
Claudia De Laia Machado and
Alessandra Rodrigues da Silva

Additional information is available at the end of the chapter

http://dx.doi.org/10.5772/67978

Abstract

In organizational management, it is highly recommended that data and information be adequately prepared to match the knowledge needed to be used in decision-making processes. However, faced with the paradigm of complexity that currently dictates the dynamics of modern organizations, there is still a search for operational solutions that allow agility and flexibility to corporate information flows to meet that desired condition. In this context, the concept of data and information governance presents itself as a fundamental premise because it systematizes, reorganizes and reorients each element of the organizational system (people, processes, structures, etc.) without losing the notion of its contexts and causalities. For this, in the conceptual modelling of governance, the concept of systemism arises to support the balance between holistic and reductionist approaches, inherent in management processes, but often considered antagonistic or contradictory. The present chapter presents and discusses a data and information governance model for research and development (R&D) organizations. The model is based upon the concepts of data, information and knowledge life cycles and knowledge mapping, recovering and valuing the ontological nature of the elements of the system under analysis and constructing a pragmatic proposal for corporate application and operation.

Keywords: knowledge mapping, semantic maps, agricultural research, data management, information management, knowledge management

1. Introduction

In the face of complexity, an in-principle reductionist may be at the same time a pragmatic holist. [1]

One of the greatest challenges of management is to align and integrate the innumerable elements that constitute the intricate system of organizational processes and, from a broader perspective, being able to assess institutional development based on performance and effectiveness of specific actions on those same elements of the system. However, the boundaries between organizational processes are often ill defined, most of them being highly interdependent and transverse, which makes convergence of efforts and coherent results more difficult to achieve.

Management processes are highly dependent on a parallel and continuous process of decision-making. Every decision, in turn, depends on the availability of data and information, which is the basis of knowledge construction. In absolute terms, there is not 'the best' decision to be taken, as this would require access to the complete and utter repertoire of available data and information about a particular subject—a superhuman intellectual effort would be necessary for processing and synthesizing such amount of information and selecting the best of all possible decisions and their expected causalities. In front of these impossibilities, it is assumed that a general knowledge management program (implicitly included, data and information management processes) is needed to support the decision-making process, directing knowledge production or recombination for use or reuse in successive decision-making cycles.

Thus, the greatest dilemma of a decision-maker at any organizational level is perhaps to reconcile and resolve the balance between analysis and synthesis or, in other words, between reductionist and holistic viewpoints to better understand the system at hand. Even when this dilemma is sorted, there remains the difficulty of operationalizing, both logically and technologically, the relevant management processes.

This chapter presents an ontological approach to organizational systems, here explored in terms of a data and information governance (DIGov) framework for a research and development (R&D) organization. This governance framework encompasses a number of management processes relating to the triad 'data-information-knowledge'.

Section 2 of this chapter offers background information about the organization that served as the context of this study (Brazilian Agricultural Research Corporation—Embrapa), while Sections 3 and 4 present the theoretical foundations of the data and information governance (DIGov) framework and the methods that were used in this research, respectively. Embrapa's DIGov model is then explained in Section 5, with the two last sections of the chapter focusing on how the model can be used in practice, with support of knowledge-map-inspired conceptual structures (Section 6) and final considerations (Section 7).

2. Context

The design and implementation of efficient corporate management processes must be supported by a logical, conceptual or even ideological framework, which mediates the causal relations among premises, values, norms and rules, logical and physical structures, costs, personal skills as well as people behaviour and attitudes. All these elements relate to the notion of 'corporate governance' [2], which adheres to the organization's strategy, therefore differing fundamentally from the 'management' system, this one being ultimately focused on operational and tactical issues, such as the monitoring of activities and results achievement.

The Brazilian Agricultural Research Corporation (Embrapa), a large governmental organization, has been developing its own conception of corporate governance. As it is probably the case with many other R&D organizations, Embrapa now finds itself as an immense, diverse and complex organization with its multi-, inter- and transdisciplinary scientific scope; its heterogeneous thematic Research Units spread all over the Brazilian territory; its staff that includes not only scientific researchers but also a wide range of support personnel and experts from many knowledge backgrounds; and its broad stakeholder network, comprised of many sectors such as the State, governments, farmers, academics, students and society as a whole, which are ever more demanding and attentive to the implications of agricultural research, making their voice heard on the most controversial issues (an example is the heated debate and influence of the public opinion on research with Genetically Modified Organisms).

Embrapa is proud to present itself to society as a knowledge-producer organization—the word 'knowledge', in this context, meaning any solution or practical response to a specific demand or problem. It turns out that the knowledge that Embrapa produces is a direct consequence of the alignment of agricultural empirical data and resulting information, which are gathered, processed, shared, reused and disseminated in a dynamic, continuous, cyclical and fed-back process, aimed at consolidating a certain kind of knowledge that, in turn, inserts more cognitive value into decision-making. This is not to be seen as a linear process, since it often involves uncertain, unforeseen and even random developments. These general properties of complex systems, inherent to organizations such as Embrapa, have the potential to hinder or delay management decisions, since required data and information are not always timely and easily accessible.

This is not to say that Embrapa's data and information management processes are inappropriate or inefficient, nor that correlate governance is missing. It can be said, though, that the input and output flow of information and the chain of activities that make up both Embrapa's management and governance processes still leave room for improvement. Particularly, the development of coherent, commonly shared practices of data and information production, sharing, reuse and dissemination is highly desirable as a means to compensate for the traditional, hierarchical organization chart and its many decision-making structures, where information flows can be greatly impaired by power microstructures and bureaucracy.

Figure 1 illustrates how corporate management processes can benefit from properly managed data, information and knowledge, through improved decision-making.

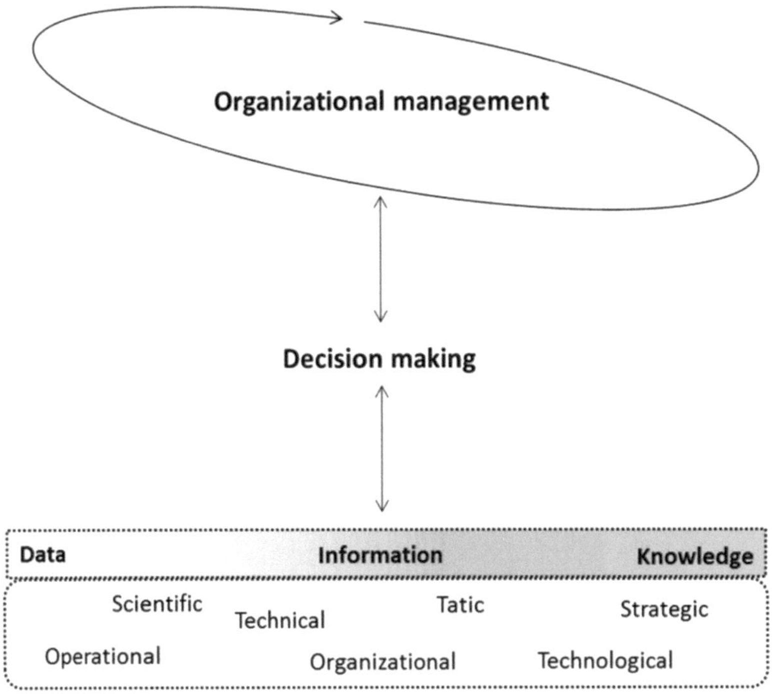

Figure 1. Attaching data, information and knowledge to organizational management through the decision-making process.

3. General approach to data gathering and analysis

Individually considered, the building blocks of Embrapa's Data and Information Governance (DIGov) model are not entirely new but relate to a range of previous conceptualizations and notions, which are detailed in Section 4. The DIGov model, however, is not only theoretically informed but also empirically grounded and based upon a deep understanding of Embrapa's information environment.

A data gathering plan was built with support of the well-known 5W2H management tool (What, Why, Where, When, Who, How and How much) and through questionnaires with both closed and open-ended questions, a large volume of data was gathered, categorized and reciprocally linked, pointing out actors; skills; logical, physical and computational structures; processes, workflows, rules and regulations; stakeholders and even potential or incipient, informal governance sub-systems.

It can be said, therefore, that this study applied both a deductive and an inductive approach [3], building upon prior knowledge and, at the same time, allowing new themes to emerge from data.

Knowledge mapping was identified as a useful tool for data analysis and representation, allowing for a complete system characterization that appreciated both the conceptual aspects of the entire complex system (level of ideas/macro-properties) and its instances (level of objects/entities). By doing so, particularities of each component could be explored without losing the sense of the whole.

Empirical data were thematically analysed [4] with support of the qualitative data analysis software Atlas.ti, and to produce a graphic representation of the interrelationships between data elements, these were translated into triple store format, A-R-B, where A and B represent the elements or concepts included in the system (entities, objects, facts, etc.), defined by terminological or textual labels; R means the relationship, defined by semantic labels and '-' can assume uni- or bi-directional paths. The triple stores were gathered and organized in a spreadsheet with three columns and innumerable rows where each row represented one triple.

For allowing the possibility of editing and visualizing a complex conceptual structure (holistic view) and then breaking it into snippets for a more detailed (reductionist) view, the software yEd (https://www.yworks.com/products/yed) was used. Besides generating high-quality diagrams and visualizations, yEd supports mathematical analysis of social relationships to provide insight into the structure of a social network. Metrics such as density and centralities (betweenness, closeness, degree, etc.), for instance, give a measure of the relevance of a particular element in the whole network.

4. Theoretical perspective

This section presents the theoretical foundations of the Data and Information Governance (DIGov) framework, exploring underpinning notions and conceptualizations to create a systemic approach to management problems at contemporary organizations, while acknowledging their ontological and complex nature. The notion of information as a complex, social phenomenon, the cognitive itinerary formed by Data-Information-Knowledge (DIK) and the conceptual alignment between the DIK life cycles form the basis of the theoretical framework, as explained in the following sections.

4.1. The corporate information environment as a complex system

The informational environment of an organization can be assumed as a complex system, that is, systems composed of innumerable autonomous but interactive elements, where the result (output) of the system is not simply the sum of the properties and particularities of its parts [5–7].

Under the systemic perspective [1, 8–10] and in the context of an organization, the corporate information environment is a social phenomenon [10, 11] and thus can be seen as a complex sub-system of another complex higher system containing, itself, other complex sub-systems within itself. As a social phenomenon, information (and, consequently, the data that originates it) assumes institutional properties and causality in the cognitive, communicative, documentary and normative or regulatory dimensions. So, one of the great challenges of complexity, when social sub-systems are involved, is [12]; since people do not act continuously and regularly in a rational way, nor are they compliant with norms and laws throughout the time, it is not uncommon for them to react in a way not intended or planned by managers and their management strategies or, at least, even if people do not disobey or do not manifest themselves contrary to superior guidelines, they may react inconsistently to corporate guidelines. These inconsistent reactions can meet random, uncertain or unpredictable situations when people are often pressured by the emergency or urgency of requested arrangements and by the huge volume of decision-making moments they experience in their daily work routines. Due to the complex interactions of these systems and the non-linear way in which their elements give rise to general behaviour patterns, complex systems can be very difficult to predict, control and manage [1, 8, 9].

It is in this context that data and information governance presents itself as a preventive, conciliatory solution, which is more concerned with guiding premises to foster good practices and less with guaranteeing results in an idealized world of strategic planning processes and deterministic projects.

4.2. An integrated look on data, information and knowledge

At R&D institutions, empirical research is an established practice. It means that one of their main concerns is to obtain and translate data into scientific knowledge, which can then be applied to solve real-world problems. For this itinerary to be complete, an improved understanding of the conceptual line between data, information and knowledge needs to be achieved.

The word 'information' is most commonly used to mean physical representations of knowledge: objects, data and documents that possess instructive character, a use that has been previously described as 'information-as-thing' [13]. Alternatively, the term is used in a wider sense, as in reference to the act of informing or becoming informed ('information-as-process'), or to what we know ('information-as-knowledge'), that is, whatever is perceived in 'information-as-process'. The interrelationship becomes then evident: it is difficult to define 'knowledge' without referring to 'information', as it is to describe 'information' without referring to 'data'. The following quotes illustrate this:

> *Knowledge is information evaluated and organized in the human mind so that it can be used purposefully. [14]*

> *[Knowledge is] information combined with experience, context, interpretation and reflection. [15]*

For taking many forms, both physical and digital, the term data can be difficult to define [16]. Among the most widely cited definitions is the following, from the National Academies of Science:

> *Data are facts, numbers, letters, and symbols that describe an object, idea, condition, situation, or other factors. [17]*

In practical terms, data are equivalent to a physically 'recorded symbol', which can be exemplified by printed characters; binary characters in magnetic, punched or optical form; spoken words; or images. Whatever the physical form may be, it becomes a recorded symbol when it is interpreted as representing something [14]. In the words of Feather and Sturges,

> *raw data is the building block, and knowledge is the construct; information is the cement. The effective management of information allows it to be stored by means that permit it to be systematically and efficiently retrieved in a format that will facilitate the tasks of the end-user. [14]*

Prior attempts to bring the concepts of data, information and knowledge closer together, in order to identify their boundaries and build a logical trajectory between them can be found in the literature of Cognitive, Information, Management and Computing Sciences. The notion of a Data-Information-Knowledge-Wisdom hierarchy [18] is opportunely recovered here, even though the philosophical discussions and implications arising from it are not addressed [19]. The hierarchical-pyramidal representation is one of the most influential perspectives, adopted in support of several lines of argumentation [19-22]. Other more cognitively elaborated appraisals represent the relation in a linear-progressive form [18]. Despite being conceptually instigating, such representations are criticized from a pragmatic point of view, as to their usefulness in supporting data, information and knowledge management in practice [19]. Conceptually speaking, the main criticism is the reasoning that, if wisdom is to be taken as an 'unquestionable and irrefutable truth', it might not be reached if the data supporting it turned out to be incorrect or untrue!

An alternative representation of the relationship between data, information and knowledge is offered in **Figure 2**. In this new conceptual set up, there is a deliberate preference, based on the logic of added cognitive value, for aligning data, information and knowledge in a circuit with a continuous feedback loop, rather than the conventional hierarchical-pyramidal or liner-progressive representations [23].

Despite their conceptual interrelatedness, however, 'data management', 'information management' and 'knowledge management' studies have specialized as different bodies of knowledge. Analogously, traditional management approaches in organizations also tend to treat 'data', 'information' and 'knowledge' separately, which might cause considerable confusion, given their high levels of complementarity and interdependence [24, 25].

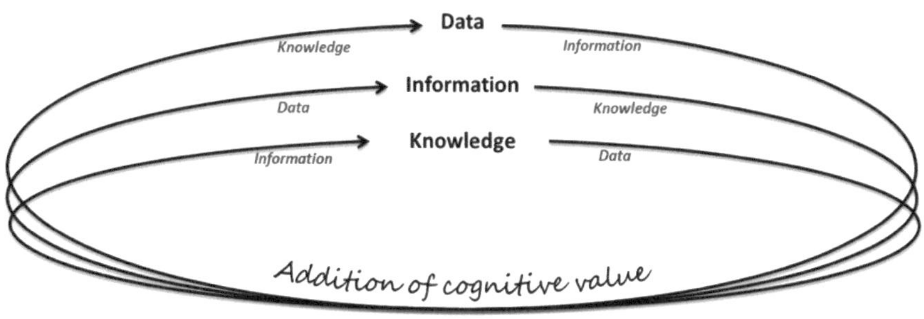

Figure 2. Data, information and knowledge in a cyclic, continuous feedback circuit. Source: Ref. [23].

To overcome this difficulty while building an integrative and systemic approach to data and information governance, these elements were arranged in a conceptual continuum—their interrelation has been acknowledged, so that their use can be maximized in the organization.

4.3. Aligning data, information and knowledge life cycles

In figurative sense, data, information and knowledge are taken here as a quantum triad: depending on the point of observation, what is seen is intellectual energy (thought, idea, cognition), or, alternatively, tangible matter (documents and media, printed or digital), which can then be collected, assembled, organized, analysed, shared, accessed and continuously reused independently of the human brain.

To better represent this perspective, the concepts of data, information and knowledge 'life cycle' emerged as a promising solution. Although offered in many different versions in the literature, these life cycles can be used, in a practical way, to support a cyclic, continuous and feedback view of the data, information and knowledge itinerary. **Figures 3–5** present examples of data, information and knowledge life cycles (DIK life cycles), as they are central to the understanding of the governance model developed in this chapter.

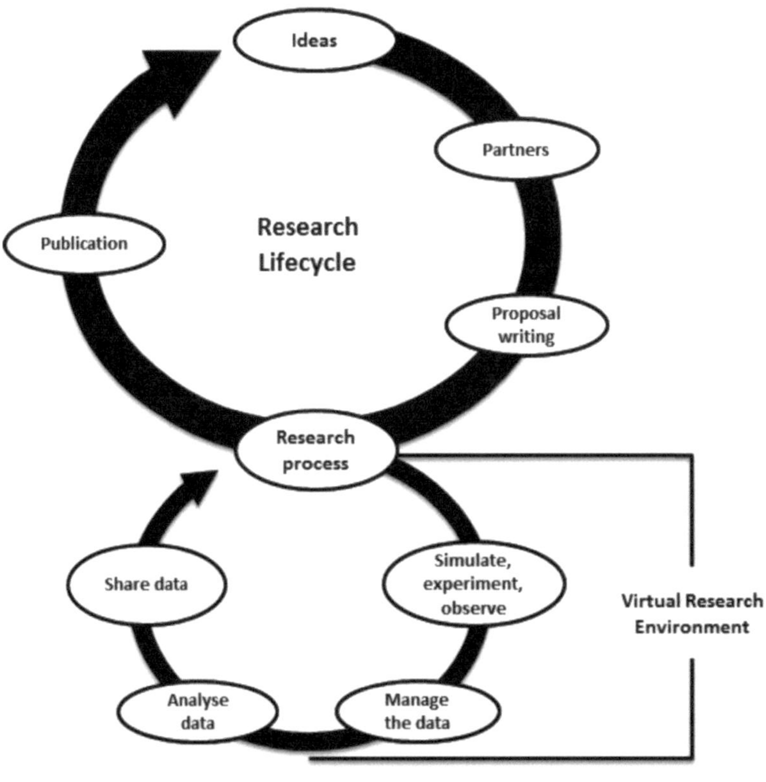

Figure 3. The data life cycle and its connection with the research process, as proposed by Tenopir et al. [26].

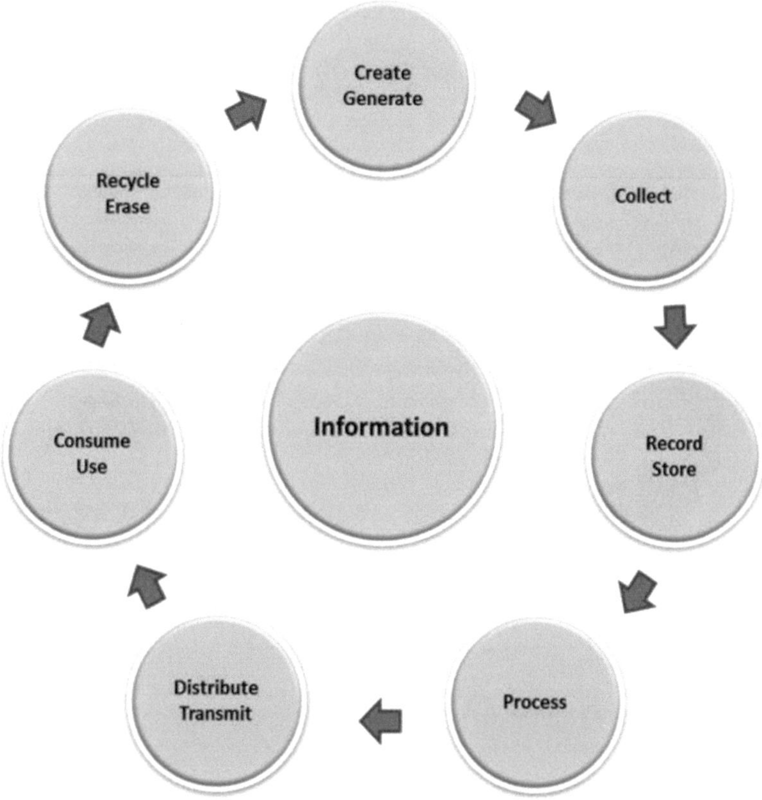

Figure 4. The information life cycle, according to Floridi [27].

On closer examination, the DIK life cycles seem comparable and have many similarities—which is not surprising, given the conceptual interrelatedness of its elements. **Figure 6** was obtained by expanding the conceptions of DIK life cycles that are available in the literature, in order to align and specify the fundamental processes (genesis, creation, production; organization; sharing; access and dissemination; appropriation, validation, evaluation). This is, therefore, a simplified view of the fundamental logic of alignment between these life cycles, here called the 'DIK Mandala', which served as a central construct to the concept of governance developed in this work.

This integrative look at the data, information and knowledge life cycles has practical significance, since it allows an appreciation of the processes involved in data, information and knowledge management, in terms of specific methodologies and technologies and parallel and progressive arrangements, as presented in **Figure 7**.

4.4. Conceptualizing data and information governance

The notion of data and information governance retrieves the understanding of governance already adopted in other initiatives of Embrapa, considering as part of a general corporate

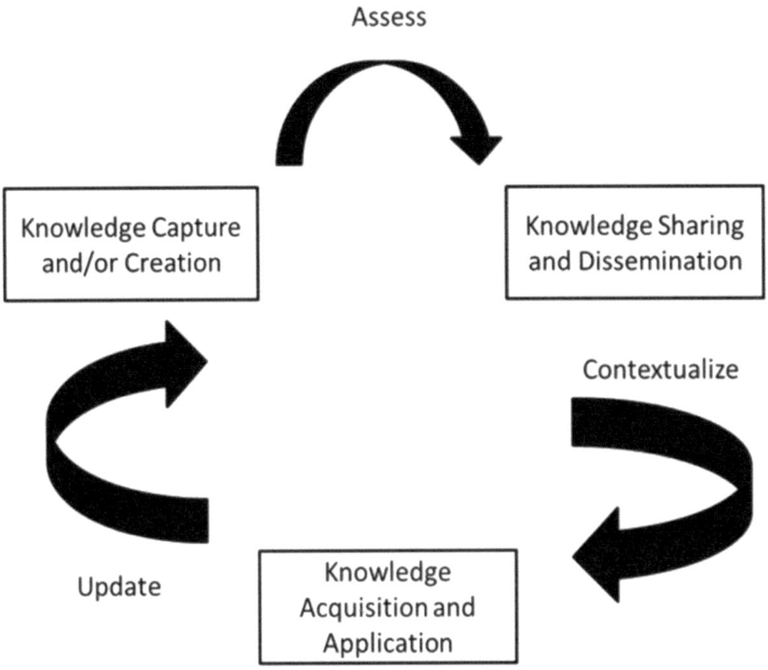

Figure 5. Knowledge management integrated cycle. Source: Dalkir [28].

governance proposal while aligns parallel to other subcategories of organizational governance, such as Information Technology governance, Human Resources governance and so forth. However, against the possible risks of creating an infinite number of instances of governance (reductionist paradigm of the organization), a systemic approach was adopted [8] to sustain the dynamics of information flows within and across organizational subunits, hierarchical levels and governance perspectives. For Embrapa, data and information governance for knowledge means: 'the determination, systematization and institutionalization of the principles, guidelines, structures, processes, culture, roles and responsibilities that drive, enable and transform data and information management in support of decision-making and the corporate governance system'.

The notion of 'governance' supported here, therefore, is not to be confused with that referring to information technology. On the contrary, it recognizes that problems related to information are often multifaceted—involving behavioural, cultural, regulatory, procedural and structural aspects that are not solved exclusively through the adoption of technological solutions.

As adopted here, data and information governance presents itself as an innovative approach that is situated in a higher and more strategic level than the operational, mechanistic and bureaucratic nature of management processes and technological tools. With constituent, morphological elements (principles, guidelines, structures, processes, cultures, roles and responsibilities) that relate to the corporate information environment, the

Figure 6. The data-information-knowledge Mandala.

data and information governance framework can be seen as a fluid, dynamic and aggregating material that permeates, integrates and interacts those elements with each other, assuming (also metaphorically) the 'physiology' of the system formed by the corporate management mechanisms, but with enough and sufficient room to deal with non-linear causalities.

This being said, the difficulty presented for the conception and development of a generic model of data and information governance was precisely to find adequate mechanisms and tools to turn these conceptual ideas into operational pragmatics. A natural way to pragmatize the DIK relation was sought, valuing its ontological nature and acknowledging, in this itinerary, the most logical solution to organize ideas around the corporate informational environment—which, in this particular case, is that of a R&D organization.

The following section presents Embrapa's DIGov model, which fills a gap in the literature of Information Science, for pursuing an ontological, systemic and conceptually integrative perspective on the reciprocal relationships of data, information and knowledge management, in the context of R&D organizations.

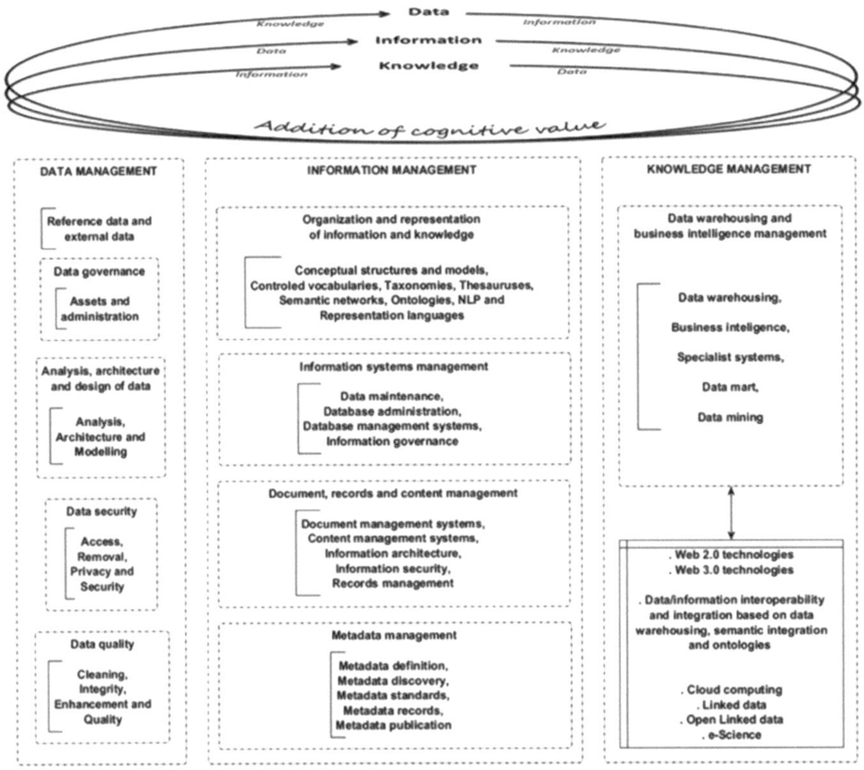

Figure 7. Alignment between data, information and knowledge management processes and activities, as a function of cognitive mechanisms and in relation to technological solutions. Source: Ref. [23].

5. Embrapa's data and information governance (DIGov) framework

The DIGov model is shown in **Figure 8**. Its main constituents and operation or physiology are described as following.

The DIGov model articulates with a series of theoretical, philosophical and conceptual notions, which are available in the literature: 'information ecology' [29], 'information policy' [30], 'informational audit' [31] and 'information culture' [32], among others. Some of these precedent approaches have arisen in parallel to the world views derived from or influenced by theories based on relationship or interdependence of system elements and global phenomena, which emerged by the end of World War II and were well consolidated in the 1990s. A creative and timely review and contextualization of the dynamics of human evolution of global knowledge over the past 70 years were presented by Brian Castellani and his work of successive editions of the 'Map of Complexity Sciences' (http://www.art-sciencefactory.com/complexity-map_feb09.html), where the main theories and scientific approaches are interrelated, as well as their authors. These theories, which support the current itineraries of knowledge that model our understanding of life and the Universe, derive from two main

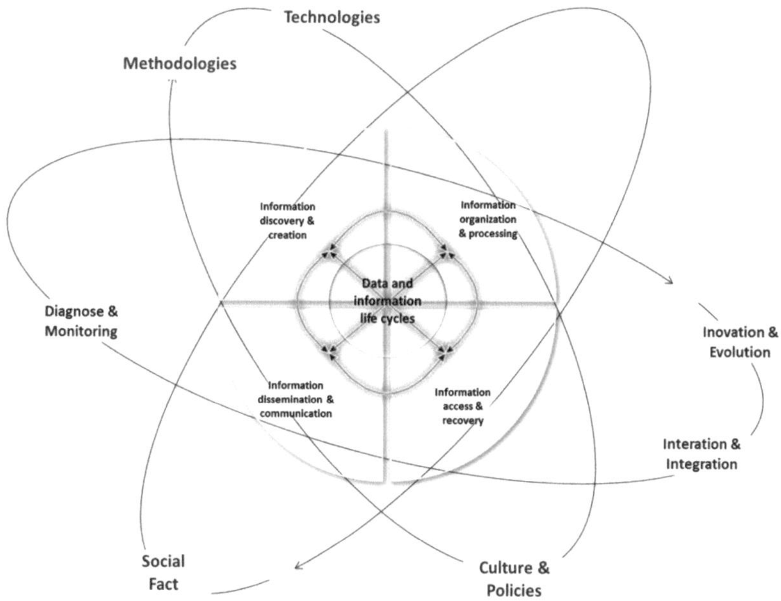

Figure 8. Embrapa's DIGov model.

intellectual strands—Systems Science and Cybernetics, both emerging in the second half of the twentieth century. The map registers the convergence of knowledge that today enables us a more systemic and organic view of the world, pointing out General Theory of Systems, Ecological Systems Theory and extending to discussions about complex adaptive systems until including, more recently, the social aspects of the knowledge development process, as in Social Systems Theory, Sociocybernetics and culminating with the e-Science and Data Science theorizations.

The influence and recovery of those chains of thought into business schools around the world have been previously analysed and contextualized [11], allowing new perspectives to emerge that make such conceptual approaches closer to the pragmatism of organizational management.

It is at this point that 'sistemism' [8] arises as one of the main theoretical-conceptual foundation of the DIGov model. It presents itself as a conciliatory solution between analysis and synthesis, the whole and the parts, holistic representations and reductionist ones, which are inherent to modelling processes, including those of organizational nature. As explained in Section 3, however, the DIGov model not only draws upon a vast theoretical background and the very definition concept adopted in this work, but it is also based upon an empirical analysis of data, information and knowledge management at a R&D organization.

The central axis of the DIGov model is formed by the data, information and knowledge life cycles—in a convergent and interrelated perspective, as explored in detail in the DIK Mandala (**Figure 6**). 'Discovery and Creation', 'Organization and Processing', 'Access and Recovery' and 'Dissemination and Communication' are, therefore, convergent dimensions of the data, information and knowledge life cycles, reflecting the managerial and operational activities that are involved in each phase of these cycles in the various organizational instances and levels. From the data collected at Embrapa, it was observed, however, that these steps, in practice, are not necessarily performed in a linear and sequential way: certain sets of data and information can be produced and immediately made available for 'access and recovery'; or, still, there are datasets and information that need to be previously organized and treated, for only then be made accessible. The several stages of the data, information and knowledge life cycles can be—and, in some cases, must be—navigated iteratively and non-sequentially, depending on the nature of the informational asset and corporate interest.

To ensure a continuous improvement of data and information management, however, it is necessary to observe trends and opportunities for improvement, so that the operation of the data, information and knowledge life cycles, which correspond to the DIGov model's 'micro-level', must be subject to the following processes, occurring in the 'meso-level': (a) continued monitoring and diagnostics of structures, skills and processes; (b) enrichment and strengthening of the interaction and integration among and between people and information and between those and available technologies; and (c) development and validation of innovations and developments in methodologies and technologies to support data, information and knowledge management.

Finally, complementing the systemic design of the DIGov model, the following components surround and guide the model in a 'macro-level': (i) culture and (ii) social fact, with regard to social aspects and people absorption and application of the model's morphology and physiology; (iii) policy, as regards the model's legal, regulatory and strategic framework; (iv) technologies; and (v) methodologies.

6. A knowledge mapping application for data and information governance

Knowledge mapping has been presented and discussed as a valuable tool for organizing, representing and retrieving knowledge, being particularly suitable for large amounts of information [33–38]. The main idea behind knowledge mapping is that facts, entities and objects of any kind can be identified, highlighted and interrelated to each other, in order to solve the deficiencies of documentary languages, which are conventionally based on categorization or classification systems. In DIGov model's scope, such deficiencies relate to: (a) the need of a conceptual framework for collective cognition and communication enhancement which respects the multidimensional and multifaceted nature of data, information and knowledge and (b) the need of mapping the numerous informational flows, emphasizing both its specific details as their general context in corporate information and knowledge management processes. Thus, knowledge mapping allows the reconciliation of reductionist and holistic paradigms, often conflicting in the choices of tools for organization and representation.

To illustrate the use of this concept and practical tool, a real-world example will be taken, among many possible ones that relate to data, information and knowledge in support of decision-making. This will be provided by the Open Access (OA) thematic, which is a recurrent, global demand to Embrapa. Acknowledged as a world reference in tropical agricultural knowledge, Embrapa is invited to present a clear, institutional position and to take practical steps towards OA to the knowledge it produces.

This was one of the main issues to emerge from the questionnaires applied in this research, which was therefore elected as one of the priority topics to be addressed by the company, so as to improve its information and knowledge management processes. In addition to other priority issues (e.g. controlled vocabularies, terminologies, semantic features and its applications; editorial process and policies; research data management; strategic information management, among others), a roadmap was designed to explore and achieve a corporative solution to the OA issue.

From the systemic point of view, which informed the DIGov model construction, a choice of tools was made to better represent this system as a complex one. Such tools are mainly editing software for conceptual structures that would allow the ontological design (concept mapping) of the represented system. In such type of representation, all of the components are assumed to be nodes and their mutual interrelationships are the vertices that connect the nodes to each other, creating a network. Embedded in these networks, it could be assumed that the corporative informational streams flow by the organization morphology (people, structures, processes) and feed its physiology, that is, the way in which an organization develops or operates its activities (*modus operandi*).

By projecting the DIGov model onto the empirical data and information that was gathered, the following framework was obtained, which forms the basis for the development and application of a knowledge map (**Figure 9**).

This higher level of abstraction and relational view of knowledge organization can still be useful in exploring the interrelationships of a system's components in the more operational level.

Figure 10(A) presents a multidimensional representation of Embrapa's data and information management panorama, mapping its main elements, as empirically observed. The large volume of data collected through the questionnaires was interconnected and their mutual interrelationships (causalities) were registered. **Figure 10(B)** highlights the contextualization of the OA issue in relation to the overall conceptual structure.

This exercise needs not to be complete and final. Being a complex system, its breadth, diversity and dynamism imposes the need of a model (and, consequently, of a representation tool) that meets the system's plasticity and allows its continued modification, due to uncertainties, randomness and unpredictabilities that characterizes the organizational time and space. However, features of this dynamics can be evidenced and captured to assist their operational management.

Figure 11 focuses on the concept of OA, isolating it from the whole it belongs to and highlighting the most relevant and immediate relationships that it establishes with other elements of the system.

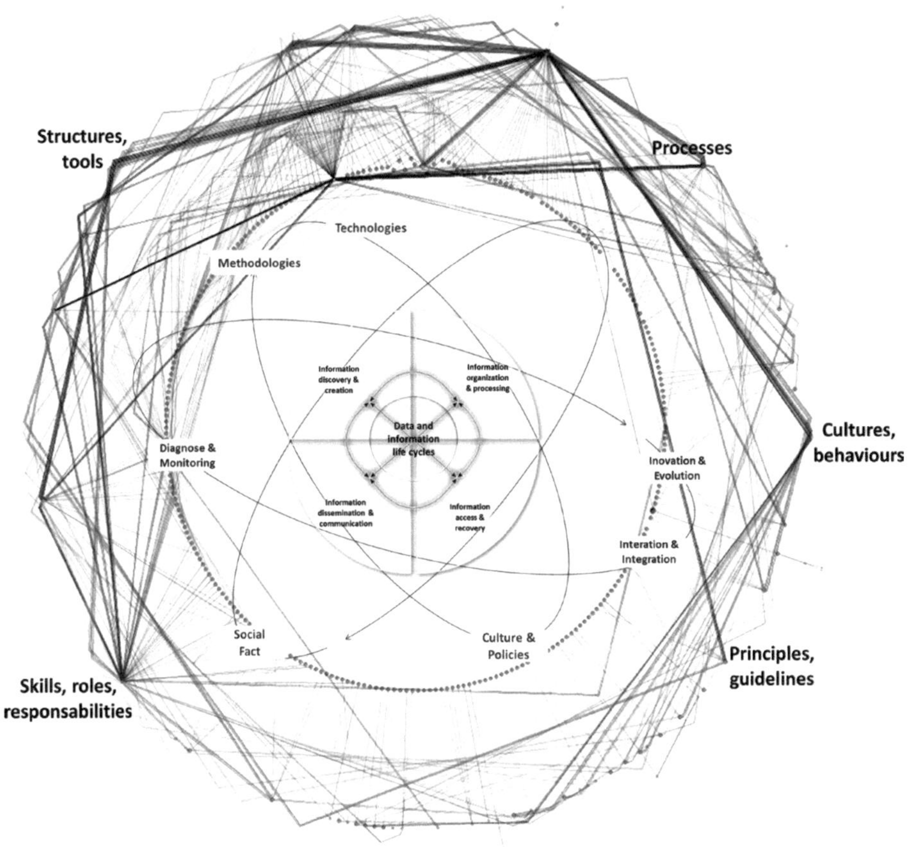

Figure 9. Contextualization of the DIGov model in a network of conceptual, procedural, structural and operational components of Embrapa's information environment.

The final stage of this exercise is to do with making concrete sense of this mapping, drawing it together with the relevant management processes. This is an intellectual, human oriented exercise, but which can be assisted by relevant tools. Doing so, the map presented in **Figure 11** can be graphically edited and semantically refined to incorporate a qualitative view of the positioning of the OA issue within Embrapa's informational environment, by identifying the elements that compose the DIGov model and designing causal relationships between them to recommend operational actions, whether to change culture and behaviour or to improve methodologies, structures or supporting technologies.

A semantic refinement of the relationships drawn in the model can and should be systematized and standardized corporately, strengthening a collectively agreed language process to ensure that the corporate learning processes become more aligned from cognitive, procedural, normative and communicational points of views. This would then result into the design that is shown in **Figure 12**—a pragmatic governance proposal to support decision-making regarding this particular issue in the corporate context.

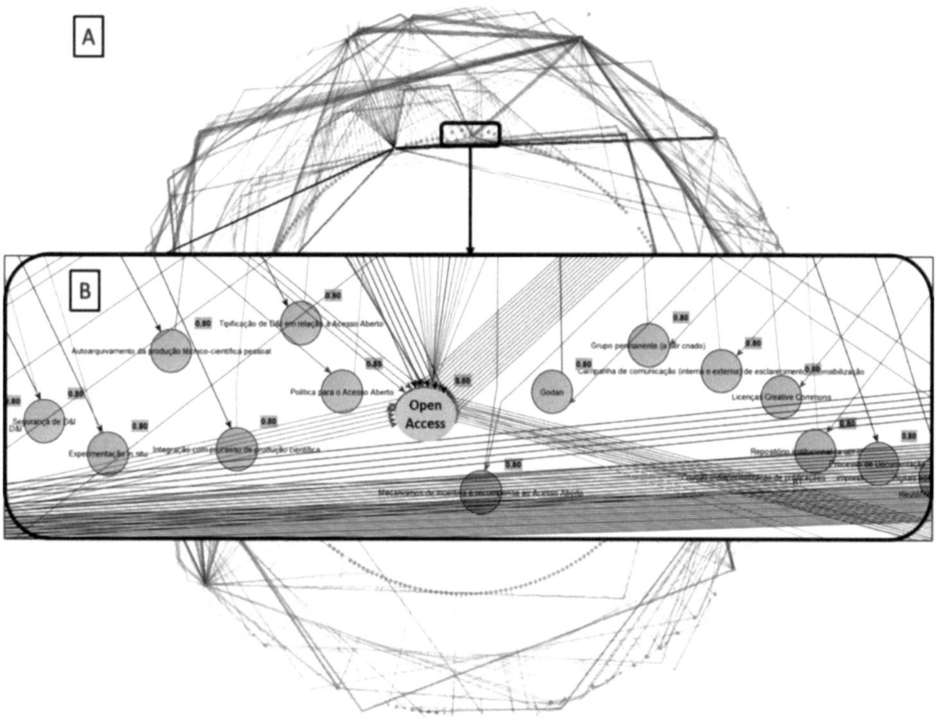

Figure 10. Conceptual representation of Embrapa's data and information management panorama (A), highlighting the positioning of the Open Access issue in relation to the other elements of the system (B).

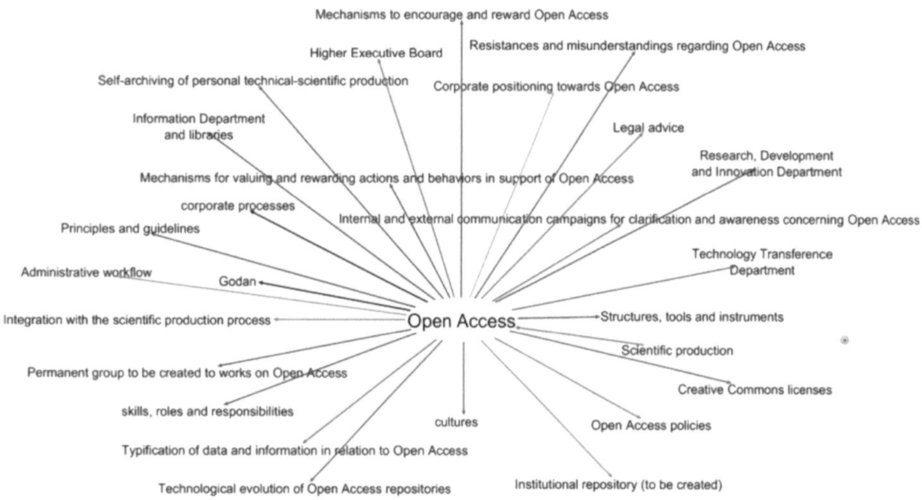

Figure 11. Apartness of the Open Access concept, identifying the most important relationships it establishes with other elements of Embrapa's informational environment.

Figure 12. Snippet view (zoom in) of the ontological structure of Embrapa's DIGov model, focusing the Open Access issue within the corporate information environment.

7. Some considerations and future avenues of development

As already mentioned, corporate management processes are inherently aligned with the decision-making process. It was also mentioned that the best decision to be made is always dependent on the assessment of possible alternatives, which are formed by the gathering and analysis of data, information and knowledge relating to the matter of interest.

Given the complexity of R&D organizations' information environment, conventional models of data, information and knowledge organization and representation, which are conventionally of the categorization or classification types (metadata systems and taxonomies, for example), have proven to limit the effectiveness of information search and retrieval, disambiguation and making sense processes. In other words, relational models such as the thesauri, multi-faceted taxonomies, semantic networks and ontologies are more appropriate options for supporting conceptual designs that can better represent the ontological nature and the multidimensionality of causal relations in a complex system [11, 39].

Recent studies have reiterated [33] knowledge mapping as an important tool for knowledge management, since they increase the recognition, systematization, communication and sharing of common corporate practices. Despite being a promising area in the fields of conceptual modelling and tools' development, the operational adoption of knowledge maps still presents shortcomings. The present chapter contributes to filling this knowledge gap, while proposing a method for modelling complex, organizational processes. Furthermore, modelling data and

http://dx.doi.org/10.5772/67978

information governance in R&D organizations such as Embrapa, with support of knowledge mapping, has still the following advantages:

- Knowledge maps are very useful when the immensity and diversity of data and information involved in a given analysis need to be structured from vast content where the encoding of the tacit knowledge has already been processed, for example, textually.
- Knowledge maps do not need to be exhaustive. In fact, they are not committed to representing the real world. Complex systems are dynamic, mutants, reactive to externalities and therefore difficult to be modelled, and, therefore, they require tools which respect their natural plasticity and which, from an operational point of view, can be easily adjusted both in relation to its component elements and in relation to the nature of interrelationships that such elements establish among themselves.
- Knowledge maps are also useful tools for inferring on the social networks implicitly contained in organizational complexity. The identification of social networks come to meet the need to enhance the social fact in the context of organizational management, recognizing its importance and the way people influence and are influenced by corporate management actions. This utility of knowledge maps can be used in support of systemic approaches [8], which have as a first general methodological rule, the commandment to put the social fact in its broader context, that is, its own system [40].

Knowledge mapping (the process) or knowledge maps (the products) are useful for meaningfully representing data, information and knowledge, where and when large amounts of data, information and knowledge are involved. Embrapa's DIGov model, as presented in this work, suggests that this process and its products can be usefully employed as a conceptual and computational model for organizing and managing extensive corporate contents. But far beyond organizing data, information and knowledge repositories, knowledge mapping can be a useful tool and basic framework for navigational purposes through corporate informational flows supporting organizational and collective intelligence applications.

Future avenues of work for the further development, implementation and use of Embrapa's DIGov model would be:

- To evolve the governance proposal in parallel with efforts to incite the desired organizational culture change, towards one that would include the understanding, absorbing and embedding of complex and system thinking as new paradigms, in support of data and information management processes.
- To evolve conventional methods of data and information management, which are still predominantly based upon uni- or bi-dimensional models of knowledge organization systems (KOS) [41] like term lists, taxonomies, categorization or classification schemes, for example, to multidimensional relationships models like thesauri, semantic networks and ontologies, which are more suitable for operationally rearrange knowledge content of large volume and high potential for use and reuse in processes of collective intelligence and institutional development.

Author details

Ivo Pierozzi Junior[1]*, Patrícia Rocha Bello Bertin[2], Claudia De Laia Machado[3] and Alessandra Rodrigues da Silva[2]

*Address all correspondence to: ivo.pierozzi@embrapa.br

1 Embrapa Agricultural Informatics, Brasília, Brazil

2 Embrapa Technological Information, Brasília, Brazil

3 EmbrapaSoils, Brasília, Brazil

References

[1] Simon HA. The architecture of complexity: hierarchic systems. Proc Am Philos Soc. 1962;**106**(6):467-82. http://scholar.google.com/scholar?hl=en&btnG=Search&q=intitle:The+Architecture+of+Complexity+Hierarchic+systems#1

[2] Daily CM, Dalton DR, Cannella Jr AA. Corporate governance: decades of dialogue and data. Acad Manag Rev. 2003;**28**(3):371-82

[3] Bhattacherjee A. Social science research: principles, methods, and practices (2nd ed.). The global text project. Tampa: University of South Florida; 2012

[4] Boyatzis RE. Transforming qualitative information: thematic analysis and code development. London: Sage Publications; 1998

[5] Waldrop MM. Complexity: the emerging science at the edge of order and chaos. New York: Simon & Schuster; 1993

[6] Mitchell M. Complexity: a guided tour. New York: Oxford University Press; 2009

[7] Casti JL. Complexification: explaining a paradoxical world through the science of surprise. New York: Harper Collins; 1994. 320 p

[8] Bunge M. Systemism: the alternative to individualism and holism. J Socio Econ. 2000;**29**:147-57

[9] Morin E. From the concept of system to the paradigm of complexity. J Soc Evol Syst. 1992;**15**:371-85

[10] Furtado BA, Sakowski PAM, Tóvolli MH, editors. Modeling complex systems for public policies. Brasília: IPEA; 2015. 396 p

[11] Stacey RD. Strategic management and organisational dynamics: the challenge of complexity. 6th ed. Harlow: Pearson Education Limited; 2011

[12] Rand W. Complex systems: concepts, literature, possibilities and limitations. In: Furtado BA, Sakowski PAM, Tóvolli MH, editors. Modeling complex systems for public policies. Brasília: IPEA; 2015. pp. 37-54

[13] Buckland MK. Information as thing. J Am Soc Inf Sci. 1991;**42**(5):351-60

[14] Feather J, Sturges P, editors. International encyclopedia of information and library science (2nd ed.). London: Routledge; 2003

[15] Davenport TH, Prusak L. Working knowledge: how organizations manage what they know. Boston: Harvard Business School Press; 1998

[16] Borgman CL. The conundrum of sharing research data. J Am Soc Inf Sci Technol. 2012;**63**(6):1059-78

[17] National Research Council – US. A question of balance: private rights and the public interest in scientific and technical databases. Washington, DC: The National Academies Press; 1999. 158 p

[18] Bellinger G, Castro D, Mills A. Data, information, knowledge, and wisdom [Internet]. Mental Model Musings. 2004 [cited 2017 Jan 1]. http://www.systems-thinking.org/dikw/dikw.htm

[19] Frické M. The knowledge pyramid: a critique of the DIKW hierarchy. J Inf Sci. 2009;**35**(2):131-42

[20] Bernstein JH. The data-information-knowledge-wisdom hierarchy and its antithesis. In: Jacob EK, Kwasnik B, editors. Proceedings from North American symposium on knowledge organization [Internet]. 1989. pp. 68-75. Available from: http://hdl.handle.net/10150/105414

[21] Rowley J. Where is the wisdom that we have lost in knowledge? J Doc. 2006;**62**(2):251-70

[22] Rowley J. The wisdom hierarchy: representations of the DIKW hierarchy. J Inf Sci. 2007;**33**(2):163-80

[23] Pierozzi Junior I, Souza MIF, Torres TZ, Oliveira LHM de, Queiros LR. Information and knowledge management. In: Massruhá SMFS, Leite MA de A, Luchiari Junior A, Romani LAS, editor. Information and communication technologies and their relations with agriculture. Brasília: Embrapa; 2016. pp. 231-52

[24] Bertin PRB. Towards effective governance of information in a Brazilian agricultural research organisation. Loughborough, UK: Loughborough University; 2014

[25] Lueg C. Information, knowledge, and networked minds. J Knowl Manag. 2001;**5**(2):151-9

[26] Tenopir C, Allard S, Douglass K, Aydinoglu AU, Wu L, Read E, et al. Data sharing by scientists: Practices and perceptions. PLoS One. 2011;**6**(6):1-21

[27] Floridi L. Information: a very short introduction. New York: Oxford University Press; 2010

[28] Dalkir K. The knowledge management cycle. In: Knowledge management in theory and practice. Oxford: Elsevier; 2005. pp. 25-46

[29] Davenport TH. Information ecology: mastering the information and knowledge environment. New York: Oxford University Press; 1997

[30] Davenport T, Eccles RG, Prusak L. Information politics. Sloan Manage Rev. 1992;(Fall): 53-65

[31] Henczel S, editor. The information audit: a practical guide. München: Saur KG; 2001

[32] Choo CW, Bergeron P, Detlor B, Heaton L. Information culture and information use: an exploratory study of three organizations. J Am Soc Inf Sci Technol. 2008;**59**(5):792-804

[33] Balaid A, Rozan MZA, Hikmi SN, Memon J. Knowledge maps: a systematic literature review and directions for future research. Int J Inf Manage. 2016;**36**(3):451-75

[34] Cook DJ, Holder LB, editors. Mining graph data. Electrical engineering. New Jersey: Wiley-Interscience; 2007

[35] Wang Z, Zhang J, Feng J, Chen Z. Knowledge graph embedding by translating on hyperplanes. In: Proceedings of the Twenty-Eighth AAAI Conference on Artificial Intelligence. Québec City, Canada; 2014. pp. 1112-9

[36] Karpicke JD, Blunt JR. Retrieval practice produces more learning than elaborative studying with concept mapping. Science (80-). 2011;**331**(6018):772-5

[37] Pulido JRG, Flores SBF, Ramirez RCM, Diaz RA. Eliciting ontology components from semantic specific-domain maps: towards the next generation web. In: LA-WEB'09 Latin American. Washington, DC: IIEE; 2009. pp. 224-9

[38] Schwendimann BA. Making sense of knowledge integration maps. In: Ifenthaler D, Hanewald R, editors. Digital knowledge maps in education: technology-enhanced support for teachers and learners. New York: Springer; 2014. pp. 17-40

[39] Ohly HP. Mission, programs, and challenges of knowledge organization. Adv Knowl Organ. 2012;**13**:25-33

[40] Kern VM. O sistemismo de Bunge: Fundamentos, abordagem metodológica e aplicação a sistemas de informação. Anais. 2011;(i):2693-709

[41] Zeng, M. L. Knowledge organization systems (KOS). Knowl Org. 2008;**35**(2-3):160-82

Chapter 5

E-Service Composition Ontology

Farzad Sanati

Additional information is available at the end of the chapter

http://dx.doi.org/10.5772/intechopen.68467

Abstract

Recently, the concept of life event was coined in the literature to describe an event in a citizen's life that would require at least one or in some cases a collection of public services from e-government service composition prospective. A system to provide the required intelligence that would be able to compose the basic e-services to build a composite service has recently become an area of debate with many solutions being proposed. This study building on prior publications is attempting to introduce and provide new technical guidelines for a new ontology that extends Ontology Web Language for Services (OWL-S) as knowledgebase and intelligent actor for creating composite services to build a life event. This chapter proposes the life-event ontology that is a logical extension of OWL-S for implementation of e-service integration modelling framework proposed in prior publications.

Keywords: ontology, e-service composition, e-government, life event

1. Introduction

An intelligent software needs to provide a platform-independent description for services that it renders, while providing the means by which the service is accessed. Then a delivery platform is needed as such where descriptions of services are made and shared and delivered to clients also in an independent platform. The delivery platform should be able to employ a standard ontology that consists of a set of basic classes and properties for declaring and describing services. Ontology Web Language (OWL) seems to be the best candidate for this from the ontology structuring mechanisms point of view. OWL provides an appropriate representation language framework within which to do this.

This chapter provides formal methods for design and proof of an upper ontology, which is of crucial importance for e-service composition framework. It discusses the definition of 'ontology', 'service ontology' and 'life-event ontology'. It gives details of what the concepts of service and service ontology mean in this study. This study explains and illustrates the overview of conceptual design for life-event ontology through the annotation used in the formal method using first-order logic to establish the main axioms and design rules for the 'life-event ontology' [1].

Ontology described in this chapter will provide technical support for implementation of life-event ontology-oriented service composition platform. Life-event ontology is a logical extension of Ontology Web Language for Services (OWL-S), extending this existing approach enables the design of a life-event metamodel, which in turn is used as an alterable workflow for composite services. The resulting ontology covers specific web services with semantic concepts to implement the conceptual life-event framework in the context of e-service composition by

1. Facilitating the construction of alternative integrated service workflows from entirely different web service vendors.
2. Enabling the repair or reconfiguration of life-event workflows in runtime.
3. The invocation of web services according to the workflow sequence.

2. Definition of ontology

In the domain of information technology, the term ontology is a word borrowed from philosophy that refers to the science of describing the kind of entities in the word and how they are related [2]. According to the Merriam Webster online dictionary, it is defined as[1]

1. A branch of metaphysics concerned with nature and the relations of beings.
2. A particular theory about the nature of being or the kind of things that have existence.

In the context of information technology, the most typical kind of ontology has a taxonomy and a set of inference rules [3]. On the other hand, a more formal definition of ontology is given by Maedche [4] as follows:

An ontology is a five-tuple as

$$O ::= (C, R, H^C, rel, A^O) \tag{1}$$

where C is a set of classes (concepts) and R is a set of relations.

Therefore, $H^C \subseteq C \times C$ is called taxonomy,

$H^C(c_1, c_2)$ means c_1 *'is-a'* c_2;

$rel : R \rightarrow C \times C$ is a function defined for other relations;

And, A^o is a logical language.

[1]http://www.merriam-webster.com/dictionary/ontology

In addition to these definitions, ontologies are used to describe a variety of models, ranging from simplest taxonomies such as Online Directory Project[2] to very complex knowledge models written in first-order logic.[3]

2.1. RDF and RDF schema

The resource description framework (RDF) is a recommendation of W3C specifications, originally designed as a metadata model. It is used as a general method for conceptual description or modelling of information that is implemented in web resources, using a variety of syntax formats.

RDF has an eXtensible Markup Language (XML)-based syntax, it provides a metadata model for ontology knowledgebase and also provides a common framework so that applications can process and exchange the information automatically through the World Wide Web.

RDF schema (RDFS) is the description of RDF language. It is also expressed in XML and provides a simple ontology of RDF concepts and property definitions. RDF provides the basis on which next generation ontology languages are developed. In other words, most new ontology languages are logical extensions of RDF.

2.2. RDF model

RDF identifies objects using Unified Resource Identification (URI) [5]. The literature describes a URI to be a series of characters that identifies an abstract or physical resource. URL is used to identify resources (available date) on the Internet, these resources be in form of html web pages or other form of data made available in the XML form. RDF uses simple property terms and their values to describe resources. RDF statements are represented as triples consisting of subject, predicate and object. The subject signifies the resource, the predicate represents the relationship between the subject and the object. The object can itself be a resource or a string literal, which represents a basic data type such as Integer or Boolean values.

RDF schema as the semantic extension of RDF describes and maps out all the relationships between resources in RDF. The resources are divided into groups or classes, which they provide a simple hierarchical classification structure, which relates these classes to each another through their properties. There is also 'Predicate' or property element, which represents the predicate and object of the statement. Its content is the object of the statement, which described as plain literal.

2.3. OWL

Recent advances have resulted in new developments in RDF towards a more cohesive approach towards new representation of knowledge. One of the most talked about is Ontology Web Language (OWL). OWL ontology is also an RDF graph and is represented by a set of RDF triples. As with any RDF graph, an OWL ontology graph has different syntactic forms. RDF

---

[2]http://www.dmoz.org/.

[3]http://www.ehealthserver.com/ontology/.

and RDF schema ontologies are extended by OWL via adding more terminology for describing properties and classes as well as cardinality, equality, relations between classes, richer property typing, property characteristics and enumerated classes.

Pure hierarchy of classes and their relationships is not the only thing that the ontology is defining; they are also used to inference class relationships such as equivalence or being disjoint.

2.4. OWL model

The root class of OWL ontology is called owlThing. Other classes defined within the ontology are subclasses of owlThing. OWL also supports a set of operators on classes such as union, intersection and complement. It also allows class enumeration and disjoint. There are two types of simple properties in owl description: one is 'data type' and the other one is 'object' properties. Relationship between class instances and RDF literals or XML schema data types is defined as data type properties. Relationship between the instances of classes is defined as object properties. There could also be logical connectivity such as transitivity, inverse and functional and symmetric connections. Similar to RDFS, an OWL class can contain instances of individuals of the class and other subclasses [6].

According to RDF, instances are defined to be the descriptions of a class with certain values in their properties. On the other hand, in OWL a class could also be defined with logical restrictions based on some properties. Classes can also be restricted by existential or universal quantifiers. For instance, the class life event may have subclasses defined with existential quantifiers on the hasService property such as 'hasService some Life-eventService' [1].

Hence, to restrict a subclass of the life-event class, one can define it as the MotorcycleLicenseLife-event class, which contains all life events that have Life-eventService as a service. This includes all the instances that have the hasService property assigned to the Life-eventService. In addition, these properties can also have cardinality restrictions. Therefore, one can safely say life event must have at least one Life-eventService but may have more than one. Thus, the hasService property can be restricted to

hasService > 1 and a life-event instance can have multiple hasService properties.

OWL has three sublanguages: OWL Full, OWL DL and OWL Lite, all described in Ref. [7]. OWL Lite is the least expressive of them. OWL Lite is somewhat more expressive than RDFS, because it provides simple constraints of classes and properties in addition to supporting a classification hierarchy. OWL DL is modelled on description logics, all conclusions are guaranteed to be computable that means, it supports maximum expressiveness while retaining computational completeness. A service class does not need to be an individual in order to represent a collection of individuals. This study suggests the use of OWL reasoners such as FaCT++ [8] to check for the accuracy of OWL documents.

2.5. OWL querying

OWL ontology can be queried in several ways. One effective way is to use a reasoner in order to create a class with certain constrains, then by classifying the class within the ontology, one can see which classes it relates to. All other relationships of this class such as equivalent classes, super classes and subclasses can also be inspected by the query processor. Reasoners can also be used to query over the OWL instances. The query processor in this method converts the query to an OWL class instance, where all the property values are the same as that of the query, where the reasoner can find all the classes that have this instance as an inferred instance. An inferred instance is known to be one that has not been explicitly instantiated within a class but is inferred to be part of a class as a result of the values and type of its properties. There are more OWL query languages that have been developed besides these methods. One example of OWL query language is the OWL-QL [9], which is a formal language and protocol that queries an OWL ontology by finding class relationships. It also allows querying and answering agents to conduct a query-answering dialogue in ontologies represented by OWL.

3. Ontology versus database

The reasoning power of ontology is the motivation behind its use for representing services rather than using simple attribute-value representations of data such as in traditional databases. An example of a query which can be done using an ontology which is difficult to do using a Simple Query Language (SQL) query is 'Given a service class, find all logically related matches to my query'. Simple Query Language (SQL) also does not support abstract data types, thus making it difficult to determine whether a certain property value belongs to a number of different classes or types. Ontologies can also be shared, re-used and changed. Ontologies can be distributed across the Internet and grow limitlessly, and they can be discovered and shared using their URI.

When new relationships are established within the ontology schema because of ontology migration or the addition of new classes, determining new relationships within the ontology is simply reduced to running a reasoner on the ontology in order to reclassify the classes. For relational databases, changes to the schema may have a fundamental impact on the existing data.

The main drawback to using ontology is that classification is expensive. As ontologies grow large, and especially when instances of classes are stored in the ontology, reasoning becomes a bottleneck. We tackle this problem by storing instances in separate ontology data-files instead of the ontology schema itself. This speeds up the classification process considerably. Moreover, a positive side effect of the distributed architecture of Life-event Ontology Oriented Service Integration (LOOSI) is that it allows each component to handle different ontologies (OWL-S and life event).

3.1. Web service ontology

In order to understand what real-world services are, we look at some works in the economic and business sciences as well as literature originating from Information and Communication Technology (ICT) area.

Hardly any of the generic concepts concerning real-world services show up in current e-commerce product classifications or standards for web services, a term that refers to Internet-based technologies, rather than business activities. Web services are loosely coupled reusable software components that semantically encapsulate discrete functionality. Web services, however necessary and useful, cannot really be seen as services in the sense of the business science literature, they are currently rather restricted to input/output interface specifications.

There are many initiatives that have made progress towards defining and organising ontologies for web services; two of which have contributed a great deal to the state-of-the-art:

1. OWL-S describes a set of foundation classes and properties that can be used for declaring and describing services. One example of that is described in W3C 2004 documentation, stating that 'an ontology for describing Web Services that enable users and software agents to automatically discover, invoke, compose and monitor Web resources offering services under specified constraints' [10]. OWL-S tries to cover the description of services in a wide sense, not focusing on a particular application domain or problem.

2. Web Services Modelling Ontology (WSMO) intended to solve the composition problem by creating ontology for describing different aspects of semantic web services, but with a more defined focus. WSMO also takes into account the specific application domains (e-commerce and e-work) in order to ensure the applicability of the ontology for these areas.

In comparison of the two standards, WSMO includes majority of the elements present in OWL-S while adding new elements in order to grow its relevance in most domains. Mediation and compensation are examples of such characteristics that are key issues yet to be solved in order to achieve the real implementation of semantic web services, in such a way to be relevant for e-commerce [11]. A more thorough look at WSMO reviles that it should provide a higher level of detail for the definition of aspects such as choreography or grounding required by web service implementation. If these elements are appropriately covered, then WSMO can become a strict superset of OWL-S that also covers relevant issues not covered by OWL-S. WSMO also intends to have an execution platform, called web service modelling eXecution (WSMX) environment, while the intentions of OWL-S in this direction are not yet defined.

A web service transaction involves three parties: the service requesters, the service provider and a mediation infrastructure facility. The service requester, who may broadly be identified as a user, seeks a service to complete its task; the service provider, who can be broadly identified as a provider, provides a service sought by the user. The user may not know of the existence of the provider ahead of time, so it relies on mediator infrastructure facilities that act like a service registry and workflow organiser to find the appropriate provider. The role of the mediator registry is to match the request with the offers of service providers to identify which of them is the best match. In Chapters 6 and 7, we will provide the details of such facilities that can act as a delivery platform for life event and a framework for using such a platform. The remainder of the section explains the detailed design for an ontology that can provide a foundation for such a framework.

Consider the utilisation of a credit card service. A customer can choose the simplest form of a credit card or a more expensive card, which offers extra services as free travel insurance, high withdrawal limits, travel assistance abroad, worldwide card replacement in the case of loss, linking the card to a preferred supplier and many more. Multiple aspects of this service offering can be facilitated by websites: ordering a card, transactions listing, buying other services and goods with the card and more.

Another example is the online organisation of events such as conferences, board meetings, executive courses and exhibitions. Their electronic facilitation requires many capabilities, including a good predefined classification of such events, together with a description of their properties, plus the constraints they impose such as suitable times and spaces (rooms, halls and room set-up).

Essentially, an ontology is needed that can define the core contents of the service. In addition, electronic facilities should provide the capability of selecting relevant supplementary services. Such services include travel insurance and high withdrawal limits in the credit card case, and coffee breaks, video facilities, Internet connection, translation, sound, technical assistance or catering, in the event organisation case. This, once more can only occur in a predefined and standardised ontology-oriented way, in a way that related additional restrictions and relationships can be automatically provided for. The other issue is where service consumer requirements regarding a service usually contain some implicit things, fuzzy statements, and often requires a substantial interpretation. This steps into the service provider's ontological terminology and the components that the service provider can actually deliver.

OWL-S has made progress towards configuration-based service composition. This study suggests that an important element of a paradigm for the support of real-world services is a generic description of services and what they provide. Simply, a service ontology that the runtime design and production of services can be simplified to a configuration task. This task of looking up configuration in order to build composite services is called service composition. This can be translated in to a collaborative e-government scenario, where the ideal is to have an intelligent support system that [12]

- ontology has service bundle contents,
- interprets the preferences and customer needs into suitable terms from the perspective of the service provider, and
- can deal with all the associated restrictions while automatically constructing the requested service in a configuration-oriented way, which supports the composition of services from different service providers into a user-controlled workflow of composite web services.

The biggest limitation of OWL-S is that it only allows for the composition of services (or operations) described in one Web Services Definition Language (WSDL). A new system of web service knowledgebase configuration would be necessary if we wanted to compose web services from different vendors. One major challenge is that the service ontology must be sufficiently generic to be useful across many application domains. We discuss below how such an ontology might look and present its logical formal description.

4. Life-event ontology description

This research defines the life-event ontology as the logical extension of OWL-S to provide extended functionality, which allows a systematic composition of e-government web services by means of abstraction in design and implementation. The advantage of such an extension is that it preserves and uses all the capabilities inherited from upper ontologies such as OWL and OWL-S, while adding more specialised ontology concepts to achieve precise results for automating the composition of e-services by means of abstraction. The design for life-event ontology will take OWL-S one step further to integrate atomic and composite services not only from one service provider but also from many, to allow the dynamic construction of a user-controlled workflow of readily available web services.

The model for life-event ontology requires two types of knowledge analysis in order to achieve a more comprehensive solution for the design of the ontology itself. This ontology needs to provide two essential types of knowledge about an event in a business or a persons' life.

Life-event ontology as a service knowledgebase is required to automate the acquisition of individual web service instances in a life-event workflow. It provides service-specific information such as availability, service type, service profile and required communication parameters to the runtime workflow construction process. A service knowledgebase could use multiple ontology descriptors (OWL-S ServiceModel) to obtain the semantic information required by the workflow for the invocation of atomic services. Life-event ontology embodies the following concepts:

A. Life event: a metamodel that provides a category of knowledge that is needed to answer the question 'In what possible alternative ways can a life event be constructed?' The answer to this question starts with the concept of life event that is the root element of the ontology inherited directly from the generic concept of thing. This ontology class is the definition of an abstract construct of all possible services that are nominated to collaborate with each other in order to solve a business problem. This ontology class has the inversed functional object property called hasService. This object property is of type class Life-eventService. The minimum cardinality of this property is one; this means that a life event must be composed of at least one service. One of the most important responsibilities of this class is to enforce the rules of government regulations to make sure that a legally acceptable workflow is provided that can be instantiated and executed to fulfil a customer request for a service. Listing 1 is the RDF code for the construction of this object property.

```
<owl:ObjectProperty rdf:about="le#hasService">
<rdf:type rdf:resource="&owl;InverseFunctionalProperty"/>
<rdfs:domain rdf:resource="le#Life-event"/>
<rdfs:range rdf:resource="le#Life-eventService"/>
<owl:inverseOf rdf:resource="le#describedByLife-event"/>
</owl:ObjectProperty>
```

Listing 1. Definition of object property hasService.

B. Life-eventInstance: one possible way of implementing a life event is defined by this concept, meaning that if we consider the life event as a metamodel that only defines the types and the order of possible web services in a workflow, then a Life-eventInstance would be one of the possible ways to create such workflow. This concept has an object property of type ServiceInstance called hasServiceInstance, with the cardinality of one. This property represents the individual invokeable instances of web services that make up the workflow of the life event at runtime. Listing 2 is the RDF code for the construction of this object property.

```
<owl:ObjectProperty rdf:about="le#hasServiceInstance">
<rdfs:domain rdf:resource="le#Life-eventInstance"/>
<rdfs:range rdf:resource="le#ServiceInstance"/>
<owl:inverseOf rdf:resource="le#partOfLife-eventInstance"/>
</owl:ObjectProperty>
```

Listing 2. Definition of object property hasServiceInstance.

C. Life-eventService: provides knowledge about the acceptable web service types and possible sets of actual service instances for every service type. In other words, this concept is the abstract construction of all service types that could potentially be instantiated as a ServiceInstance at runtime. As it is strongly acknowledged by other research literature [13], the diversity of structures, regulations and procedures affecting networks of heterogeneous administrative units, represents a challenge for semantic composition. This type of knowledge is specifically related to e-government service composition, since every Life-eventService participant in any life event may enforce or be affected by one or more government regulations. These regulations are the governing rules of composite services in the e-government domain, specifically because regulations are one of the integral parts of inter-agency processes (i.e. where the life-event process flow crosses multiple agencies). Furthermore, regulatory knowledge is required for designing an inter-agency workflow that crosses the boundaries of local, state and federal agencies. It has three object properties:

1. hasPrerequisite provides the knowledge about the order of services in the workflow or possible required action or documentation prior to the invocation of the web service. Listing 3 is the RDF code for the construction of this object property.

```
<owl:ObjectProperty rdf:about="le#hasPrerequisite">
<rdfs:domain rdf:resource="le#Life-eventService"/>
<rdfs:range>
<owl:Restriction>
<owl:onProperty rdf:resource="le#hasPrerequisite"/>
<owl:someValuesFrom rdf:resource="le#Prerequisite"/>
</owl:Restriction>
</rdfs:range>
</owl:ObjectProperty>
```

Listing 3. Definition of object property hasPrerequisite.

2. hasServiceType and (3) hasServiceSubType provide knowledge about the type of LfeEventService. Listing 4 is the RDF code for the construction of these two object properties.

```
<owl:ObjectProperty rdf:about="le#hasServiceSubType">
<rdfs:domain rdf:resource="le#Life-eventService"/>
<rdfs:range rdf:resource="le#ServiceSubType"/>
<rdfs:subPropertyOf rdf:resource="&owl;topObjectProperty"/>
</owl:ObjectProperty>
<owl:ObjectProperty rdf:about="le#hasServiceType">
<rdfs:domain rdf:resource="le#Life-eventService"/>
<rdfs:range rdf:resource="le#ServiceType"/>
<rdfs:subPropertyOf rdf:resource="&owl;topObjectProperty"/>
</owl:ObjectProperty>
```

Listing 4. Definition of hasServiceSubType and hasServiceType.

D. ServiceInstance: it is a personalised instance of the Life-eventService and provides knowledge about the user preferences at runtime. It implements all the prerequisites of the web service that are enforced by the Life-eventService. ServiceInstance extends Life-eventService and represents one of many possible runtime instances of the Life-eventService. This ontology class has a property partOfLife-eventInstance that points to a class Life-eventInstance described in Listing 3 as the inverse functional property of hasServiceInstance. It is through this property that we can obtain knowledge about actual web services participating in a Life-eventInstance. It is our view that any problem a life event seeks to address can be fitted to two main areas of concern:

(I) For life-event users, it should describe how to ask for an OWL-S service and what happens when the workflow is being executed. By 'what happens' we mean what are the particular technical and legal requirements of invoking any of the web services in the life-event workflow.

(II) For managing the workflow, life event uses a logical description to perform four different functions:

1. To create a composite service workflow from multiple services in order to perform a specific complex task. It is important to note that 'composing OWL-S services' as a life-event is different from 'composite services' described in OWL-S specifications. The composite services described in OWL-S are provided by one service provider and specified in one WSDL grounding specification, whereas a life event comprises services from totally different providers with separate WSDL grounding specifications.

2. To manage the status and results of executing a complete or a partial life-event workflow of web services. This means that a citizen can request an invocation of a life event but does not necessarily complete the whole life event in one go. The

http://dx.doi.org/10.5772/intechopen.68467

user also has the ability to choose to invoke any of the operations listed in a web service descriptor.

3. To coordinate the activities of different service participants (requester, provider and mediator) during the course of the web service enactment.

4. To monitor the execution of the web service and compensate for any web service failures at runtime. This is made possible by the fact that a life event is a metamodel and it can be instantiated in many possible ways depending on the availability of different actual ServiceInstances for a particular Life-eventService. There are two object properties of ServiceType and ServiceSubType that can provide essential knowledge about a particular ServiceInstance that enables a Life-eventInstance and make a decision on substituting a failed ServiceInstance with a new one that is the closest match in terms of its object properties (hasServiceType and hasServiceSubType).

The ontology illustrated in **Figure 1** displays the main concepts of life event. The abstract concept of life event is extended by Life-eventInstance. Life event is a 'metamodel' representing a generic event in a typical citizens' life. This concept points to one Life-eventService. A Life-eventService is the conceptual representation of a web service that holds information about the service type by

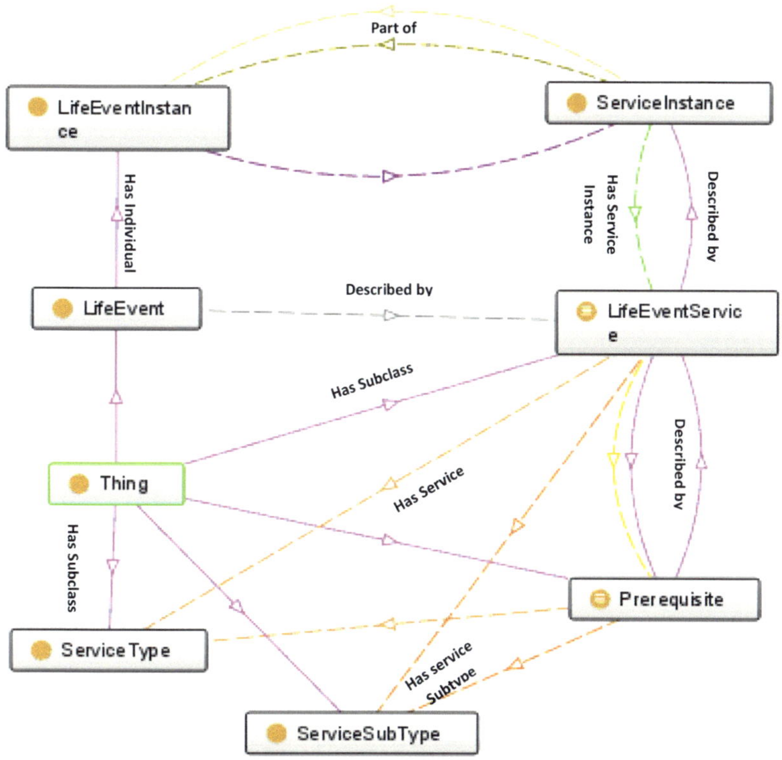

Figure 1. Life-event ontology conceptual graphs.

pointing to an instance of a class ServiceType and an instance of class ServiceSubType. Life-eventInstance is also aware of the position of its corresponding web service within the execution workflow at runtime. Life-eventService represents one element in a possible set of 'n' elements that makes up the life-event workflow.

A Life-eventService can be instantiated in many ways since it would be pointing to one or possibly more than one Life-eventInstance through ServiceType and ServiceSubType concepts.

In order to lay down a legally acceptable foundation for invocation of any government web services and to attain a legal outcome of such invocation, one needs to satisfy a set of legally binding regulatory requirements. We achieve this by setting up the rule: 'every element in this workflow must point to at least one prerequisite'. This rule is modelled as a concept called 'prerequisite'. This new concept extends the concept 'thing', therefore it could represent anything including but not limited to document, payment or, in most cases, another Life-eventService. This rule creates a linked list of services in which every Life-eventService has an object property hasPrerequisite, which is of type 'prerequisite'.

It is important to stress that the concept of prerequisite is very different from the property of 'precondition' described in OWL-S specifications; this difference is illustrated in Listing 4. OWL-S defines the property precondition to be represented as logical formulas like expressions as literals, either string literals or XML literals. The latter case is used for languages whose standard encoding is in XML such as Semantic Web Rule Language (SWRL) or RDF.

```
<Description rdf:about="#process2">
<hasPrecondition>
<expr:KIF-Expression>
<expr:expressionBody>
(!agnt:know_val_is
(!ecom:credit_card_num?cc)
?num)
</expr:expressionBody>
</expr:KIF-Expression>
</hasPrecondition>
</Description>
```

Listing 5. Implementation of property hasPrecondition in OWL-S.

If an OWL-S process has a precondition, then the process cannot be performed successfully unless the precondition is true. The difference between the precondition properties of OWL-S and the prerequisite concept of life event falls into two major areas:

1. Consider a process that charges a credit card. The charge goes through if the precondition (card is not overdrawn) is true. If it is overdrawn, the only output is a failure notification. This means that the precondition is an expression of whether to allow the invocation of a

service to go ahead, whereas the concept prerequisite of Life-eventService extends the concept thing, therefore it could be anything, including another Life-eventService. A Life-eventService can be invoked if and only if the prerequisite is not itself and the property isFulfilled of the prerequisite service is set to true.

2. The other important difference between the two concepts is that the concept of precondition is confined within the domain of one web service, whereas a prerequisite goes beyond the domain of one web service and includes a much larger area of the universe of discourse under the domain of life event. In next sections, we will explain the significant role of the concept prerequisite where it is of the type Life-eventService. Listing 6 is a snippet of the owl tag for the class prerequisite.

```
<owl:Class rdf:about=le#Prerequisite”>
<rdfs:comment>
This class could constitute anything and is the root element of all classes
that enforce workflow regulations for the life-event ontology
</rdfs:comment>
</owl:Class>
```

Listing 6. Class prerequisite in life-event ontology.

Catering for the possibility of service substitution in runtime is made possible by the concept Life-eventService, which points to one or more ServiceInstance; this allows for the substitution of similar web services with some degree of similarity, depending on web service availability or user preferences at runtime.

5. Life-event ontology formalisation

We find it convenient to be able to speak about ontologies as objects and to have a theory of these objects. We will use a first-order language that contains the usual logical operators and symbols: for negation, for conjunction, for disjunction, $\rightarrow$ for material implication, $\leftrightarrows$for logical equivalence, $=$ for equality ($\neq$ will abbreviate its negation), for the universal and for the existential quantifier. In due course, we will introduce non-logical symbols for the relevant predicates and relations if required. We shall use x, y and z as variables ranging over existing entities, and a, b and c will be constants denoting such entities. We will use ω and ω' as variables ranging over ontologies, and α, β and γ will be constants denoting ontologies.

We do not offer a full logic, and in particular, there will be no consideration of a deductive system. For the rest, unbound variables are assumed to be within the scope of universal quantifiers.

Life-event candidate is an abstraction of a complex workflow consisting of a number of composite or simple web services. Life-event candidate can use OWL-S descriptors of web services provided by service provider including the required government regulatory information, which is required to guarantee a legally acceptable outcome whenever the service is executed.

In the following, we provide a formal description for the main concepts (classes) of our life-event ontology followed by their description logic:

Life-event = LE

Life-eventInstance = LEI

Life-eventService = LES

ServiceInstance = SI

Prerequisite = PR

ServiceType = ST

ServiceSubType = SST

We shall use the predicate 'concept' in order to denote concepts, thus 'concept(x)' is to be read, 'x is a concept', and a concept can be from any of the following types: (LE, LEI, LES, SI, PR, ST and SST). We will use x, y and z as variables ranging over concepts.

Symbolically, the first axiom is an existential one, which asserts that there is at least one entity of a certain type. Here, we indicate that there exists ontology ω and there exists entity x that is of concept (class) life event in a variable ontology ω.

$$\exists\omega, \exists x[\Omega(\omega) \wedge LE(x)] \tag{2}$$

We use the predicate Ω in order to denote token, thus '$\Omega(\omega)$' is to be read 'ω is an ontology'. An instance of a given ontology token α is an entity whose existence is recognised by α. We will write 'inst(x, α)' which is to be read 'x is an instance of α'. Hence, there is no empty life-event ontology.

$$inst(x, \omega) \rightarrow [consept(x) \wedge \Omega(\omega)] \tag{3}$$

In addition, any existence is a constituent of ontology.

$$\Omega(\omega) \rightarrow \exists x[consept(x) \wedge inst(x, \omega)] \tag{4}$$

The predicate 'realises' denotes the instances of associated LES concepts within the life-event ontology. While each instance may be a model on its own, a combination of LESs may be aggregated to constitute a composite model. In that case, the services are considered to be the components of a model. LES (y) play role (r) that requires skills (s) needed to perform their role.

http://dx.doi.org/10.5772/intechopen.68467

$$\exists y[LES(y) \wedge (plays(y, r) \wedge has(r, s))] \tag{5}$$

Given that LES provides a set of specific operations O and x is a variable over this set to fulfil a t that is a variable over the set of tasks T, it would be required to have a subset S′ from the skill set of S.

$$[LES(y) \rightarrow (provids(y, x) \wedge (O \vee S))] \tag{6}$$

We must ensure that every LES carries enough semantic information to facilitate the runtime reconfiguration in the case of a web service failure during the LEI execution. Every LES has an object property 'hasPrerequisite' that makes one LES the prerequisite service of the value of this property in the workflow of LESs. Each of these object properties points to another LES, essentially creating a linked list of LESs in which every LES is aware of its place in the list through the data property called WorkflowPosition. In other words, a life event is the construct of a two-dimensional linked list, in which the first dimension is the list of meta-services and the second dimension is the list of service instances for each meta-service.

6. Life-event ontology evaluation

There is no restriction on the complexity of the logic that may be used to state the axioms and definitions of concepts in ontology. The distinction between terminological and formal ontologies is one of degree rather than kind. Life-event ontology tends to be smaller than terminological ontologies, but its axioms and definitions can support more complex inferences and computations. We conduct the experimental evaluation of the life-event ontology in two stages. We use the ontology editor tool Protégé to design and develop the life-event ontology schema as the preparation for evaluating the life-event ontology. We use the FaCT++ reasoner plug-in from within Protégé to perform structural validation of the schema. To evaluate the efficiency of life-event ontology, an experiment is conducted to measure the complexity of the ontology through a set of well-known formal methods and demonstrate the results in a numerical as well as graphical representation. We compare the life-event ontology to OWL-S ontology since it is the most conceptually similar to it.

6.1. Methods of measuring the ontology complexity

As ontologies grow in size and number, it is important to be able to measure their complexity quantitatively. Quantitative measurement of complexity can help ontology developers and maintainers better understand the current status of the ontology, therefore allowing them to better evaluate its design and control its development process. We are using a suite of ontology metrics [11], at both the ontology level and the class level, to measure the design complexity of life-event ontology. This ontology complexity measurement metric was evaluated in an empirical analysis on public domain ontologies to show the characteristics and usefulness of the metrics. The proposed metric suite is useful for managing the life-event ontology development projects.

6.2. Ontology level metrics

We use three different ontology level metrics to measure the complexity of the ontology:

Size of vocabulary **(*SOV*)** measures the amount of vocabulary defined in ontology. Given a graph representation $G = (N, P, E)$ of an ontology, where N is a set of nodes representing classes and individuals; P is a set of nodes representing properties and E is a set of edges representing property instances and other relationships between nodes in the graph G. In this measurement, SOV is defined as the cardinality of the named entities N_n and P_n in G: $SOV = |N_n| + |P_n|$, where N_n represents named classes and individuals and P_n represents user-defined properties.

Edge node ratio **(*ENR*)** measures the connectivity density. In this measurement, ENR tends to increases as more edges are added between nodes. The greater the ENR, the greater the complexity of an ontology. ENR is calculated as follows:

$$ENR = \frac{|E|}{|N|}, \tag{7}$$

as the division of the number of edges ($|E|$) by the number of nodes ($|N|$).

Tree impurity**(*TIP*)** measures how far ontology's inheritance hierarchy deviates from being a tree and it is defined as being:

$$TIP = |E'| - |N'| + 1, \tag{8}$$

where $|E'|$ is the number of *subclass* edges and $|N'|$ is the number of nodes in an ontology's inheritance hierarchy.

6.3. Class level metrics

This metrics are mostly concerned with the class level specific statistics, the most popular technique in this method is known as ***number of children*** **(*NOC*)**, as such to calculate NOC for a given class C, NOC measures the number of its immediate children in the ontology inheritance hierarchy given, as follows:

$$NOC_c = \#\{D | D \in N' \wedge (D, rdfs : subClassOf, C) \in E'\}, \tag{9}$$

where $C \in N'$ and symbol # denote the cardinality. And, the E' denotes the set of entities.

6.4. Experiment preparation

This section will describe the preparation for a comparative evaluation of life-event ontology against OWL-S using the methods described in Sections 6.2.2 and 6.2.3.

Step 1: Building the ontology. It aims to prepare for the evaluation of the life-event ontology. The choice of ontology editor was made mainly due to the fact that Protégé is open source software and was more suited to our purpose [14]. This tool is developed and maintained by

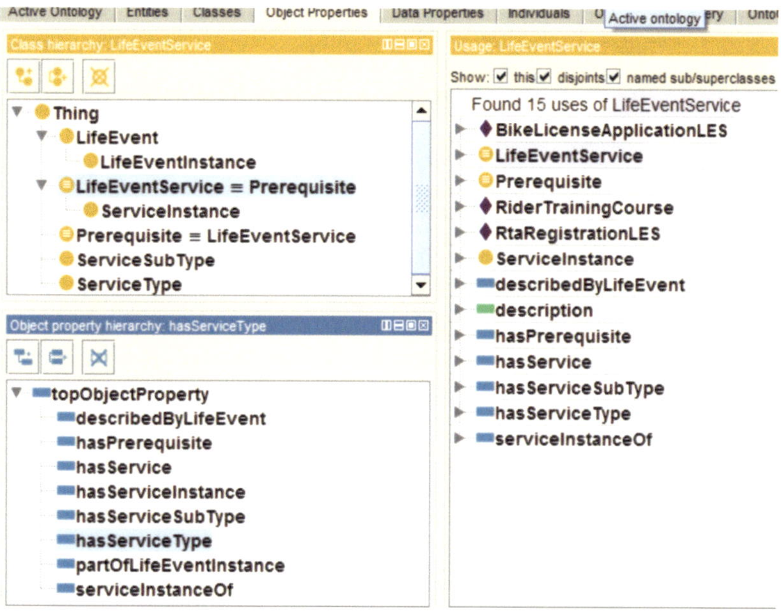

Figure 2. Life-event ontology built by Protégé.

Stanford University. We used version 4.1, which was more advanced, intuitive and easier to use than other available ontology editors. **Figure 2** shows a screenshot of our developed ontology, which illustrates the concepts, their relationships with object properties and data properties in the Protégé ontology editor.

Step 2: Comparable ontology. This step is to select an ontology that is conceptually similar to life-event ontology. OWL-S is chosen because it is not only conceptually very similar to the life-event ontology but also functionally designed to perform a similar work. This ontology is also used by the LOOSI platform to provide knowledgebase support for the web service enactment functionality of the system. The diagram shown in **Figure 3** is the graph representation of OWL-S conceptual schema version 1.1.

In this comparative evaluation of life-event ontology with OWL-S, we use numerical value results from applying the metrics in Sections 6.2.2 and 8.2.3 on both ontologies to illustrate the measurement of efficiency and complexity of the life-event ontology in compare to the OWL-S.

The experiment starts with creating and adding five named individuals that are the representatives of five individual web services that are published by the Australian Government agencies and other businesses. One more named individual is created only in life-event ontology as the first instance of the schema to point to the Life-eventServices. The list of these named individuals is described in **Figure 4**.

Considering the populated OWL-S ontology and the life-event ontology, we use the actual measurements with the methods described in Sections 6.2.2 and 8.2.3 and calculate the results as follows:

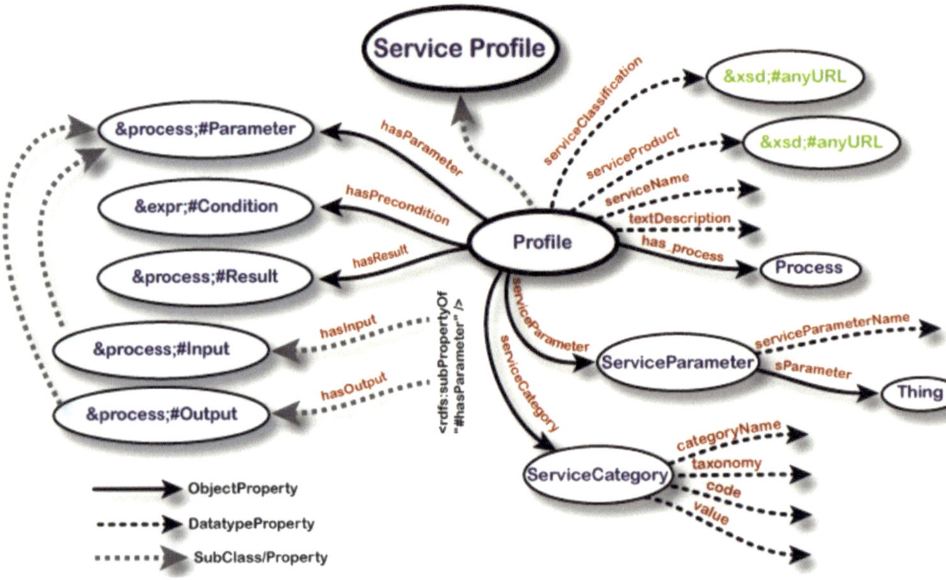

Figure 3. OWL-S ontology schema [10].

Based on the SOV method, we measure the SOV value of the life event to be $7 + 8 = 15$, and for OWL-S to be $12 + 9 = 21$, this means that if we consider the growth ratio for the life event as being the base $15/15 = 1$ then this for the OWL-S would be $21/15 = 1.4$. **Table 1** details the numerical representation of the growth of ontology data in both ontologies.

We register the statistics in **Table 1** by assuming the initial SOV as to be the sum of the nodes, plus object properties in the ontology schema. Then we increased this number five times as per the number of named individuals representing the web services created for this experiment, each time by the amount of SOV ratio, representing the linear growth in the volume of ontology data.

Figure 5 shows the comparative graph representation that illustrates the trend of growth in the life-event ontology data and the OWL-S ontology data. It is shown that the rate of growth in the volume of data in the life event is dramatically less than the OWL-S, after a fivefold increases in the number of named individuals.

a. Based on the ENR method, we measure the ENR value of both ontologies in question to be as follows:

$$\text{Life} \quad -\text{event} = \frac{|15|}{|7|} = 2.5, \circledcirc\text{OWL} \quad -\text{S} = \frac{|21|}{|8|} = 2.63. \tag{10}$$

Table 2 shows the growth of ontology data in both ontologies in terms of ENR in numerical terms. The statistics shown in **Table 2** is obtained by initial ENR 1 is increased five times as per the number of web service named individuals, created for this experiment, each time by the amount of ENR ratio.

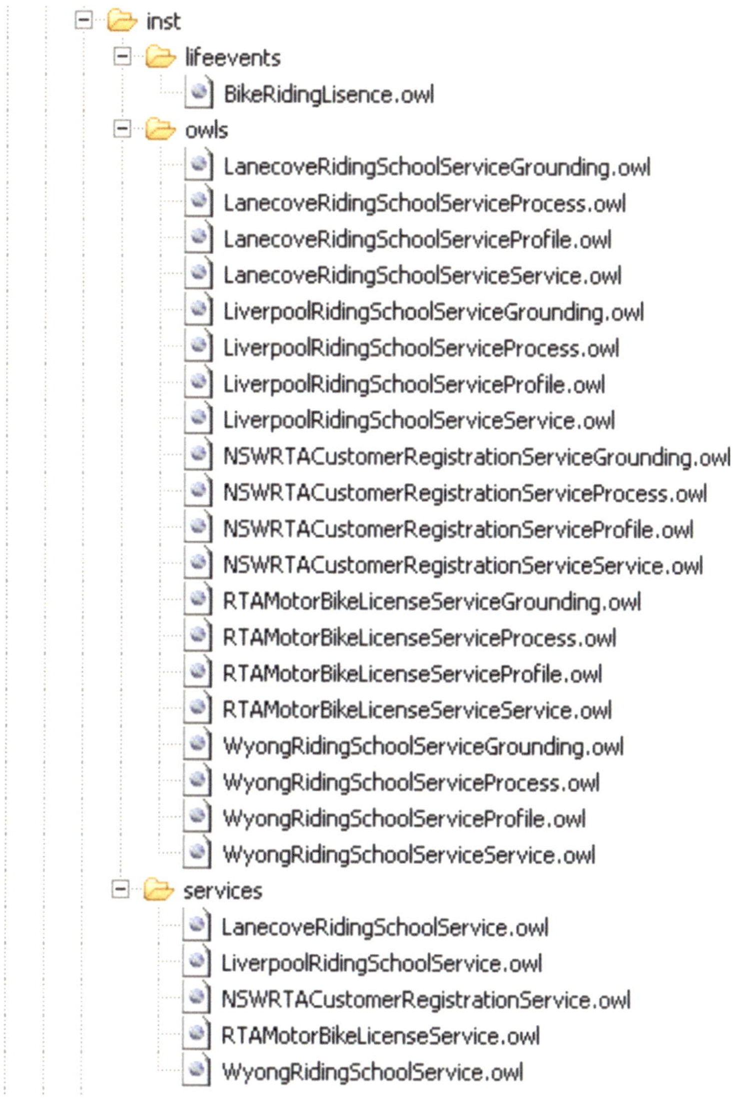

Figure 4. Life event and OWL-S named individuals.

Life event	OWL-S
15	21
30	36
60	86.4
120	207.36
240	497.7

Table 1. Numerical representation of ontology growth as per SOV ratio.

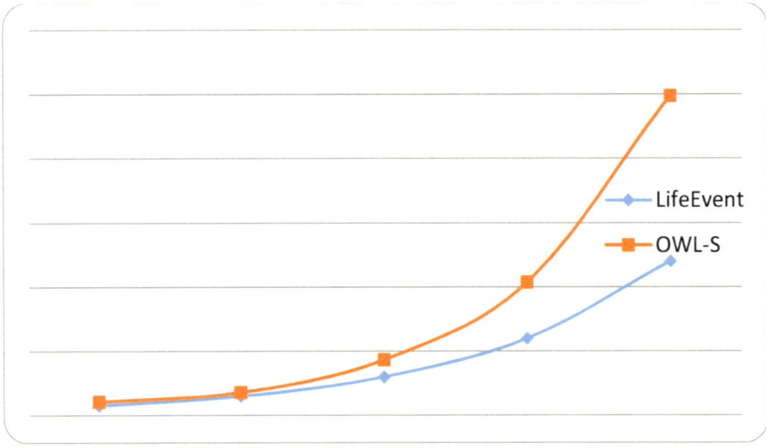

Figure 5. Physical representation of growths in ontology data as per SOV ratio.

Life event	OWL-S
2.5	2.63
6.25	6.9
15.63	18.2
39.1	47.8
97.75	125.8

Table 2. Numerical representation of physical growth for ontology as per ENR ratio.

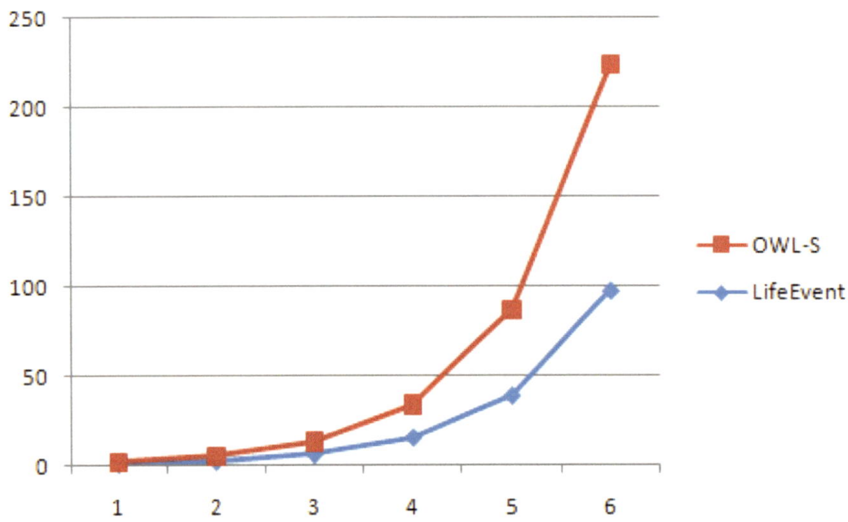

Figure 6. Physical representation of growths in ontology data per ENR ratio.

Figure 6 shows the comparative graph illustrating the trend of growth in ENR for the life-event ontology and OWL-S ontology in the event of growth in ontology data. It is shown that this increase in life-event ontology is less than OWL-S after a few fold increases in the number of named individuals.

b. Based on the TIP method, we measure the value of 'how far life event deviates from being a tree?' to be $(15 - 7 + 1 = 9)$, and for OWL-S to be $(21 - 8 + 1 = 14)$. As it is shown that this value is greater for OWL-S than for life-event ontology.

c. Using the NOC method, we calculated the number of immediate children (*rdf: subClassOf*) for the class *Parameter* that is the most frequently used in web service invocation to be 3. The value of NOC calculated for Life-eventService, which is the most used class in life-event ontology, is 2. **Table 3** shows the complexity growth of ontology data for class parameter in OWL-S in comparison with the class Life-eventService in life-event ontology in terms of the NOC ratio. The statistics shown in **Table 3** is obtained by initial NOC 1 increased five times as per the number of web service named individuals, created for this experiment, each time by the amount of NOC ratio.

Life event	OWL-S
2	3
4	9
8	27
16	81
32	243

Table 3. Numerical representation of physical growth for ontology classes as per NOC ratio.

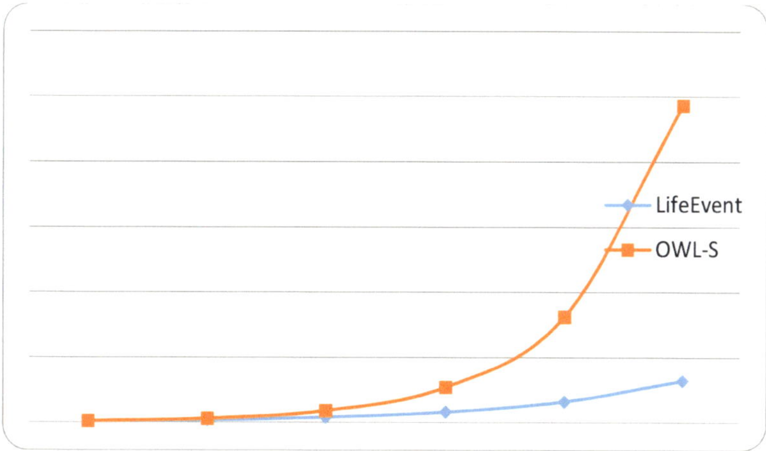

Figure 7. Physical representation of growths in complexity of ontology data as per NOC ratio.

Figure 7 shows the comparative graph illustrating the trend of growth in complexity as per the NOC ratio for class parameter in OWL-S in comparison with the class Life-eventService in life-event ontology in the event of growth in ontology data. It is shown that this increase in life-event ontology is less than OWL-S after a few fold increases in the number of named individuals.

7. Summary

In this chapter, we outlined our design strategies to extend the OWL-S in order to propose life-event ontology as an abstract design and execution unit for composing e-services. We introduced an ontology that accommodates the concept of life event within the process of e-services composition. The idea was to introduce an innovative approach towards the whole process of e-service composition and delivery.

We put forward a formal design for an ontology knowledgebase to manage the workflow of composite web service workflows in a linear approach. Nevertheless, this research also recognises that more research is required to specify and formalise the design of more complex types of web service composition such as parallel service processes in complex workflows.

Author details

Farzad Sanati

Address all correspondence to: f_sanati@yahoo.com

The American University of Iraq, Sulaimani, Iraq

References

[1] Sanati, F. and J. Lu, An ontology for e-government service integration. International Journal of Computer Systems Science And Engineering. 2012;**27**(2):89-101

[2] Smith MK, Welty C, McGuinness DL. Owl Web Ontology Guide. 2003 [cited 2011]

[3] Berners-Lee T, Hendler J, Lassila O. The semantic web. Scientific American. 2001;**2845**:34-43

[4] Maedche A. Ontology Learning for the Semantic Web. Kluwer International Series in Engineering and Computer Science; SECS665. Boston: Kluwer Academic; 2002

[5] Berners-Lee T, Fielding R, Masinter L. Uniform Resource Identifiers (URI): Generic Syntax. RFC Editor 1998

[6] Valencia-Garcia R, et al. OWLPath: An owl ontology-guided query editor. IEEE Transactions on Systems, Man, and Cybernetics—Part A: Systems and Humans. 2011;**41**(1):121-136

[7] McGuinness DL. OWL Web Ontology Language Overview [Internet]. 2004. Available from: http://www.w3.org/TR/2004/REC-owl-features-20040210/

[8] Tsarkov D, Horrocks I. FaCT++ description logic reasoner: System description. In: Proceeding of the International Joint Conference on Automated Reasoning (IJCAR 2006). 2006. Springer

[9] Koponen T, Virtanen T. A service discovery:A service broker approach. In: 37th Annual Hawaii Internation Conference on System Science. 2004: Hawaii, USA. pp. 284-290

[10] W3C. OWL-S: Semantic Markup for Web Services. 2004 [16 November 2010]

[11] Zhang H, Li Y-F, Tan HBK. Measuring design complexity of semantic web ontologies. Journal of Systems and Software. 2009;**83**(5):803-814

[12] Ferrario R, Guarino N. Towards an ontological foundation for services science. In: Future Internet Symposium. 2008. Springer

[13] Lytras MD, García R. Semantic web applications: A framework for industry and business exploitation—What is needed for the adoption of the semantic web from the market and industry. International Journal of Knowledge and Learning. 2008 Jan 1;**4**(1):93-108

[14] Stanford-University. Protégé. 2009. Available from: http://protege.stanford.edu/. [Accessed: 2010]

Chapter 6

Ontology in IT Projects Based on OSM

Frank Stumpe

Additional information is available at the end of the chapter

http://dx.doi.org/10.5772/intechopen.72729

Abstract

Project management is the discipline of initiating, planning, executing, controlling, and closing the work of a team to achieve specific goals and meet specific success criteria. However, there can exist a considerable amount of uncertainty in decision making for project management stemming from the typical complex characteristics of projects. This study focused on two primary objectives: (1) to understand the role of project management in complex situations and (2) to offer a more robust model for project management. Pertinent literature on models for project management was collected and synthesized for application in complex situations. A cybernetic-based model is then developed. This model enables a manager to focus on internal organizational complexity while paying enough attention to external perturbations. The utility of the model is demonstrated in a case application in an organization in Belgium.

Keywords: project management, ontology, cybernetic management, complex systems

1. Systemic management models and their link to project management

Today, a project is defined by a defined start and end, constrained by time, funds, and measured by expected deliverables. So, the project organization within an organization takes place within the confines of operations with a bearing on project management.

Aim of projects is to deliver value to customers. The task necessary to deliver value is intricately related to many factors, some of which can be beyond the scope of the project itself as it is related to being a temporary organization within an organization. Enterprises today are socio-technical systems, constantly interacting with an increasingly complex environment. Investments are often done within specific projects as a temporary organization within an organization. The OSTO® System Model (OSM) deals with processes that are strongly interrelated and is a result of a combination of technology, work organization, and human communication. The OSM is robust and mature model used over years in several management reorganizations [1].

As mentioned above, a project is aimed to delivers outputs as deliverables. In a good design, the output is the customers expected out-come, following the objectives. In the OSM, the objectives are injected into the system as a target to be reached while the system delivers the output. One should deliver what is requested, in the scope, quality, timing, and within budget, for the system to be considered reliable. Thus, one can conclude that an output is not sufficient but necessary. Clearly, other terms need to be considered. These include *mission statements* involving *reason of existence* and *meaning*. Reason for system existence relates to the needs or expectations of customers to make use of the products or services of the business system (**Figure 1**). It is imperative that system actors know the "reason of existence" of the system. This involves long-term value-creation of the system leading to future-oriented execution of output, long-term thinking, and looking forward at the wider context rather than exclusively considering the economic reality of today [2].

As previously mentioned, system components interact among themselves with a given system, as well as interacting with the environment. There is the need for stability and orientation within investment management. This orientation can only be given on a vision level through the statement of the system *meaning*. As suggested by a cybernetic model of a system, long-term survival of the business depends on having defined sustainable and future-oriented *meaning* statements. The focus here is on the system usefulness in terms of sustainability involving context of individual, cultural, ethical questions, and expectations within society. Such *meaning* statements imply that there are values defined for the owner of the investment. In this case, values are one-dimensional for measuring effectiveness. Effectiveness is assessed by *quality* metric, and *efficiency* is also measured as a *productivity* metric. Quality of output, in this perspective, is related to products or services especially the value assigned by the customers.

Beyond the original OSM, two new artifacts are introduced in the system model: Actor and Sensor. The *actor* has the responsibility to understand certain orders (e.g., management decisions)

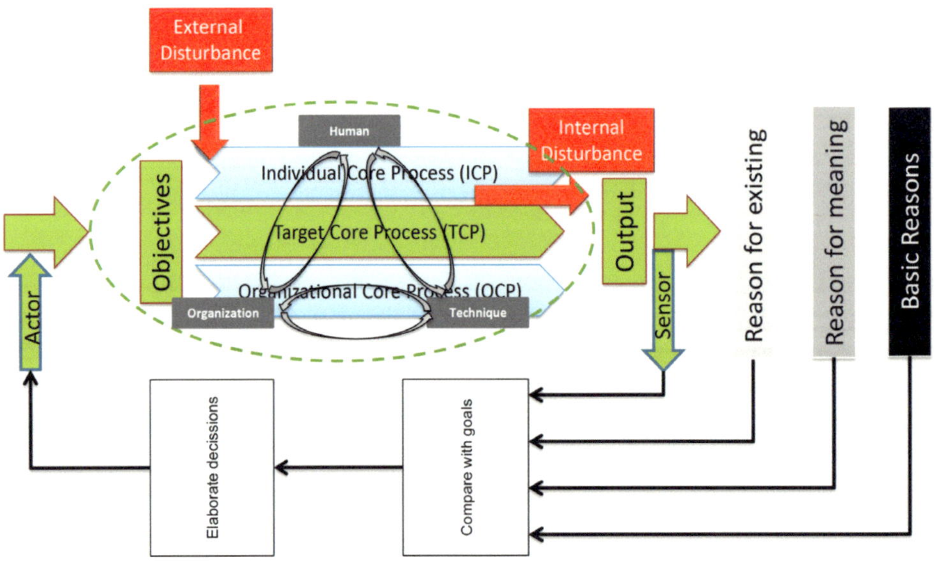

Figure 1. Complex cybernetic investment management framework based on OSM.

and translate them into actions. As the *actor* injects signals into the system, the *sensor* extracts information from the system and its output, and changes this information into a certain language to allow closing the cybernetic loop toward the *actor*.

A project as system consists of at least three main elements: *objectives, inputs*, and *outputs*. Objectives include a description of a situation beyond project conclusion. In objectives, there is also need to consider constraints that would enable or hinder the project as well as ensuring enough focus to enable delivery of the expected outcomes. Furthermore, objectives might depend on non-linearity of the situation which could be dominated by "the butterfly effect." For a project manager, this implies that managing of a project is not static, since objectives could change based on individual, social, and environmental factors.

Inputs describe everything the project gets to execute, including all necessary actions and tasks, to deliver outputs according objectives. As the project is being executed, inputs are expected to change. Therefore, input is not fixed in time but is dynamic. Additionally, and in complex projects, it is expected that resources, associated with inputs, will change during execution. Reasons associated with such changes include, but not limited to capabilities, contractual obligations, and illness to stakeholders. Moreover, the scope could be redefined by the newly discovered insights in design and unforeseen circumstances. Outputs are everything the project produces. This involves physical and theoretical outputs. Physical outputs are the deliverables including documents, software, and equipment. Theoretical outputs include insights, knowledge, and experiences. In this case, projects, like complex systems, will have interacting components and processes, influencing output.

The OSM identifies three processes: Target Core Process (TCP), Individual Core Process (ICP), and Organizational Core Process (OCP). TCP combines all activities, communication, and tasks necessary to produce the expected output. This is known as one-dimensional project management. ICP is influenced by the mood of each individual human, which can be influenced by situations within and outside the system. OCP considers interactions among individuals, system organization, and the project itself [3].

As previously suggested, there are "hard" and "soft" elements and that these interact in project management. The sensor interprets the output of the system and provides measurements for the management. The sensor also looks on other steering parameters like objectives, reason for existing, reason for meaning and basic reason, as well as their changes. However, each sensor has a limited view of the system by its own boundaries. The actor gets the results of the project managers decisions based on the data of the sensor. These results will be transformed into steering input. Then, the actor injects this into the system in a structured way to steer the project. However, this planning is with uncertainties. Moreover, the system must contend with external disturbances, involving inputs not planned for or foreseen by the steering. These disturb the efficiency and effectiveness of the system.

2. Model of the system

Starting with the abstraction that the probability of each state of a system is 100%, it is possible to model system dynamics and interactions. Any process or change in state of the system is represented as a transformation. We define the function T as one-to-one which means that an initial state $S_{(t+1)}$ always mapped onto a single state $S_{(t)}$. The function can be used as a dynamical representation to model the interactions between components of a system. The project manager is a system, represented as a Project Manager. He affects the system P or the project itself. We assume that the state of P, at time t + 1, is dependent on the state of the project at time t.

$$T: S_{PM} \times S_P \to S_P: (S_{PM}(t), S_P(t)) \to S_P(t+1) \quad (1)$$

S_{PM} plays the role of the input of the project. In general, the project will not only be affected by an outside system, but also be effected by other systems causing external disturbance (S_{ED}).

$$T': (S_{PM}, S_{ED}) \times S_P \to S_P: \left(S_{PM}(t), S_{ED}(t), S_P(t)\right) \to S_P(t+1) \quad (2)$$

The project is aimed to produce output which is system S_O. This leads to the transition

$$T'': T'': (S_{PM}, S_{ED}) \times S_O \to S_O: \left(S_{PM}(t), S_{ED}(t), S_O(t)\right) \quad (3)$$

a project is a process that transforms input into output. If the observer does not know the states of the project, and precise transformations T and T′, then the project acts as a black box for the observer. By experimenting with the sequence of inputs $S_{PM}(t)$, $S_{PM}(t+1)$, $S_{PM}(t+2)$, etc., and observing the corresponding sequence of outputs $S_O(t+1)$, $S_O(t+2)$, $S_O(t+3)$, …, the observer may try to reconstruct the dynamics of the project. In some cases, the observer can determine a state space SP so that both transformations become more deterministic, without being able to directly observe the properties, processes, or components of the project. Internal disturbing make modeling black-box a difficult endeavor.

A project manager is seen as the Observer. This notion is said to hold true for all decisions taken by a project manager in any project management process. Managers see the system as a linear one and try to master the feedback loop. However, since projects are nonlinear in nature, a project manager serving as observer, needs to be more trained to deal with uncertainty of nonlinear systems and focus on positive feedback of the project. This suggests that they might let the system freely float to a certain degree or even intentionally destabilize the system to learn the equilibriums and the resistance to change. Operating at the verge of chaos has been suggested as the most successful strategy to dealing with non-linear systems. Nonlinearity is based on the internal disturbance as well as parallel active processes. This suggests that traditional objectives of a project can have dependencies which are often beyond internal control mechanisms of the system including elements of reason for existing, reason for meaning, and basic reason. In such a case, a non-linear model of OSM is necessary.

At the beginning of the project (t = 0), the project manager provides the necessary input for the project. This input is, in the first place, clearly defined in objectives (i.e., what to deliver). In the second place, project manager provides the scope (i.e., how to deliver), resources (i.e., with what to deliver), and timings (i.e., when to deliver). These inputs are based on the planning of the project. After a control period, the project manager gets information out of the system SP(t) as output $S_O(t)$. With this information, the project manager, S_{PM}, can make certain decisions.

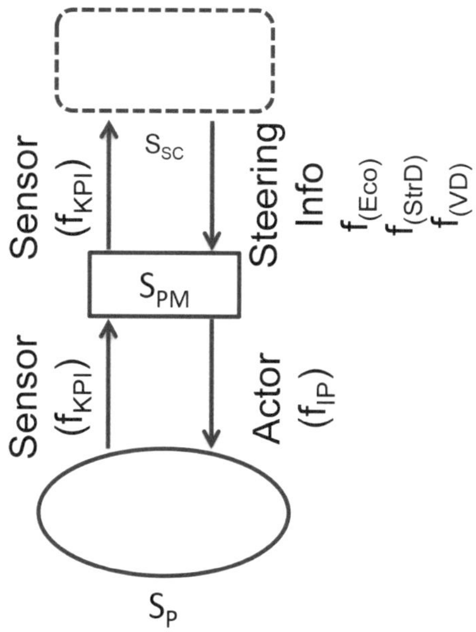

Figure 2. A basic organizational hierarchical model of a project.

These decisions must be translated into input parameters. This enables the project S_P to change into the state t + 1.

This reflex is also basic for project organization. A team of project experts can be seen as system, S_P, while the decision makers as system, S_{PM}. The decision makers can get their guidance through higher level system representations of reason for existing, reason for meaning and basic reason. This system is normally known as steering committee (S_{SC}) (**Figure 2**). When these systems are logically separate, a hierarchy is evident as shown in a basic organizational model [4].

3. Ontology of a project system

It is safe to say that each project starts with objectives. These objectives are a combination of different types of statements based on assumptions regarding the environment, E. These are realis moods of domain assumptions describing the environment of the requirements engineering problem as it is known. The second type of statements in objectives is irrealis mood statements describing situation-to-be, how the situation and environment should look like. These irrealis mood statements prescribe what the outcome of the project should be. **Figure 3** shows that objectives can be described in functional requirements which are defined as goals (g) and non-functional requirements, which are divided into soft goals (f) and quality constraints, q [5].

With a *justified approximation* (jappr), it is possible to define softgoal, F, a quality constraint, Q, that can exist for which it is justified to assume that if the quality constraint, Q, is met, then the softgoal, F, is also automatically fulfilled as described in $jappr(f, q) \Rightarrow (q \Rightarrow f) for\ all\ f \in F, q \in Q$.

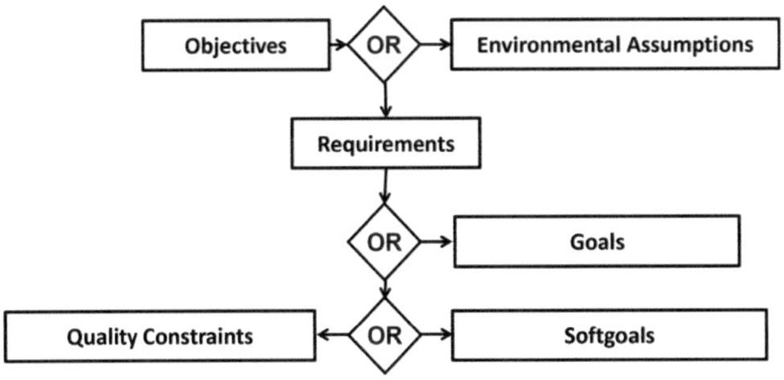

Figure 3. Types of statements within objectives.

Additionally, one can define a *requisite* (req) relation as an asymmetric relation defining that in order to make a certain statement true, another statement also needs to be true. This is valid for all statements within requirements (q, g, and s) but not for domain assumptions $req(r_1,r_2) \Rightarrow (r_1 \Rightarrow r_2)\ for\ all\ r_1,r_2 \in R$ for requirements. Similar equations are necessary for **S** (soft goals) and **Q** for quality constraints. Such requisite relations are important if there are hidden objectives. In this case, there are certain quality constraints, goals, or soft goals identified, which are not directly linked to the objectives, that could be an indicator for an implicit objective based on assumptions. Similar to the requisite relation, an *exclude* (excl) relation defines a symmetrical relation stating that some statements can exclude each other. These are indicators for conflicting objectives and not valid for quality constraints $excl(r_1,r_2) \Leftrightarrow \neg(r_1\ AND\ r_2)\ for\ all\ r_1,r_2 \in$ for requirements. And again, similar equations are necessary for **S** (soft goals) and **Q** for quality constraints.

In project work, one can make a separation between domain assumptions, goals, soft goals, and quality constraints as objectives and the realized deliverables as linked output. For all objectives, O, there can be a corresponding objective (r_n, d_n, s_n) at least one deliverable d_m within the full set of deliverable, D, to fulfill a given objective. Notice that each deliverable is linked to one or more objectives and is the proven fulfillment of the objective.

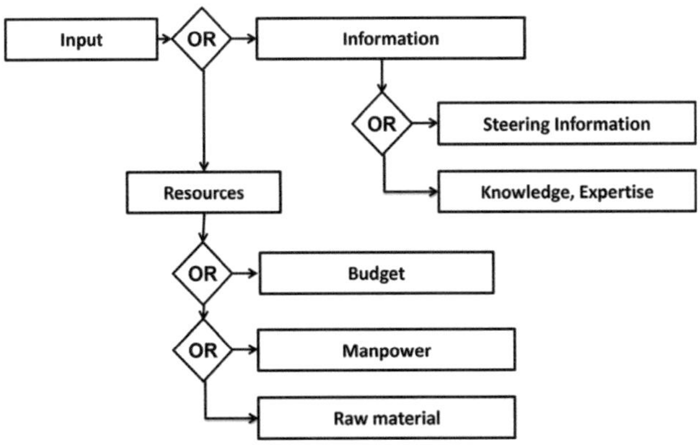

Figure 4. Different types of input.

This relationship can be described in by $\forall o \in \boldsymbol{O}$ ***and*** $\boldsymbol{d} \in \boldsymbol{D}\ \exists d \vdash \boldsymbol{o}$. The full set of all deliverables, D, is the result of processes executed by resources with a necessary input. **Figure 4** depicts type of expected inputs. This input is either information (both steering information or knowledge and expertise) or resources as describes in **Figure 4**.

In analogy with the objectives, depicted in the equation above, one can define a *justified approximation* (jappr) between expertise "**e**," and knowledge, "**k**".

$$jappr(e,k) \Rightarrow (e \Rightarrow k) for\ all\ e \in E, k \in K \tag{4}$$

We can also define similar requisite relations among budget, manpower, and raw material, as well as some *exclude* (excl) relation. Additionally, raw material, in each process step after the first process step, is also the deliverable of the first process step.

$$\forall\, i \in I \begin{cases} n = 1\ i_n = i_{RM_n} + i_{MP_n} + i_{Bud_n} + i_{k_n} + i_{e_n} \\ n > 1\ i_{n+1} = (i'_{RM_{n+1}} + d_n) + i_{MP_{n+1}} + i_{Bud_{n+1}} + i_{k_{n+1}} + i_{s_{n+1}} \end{cases} \tag{5}$$

With these inputs, output, transformation processes, and steering, one can model the traditional project based working. The transformations follow an environmental adapted approach. This could be traditional waterfall (sequencing) or agile approach (iterative):

$$\forall\, d \in D \begin{cases} n = 1\ d_n = f(\,i_n, o_n)\ with\ t \in T \\ n > 1\ i_{n+1} = \ d_n = f(\,i_n, o_n, d_{n-1})\ with\ t \in T \end{cases} \tag{6}$$

When comparing linear model with the real-life system, one can see that some additional artifacts are necessary to create a more accurate model. As the objectives are defined to contribute to a defined strategy, each transition must bring an added value. As we have defined the transition: $T\colon (S_{PM}, S_{ED}) \times S_P \rightarrow S_O\colon (S_{PM}(t), S_{ED}(t), S_P(t)) \rightarrow S_O(t+1)$ with $y_{t+1} = f(y_t) \equiv T$. The transition is not a linear one as assumed above. The transition depends on three processes and internal disturbances as shown below. Internal disturbance is unknown transitions of the systems generating risks. In this case, risk is the possibility of not being able to fulfill the objective as expected and not to deliver the deliverables linked to the objective:

- Target Core Process (TCP) with $y_{t+1} = f_{TCP}(y_t, i)\ with\ i \in I$
- Individual Core Process (ICP) with $y_{t+1} = f_{ICP}(y_t, i)\ with\ i \in I$
- Organizational Core Process (OPC) with $y_{t+1} = f_{OCP}(y_t, i)\ with\ i \in I$
- Internal disturbance (ID) with $y_{t+1} = f_{ID}\,(y_t, i)\ with\ i \in I$

This led to an unsolvable equation based on the odd number of functions *f* and inputs *i*. This is in fact a characteristic for complex systems. Each of these transitions contributes to the delivery of the expected deliverable. Additionally, the external disturbance can be seen as input i_{ED} and depends on unknown environmental changes or changes brought about by stakeholders.

$$i_{ED} \rightarrow \Delta Environment\ or\ \Delta Stakeholders \quad (7)$$

This input can also be seen as a risk, since it is unknown to the system and similar modeled as other inputs.

Objectives are derived from strategic drivers. These strategic drivers, *sd*, are the concretization (detailed description) of the strategy, *S*. Each strategy has at least one strategic driver and at least one objective. The contribution of the objective to the strategic driver is an estimation, since the use of the deliverables linked to the objective is in the future. This estimation is mostly done in a matrix with value areas so that the contribution can be estimated [6].

The result of the estimation is mainly in odd categories (e.g., low, medium, and high) added by "non." For each estimated contribution, a financial analysis of efficiency (e.g., Net Present Value and Return On Investment) is done to estimate the revenue. Within this calculation, a link is made among the necessary input of the project, the expected delivery, and the estimated revenue. This is done in the Business Case. This Business Case is the economical *reason for existing* (i.e., RFE) of the project. The calculation is based on the link between all elements of the input, *I*, necessary for all deliverables, *d*, linked to objective, *o*, in relation to the estimated contribution [7].

$$RFE \leftrightarrow \bigcup f(\hat{p}_{(o_n, sd_m)}, I_n, d_n, o_n, t) \quad \forall d \in D, \forall o \in O\ and\ I \rightarrow D \quad (8)$$

As scope, timing, and resources (input) are related to each other by the "Devil's triangle," we can calculate each point as a variable of the two other points leading to the function to calculate the timings of the project:

$$t \vdash f(\hat{p}_{(o_n, sd_m)}, I_t, d_n, o_n, RFE) \quad (9)$$

This unsolvable loop of equations can be approximated by different iterations and adapted estimations during the project definition. In case a level of uncertainty (at the stakeholders) is reached, the iterations will stop and the project is defined with all necessary information to execute the transition, *T* (process all input *I* to the desired deliverables *D*). The system is ready defined by Objectives $o \in O$, expected deliverables $d \in D$, Scope (transitions), $T \cup T_{TCP}, T_{ICP}, T_{OCP}$, Resources and input $i \in I$, Risks (external and internal disturbance) TID and i_{ED} as well as Timings $t \vdash f(\hat{p}_{(o_n, sd_m)}, I, d, o, RFE)$. Similar to the definition of the link between objective and deliverable as $\forall o \in O\ and\ d \in D\ \exists d \vdash o$.

The link between objective and strategic driver/strategy, objective and Business Case, strategic driver/strategy and Mission, and Mission and Vision can be described similar. Mission is a foundational statement that describes the purpose of projects existence. It answers questions such as *"why do we do what we do"* and *"who do we serve."* For each project, this is the *Business Case* that should distinguish one project from another. Within a Business Case, different statements are made, as seen in **Figure 5**. Beside measurable economical facts, there is a

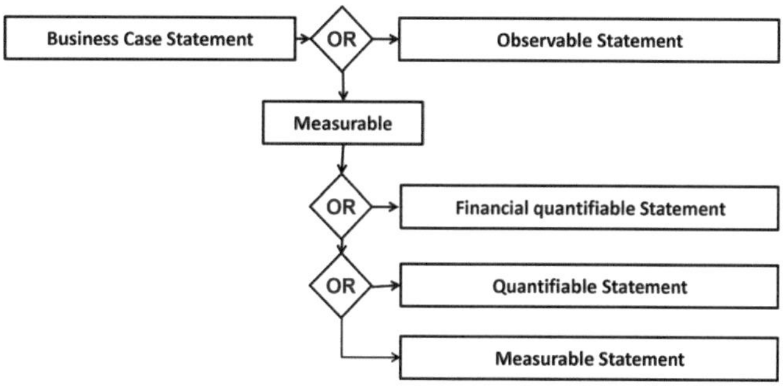

Figure 5. Statements in a Business Case.

possibility for quantifiable, measurable, and observable parameters. Additionally, all needed measurements need to be covered by having parameters concerning output, people, and organization [8].

Vision can be described as an image or description of the customers' system after the implementation of the deliverables of the project. In this vision, a strategy is essential and takes different forms. It requires the use of strategic drivers to translate the strategy into the project objectives. Traditional approaches, as described above, or the use of moving averages can be used to define the strategic drivers, which are shown in **Figure 6**.

The *Sensor* must be able to measure all outputs of the system. In this case, a Sensor, s, of the Target Core Process (Sensor $_{TCP}$) extracts all the necessary information from the system and prepares this information for management decision of the project manager who deals with system feedback: $\boldsymbol{Info_{Sensor(TCP)} \vdash f\left(inf_{d_{(t)}}, inf_{o_{(t)}}, info_{bc_{(t)}} inf_{sd_{(t)}}, inf_{vd_{(t)}}\right)}$, with $\boldsymbol{inf_{d_{(t)}} \vdash D_t, inf_{o_{(t)}} \vdash O_t, inf_{sd_{(t)}} \vdash S_t \text{ and } inf_{vd_{(t)}} \vdash V_t}$,, and $\boldsymbol{inf_{bc_{(t)}} \vdash BC_t \approx f(\hat{p}_{(o_n, sd_m)}, I, d, o, t)}$.

The Sensor, s, for the Individual Core Process ($Sensor_{ICP}$) and for the Organizational Core Process ($Sensor_{OCP}$) identifies, similar to the Sensor $_{TCP}$, data according to parameters defined.

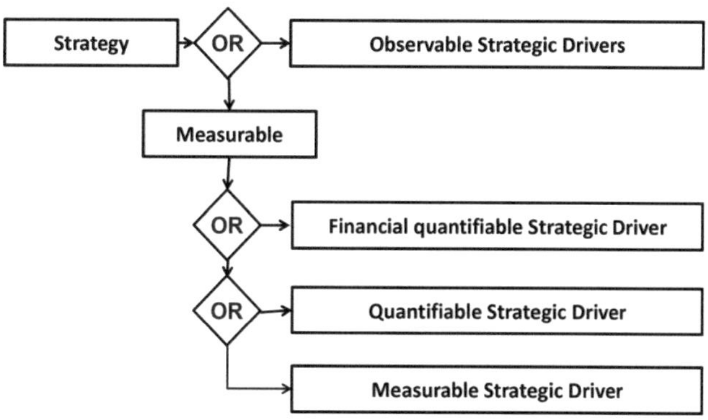

Figure 6. Strategic drivers.

As these are not always objective, other measurements are necessary. For the $Sensor_{ICP}$ possible examples are, among others, Employee Satisfaction Surveys, Bilateral meetings, Coaching moments, Evaluations, and follow-up discussions.

For the $Sensor_{OCP}$ possible examples are, among others, Outstanding reorganizations, "Over the fence" management of departments, and Leadership Decision Management Systems.

In reality, most of the sensors are focused on TCP second on OCP, and there is a minor group measuring the ICP. In opposite to that, studies show that the organizational aspects as well as the individual integration in the team are significantly impacting the result of the project. This is even more visible when looking the output in general. The output of the system is not only a set of deliverables but also changes in knowledge, experiences, and other insights [9].

However, different measurements can be combined and considered in a multi-dimensional matrix. The change periods, *CP*, is related with each other. An exact relation depends on the environment. Obvious in fast changes environments (e.g., mobile application development) the period is much shorter than in slow changing environments (e.g., industrial plant investments). This discussion provides a basis for linking different elements including sensors and system vision. A systematic overview of possible sensors is given in **Figure 7**.

Up to this time, time aspect of dependency has been overlooked. However, this aspect is introduced by the *Business Case* which accounts for maximum in project duration and the return period. For the project, *Business Case* is translated into a "plan in time." The plan is part of the steering and is indicated by the dotted line (box). Taking the picture **Figure 7**, one can reduce the information into a class model **Figure 8** to be able to design the system.

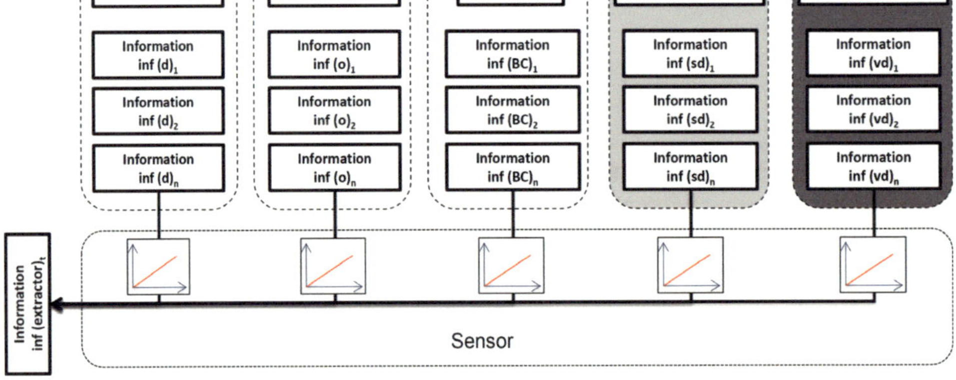

Figure 7. Relating sensor and deliverables, objectives, reason for existing, mission as well as vision.

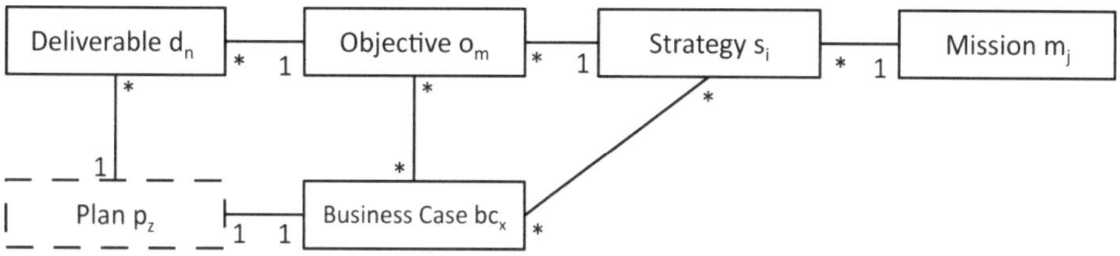

Figure 8. Class model for deliverables, objectives, reason for existing, and vision.

As the information of the *Sensor* is multidimensional, it can be seen as a vector of information. The project manager executes a transformation of the information to create an input to the system:

$$\overrightarrow{INF_{ext.t}} = \begin{pmatrix} inf_{(d).t} \\ inf_{(o).t} \\ \vdots \end{pmatrix} \text{ and } \overrightarrow{INF_{inj.t}} = \begin{pmatrix} i_x \\ \vdots \\ i_y \end{pmatrix} \text{ with } \overrightarrow{INF_{inj.t}} = S_{PM} \times \overrightarrow{INF_{ext.t}} \text{ with } S_{PM} = \begin{pmatrix} t_1 \\ t_2 \\ \vdots \\ t_n \end{pmatrix} \forall t \in T_{PM}.$$

In this transition, T_{PM}, project manager, S_{PM}, converts the information of the Sensor into input of the system. All necessary processes can be found in process-based method for effective project management. The output of this processes will be injected back into the system project SP by a translation *f(IP)*. This translation helps in ensuring that missing resources are injected or that more material is provided.

4. Briefly use case

In this section, we provide an application of the developed model. A non-disclosure agreement prevents us from disclosing certain detailed information regarding the company (entity) of analysis. Therefore, some information is masked. However, we provide sufficient information to demonstrate the usability of the model. Within this company, different and sometime conflicting core activities are present. The global mission statement is translated into global strategic statements within each business unit and has a defined strategy for fulfilling the requested group strategy. Measurable strategic drivers are given and defined as Performance (mainly driven by Cost/income ration), Empowerment (mainly driven by maturity levels), Accountability (mainly cultural driven), Responsiveness (*time2market*), and local embeddedness (local compliance).

Additionally, the company wants to "aim to be the first company TOMORROW to be the reference … TODAY." The given drivers on group level are defined on coarse grain level. Each Unit determined their own strategy to fulfill the expected groups' strategy. Therefore, they defined meso-grain drivers to evaluate their own operations and investments, the so called "Rose." This level is the strategy of the Business Unit and represents the next detailed level.

At this level, the link to the Business Case is already implemented as drivers for the investment analysis as analysis of efficiency or Business Case. The other drivers are defined for the purposes of ranking initiatives according to an added value without executing a detailed Business Case—called back-log. These drivers are separated into two groups (compare **Figure 9**). The first group is the "Externally drivers" and provides KPIs related to the company outside world, while the others took on "Internal aspects" of the organization.

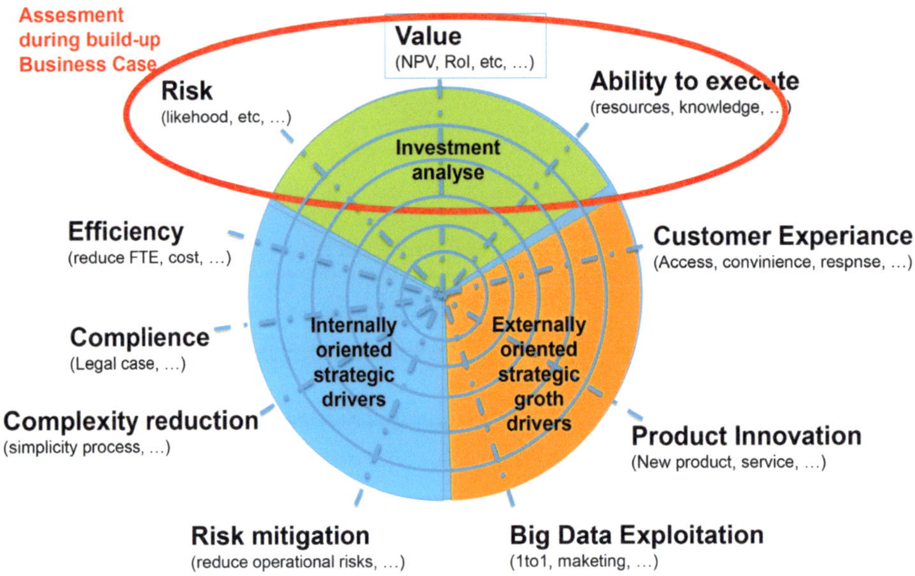

Figure 9. An example of statements, the case emerging from mission statement.

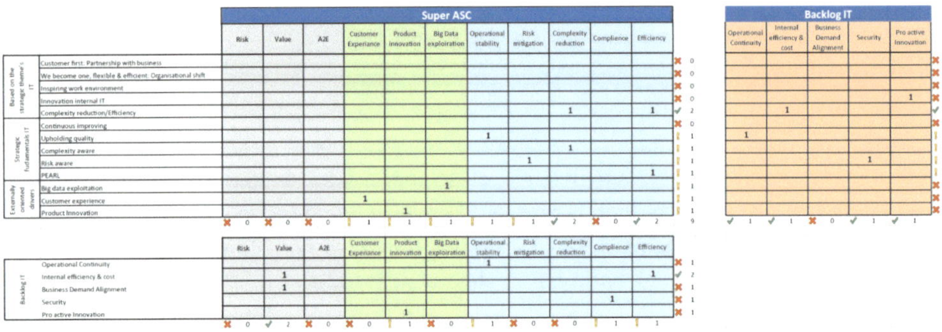

		Super ASC													Backlog IT						
		Risk	Value	A2E	Customer Experiance	Product innovation	Big Data exploiration	Operational stability	Risk mitigation	Complexity reduction	Complience	Efficiency			Operational Continuity	Internal efficiency & cost	Business Demand Alignment	Security	Pro active Innovation		
Based on the strategic theme's IT	Customer first: Partnership with business												✗	0						✗	0
	We become one, flexible & efficient: Organisational shift												✗	0						✗	0
	Inspiring work environment												✗	0						✗	0
	Innovation internal IT												✗	0					1	✗	1
	Complexity reduction/Efficiency									1		1	✓	2		1				✓	5
Strategic fudamentals IT	Continuous improving												✗	0						✗	0
	Upholding quality							1					!	1	1					!	2
	Complexity aware									1			!	1						!	2
	Risk aware								1				!	1				1		!	3
	PEARL											1	!	1						!	2
Externally oriented drivers	Big data exploitation						1						!	1						✗	1
	Customer experience				1								!	1						✗	1
	Product Innovation					1							!	1						✗	1
		✗ 0	✗ 0	✗ 0	! 1	! 1	! 1	! 1	! 1	✓ 2	✗ 0	✓ 2		9	✓ 1	✓ 1	✗ 0	✓ 1	✓ 1		

		Risk	Value	A2E	Customer Experiance	Product innovation	Big Data exploiration	Operational stability	Risk mitigation	Complexity reduction	Complience	Efficiency		
Backlog IT	Operational Continuity							1					✗	1
	Internal efficiency & cost		1									1	✓	2
	Business Demand Alignment		1										✗	1
	Security										1		✗	1
	Pro active Innovation					1							✗	1
		✗ 0	✓ 2	✗ 0	✗ 0	! 1	✗ 0	! 1	✗ 0	✗ 0	! 1	! 1		

Figure 10. A list of strategic drivers used in a business unit and IT-related drivers.

Besides business (BUS)-related drivers, the company also has information and technology (IT)-related drivers. These drivers are also defined on strategic level. **Figure 10** shows a mapping indicating where drivers are complementary and where the drivers are supplementary.

As previously mentioned, all cases are listed in a "back-log." In this back-log, all scope-items are listed and are prioritized according the drivers of the Business Unit as indicated above. While some of these items can be executed separately, others require a "project" approach. To define the priority, the value of each driver is defined and described along with the degree of performance.

The use of this methodology provides insights into the expected deliverables as well as the objectives. The deliverables are mentioned as a single line and describe the expected outcome of the task as clusters defining objectives. The objectives are mentioned as numbers in the list.

http://dx.doi.org/10.5772/intechopen.72729

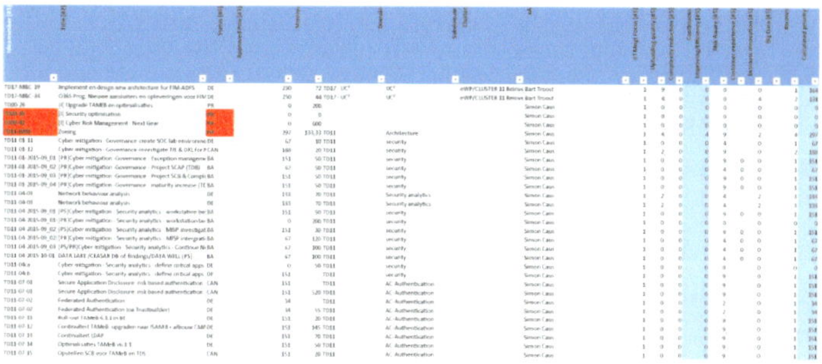

Figure 11. Project links among sensor and deliverables, objectives, reason for existing, mission and vision.

The methodology can be seen in **Figure 11**, but on confidentiality reasons the detail-content is blanked.

At this level, we have identified several projects scope items with the exclusion of approximate relations between drivers. Interestingly, as some IT-related drivers are fulfilled, Business Unit drivers are also fulfilled. However, there can be contradictions among drivers. This is the case when, in one project, the meso-grain drivers are detailed into fine-grain drivers within the Business-Case. **Figure 12** shows an example for strategic statements. The first statement was "*to become the first with easy access techniques for the customers*." This follows the driver "*to be the reference and the first of this easy-access today*." On the next level, the management decided that "*using other identification and authentication technique*" allows to assume (*justified approximation*)

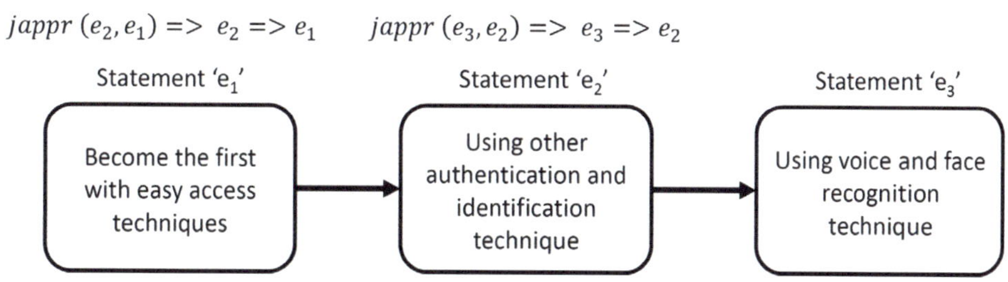

Figure 12. An example of statements in the case of starting from mission statement.

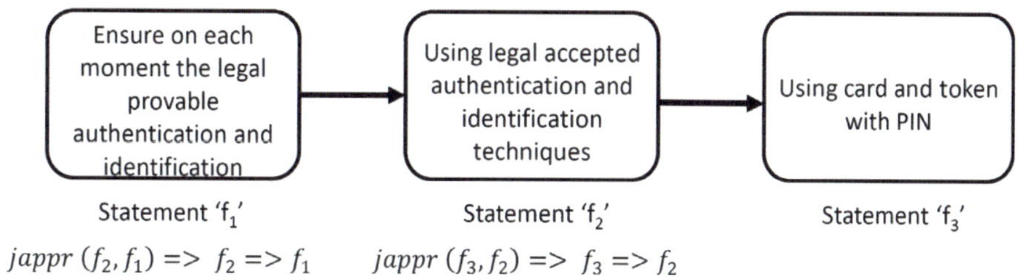

Figure 13. A second example of statements in a case starting from mission statements.

that these techniques will increase the easy access. Finally, a similar assumption is made to "*use voice and face recognitions for identification.*"

Similar to this depicts another strategic statement (**Figure 13**). Here, the company is obligated to fulfill the regulators request to be able provide legal provable identification and authentication. This follows the local embeddedness and compliance with the local regulations. The next management level assumed that only using legal accepted techniques can give evidence that the mission statement is fulfilled. This statement leads to the conclusion that old existing technique is actually the only technique for fulfilling the statement.

Taking e_1 and f_2 as independent from each other in one system, the mission statement is without exclusions. On the next level, one sees that the statements are excluding each other *excl* (f_2, f_2) and *excl* (f_3, e_3)]. If a project, in this case, starts to increase easy access to the system, then the same project will be confronted with statements which will not allow the project to deliver successfully. The project manager needs to detect this exclusion and create another input into the system. This input is considered new information coming externally as information from another system, the company S_{ED}. The project itself faces the problem (S_P) and the Project Manager transforms this into the scope change (S_O). We can conclude that the project manager transforms information received, the exclusions, to allow for a change in scope, S_O, which results into a new scope, $S_O(t + 1)$, as described. The project will deal with the highest exclusion. This means dealing with clarification of any legal provisions and authentication techniques. Once the exclusion of e_2 and f_2 *excl* (f_2, e_2)] is met, the project will deliver a solution which fits more to the mission of the company.

Another example of a project is a company deciding to respond to local markets with local front-ends in local language. This should increase the local embeddedness and *time2market* as the local developers do not need to translate. Subsequently, such a project reduces costs for the company. This type of a project also presents a unique opportunity in terms of using the same solution in other markets (i.e., regions and countries) that uses a different language, for

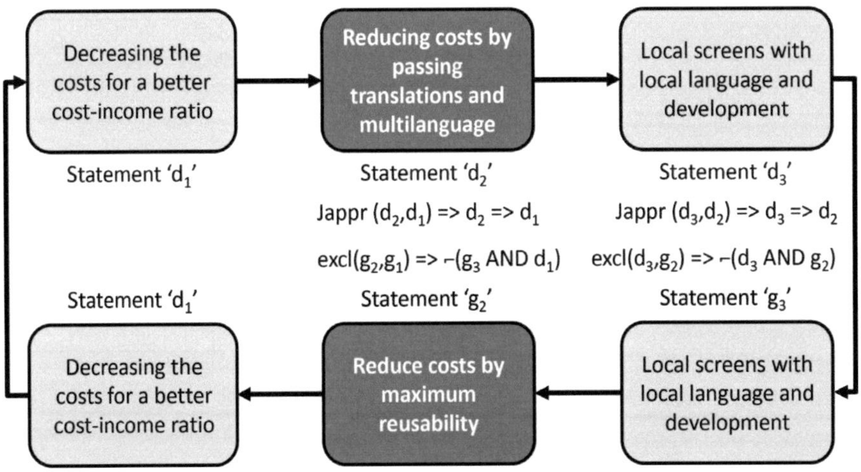

Figure 14. Two project sequences in different entities using the same mission statement.

example. In the case study, two different projects were defined from the "back-log" and the dilemma, as shown in **Figure 14**. One project is a local implementation on the same SharePoint tenant as an international implementation. However, both projects are defining their case separately as described.

However, during the local translations and the concrete implementation in the BUS-Case, both the projects used different statements, d_2 and g_2. Obviously, both PM's have different ways to deal with the issue of the excluding statements d_2 (passing translations and Multilanguage) and g_2 (maximizing reusability) to reach the statement d_1 (decreasing costs). Each might view the other statement "d_2" or reverse "g_2" (the decision) as a disturbance, and therefore try to mitigate its impact. On the other hand, both PM's could elevate the issue to a higher level by using appropriate feedback loops. In the case study, both PM's decided to escalate issue via their steering committee. These committees decided to escalate on an international level, where problems could be solved. This approach was taken since projects where able to show logical link of their own drivers to the drivers of the Business Unit and drivers on group level. The group steering committee decided that reusability should be implemented. This enabled savings of the second project to be used as subsidies to the first project. As expected, both projects received changes to the inputs including change in scope, change in budget, and change in resources.

5. Conclusion

The discussed model provides a clear overview about influencing parameters, disturbances, and processes executed during a project. The offered more robust model for project management in complex situations allows the project manager to understand more the role of project management and provides possible steering once the system is implemented in real projects. Within a brief use-case, the focus on internal organizational complexity is shown.

The model not only proved the usability but also shows the effort necessary to be implemented. As the elements of the system are not clear enough in the beginning, the implementation takes some experience and time to be valid enough for use. Within the presented case, the usability of the model was reached after 2 years and proves the value in prediction of the impact of steering. This means a more practical implementation guide as well as supporting documentation is necessary to use this model more in practice. Here, additional work is necessary.

Author details

Frank Stumpe

Address all correspondence to: frank.stumpe@kbc.be

KU Leuven, KBC Group NV, Mechelen, Belgium

References

[1] Schwaninger M. System theory and cybernetics: A solid basis for transdisciplinarity in management education and research. Kybernetes. 2001;**30**(9/10):1209-1222

[2] Crownover MWB. Complex system contextual framework (CSCF): A grounded-theory construction for the articulation of system context in addressing complex systems problems [Dissertation]. Norfolk, VA, United States: Old Dominion University; 2005

[3] Stumpe F, Polinpapilinho FK. A cybernetic ontology for project management. International Journal of System of Systems Engineering. 2017;**8**(1):42-73. DOI: 10.1504/IJSSE.2017.083937

[4] Hartman F, Ashrafi RA. Project management in the information systems and information technologies industries. Project Management Journal. 2002;**33**(3):5-15

[5] Huysegoms T, Snoeck M, Dedene G, Goderis A, Stumpe F. Visualizing variability management in requirements engineering through formal concept analysis. Procedia Technology. 2013;**9**:189-199. DOI: 10.1016/j.protcy.2013.12.021

[6] Keating CB, Katina PF, Bradley JM. Complex system governance: Concept, challenges, and emerging research. International Journal of System of Systems Engineering. 2014;**5**(3):263-288

[7] Stumpe F. Entwicklung und betrieb von neuen sattelanhänger-waggon kombinationen für zukunftsfähige intermodale transportketten in Europa [Dissertation]. Aachen: RWTH Aachen University; 2003. Retrieved from: http://publications.rwth-aachen.de/record/62709

[8] Stumpe F. Uniformity in project-based working. The Journal of Modern Project Management JMPM - Number 5 - September/December. 2014;**2**(2)

[9] Katina PF, Keating CB, Jaradat RM. System requirements engineering in complex situations. Requirements Engineering. 2014;**19**(1):45-62. DOI: 10.1007/s00766-012-0157-0

Chapter 7

Ontology: Core Process Mining and Querying Enabling Tool

Kingsley Okoye, Syed Islam and Usman Naeem

Additional information is available at the end of the chapter

http://dx.doi.org/10.5772/intechopen.71981

Abstract

Ontology permits the addition of semantics to process models derived from mining the various data stored in many information systems. The ontological schema enables for automated querying and inference of useful knowledge from the different domain processes. Indeed, such conceptualization methods particularly *ontologies for process management* which is currently allied to *semantic process mining* trails to combine process models with ontologies, and are increasingly gaining attention in recent years. In view of that, this chapter introduces an ontology-based mining approach that makes use of concepts within the extracted event logs about domain processes to propose a method which allows for effective querying and improved analysis of the resulting models through semantic labelling (annotation), semantic representation (ontology) and semantic reasoning (reasoner). The proposed method is a semantic-based process mining approach that is able to induce new knowledge based on previously unobserved behaviours, and a more intuitive and easy way to represent and query the datasets and the discovered models compared to other standard logical procedures. To this end, the study claims that it is possible to apply effective reasoning methods to make inferences over a process knowledge-base (e.g. the learning process) that leads to automated discovery of learning patterns and/or behaviour.

Keywords: ontologies, semantic annotation, semantic reasoning, process querying, process mining, event logs, process models

1. Introduction

Ontologies has been proven to be one of the essential tools used for semantic-based process mining. The schema is a useful technique towards improving information values of process models and their analysis by means of conceptualization. The conceptual system of analysis allows the meaning of process elements to be enhanced through the use of property characteristics and classification of discoverable entities, to generate inference knowledge that could be used to determine useful patterns as well as predict future outcomes.

Indeed, the ability to mine useful or worthwhile knowledge from readily extracted data in current information systems is a challenge, due to the exponential increase in volume of data that is continuously generated. Moreover, many of such organizations data collection systems and procedures for the process analysis is proving to be more and more complex. In consequence, this has spanned the need for a richer or advanced description of real-time processes that allows for flexible exploration of the large volumes of data targeted at improving the systems performance and of course the main business operations. Such process-related analysis means there is also need for techniques that are capable of extracting valuable information from the event logs and the resulting models about the real time processes in view.

More or less, most organization have invested in projects to model their various operational process. However, most of the derived process models are often unfitting, non-operational, or represents a form of reality that are pointed towards comprehensibility rather than covering the entire actual business process complexities. Perhaps, according to the works in Refs. [1–4] an accurate exploration or analysis of the extracted events log is capable of providing vital and valuable information with regards to the quality of support being offered for the so-called organizations and their information knowledge-base or system at large. For example, revealing the underlying relationships the process elements or resources share amongst themselves within the information knowledge-base.

Recently, the Process Mining [3] or yet still Process Querying [5] notion has become a valuable technique used to discover such kind of meaningful information from the event data logs and the derived process models. However, the study carried out in [6] observes that a shared challenge with most of the existing process mining techniques is that they depend on tags/labels in event logs information about the processes they represent, and therefore, to a certain extent are limited because they lack the abstraction level required from real world perspectives. This means that the techniques do not technically gain from the real knowledge (semantics) that describe the tags or labels in events log of the domain processes [6]. Practically, majority of the process mining techniques in literature are purely syntactic in nature, and to this effect are somewhat vague when confronted with unstructured data.

For that reason, this work explores the technological potentials and prospects in using ontology as a core process mining and querying enabling tool by pursuing to address such challenges posed by the lack of semantic information through provision of a method for formal structuring of the readily available datasets. In other words, the work in this chapter addresses the above challenges i.e. (i) lack of process mining or querying tools that supports semantic information retrieval, extraction and analysis, and (ii) mining of event logs and models at a much more conceptual levels as opposed to the syntactic nature or methods for process mining. The purpose is mainly as a way of providing formal structures for the datasets used for process mining and enhancement of the analysis and integration of the resulting process models. Such an ontology-based approach is significant because, indeed, it involves semantic descriptions and/or reformulation of the meanings of the labels within the event logs and process models, as well as their comparisons for the purpose of improving the usefulness and performance of the entire domain processes in question particularly during the information retrieval, processing, and extraction process. In short, the propose approach in this chapter supports the augmentation of the informative values of the resulting models by semantically annotating the process elements with concepts they represent in real time, and linking them to an ontology in order to allow for analysis of the extracted data logs and models at a much more conceptual level.

In turn, the conceptual method of analysis provides an easy way to analyse the datasets (i.e. the event logs and models), and even more allows the meaning of the process elements to be enhanced through the use of property descriptions languages or syntax—such as the Ontology Web-Rule Language (OWL) [7] Semantic Web Rule Language (SWRL) [8], Description Logic (DL) queries [9], and classification of discoverable entities or taxonomy [4] in order to make available inference knowledge that could be utilized to determine useful patterns by means of the semantic reasoning aptitudes. On the other hand, the semantic modelling (*ontological representations*) and analysis techniques provide us with the opportunity to develop intelligent algorithms and tools which are capable of enhancing the resulting process models through explicit specification of the concepts (often referred to as *conceptualisation*) [5, 10, 11] in order to identify appropriate domain semantics and relationships amongst the process elements.

Finally, the work applies the proposed method on the case study of learning process domain to demonstrate the usefulness of the semantic-based approach. The study takes into consideration the different stages of process mining and its application—from the initial phase of collecting and transformation of the readily available event data to discovered process models, and then to semantically preparing the extracted models for further analysis and process querying at a more abstraction level. In essence, the chapter shows by using the case study of *Learning Process*—how the data from the various process domains can be extracted, semantically prepared, and transformed into mining executable formats to support the discovery, monitoring and enhancement of real-time processes through further semantic analysis of the discovered models. Indeed, the proposals and outcomes of the study shows that a system which is formally encoded with semantic labelling (annotation), semantic representation (ontology) and semantic reasoning (reasoner) has the capability to enhance process mining analysis and results from the syntactic level to a much more conceptual level.

Over the following section, the study looks at the ontological concepts and its main functions, and the describe how the work has utilised the schema to develop the proposed semantic-based process mining approach.

2. Ontologies

As a collection of *concepts* and *predicates*, ontology has the ability to perform logic reasoning and bridge the underlying challenges (semantic gaps) beneath event logs and models discovered especially through conventional process mining techniques with rich semantics.

To make the semantic knowledge available, ontologies are incorporated with the process models in order to pre-determine the model structure. Besides, the method also serves as a way of representing or bridging the distances between the labels within the process models and concepts in the defined ontologies.

Indeed, an ontological schema aims to transforms a process map into a *bipartite graph* (also referred to as Ontograph) to denote both the process models and its elements in a uniformed structure. So, whenever an inference (semantic reasoning) is made, a generalized associations (classification) of the process elements is created, and in consequence, infers the class hierarchies as well as performs a consistency check for those predicates. Besides, the sets of constraints (i.e. Object or Datatype property restrictions) driven by the ontology have the capacity to recognize inconsistent data and outputs particularly during the pre-processing stage, the algorithm executions, filtering or interpretation stage, and the results generation.

Several application and definition of the ontology term has been proposed in literature which most of the time concerns the varied domains of interest. According to Ref. [12] the term ontology is borrowed from the philosophy field which is concerned with being or existence study. The author mentions that in the context of computer and information science, ontology symbolizes as an artefact that is designed to model any domain knowledge of interest.

Even more, Ref. [13] refers to the ontological term as a formal explicit specification of a conceptualisation, and till date has been the most widely cited definition of ontology in the computer field. The definition means that ontology is able to explicitly define (i.e. specifies) concepts and relationships that are pertinent for modelling any domain of interest. Moreover, such specification can be represented in the form of *Classes, Relations, Constraints* and *Rules* to provide more meanings to use of the different expressions or relations. So therefore, ontology performs the following three functions, namely: *Formal—Explicitness—Conceptualisation*—to provide hierarchical structures and representation of information or knowledge.

In principle, ontology helps in description of the various concepts as well as the associations that holds amongst those concepts within a process domain. Hence, ontologies range from taxonomies, classifications, database schemas to fully axiomatized theories which state facts. Moreover, ontologies are nowadays an essential tool to a lot of systems or algorithms that are used for information retrieval and extraction, information management and integration of systems, scientific-knowledge portals, including e-commerce and web services.

Equally, ontology has been broadly used in many other sub-fields of computer science and AI, particularly in areas that concerns Information Retrieval (IR) [14] and Information Extraction (IE) [15], Ontology-Based Information Extraction (OBIE) [16], database management systems [17], information management and intelligent systems integration [18], knowledge representation [19], and in context of this study, Semantic-based Process Mining [2, 4, 6].

Clearly, the representation of knowledge using ontologies helps in organising datasets of complex structures (e.g. the fuzzy models). Moreover, the work in this chapter claims that by using the ontology as a conceptual consistency constraint, a fuzzy model with unlabelled data can be tuned into one (semantic model) that have the best consistency based on the prior knowledge or information. In addition, the formal representations and the resulting metadata (process descriptions) allows for automatic reasoning of the whole ontology with the aim of retrieving meaningful and useful knowledge that are inferred. Apparently, such reasoning disposition ensures that the process elements specifications within the ontologies are logically interpreted in a suitable manner that enables the automatic reasoning over the explicit knowledge about the domain processes in view [13].

Therefore, the main benefits of ontologies can be summarised in two forms:

i. encoding knowledge about specific process domains, and

ii. advanced analysis and reasoning of the processes at a more conceptual levels.

Likewise, one of the main benefits of ontologies particularly the OWL is that the schema is capable of declaring the different *classes* and *object/data properties* in any given process domain. In turn, it classifies those classes or properties into a taxonomy (i.e. *subClass* and *subProperty* hierarchy) by assigning the *domains* and *ranges* in the same way as the RDF schema [7]. Moreover, the resulting logical models allows the use of a *reasoner* to check if or not all of the definitions or expressions within the ontologies are equally consistent and recognises which concepts fits under which class, as well as, what the meaning of the individual specific properties are [19]. To end with, state of the art tools used for constructing ontologies (e.g., Protégé, SWOOP, and TopBraid Composer) makes use of those reasoners to make available the inference knowledge (i.e. the underlying inferred classes) to the developers or users predominantly in understanding the logically impacts or implications of their developed ontologies and design frameworks [18, 20].

3. Semantic reasoning

The main benefit of OWL ontologies is the capability to automatically compute the class hierarches (i.e. taxonomy) and the underlying relationships that exist amongst the different process elements (entities) by making use of a *reasoner*. Truly, *Reasoners* [2, 9] are essentially used to infer and check if a specific class is a subClass, or superClass of another, or not at all within the ontology, and as such automatically computes the inferred class hierarchy [4, 12].

Indeed, an additional function offered by the reasoner especially as used in this study is *consistency checking* of the process elements and parameters. This means that based on the *process description* or *attributes* within the ontology, the reasoner is able to use the underlying information to *check* if it is possible for any instances (individuals) to become a member of a class. Hence, a class is classified as being inconsistent if it cannot perhaps have any instance.

Moreover, a reasoner is every now and then also referred to as *classifier*. According to Ref. [3] a classifier is a function that maps the attributes of an event onto a label used in the resulting process model. Therefore, in context of ontology-based systems, a classifier (i.e. the reasoner) maps the taxonomy of the defined domain process by matching the various classes with their resulting process instances and/or attributes. In short, the process of computing the inferred class hierarchies in an ontology is typically known as *classifying the ontology*. Henceforth, the reasoner is regarded as the *classifier* or the *inference engine* used in querying and manipulation of the whole ontology.

Thus, the main function of the reasoner is summarized as follows:

- *Classifier*—used in computing the class hierarchies i.e. taxonomy
- *Consistency Checking*—for the inferred process elements, relations and parameters.

4. Ontology-based method and design framework

This study claims that the quality augmentation of process models is as a result of employing *semantic process mining* or better still ontology-based approaches and querying methods which encodes the envisaged system with the three rudimentary building blocks—semantic labelling (annotation), semantic representation (ontology), and semantic reasoning (reasoner) as described in the following section.

4.1. *Semantic process mining* framework: the 2-D rhombus approach

The design of the semantic-based process mining approach is primarily constructed on the following building blocks as shown in **Figure 1**.

In **Figure 1**, the work introduces the framework for the proposed sematic approach (also referred to as 2-Dimensional Rhombus approach) which integrates the following:

- extraction of process models from event data logs: the derived models are represented as a set of annotated terms that links and relates to defined terms in an ontology, and in so doing, encodes the process logs and the deployed models in the formal structure of ontology (semantic modelling).

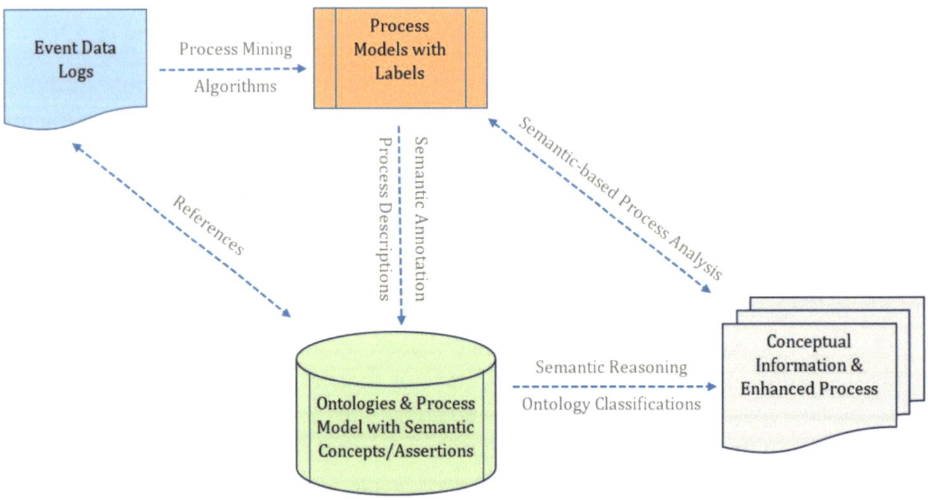

Figure 1. Proposed Framework for the semantic-based (ontology) process mining and querying method.

- the Reasoner (inference engine): which is designed to perform automatic classification of task and consistency checking to validate the resulting model as well as clean out inconsistent results, and in turn, presents the inferred (underlying) associations.
- the inferred ontology classifications helps associate meanings to labels in the event data logs and models by pointing to the concepts (references) defined within the ontology.
- the conceptual referencing supports semantic reasoning over the ontologies in order to derive new information (or knowledge) about the process elements and the relationships they share amongst themselves within the knowledge base.

Therefore, to summarize the design framework, the work shows that the application of semantic-based or better still ontology-based process mining and querying methods must focus on feeding the algorithms with two key core elements:

1. Event Logs and process models which their labels have references to concepts in an ontology, and.
2. Reasoners which are invoked to reason over the resulting ontologies for the event logs and models.

Indeed, the use of such framework and its application have gained a significant interest within the field *semantic process mining* in recent years. On the one hand, the proposed framework trails to make use of the semantics captured in event data logs (i.e. metadata) to create new techniques for process mining or yet still support the enhancement of existing ones in order to assist humans in gaining a novel and much more accurate results. On the other hand, the semantic-based analysis helps to provide the process mining and querying results at a much more level of abstraction so they can be understood easily by the process owners, process analysts, or IT experts. Besides, event logs from various process domains usually carry domain specific information (semantics), but quite often, the traditional process mining techniques and algorithms lack the ability to identify and make use of such semantics across the different domains. Nonetheless, the work in this chapter shows through the proposed approach in Section 4.2 and the semantically motivated algorithms in Section 4.3—that by annotating and encoding process models with rich semantics and the integration of semantic reasoning, that it is possible to specify useful domain semantics capable of bridging the semantic gap conveyed by the traditional process mining techniques. Thus, with the semantic-based approach, useful information (i.e. semantics) about how activities depend on each other in a process domain is made possible, and essential for extracting models capable of creating new and valuable knowledge.

To this end, the next section of this chapter presents the main components and architecture of the proposed approach in details, as well as, explain how the study have used the method to support the implementation of the proposed approach and algorithms.

4.2. Main components of the proposed semantic-based approach

This section looks at the general architecture of the semantic-based approach and how the main building blocks (i.e. annotated logs/models, ontology, and semantic reasoning) has been integrated in the development of the system. Clearly, the work summarizes in **Figures 2** and **3** the various components of the proposed system and its implementation as follows:

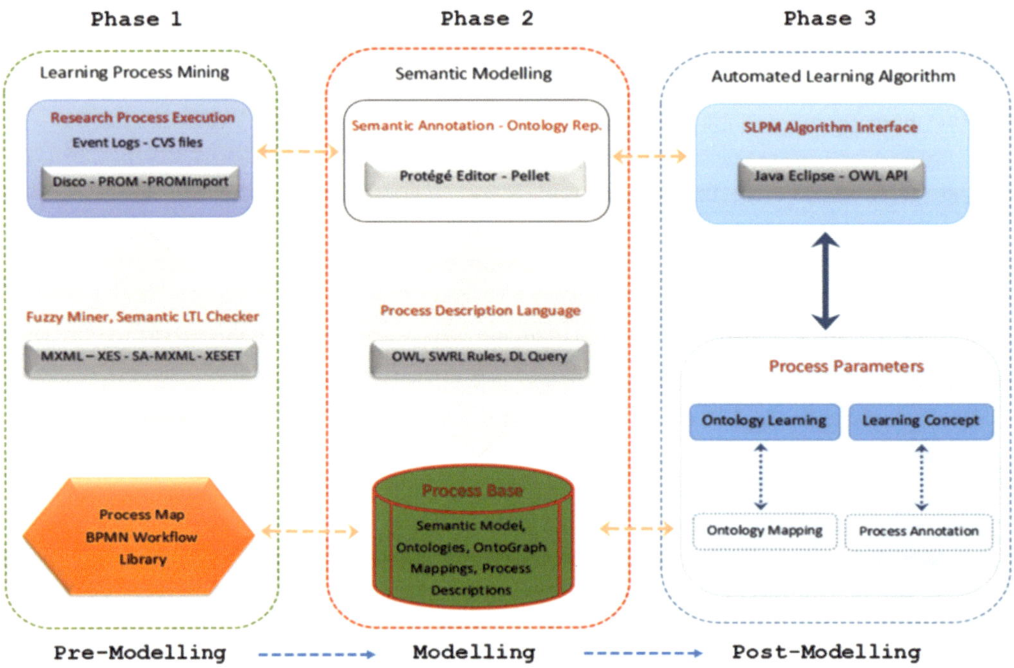

Figure 2. Architecture of the proposed semantic-based process mining and querying approach.

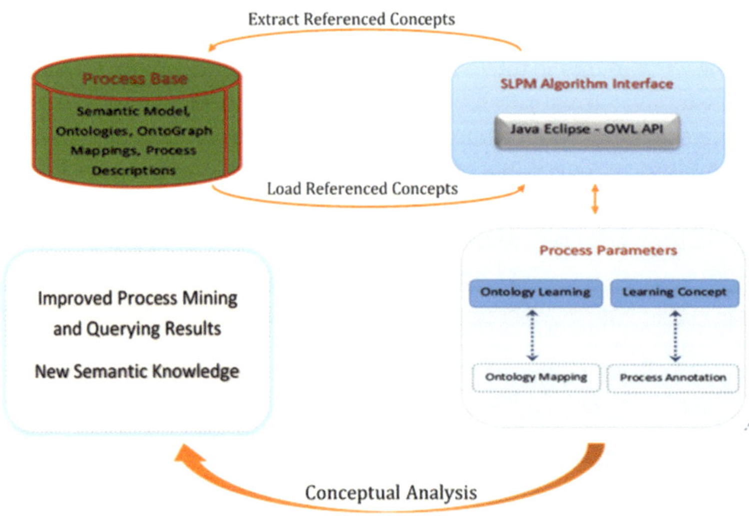

Figure 3. Practical aspects of implementing the proposed system and its main functions.

Figures 2 and **3** represents an overview of the various components of the semantic-based approach proposed by this study including the different stages of its development and implementation, as follows:

In Phase 1: the study applies the *process mining* techniques in order to make available the process mappings for the learning process, and check its conformance with the event logs based on the Fuzzy Miner as described in Ref. [4]. The main reason is that the resulting process map allows us to quickly, and interactively explore the processes into multiple directions and to show the individual *activities workflow*, and then provide platform for semantic annotation of the different process elements within the knowledge base.

In Phase 2: the work performs *semantic modelling* of the resulting process mappings in terms of the annotated terms. Thus, the semantic model represents the domain knowledge about the various activities and sequence workflows including the concepts defined in an *Ontology* by using process description languages such as the OWL [3] and SWRL [7]. In addition, the approach also makes use of the *Reasoner* i.e., Pellet—to infer the different process instances and the ontological representation (taxonomy) of the learning process model in reality [6].

In Phase 3: the study implements the semantic-based application used for extraction and automated mining or querying of the learning concepts. The work uses the Eclipse Java Runtime Environment to create the methods and interface for loading the *Process Parameters* (i.e. the ontology concepts). Essentially, the work makes use of the OWL Application Programming Interface (OWL API) to extract and load the inferred concepts within the ontology. The purpose is to match the questions one would like to answer about the relationships or attributes the process instances share amongst themselves by linking to the inferred *concepts* within the defined *ontology*.

4.3. Proposed semantic-based algorithms and its formalization

The semantic depiction (*representation*) of processes in an ontological form is a very important step in the proposed approach in this study. The method is aimed at unlocking the information value of the event logs and the derived models by way of finding useful and previously unknown links between the process elements and the deployed models. Moreover, the use of the reasoner to infer the individual process instances relies exclusively on the ability to represent such information in a formal way (ontology) to create platform for a much more conceptual analysis of the process instances.

The following Algorithm 1 describes how this work generates the ontology from the process models and event logs:

Algorithm 1: Developing ontology from process models and event logs

1: For all defined models $\boldsymbol{M}$ and event log $\boldsymbol{EV}$

2: **Input:** C—different classes for all process domain

R—relations between classes

I—sets of instantiated process individuals

A—sets of axioms which state facts

3: **Output:** Semantic annotated graphs/labels & an ontology-driven search for process models and explorative analysis

4: **Procedure**: create semantic model with defined process descriptions and assertions

5: **Begin**

6: **For all** process models ***M*** and event log ***EV***

7: **Extract** Classes ***C*** ← from ***M*** and ***EV***

8: **while** no more process element is left **do**

9: **Analyze** Classes ***C*** to obtain formal structures

10: **If** *C* ← Null **then**

11: obtain the occurring Process instances **(*I*)** from ***M*** and ***EV***

12: **Else If** *C* ← 1 **then**

13: create the Relations **(*R*)** between subjects and objects // i.e. between classes ***C*** and individuals (***I***)

14: **If** relations ***R*** exist **then**

15: **For** each class ***C*** ← semantically analyse the extracted relationships **(*R*)** to state facts i.e. Axioms **(*A*)**

16: create the semantic schema by adding the extracted relationships and individuals to the ontology

17: **Return**: taxonomy

18: **End** If statements

19: **End** while

20: **End** for

According to Ref. [13] ontologies, i.e. $Ont \in Onts$, are formal explicit specification of shared conceptualization that can be applied in any context, for example, as exploited in this study to model the case study of the learning process. Indeed, the semantic annotated logs and models are very fitting for further steps of semantically enhancing and accurate analysis of the process models, because at this stage, the input data are presented in a formal and structured format that can connect to referenced concepts within the ontologies.

Ultimately, from the described Algorithm 1, we recognize that ontology is a quadruple, i.e.

$$Ont = (C, R, I, A)$$

which consists of different classes C and relations *R* between the classes [13, 21]. Perhaps, a relation *R* trails to connect a set of classes with either another class, or with a fixed literal and is capable of also describing the sub assumption hierarchy (i.e. taxonomy) that exists between the various classes and their relationships. In addition, the classes are instantiated with a set(s) of individual, *I*, and can likewise contain a set(s) of axiom, *A*, which states fact (e.g. what is true and fitting within the model, or what is false and not fitting in the model).

Therefore, to achieve this importance step in this work, it was necessary to:

- Create the various process domain ontologies, workflow ontologies, and the Individuals classes that will be inferred
- Provide Process Descriptions for all the Objects and Data Types that allows for Semantic Reasoning and Queries (i.e. CLASS_ASSERTIONS; OBJECT_PROPERTY_ASSERTIONS; DATA_PROPERTY_ASSERTIONS)
- Create SWRL rules to map the existing class ontologies with concepts that are defined in the ontologies.
- Check for Consistency for all Defined Classes within the Model using Description Logic Queries.

Obviously, the defined concepts and process descriptions as explained in the steps above means that the *semantic annotation* is also another essential component in realizing such an ontology-based approach that supports automated process mining and querying by automatically conveying the formal semantics of the derived process models and extracted logs [21]. In other words, the annotated process models or logs are necessary for the semantic-based analysis, process querying and further steps of enhancing the model.

Essentially, *semantic annotation(SemAn)* is defined formally as a function that returns a set of concepts from the ontology for each node or edge in the graph [21]. Thus,

$$SemAn :: N \cup E \rightarrow COnts$$

where: *SemAn* describes all kinds of annotations which can be input, output, meta-model annotation etc. It is also important to note that semantic annotations could be carried out either manually or automatically computed bearing in mind the similarity of words [22] to generalize the individual entities within the domain process in view. Therefore, a *semantic annotated graph* (see **Figure 4**) is defined as follows:

$$\begin{aligned} Gsem &= (Nsem, Esem, Onts) \text{ with } Nsem = \{(n, SemAn(n)) \mid n \in N\} \text{ and } Esem \\ &= \{(nsem, n\_sem) \mid nsem = (n, SemAn(n)) \wedge n\_sem \\ &= (n\_, SemAn(n\_)) \wedge (n, n\_) \in E\} \end{aligned}$$

In fact, semantically planning of any ontology-based system requires that all process actions within the defined ontology must perhaps include some form of semantic annotation. Thus;

According to the definitions in Ref. [21] if we Let *A* be the set of all process actions. A process action $a \in A$ is characterized by a set of input parameters $Ina \in P$, which is required for the execution of *a* and a set of output parameters $Outa \subseteq P$, which is provided by *a* after execution. All elements $a \in A$ are stored as a triple (*namea, Ina, Outa*) in a process library *libA*.

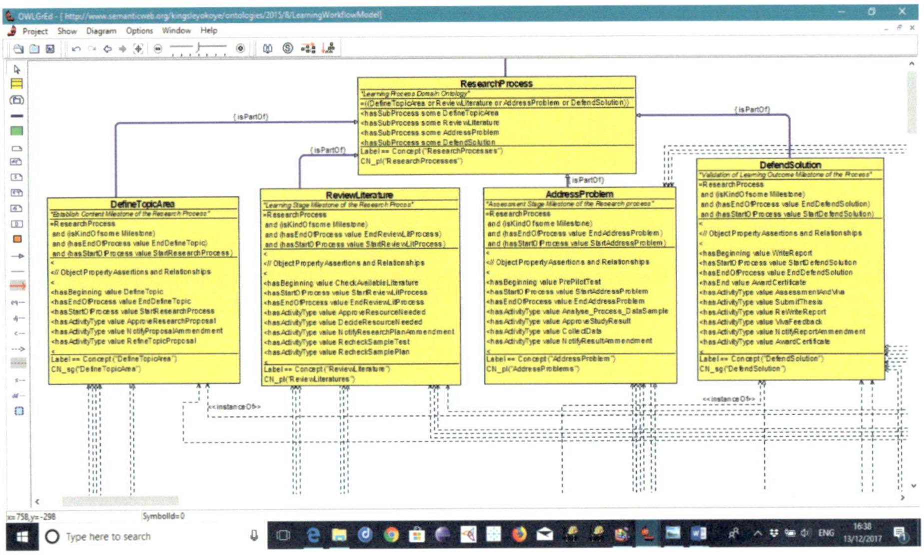

Figure 4. Research process domain with description of the learning activity concepts and relationships.

To this end, the last essential component in realizing the ontology-based approach is the capability of performing *semantic reasoning* to classify and even more check for consistency for all the defined classes and relationships that exist within the model. This means that based on the process description (i.e. assertions) within the domain ontology, the *reasoner* is able to use the underlying information to check if it is possible for any process instances (individuals) to become a member of a class, and to provide the necessary results or associations as requested based on the executed queries or information retrieval process.

Accordingly, the following Algorithm 2 describes how this study makes use of the reasoner to classify and infer the necessary associations to produce the outputs:

Algorithm 2: Reasoning over Ontologies and Classification of Entities and Outputs

1: For all defined Ontology models ***OntM***

2: **Input:** classifier e.g. Pellet Reasoner

3: **Output:** classified classes, process instances and attributes

4: **Procedure**: automatically generate process instance, their individual classes and Learning concepts

5: **Begin**

6: **For all** defined object properties *(**OP**)* and datatype properties *(**DP**)* assertions in the model (***OntM)***

7: **Run** reasoner

8: **while** no more process and property description is left **do**

Input the semantic search queries ***SQ*** or set parameter ***P*** to retrieve data from ***OntM***

Execute queries

If *SQ* or ***P*** ← Null **then**

re-input query or set the parameter concepts

Else If *SQ* or ***P*** ← 1 **then**

infer the necessary associations and provide resulting outputs

Return: classified Concepts

End If statements

End while

End for

Indeed, as shown in the Algorithm 2, semantic reasoning (or better still *ontology classifications*) helps to infer and associate meanings to labels within the defined ontologies by referring to the concepts assertions (i.e. Objects and Datatype properties) and sets of rules/expressions that are defined within the ontologies in order to answer and produce meaningful knowledge, and even in most cases, new information about the process elements and the relationships they share amongst themselves within the knowledge base.

5. Use case scenario and implementation

The use case scenario in this chapter is based on running example of a *Research Learning Process*. The work makes use of the events log about the research process to prove how the proposed approach is applied to represent and answer real time questions about a learning process. In the case study example as presented in our previous study in [6], the work shows that the first step to conducting a research is to decide on what to investigate, i.e. research topic, and then go about finding answers to the research questions. At the end of the process, the researcher is expected to be awarded a certificate. Basically, these process involves the workflow of the journey from choosing the research topic to being awarded a certificate, and comprises of sequence of practical steps or set of activities through which must be performed in order to find answers to the research questions [6].

Indeed, as shown in [6] the workflow for those steps are not static, it changes as a researcher travel along the research process. At each phase or milestone of the process, the researcher is required to complete a variety of learning activities which will help in achieving the research goal. Even more, from the process mining perspective, the derived process models may not disclose to us some of the valuable information at the semantic or abstraction levels, despite all of the mappings from mining the process. For example, the process maps may not disclose how the individual process instances that makes up the model interact or differ from each other, which attributes they share amongst themselves within the knowledge base, or the activities they perform together or differently. In turn, questions like—who are the individuals that have successfully completed the research process? may not be established. For such reason, the study in [6] has shown that by adding semantic knowledge to the deployed models, it becomes possible to determine and address the identified problems. To explicate such tactics, we presume that for a research process to be classified as successful, it is necessary that the researcher must complete a given set(s) of milestones in order to be awarded the degree. Moreover, in any case whereby the researcher has not completed the set(s) of milestone which is necessary to ensure the research outcome, such learner can be classified as incomplete. In such formal way, it becomes possible to logically ascertain which individuals has successfully completed the research process or not.

Therefore, the following section explains how the work uses the case study of the Research Process domain to demonstrate the capability of the ontology-based approach and algorithms by analyzing the learning activity logs based on concepts. Henceforth, presenting the process mining and querying results at a much more conceptual level.

5.1. Semantic representation and modelling of research learning process

In this section, the work implements the semantic-based approach to find out patterns/behaviour that describes or distinguishes certain entities within the learning knowledge base from another. Thus, by recognizing what attributes/paths the learners (i.e. process instances) follow or have in common, or what attributes distinguishes the successful learners from the incomplete ones. The purpose is not only to answer the specified questions by using the semantic-based approach, but to show how by referring to attributes (concepts) and the application of semantic reasoning, it becomes easy to refer to a particular case (i.e. certain group of learners). Principally, the study focus is therefore on the use case scenario of the *Successful* and *Uncomplete* learners.

Apparently, the work in [6] describes that the flow of the research process from the definition of research topic to being awarded a certificate; consist of different learning steps which a researcher has to or partly perform in order to complete the research process. In view of that, the work provides the four milestones; Establish Context → Learning Stage → Assessment Stage → Validation of Learning Outcome (as illustrated in **Figure 4**) in order to determine and explain the steps taken during the research process. Thus, from Defining the Topic Area –to- Review Literature –and- Addressing the Problem –then- Defending the Solution [6].

These milestones consist of sequence of activities, and the order in which the individual learning activities are carried out has the capability of determining the research outcome [6]. Henceforth, as described in **Figure 4** the work shows the *Learning Activity* concepts that are defined in the learning model ontology, and how they are mapped to the various milestones of the Research Process to ensure sequence of transitions during the entire learning process.

Indeed, the drive for such semantic mapping of the activity concepts is that the method allows the meaning of the learning objects and properties to be enhanced through the use of property descriptions (semantic annotations) and classification of discoverable entities (reasoning).

For instance, to address the real time learning questions the work have identified in Section 5 in relation to the successful and uncomplete learners. We refer to the deployed model, and to that effect, describe that a "Successful Learner" is a subclass of, amongst other NamedLearnerCategory, a Person that performs some LearningActivityConcepts, who has a universal object property restriction or relationship with the four milestones of the ResearchProcessClass (i.e. from Defining the Topic Area –to- Review Literature –and- Addressing the Problem –then- Defending the Solution) [6].

Moreover, as shown in **Figure 5**—the necessary condition is: if something is a Successful Learner, it is necessary for it to be a participant of the Learning ActivityConcept class and necessary for it to have a kind of sufficiently defined condition and relationship with the ResearchProcessClass: DefineTopicArea, ReviewLiterature, AddressProblem and DefendSolution [6].

Accordingly, to ascertain the class of the "uncomplete learners", it was also necessary to refer the object properties in order to determine what attributes distinguishes such learners from the Successful ones.

Therefore, the work describes that an Uncomplete Learner is a subclass of, amongst other NamedLearnerCategory, a Person that performs some Learning ActivityConcept who has a universal object property restriction/relationship with only some of the milestones of the ResearchProcess Class but not all of the classes [6].

As shown in **Figure 6**—the necessary condition is: if something is an Uncomplete Learner, it is necessary for it to be a participant of the Learning ActivityConcept class and necessary for it to have a kind of sufficiently defined condition and relationship with only some of the Class, i.e. DefineTopicArea, ReviewLiterature, AddressProblem but not all of the four classes [6].

Ideally, we observe in **Figures 5** and **6** that the Object Property Restrictions are used to infer anonymous classes that contains all of the individuals that satisfies the restriction. In essence, all of the individuals that have the relationship required to be a participant or member of a

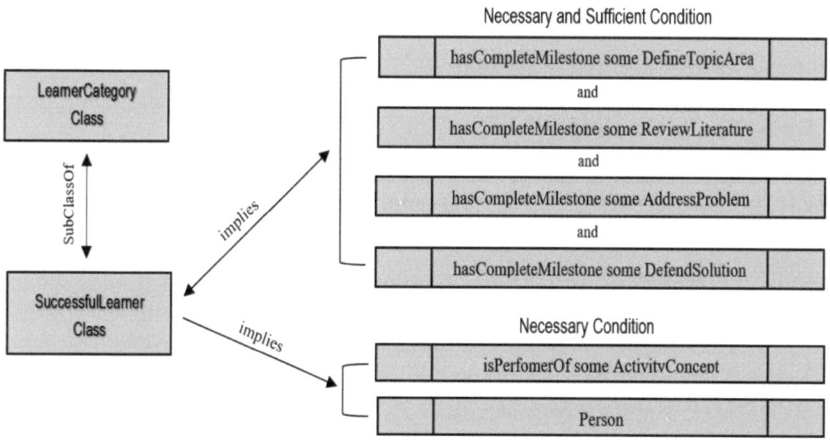

Figure 5. Attributes/object property assertions for the SuccessfulLearner Class.

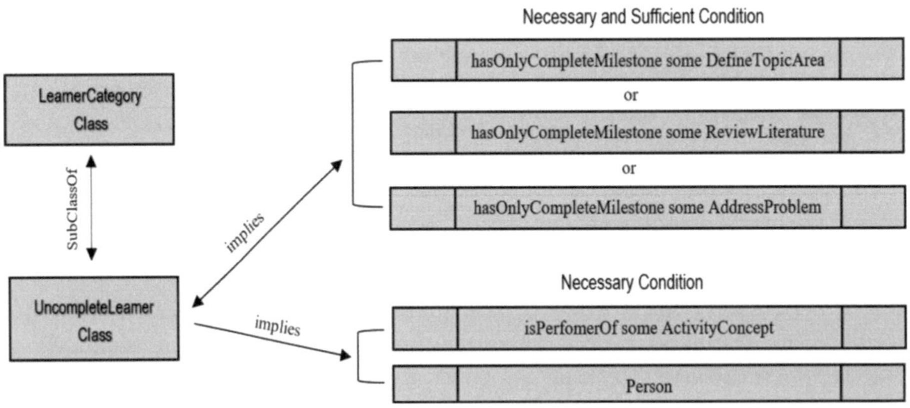

Figure 6. Attributes/object property assertions for the UncompleteLearner Class.

specific class e.g. the successful or uncomplete learner class. As noted in Ref. [6], the consequence is the *necessary* and *sufficient* condition: which makes it possible to implement and check for consistency in the model. Meaning that it is necessary to fulfil the condition of the universal or existential restriction—for any individual to become a member of the class, as we have used to answer the real life learning question identified in Section 5.

Indeed, property restrictions (structured organisation) and semantic labelling serves as a good practice for representation of the learning process information by providing a formal way of determining the individual process instances within the learning knowledge base.

For example, the following are description of the implemented ontology concepts and axioms for the "successful learner" class within the learning model following the definitions in **Figure 7** including the OWL XML file syntax as follows:

```
1: ontology ResearchProcess

2: concept SuccessfulLearner

3: hascompleteMilestone ofType {DefineTopicArea, ReviewLiterature, AddressProblem, DefendSolution}

4: isPerformerOf some LearningActivity

5: is ofType Person

6: hasInstance members {Mattew, Isaac}

7: axiom DefinitionOfSuccessfulLearner

<EquivalentClasses>

<Annotation>

<AnnotationPropertyIRI="http://attempto.ifi.uzh.ch/acetext#acetext"/>
```

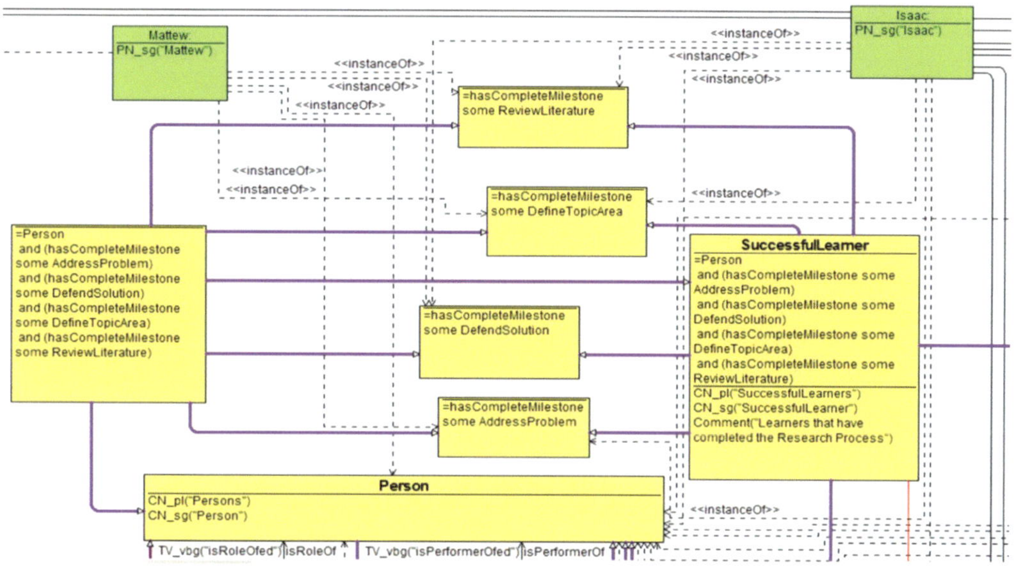

Figure 7. Concept assertions and the different formal relationships for the SuccessfulLearner Class.

```
<Literal datatypeIRI="&xsd;string">Every SuccessfulLearner is a Person that hasMilestones an AddressProblem and that hasMilestones a DefendSolution and that hasMilestones a DefineTopicArea and that hasMilestones a ReviewLiterature. Every Person that hasMilestones an AddressProblem and that hasMilestones a DefendSolution and that hasMilestones a DefineTopicArea and that hasMilestones a ReviewLiterature is a SuccessfulLearner.</Literal>

</Annotation>

</EquivalentClasses>
```

On the other hand, the work also provides example description of the implemented ontology concepts and axioms for the "uncomplete learner class" within the learning model following the definitions in **Figure 8** including the OWL XML file syntax as follows:

1: **ontology** ResearchProcess

2: **concept** UncompleteLearner

3: hasOnlycompleteMilestone ofType {DefineTopicArea, Or ReviewLiterature, Or Address Problem, Not DefendSolution}

4: isPerformerOf **some** LearningActivity

5: is ofType Person

6: hasInstance **members** {Paul, Danny, Mark, Gregory, John}

7: axiom DefinitionOfUncompleteLearner

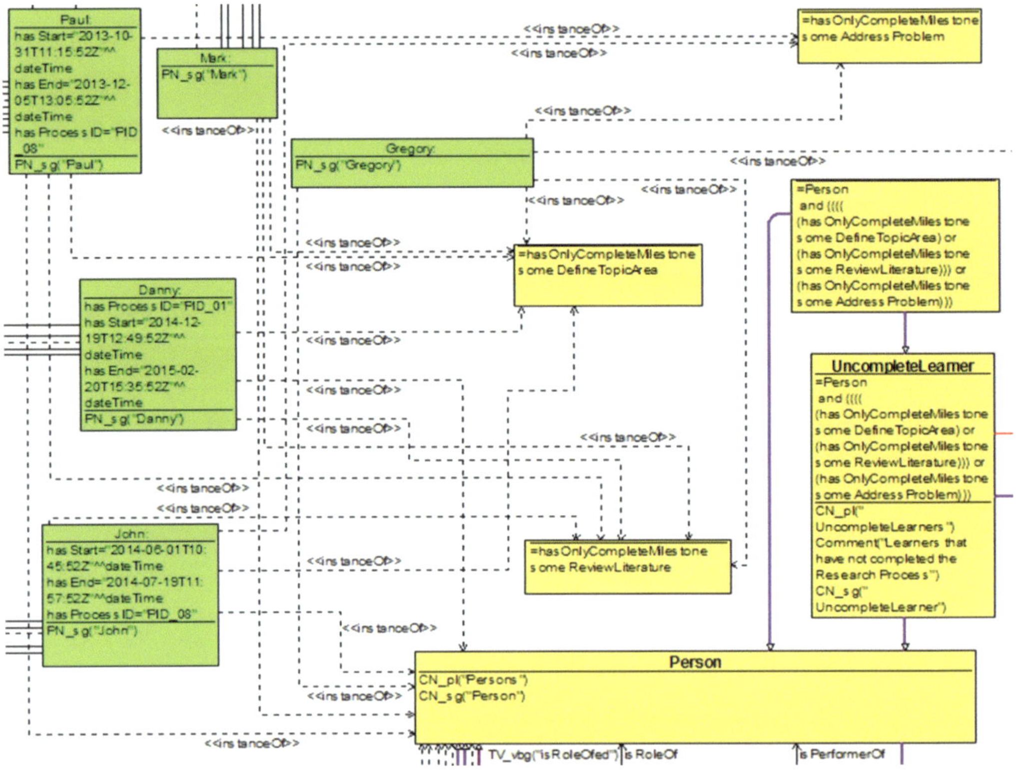

Figure 8. Concept assertions and the different formal relationships for the UncompleteLearner Class.

```
<EquivalentClasses>

<Annotation>

<AnnotationProperty IRI="http://attempto.ifi.uzh.ch/acetext#acetext"/>
<Literal datatypeIRI="&xsd;string">Every UncompleteLearner is a Person
that onlyHaveMilestones an AddressProblem or that onlyHaveMilestones
a DefineTopicArea or that onlyHaveMilestones a ReviewLiterature. Every
Person that onlyHaveMilestones an AddressProblem or that onlyHaveMile-
stones a DefineTopicArea or that onlyHaveMilestones a ReviewLiterature
is an UncompleteLearner.</Literal>

</Annotation>

</EquivalentClasses>
```

5.2. Description logic queries and process reasoning

The Description Logic (DL) query [9] is a process description language or syntax that could be used to check for consistency for all defined entities within the ontology model. It makes use of the *Reasoner* as previously explained in Section 3 to perform automatic classification of the relationships (i.e. property assertions) that are described within the ontology.

Likewise, this work makes use of the syntax to compute and ascertain the inferred classes and individuals within the learning domain ontology [23]. The queries are implemented in order to check that all parameters (entities) within the defined classes are true and at least falls within the universal restriction of validity by definition, and that there are no inconsistency of data or repeatable contradicting discovery.

Consequently, the study as shown in Ref. [23] provides the following example queries to explain how it employs the DL queries to perform automatic classification and/or retrieval of the process instances (entities) within the ontology. Thus:

DQ1. Is DefineTopic an Activity of the first Milestone (DefineTopicArea)?

DL Query: `ActivityConcept and is ActivityType Of some DefineTopicArea`

== the DL query checks if the activity of the first Milestone equal to Define Topic, thus compares the activity of the first Milestone DefineTopicArea with Activity Concept (DefineTopic)

DQ2. Is the Last Activity of the Research Process Award Certificate?

DL Query: `(i) ResearchProcess and hasEnd value AwardCertificate`

`(ii) ActivityConcept and isEndOf some ResearchProcess`

== the query computes and checks the last Milestone of the research process and compares if the last activity is equal to Award Certificate. Hence, compares the activity of the last Milestone DefendSolution with AwardCertificate

DQ3. Is CollectData an Activity of the Third Milestone Address Problem?

DL Query: `ActivityConcept and isActivityTypeOf some AddressProblem`

== computes and check the activities of the Third Milestone AddressProblem, thus compare if the result is equal to the Activity Concept CollectData

DQ4. Does Person P Activity A?

Example: Does Person (Richard) Activity Approve Research Proposal?

DL Query: `Person and hasActivityType value ApproveResearchProposal`

== the query computes and check persons related to the Approve Research Proposal and then compares if person (Richard) does the activity ApproveResearchProposal.

DQ5. Does person P activity of activity A and B?

Example: Which Persons does Activity RecheckSamplePlan and ReWriteReport?

DL Query: `Person and hasActivityType some {RecheckSamplePlan, ReWriteReport}`

== computes and check which persons in the model does activity RecheckSamplePlan and ReWriteReport.

DQ6. Does Person P activity A and then B and then C?

Example: Does person Paul activity of type CollectData and then Edit_Code_Data Sample and then Analyse_Process_Data Sample?

DL Query: `Person and hasActivityType some {CollectData, Edit_Code_Data Sample, Analyse_Process_Data Sample}`

= the query computes and check if person Paul does the activity {Collect Data, Edit_Code_Data Sample, Analyse_Process_Data Sample} [23].

6. Related works

Process querying is an emerging method for automated management of real-world and envisioned processes, models, repositories, and knowledge within the field of business process management and organisational data analysis [4, 5, 24]. According to [24] the process querying techniques concerns automatic methods for handling (e.g. filtering or manipulating) repositories of models of observed and unseen processes as well as their relationships, with intension of transforming the process-related information into decision making capabilities.

In practice, Ref. [5] notes that the process querying research spans a range of topics from theoretical studies of algorithms and the limits of computability of process querying techniques to practical issues of implementing the querying capabilities in software products [2–4, 17, 19, 25]. Also, Ref. [5] observes that such approaches which trails to combine process models and ontologies (particularly *ontologies for process management*) are increasingly gaining attention in recent years. According to the authors one reason for such growing interest, is that ontologies permits the adding of semantics to discovered or existing process models which in turn enables the automated inference of knowledge from the domain processes in question. Consequently, the derived knowledge (semantics) could then be used to manage any process (e.g. business processes) both at design and/or execution time.

In view of that, the authors in [5] propose a process querying framework used for enabling business intelligence through query-based process analytics. The framework structures the state of the art components built on generic functions that can be configured to create a range of querying techniques, and also points to gaps in existing research and use cases within the BPM and BI fields [3]. According to [3, 5] process querying methods need to address those gaps. For instance, organizations often fail to convert the high volume of data recorded in the information system into strategic and tactical intelligence. This is due to the lack of dedicated technologies that are designed to effectively manage the information about the instances (entities) encoded within the envisioned process models or data records, in order to better support strategic decision-making and provide the next generation of Business Intelligence. Interestingly, the proposed framework listed in [5] is an abstract system in which components can be selectively replaced to result in a new process querying method.

For the purpose of the work done in this chapter, our focus is particularly on the *Process Querying with Rich Annotations* [24] which studies the use of rich ontology annotations of process models for the purpose of process querying. Besides [11] notes that a trace abstraction technique for semantic-based process mining and model analysis should present methods or design frameworks which are able to convert actions found within the discovered models into higher level concepts based on the domain knowledge, thus, the term *conceptualization*.

7. Discussion and conclusion

The study in this book chapter introduces a design framework, method and algorithms used for implementation and semantic integration of process models in order to improve their analysis and querying process. Typically, the work recognizes that much of the effort in developing sematic-based process mining or better still ontology-based systems and approaches, relies mainly on constructing an effective system that integrates the three main building blocks (i.e. annotated logs or models, ontology and semantic reasoning). Hence, whilst the *semantic annotation* process is focused on describing the meaning of the process models and its entities or attributes, the *ontology* is devoted to binding together the different concepts, classes and properties in a way that maximizes their influence and outcomes. The work notes that the best way to create such systems is to make use of tools that supports the different components particularly the ontology which every now and then are required to maintain consistency of the process elements and formal hierarchy. Without a doubt, the use of a *reasoner* to compute relations between the various entities (process instances) in the ontology is practically possible, especially when building huge ontologies with numerous entities in them. Perhaps, without an automated classification process (semantic reasoning) it may become very challenging to manage those massive ontologies particularly in a precise logic way. Moreover, not only does this kind of ontology-based approach supports the application of rules and languages such as the OWL, SWRL and DL queries and/or re-use of an ontology by another ontology, but it also minimalizes the level of human-errors which are every now and again present especially when managing the manifold existence of entities or concepts within the ontologies or process knowledge-base.

Even more, the work has shown how the proposed semantic-based approach is applied to answer real time questions about the process domains as well as the classification of the individual process elements that can be found within a process knowledge-base. The study illustrates this through the use case scenario of the learning process. Significantly, such method of quality classification for individual traces within the learning process base can be utilized by the process analysts or IT experts as a way of performing useful information retrieval and/or query answering in a more efficient, yet effective way compared to other standard logical procedures. Practically, it is shown that the classification performance is not only comparable to the outcome of just a reasoner, but also a classifier that is able to induce new knowledge based on previously unobserved behaviours.

In summary, the use of ontologies and the relations between the concepts in the ontologies can be utilized to collectively combine tasks and compute process models in a hierarchical form (taxonomy) including several levels of abstraction The main idea is that for any ontology-based system such as the semantic-based process mining approach, these aspects of aggregating the task or computing the hierarchy of the process models should not only be machine-readable, but also machine-understandable. This means that the process models are either semantically annotated, or already in a form which allows a computer (i.e. the reasoner) to infer new facts by making use of the underlying ontologies.

Author details

Kingsley Okoye*, Syed Islam and Usman Naeem

*Address all correspondence to: k.okoye@uel.ac.uk

School of Architecture Computing and Engineering, Docklands Campus, University of East London, London, UK

References

[1] Dou D, Wang H, Liu H. Semantic data mining: A survey of ontology-based approaches. In: 9th IEEE International Conference on Semantic Computing; California, USA; 2015. pp. 244-251

[2] de Medeiros AKA, Van der Aalst WMP, Pedrinaci C. *Semantic Process Mining* Tools: Core Building Blocks. In: ECIS; June 2008; Galway, Ireland; 2008. pp. 1953-1964

[3] Van der Aalst WMP. Process Mining: Data Science in Action. 2nd ed. Berlin: Springer-Verlag Berlin Heildelberg; 2016

[4] Okoye K, Tawil ARH, Naeem U, Islam S, Lamine E. Semantic-based Model Analysis towards Enhancing Information Values of Process Mining: Case Study of Learning Process Domain. In: Abraham A, Cherukuri AK, Madureira AM, Muda AK, editors. Advances in Intelligent Systems and Computing book series (AISC, volume 614). Springer International Publishing AG; 2017. pp. 622-633

[5] Polyvyanyy A, Ouyang C, Barros A, van der Aalst WMP. Process querying: Enabling business intelligence through query-based process analytics. Decision Support Systems; 2017;**100**(1):41-56

[6] Okoye K, Tawil ARH, Naeem U, Islam S, Lamine E. Using semantic-based approach to manage perspectives of process mining: Application on improving learning process domain data. In: Proceedings of 2016 IEEE International Conference on Big Data (BigData); Washington, DC; 2016. pp. 3529-3538

[7] W3C. OWL Web Ontology Language [Internet]. 2004. Available from: http://www.w3.org/TR/owl-ref/ [Accessed: September, 2017]

[8] Horrocks I, Patel-Schneider PF, Boley H, Tabet S, Grosof B, Dean M. SWRL: A Semantic Web Rule Language Combining OWL and RuleML. W3C Member Submission [Internet]. 2004. Available from: http://www.w3.org/Submission/SWRL/ [Accessed: September, 2017]

[9] Baader F, Calvanese D, McGuinness DL, Nardi D, Patel-Schneider PF. Description Logic Handbook: Theory, Implementation, and Applications. 1st ed. New York, NY, USA: Cambridge University Press; 2003

[10] Balcan N, Blum A, Mansour Y. Exploiting ontology structures and unlabeled data for learning. In: Proceedings of the 30th International Conference on Machine Learning; Atlanta Georgia, USA; 2013. pp. 1112-1120

[11] Montani S, Striani M, Quaglini S, Cavallini A, Leonardi G. Knowledge-based trace abstraction for *semantic process mining*. In: ten Teije A, Popow C, Holmes J, Sacchi L, editors. Artificial Intelligence in Medicine. AIME 2017. Lecture Notes in Computer Science. Vol. 10259. Australia: Springer, Cham; 2017, pp. 267-271

[12] Hashim H. Ontological structure representation in reusing ODL learning resources. Asian Association of Open Universities Journal. 2016;**11**(1):2-12

[13] Gruber TR. Toward principles for the design of ontologies used for knowledge sharing. International Journal of Human Computer Studies. 1995;**43**(5):907-928

[14] Manning CD, Raghavan P, Schütze H. Introduction to Information Retrieval. Cambridge, UK: Cambridge University Press; 2008

[15] Cunningham, H. Information Extraction, Automatic, University of Sheffield, UK [Internet]. 2005. Available from: http://citeseerx.ist.psu.edu/viewdoc/download?doi=10.1.1.66.8785&rep=rep1&type=pdf [Accessed: August, 2017]

[16] Calvanese D, Montali M, Syamsiyah A, van der Aalst WMP. Ontology-driven extraction of event logs from relational databases. In: Reichert M, Reijers H, editors. Lecture Notes in Business Information Processing. BPM Workshops 2015. Springer, Cham; 2016. pp. 140-153

[17] Alkharouf NW, Jamison DC, Matthews BF. Online analytical processing (OLAP): A fast and effective data mining tool for gene expression databases. Journal of Biomedicine and Biotechnology. 2005;**2005**(2):181-188

[18] De Giacomo G, Lembo D, Lenzerini M, Poggi A, Rosati R. Using ontologies for semantic data integration. In: Flesca S, Greco S, Masciari E, Saccà D, editors. A Comprehensive Guide Through the Italian Database Research Over the Last 25 Years. Studies in Big Data. Springer, Cham; 2018. pp. 187-202

[19] Kumar AP, Abhishek K, Vipin Kumar N. Architecting and designing of semantic web based application using the JENA and PROTÉGÉ – A comprehensive study. International Journal of Computer Science & Information Technologies (IJCSIT). 2011;**2**(3):1279-1282

[20] Horrocks I. Ontologies and the semantic web. Communications of the ACM. 2008;**51**(12): 58-67

[21] Lautenbacher F, Bauer B, Forg S. Process mining for semantic business process modeling. In: 13th Enterprise Distributed Object Computing Conference Workshops; Auckland; 2009. pp. 45-53

[22] Born M, Dörr F, Weber I. User-Friendly semantic annotation in business process modeling. vol. 4832. In: Weske M, Hacid M, Godart C, editors. Web Information Systems Engineering – WISE 2007 Workshops. WISE 2007. LNCS Series, Berlin, Heidelberg: Springer; 2007. pp. 260-271

[23] Okoye K, Tawil ARH, Naeem U, Lamine E. Discovery and enhancement of learning model analysis through *semantic process mining*. International Journal of Computer Information Systems and Industrial Management Applications. 2016;**8**(2016):93-114

[24] Polyvyanyy A, et al. Process Querying [Internet]. 2016. Available from: http://process-querying.com/ [Accessed: July, 2017]

[25] Okoye K, Tawil ARH, Naeem U, Lamine E. A semantic reasoning method towards ontological model for automated learning analysis. In: Pillay N, Engelbrecht A, Abraham A, du Plessis M, Snášel V, Muda A, editors. Advances in Intelligent Systems and Computing. NaBIC 2015. Switzerland: Springer; 2016. pp. 49-60

Chapter 8

Generating Scientifically Proven Knowledge about Ontology of Open Systems. Multidimensional Knowledge-Centric System Analytics

Tamara L. Kachanova, Boris F. Fomin and
Oleg B. Fomin

Additional information is available at the end of the chapter

http://dx.doi.org/10.5772/intechopen.72046

Abstract

Physics of open systems overcomes real complexity of open systems, perceives them in natural scale without resorting to expert knowledge, subjective analysis and interpretations. Its scientific methods and technologies produce scientifically proven ontological knowledge from the systems' empirical descriptions that in turn are gathered from a huge amount of semi-structured, multimodal, multidimensional, and heterogeneous data, provide scientific understanding and rational explanation of obtained knowledge, research its value (correctness, fullness, and completeness), and carry out a deep and detailed analytics of multidimensional open systems on the basis of knowledge about their ontology.

Keywords: open systems, Big Data, physics of open systems, ontological knowledge, knowledge mining from empirical data, value of ontological knowledge, multidimensional knowledge-centric system analytics

1. Introduction

Open systems are being exchanged with environment by substance, energy, and information. The fundamental laws still unknown to science define organization, existence, states, and evolution of such systems. For producing reliable knowledge about open systems, it is necessary to have a well-developed theory. Such theory has arisen within the frame of interdisciplinary branch "Physics of Open Systems" (POS) [1]. Its top purpose is a scientific understanding of the essence of complexity and rational explanation of deep relationship of complexity with laws of nature. POS perceives complexity of systems as complexity of movement.

Big Data about open systems are created and continue to be incrementally created by empirical science. A new direction of POS came into being in the mid-1990s. Within it, the formation of cyber-physical paradigm of systemology, whose goal is to research open natural, social, anthropogenic, and complex technical systems, given by empirical descriptions, goes on [2–4]. *Further talk is only about this new paradigm of POS.* POS can be used for any self-sufficient totality of empirical data representing a certain slice of the system being researched in its natural scale and real complexity. Its main purpose is to overcome the fundamental complexity of open systems.

Scientific knowledge cannot be obtained from empirical data by purely logical means. Ontologies of scientific and empirical knowledge are significantly different. POS generates scientifically proven knowledge about the ontology of open systems from a huge amount of semi-structured, multimodal, and heterogeneous data. Scientific methods of POS are implemented: in technologies to automatically mine ontological knowledge about open systems directly from empirical data; in technologies of both scientific understanding and rational explanation of obtained knowledge; in technologies to analyze the value (correctness, fullness, and completeness) of knowledge; and in technologies for applying ontological knowledge about open systems in analytical, projective, and cognitive activity. On the basis of POS, the following activities are being performed: the mastering of a huge amount of data that are collected by empirical science; creating and exploiting the knowledge bases containing a scientifically proven ontological knowledge; and producing informational, intellectual, cognitive, and technological resources of knowledge as well as resources for solving complex system problems. POS assists in overcoming technological barriers of interdisciplinary interaction, helps to accelerate dynamics and improve flexibility of collaborative researches related to large-scale system problems in different branches of knowledge. Methods and technologies of POS has led to formation of multidimensional knowledge-centric computer analytics of open systems, that works with hundreds and thousands of variables, and operates automatically, without resorting to expert knowledge, subjective analysis and interpretations.

2. Conception of POS

Concept "System" is the initial and main concept of POS where a universal concentrated image of senses of the phenomena of the real world obtains its expression, and through which both scientific understanding and rational explanation of empirical facts are being achieved. At conceptualization of POS the following concepts play a key role together with the concept "System:"

- *relation*—is a condition of systemacity of the real world; an implementation of the principle of relationship universality; a manifestation of the unity of the whole; a carrier of regularity;
- *harmony*—is the fundamental basis of the unity of the whole comprehended through self-consistency, self-movement, inner conditionality, and orders;
- *symmetry*—is a particular physical equivalent of harmony; a harmonically conjugate unity based on the idea of form; the fundamental regularity; a tool to discover both hidden forms of system organization and higher synthetic system unity;

- *interaction*—is a fundamental understanding of the system's genesis; an interpretant of universal mechanisms of the system's self-movement and which discloses the system's senses encrypted in constructs that also are referents;
- *constructs*—are referents of deep system senses; polyadic system-forming relations endued with a characteristic symmetry and special system attributes;
- *structure*—is the base for existence of reality, the base that includes a multiplicity of steady relations; elements of at-oneness arising as a result of form-making processes.

2.1. Scientific approach

There are three ideas that shaped the scientific approach of POS:

- a scientifically proven knowledge about the ontology of open systems can be mined from big sets of semi-structured multimodal heterogeneous multivariate empirical data;
- a fundamental barrier of open systems' complexity can be overcome by identifying characteristic symmetries that disclose systems ontology;
- an open system obtains full, complete figuration in the state space whose organization is defined by the system's ontology.

Initially, the concept "System" arises without definition. A central problem of POS is to develop a scientific definition of this concept, to organize semantic sphere of system knowledge, and also its constructive figuration, and to reconstruct the system's essence as a one whole (**Figure 1**) [5, 6].

The triad "*Symbol – Word – State*" expresses an idea of cognition, understanding, and explanation of system's ontology. Semantic organization of the system ("Symbol") discloses organization of

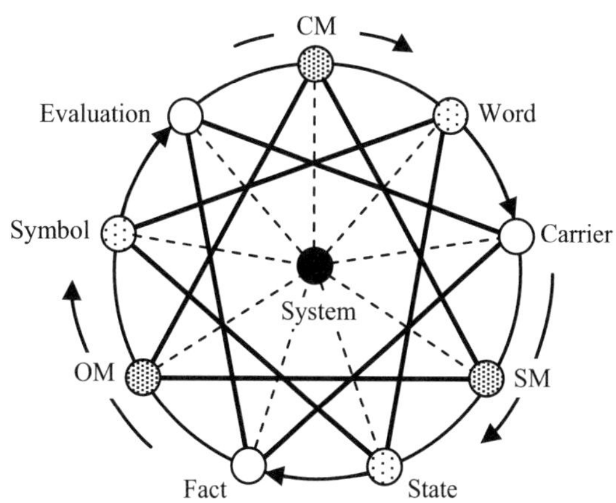

Figure 1. Definition of concept "system".

system's multiqualitative unity. Semantic activity of the system ("Word") is being manifested through qualities and properties of all elements and all parts of the system organization which are generating the system's language. Semantic forms of the system ("State") define formal synthetic image—reconstruction of the system unity able to be embodied in objects of reality. Ideal abstract forms of representing ontological knowledge have an absolute value. Through the concept "Symbol," the sense of concrete system went over into "expressive sphere," knowledge has obtained an adequate figuration, like a "*system in itself*." Through the concept "Word," the semantic significance of elements of ontological knowledge is disclosed to be understood like a "*system for itself*." Through the concept "State," both the states and regularities of generation of system's states became understandable ("*system for others*").

The triad "*Symbol – Word – State*" has its reflection in the triad "*Fact – Evaluation – Carrier*." This triad is engrained in observed reality ("Fact"), is in contact with reality through objects of reality ("Carrier") and establishes measures to express ability of the fact to perceive and undertake senses embodied in the carrier ("Evaluation"). The first concept of the triad ("Fact") expresses *hypothesis about the system* manifested in observed reality. The third concept of the triad ("Carrier") *connects hypothesis about the system with defining the system taken as "a whole" through system actual states*. The second concept of the triad ("Evaluation") evaluates *validity of this hypothesis*.

The triad "*OM – CM – SM*" is a modeling triad presenting methods of cognition of system's ontology (*ontological modeling—OM*), methods of understanding of system's senses (*communicative modeling—CM*), and methods of figuration of system's idea (*states modeling— SM*).

Both, the second concept "Evaluation" and relationship between concepts "Fact" and "Carrier" (triad "Fact – Evaluation – Carrier") demand that the definition should be extended [7] (**Figure 2**).

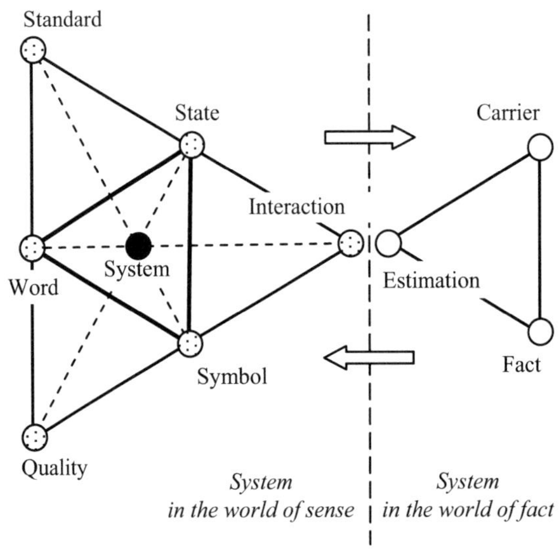

Figure 2. Extension of definition of the concept "system".

Such extension creates *axiological level of knowledge* [8]. At the axiological level of knowledge, the problem of value (correctness, fullness, and completeness) of ontological knowledge is solved. This level of knowledge is specified by the triad "Quality – Standard – Interaction." In measures of truth of sense and value of ontological knowledge it expresses a relationship between the worlds of system's sense and system's fact [9]. As a result of extending the system's definition, the triad "OM – CM – SM" includes (together with cognition, understanding, and explanation of ontological knowledge) also a value analysis of this knowledge. Application of the scientific method of POS to concrete system produces true knowledge to which certain value corresponds. The moment "Quality" define degree of the value of obtained forms in measures expressing the fullness of manifestation and depth of insight into the system's senses. The moment "Standard" states the measure of comprehension of disclosed and understood system senses by its real carriers. The moment "Interaction" measures degree of reconstructing the system's unity (as a whole), from the set of the system's states.

2.2. Methodological foundations

POS has proposed a logically complete system of concepts that are revealing sense of system's genesis. The following has become methodological foundation for this system [4, 5, 10]:

- a constructive definition of the concept "*System;*"
- a philosophical system of doctrines and fundamental concepts about senses and relationship between senses of the system in the chain of acts of cognizing the system's ontology (*doctrinal model*);
- basic concepts in their dialectical relationship that form a unified, holistic, and hierarchically arranged conceptual structure (*dialectical model*);
- stages of both cognition and creation of structural images of the system's senses on the basis of measure category and universal principle of symmetrization-dissymmetrization (constructive-methodological model);
- a set of sense relations that transfer all specific intrasystem regularities by way of generative and expressive moments (*symbolic model*);
- agreements about organization and use of the systems language (*language convention of POS*).

2.3. Principles to which POS conforms

POS is aimed at researching complex large-scale objects (phenomena and processes), they can be not only (and not necessarily) of physical nature. POS proceeds on the assumptions that if there is empirical description of object properties, its states, and conditions of its existence, that is enough to discover the essence of this object. POS considers the system as a tool for cognition of complexity and as special dimension of reality. POS, in its becoming and development, is based on the following principles:

- *principle of systemacity* (all objects that are carriers of the system states are ontologically united);
- *principle of holism* (system integrity is being stated);
- *principle of objectivity* (empirical fact is a unique source of objective data about system);
- *principle of compliance for system's observation channels* (uniform set of states variables; indicators sensitivity to various states; unified procedure for scaling measurements);
- *principle of counting quantities* (counting quantities are structural elements of every kind at each stage of cognition, understanding, explanation, and estimation of the system's ontology; the number of counting quantities is of special importance);
- *principle of complexity actualization* (initially, structures of binary relations of variables of the system's state are the carriers of heterogeneity intrinsic to the system);
- *principle of symmetry* (structures of binary relations in the system are being harmonized);
- *principle of subordination* (order parameters of the system define behavior of all system parts and elements);
- *principle of denotation* (referents of standards of states of the system's eigen qualities are the carriers of the system's state);
- *principle of desemantization* (ontological knowledge about the system is being transformed into understanding and rational explanation of the system's phenomenon);
- *principle of value* (relation of correctness, fullness, and completeness of ontological knowledge);
- *principle of assembling* (in each state, the system is a whole; reconstructing each system state is an assemblage of standards of states of the system's eigen qualities).

2.4. Axioms of the system

The base of POS is the system's axioms—are predicates of harmonization and systemacity, which explain the general idea to resolve heterogeneity inherent in the system, they assert statements of fundamental properties inherent in the system at various levels of cognition of its ontology [2–4].

- *pre-image axiom* (universal principle of harmony and the law of analogy);
- *axiom of relations harmonization* (in the system, all quantities are conjugate and proportionate, their variability is consistent);
- a*xiom of role contingency* (all quantities in the system have role definiteness; the system is able to change role definiteness of its quantities);
- *axiom of orientation* (fundamental carriers of the system's senses have spatial orientation; conditions when mechanism of inner orientation is being manifested in the system, are postulated);
- *axiom of determination* (the system in each of its qualitative definiteness knows unique dividing line between the big and the small at quantities variability).

2.5. Symmetries of forms of system organization

Symmetry displays harmony at the level of such categories as "the part" and "the whole," and manifests itself as unity of identity and distinction, conservation, and change. Cognition process of system ontology is being understood as disclosing more deep and general symmetries. Ascension from the symmetry of one level to another is related to discovering dissymmetry and to comprehension of facts of dissymmetry that are considered as variety sources, and which are subordinated to other deeper and general symmetries.

POS has discovered symmetries of forms of system organization [2–4]:

- *signed balance* (it states system attribute named "*Level of quantity values*");
- *symmetry of singlet* (main axial symmetry; it states system attribute named "*Role charge;*" it generates all kinds of system units);
- *symmetry of doublets* (it reveals senses of role charges: mirror symmetry (it states base interaction named "*Similarity*"); mirror-mirror symmetry (it states base interactions that named "*Switching*" and "*Absorption*"); axial symmetries 1 and 2; symmetry of rotation);
- *symmetry of triplets* (it states types of orientation: general axial symmetry (it states system attribute named "*Orientation*"); planes of symmetry 1 and 2);
- *symmetry of system units* [*point of symmetry* (*it introduces order center*); main axial symmetry (it reveals system organization in each *qualitative definiteness* of the system)].

3. Scientific foundations of POS

3.1. Reconstructive analysis

Solving of the general problem of reconstructive analysis of open systems on their empirical descriptions became the basis for creating POS. Method of reconstructive analysis has overcome the barrier of complexity of open systems and has provided the possibility to mine scientifically proven knowledge (about the ontology of open systems) from the big polymodal sets of heterogeneous empirical data with hundreds and thousands of variables [4, 11, 12]. Method of reconstructive analysis is not resorting to expert knowledge, subjective analysis and interpretations. Models of cognition of open systems, also systems axioms and principles of system's genesis act as a methodological base for reconstructive analysis. On their basis, *the semantic generatrices of the system, full reconstructive set of system models, and families of interaction models* are produced.

Semantic generatrices of the system are represented by *families of formal constructs with characteristic symmetries of forms of system organization*. Each model of reconstructive set of system models is:

- an underlying structural invariant of open system;
- a part of one whole (of the system) and also—all whole (of the system) in the context of this part;

- n-ary relation with fixed structure and morphology, axial symmetry and order center;
- a unique feature of the system, an abstract form of expressing certain quality inherent in the system.

The families of interaction models are 0-, 1-, 2-, 3-ary simplexes with *specific symmetries revealing the mechanisms of system's genesis*. Method of reconstructive analysis reveals multi-qualitativeness (complexity) of the system, presents the system in all its qualities, discloses the full families of models of intra-system interactions forming one whole from the set of all qualities inherent in the system.

3.2. Language of systems

A creation of systems language was of fundamental importance for POS, when it formed and developed as a "scientific method." The systems language has led to scientific understanding of ontological knowledge and to defining its value (correctness, fullness, and completeness).

Inner systems code manifested in ontological knowledge was revealed and understood. Language of systems overcame differences of methodological bases and eliminated technological barriers of scientific understanding of open system. Understood senses of systems became equally accessible to experts in different domains of knowledge. Through the language, the *postulates of reconstructive analysis have obtained the status of postulates of scientific theory*.

Language of systems is characterized through: lexical composition (*words, concepts, concepts qualities*); nominative units; paradigmatic and syntagmatic relations; assessment systems (*evaluation aspects, ideals, evaluative propositions, and assessment scales*); and computability of concepts qualities, concepts and words of the systems language (*axiological operators*). Language of systems has formalized and organized system thinking, has increased interdisciplinary interaction, has led to scientific understanding of the ontology of open systems and value of ontological knowledge obtained from empirical data. Both, reconstructive analysis and language of systems *became the scientific basis for creation of informational, intellectual, cognitive and technological resources of system knowledge* [5, 7, 13].

3.3. States, properties, and evolution of systems

Solving the general problem of rational explanation of ontological knowledge about open systems became the third essential result in formation of POS [7, 14]. The answer to the question—"… how system-wide, abstract, extra-subject, ontological knowledge about open systems (in force field and in relation to order parameters) is related to key concepts in the real world of systems (variables, states, properties of variables, properties of states, variability of quantities, variability of states, and variability of properties)?"—was obtained. The system regularities determine variability in "order parameters." Variability in "force field" is explained by the spectrum of system's possibilities. As a result of this decision, POS gives a rational explanation for relationships: between system's ontology and reality, system regularities and properties of system's carriers, system-wide regularities and predeterminacy of system's phenomenon.

3.4. Representation forms of system

POS works with systems' representations defined in feature space, space of qualities, linguistic space, state space, and space of system's behavior. In each space, the system has its own special forms of implementation [7, 14] (**Figure 3**).

System in Data is given in actual states by values for variables of state and environment (initial representation of the system). *System in Relations* is defined through attributed binary relations between variables (this initial abstract representation of the system is obtained directly from the System in Data). *System in Qualities* is given as a full set of its eigen qualities (this representation of the system arises as a result of overcoming the complexity of open systems). *System in Standards* is represented by images of ideal states of its eigen qualities able to transfer onto actual states of the system. *System in Linguistic Space* is represented by words, concepts, concepts qualities, and evaluations of concepts qualities of the systems language. *System in Forms of Standards Implementation* is shown by a full model set of the forms of standards implementation in the system's carriers. *System in States* is displayed by a full model set of system's actual states (states' reconstructions).

3.5. Ontological knowledge

Ontological knowledge represents system in three spaces: qualities space, linguistic space, and state space [5, 7].

Model of Qualities Space reveals complexity of the system taken as a multiqualitative essence, through a full set of formal system models and full sets of the models of intrasystem interactions.

Model of Linguistic Space gives a reasoned and scientifically understood space of eigen qualities of the system. The problem of reference of this space is solved by means of the systems language. Words and concepts of systems language as well as explications of semantic content of

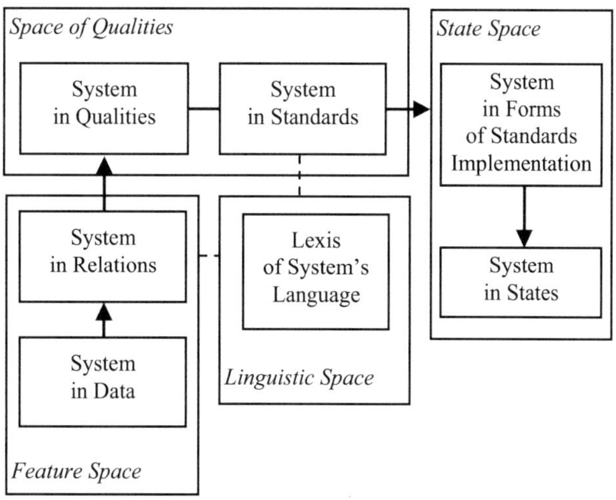

Figure 3. System in spaces of POS.

the system define Lexical Portrait of System. Evaluations of Concepts Qualities establish the relationship between linguistic space and qualities space.

Model of States Space constructively identifies system as "a whole" through system states and system-making interactions, and sets the conditions, rules, and limitations on forming and changing states of the system. States Reconstructions explicitly represent scientifically proven knowledge about actual states of the system. Models of Implementation Forms of standards map the space of eigen qualities of the system to its feature space. The feature space is structured. Obtaining reconstructions of all actual and potential states of the system is provided. Ontological knowledge has a two-level structure—knowledge elements and a base knowledge (**Figure 4**).

On the level of "Knowledge Elements" the sets of formal constructs—semantic generatrices of the system—are presented. The level "Base Knowledge" contains models of eigen qualities of the system, interaction models, and models of the system's states.

3.6. Axiological knowledge

Including axiological knowledge into explicative statements leads to objective description of open systems considering them as man-sized objects. Axiological knowledge represents evaluations of knowledge resources [5, 7] (**Figure 5**).

Information resource of knowledge sees the system as an empirical reality, defines the ability of system's empirical description to manifest, and express senses of the system in full and complete form. *Intellectual resource of knowledge* includes families of formal models of the system's qualities and models of interaction, provides qualimetric measures of the system models. *Cognitive resource of knowledge* contains collections of elements providing creation of constructively defined formats for cognitive schemas of intrasystem mechanisms. *Technological resource of knowledge* covers models of both states and properties of the system as a whole, and gives variety of evaluations to characterize completeness and adequacy of states models of the system as an integrated whole, in the context of relatedness of empirical fact and system sense. Axiological knowledge consists of the following:

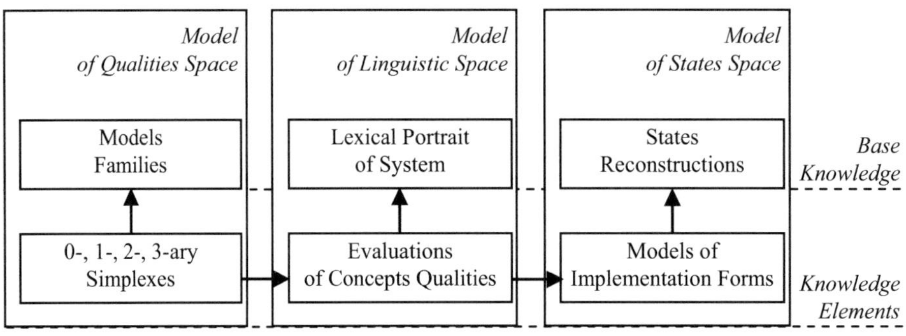

Figure 4. Organization of ontological knowledge.

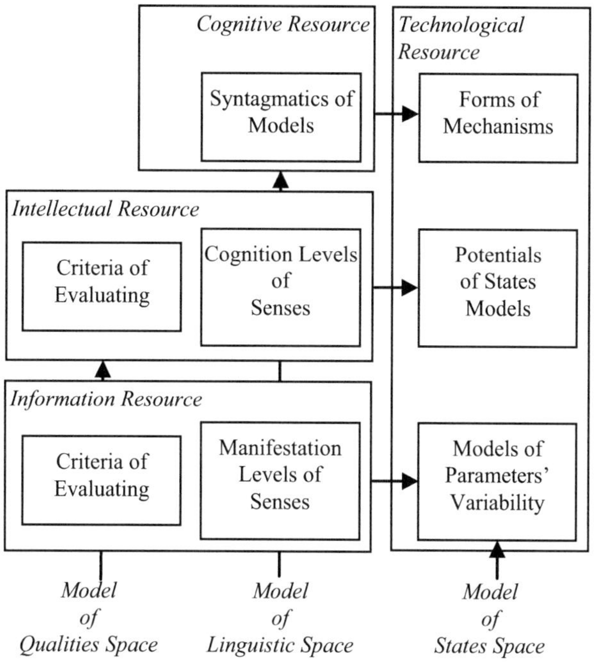

Figure 5. Evaluations of knowledge resources.

values of representation forms of the system; ideals and norms of these forms; measurement scales and procedures of estimating the value; and characteristics of correctness, fullness, and completeness of system knowledge. Value-based orientations discern the real and ideal; they discriminate correct knowledge from incorrect one; full knowledge from insufficient one; complete knowledge from incomplete one; as well as significant and essential knowledge from insignificant and inessential one.

4. Analytical core of POS

4.1. Possibilities of analytical core. Composition and structure

Analytical core of POS (AC POS) is an "intelligent machine" that is able [7, 11]:

- to automatically discover scientifically proven knowledge about the ontology of open systems from huge multidimensional sets of multimodal heterogeneous empirical data, without resorting to expert knowledge, subjective assessment, simplifications, and interpretations;
- to automatically provide a scientific understanding and rational explanation of obtained ontological knowledge;

- to automatically research the value (correctness, fullness, and completeness) of both revealed and scientifically understood ontological knowledge;
- to automatically generate informational, intellectual, cognitive, and technological resources of knowledge about the ontology of open systems.

AC POS includes three components (**Figure 6**):

- integrative component (it organizes interrelationship and uses elements of AC POS, and it will not be considered further);
- technological component;
- qualimetric component.

Ideas, approaches, and scientific methods of POS have been fully implemented in technologies of technological and qualimetric component. Technologies of *technological component* produce ontological knowledge, whose attributes are: truth, thingness, determinacy, concreteness, logical substantiation, verifiability, theoretical and empirical validity, and applicability. Technologies of *qualimetric component* create axiological knowledge, whose characteristics are the categories of value. Technologies of POS are universal and used in various areas of knowledge for large scale and deep research of natural, social, anthropogenic, and complex technical systems.

Empirical data systems (EDS), at input of AC POS, represent comprehensive empirical contexts of certain open systems and certain system problems related to these systems. For each open system, its data set complying with the requirements of POS is being formed. Its preparation consists of gathering empirical data, integrating, and systematizing collected data, and forming big data sets covering all basic aspects of systems' existence within a changing environment. POS don't consider solving these problems as its problems. Their solution is provided by Big Data technologies that have necessary functionality (for example, open

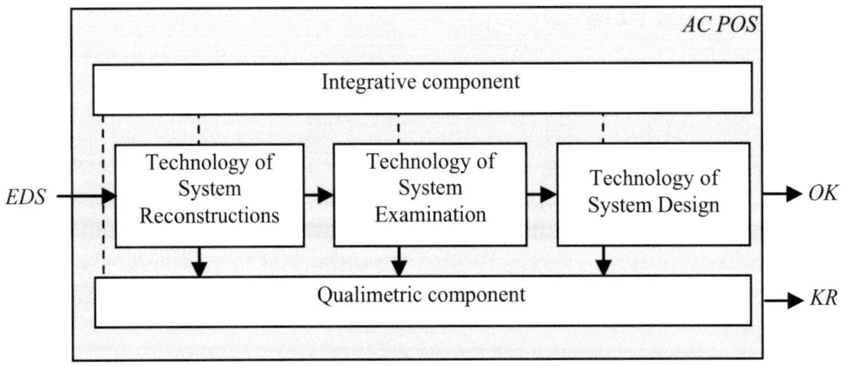

Figure 6. Layout of AC POS: *EDS*—empirical data system; *OK*—ontological knowledge; *KR*—knowledge resources.

platform Hadoop (IBM) or a product set of Oracle Corporation used to gather data and to systematize them). Interests of POS cover problems related to forming empirical contexts of open systems:

- vision development of systems and system problems, also their verbalization, isolation, and estimating scale and complexity;
- determining volume and nature of empirical data which, according to opinion of subject-matter experts, are appropriate for producing knowledge about the system and about system problems;
- discovery of possibilities, sources, conditions, rules, ways, and technologies for data supply that are used to form the empirical contexts of high quality.

Ontological knowledge and resources of knowledge at output of AC POS are results of the technological and qualimetric component. On their basis the scientific methods and computer technologies of multidimensional knowledge-centric system analytics of POS are being created.

4.2. Technologies of cognition, scientific understanding, and rational explanation of the ontology of open systems

Technology of System Reconstructions (*TSR*) on the basis of initial empirical context of the system produces the system's representation in eigen qualities and creates a complete set of models of intrasystem interactions [15]. *Technology of system examination* (*TSE*) transforms the system's representation given through eigen qualities, to representation of the system in standard states of its eigen qualities [14, 15]. *Technology of system design* (*TSD*) synthesizes adequate models of actual states of the system, researches emergent properties of the system, generates, shapes, and represents ontological knowledge about the system for further use [14, 15]. The organization of each of these technologies is disclosed according to unified scheme, beginning with the technology model and finishing by the patterns for automatically generated normative documented reports about obtained ontological knowledge [7, 12, 14]:

- *technology model*—sets the scheme of cognitive process [*process of ontology cognition* (for TSR), *process of understanding ontology* (for TSE), *and process of ontology explanation* (for TSD)] in its main concepts that are structured by categories of the system's representation and deployed according to stages of the process;
- *dual way* of cognitive process [*process of cognition* (for TCR), *process of understanding* (for TSE), *process of explanation* (for TCD)]—includes two stages (the *ascending* from fact to sense, and the *descending* from sense to fact). Each stage in a special way expresses inter-conditionality between the two worlds of the system—i.e., world of facts and world of senses;
- *key objects of technology*—represent (for TSR, TSE, and TSD accordingly) main concepts of the technology model in constructive and computable forms;

- *technology method*—sets computational procedures (for TSR, TSE, and TSD accordingly) that are needed to automatically generate the technology objects and their attributes, the procedures are based on own scientific apparatus of POS and on additional external methods of measurement theory, mathematical statistics, graph theory, set theory, mathematical logic, estimation theory, qualimetry, and computer visualization;
- *measurement scales*—represent values of attributes of technology objects: scale of values, and groupings scale—are tools for measuring the system's properties in TSR; scale of levels and scale of level's numerical forms—are used to evaluate concepts qualities in TSE; also a complete scale of level's numerical forms, weight scale, scale for measuring proximity to standard, also scale of level's predominance, scale of level's predetermination, and scale of significance and mobility of level—are instruments to measure the system's states in TSD;
- *patterns for normative documented reports of technology*—set the structure, sections content, and formats of knowledge representation.

In the case of TSR, normative reports represent *the system's portraits expressing ontological knowledge that has been revealed*: empirical portrait, statistical portrait, structural portrait, system portraits (ones of type, and ones of type forms), and realistic portrait. In the case of TSE, normative reports represent *scientifically understood ontological knowledge*: knowledge quality, knowledge volume, and each aspect of knowledge. In the case of TSD, normative reports represent *shaped ontological knowledge*: knowledge about the system as a whole, knowledge about the system's standards, and knowledge about the system's states.

4.3. Technology to analyze the value of ontological knowledge

Qualimetric component of AC POS performs multifaceted research on the value of obtained ontological knowledge and generates axiological knowledge about the system. In the ideal case, the system initially is represented by complete representative system of empirical data. After this, the technologies of cognitive processes of AC POS guarantee production of scientifically proven (formally correct), full, complete ontological knowledge about the system. In real situation, the technologies of AC POS generate correct knowledge that is not full and complete. Value-based and evaluative aspects of axiological analysis of the system's ontology discovered by cognitive processes are being researched in all such cases and in full.

Formal correctness is an important moment of ontological knowledge. Besides correctness, knowledge possesses value. These two moments oppose each other, complement one another, moreover none of them cannot be reduced to or replaced by another one. *Correctness relation* is being established between the object vision and the object itself, and is expressed through abstract descriptions. The object is the main thing here (an unchangeable element of correctness relation). The object vision is a variable element of correctness relation. *Value relation* is being established between the object and the statement about the object, and is given in evaluations. The evaluative statement about the object is the main thing here. If correspondence between elements of the relation is absent, then the object (but not the evaluation) should be changed.

Essence of value (value of element of system knowledge); *existing value* (subject-object relation between the system analyst and the object)—they serve as aspects of value. Essence of value reflects *potential value*, whereas existing value manifests *actual value*. Qualimetric component of AC POS computes estimates of potential value of knowledge. The question about actual value is related to choice of orientation at applying knowledge. Actual value is corresponds to the concepts of usefulness, degree of intensity, and tension measures. The system analyst addresses these concepts at certification of valued knowledge.

Technologies that form the technological component of POS disclose ontological knowledge about the system through the objects ("Models," "Attributes," "Words," "Concepts," "Concepts Qualities," "States," and "Properties"). They take a certain form for each system being researched [5, 7] (**Figure 7**).

Element "*Definiteness*" of the process of knowledge assessment forms value vision of elements of system knowledge that characterize the system as a whole. Element "*Order Existence*" describes value of knowledge about the system in whole and in parts of the whole. Element "*Explanation*" expresses the value of any element of disclosed scientifically understood and rationally explained knowledge about the ontology of open system. Organization of each element of value-based and evaluative process is being described according to unified scheme: element's model; knowledge value; process of evaluation; ideals (norms and samples); estimates; evaluation scales; and patterns for normative reports.

Element's model discloses a process of generating objects of each technology that is part of technological component of AC POS, evaluates these objects, and, where possible, improves objects being evaluated, thus improving the quality of generated knowledge.

The *value* is an essential property of ontological knowledge. Principles of value gradation are the following: knowledge *orientation* (disposition "well/badly"); *intensity* (expressiveness degree of value of knowledge elements); *preferability* (a value distinction and establishing an order for value); *includability* (consistency of given value with other values). Value is expressed in *evaluative proposition*. It includes: the object of evaluation (knowledge element); character

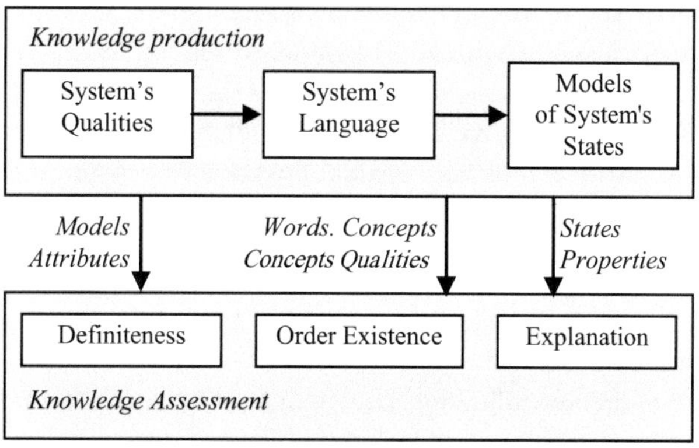

Figure 7. Relationship of cognitive process with value-based, evaluative process.

of evaluation (absolute or comparative); basis of evaluation (aspect of estimating); and the subject of evaluation. *Absolute evaluation* is being applied towards one evaluative object, is expressed in terms of "well/badly," and uses a concept of ideal. *Comparative evaluation* is being applied to at least two objects or two states of the same object, and is expressed in terms of "better/worse." Preference relation is being introduced through comparative evaluation. In general case, an absolute evaluative concept cannot be defined through comparative evaluative concept and vice versa.

Ideal is the starting point in forming absolute evaluations. Ideal is being perceived as a methodological construction which is constitutive for evaluation process and plays role of semantic invariant for different certain forms of the system's representation. Such invariant discloses value content and sets an absolute expression of value or the expression that should be. Ideal is a form of rational understanding, creating, and transforming techniques of the system's representation. Rationality and constructibility of ideal are being manifested through concepts of essentiality, allness, fullness, perfection, and integrity of knowledge. Ideals are always unconditional, absolute, and self-sufficient. A concept "*Sample*" is introduced for rational figuration of the sense of ideal. If the system's senses in ontological knowledge obtain certain figuration, but at the same time some semantic moments of the values have not obtained absolute and unconditional expression then ideal is being replaced by norm. *Norm* is a concept similar to ideal but it differs by its concreteness, attachment to forms of the system's representation. Norms is being determined on the basis of rules and implemented in samples.

Estimating a value is inextricably linked with estimate (a tool of value perception). Evaluation arises from comparison act and recommendations about how to choose what can be recognized as a value. Formed judgments about utility or harm, correctness or incorrectness, necessity or non-necessity of that which is being estimated are the result of such estimation. Axiological evaluations link theory and its application in practice. Emphasis is made on the practice.

The formalism of scientific method is provided by the action schemes with knowledge elements whereby the method applicability with evaluated level of quality of obtained knowledge is being achieved. The nature of evaluations can be qualitative and quantitative. Each value estimate conveys the intensity degree of value expression on the basis of *relevant graduated scale*. Scales that are used at absolute evaluations fix position of the ideal or norm. The ordinal scales are used at comparative evaluations. Both evaluations characterize the relation of evaluation object to the ideal (absolute evaluations) or to the beginning of order (comparative evaluations). *In POS, for each evaluation basis, the special scale is being created*. All objects being estimated in accordance to this basis are comparable on this scale.

Knowledge about the system is being represented in three formats: *data base and knowledge base*; *panels to display knowledge*; and *normative documented reports*. System knowledge in all its forms of representation creates following knowledge resources: information resource; intellectual resource; cognitive resource; and technological resource.

Information resource—represents empirical data about the system, ones being evaluated through fullness and representativeness using technology of forming system's context. A variable of the system's state is the central object of information resource. Technologies of AC POS form the system context of each quantity. This context includes variables' attributes and evaluative propositions about variables. Into this context, TSR introduces knowledge about system roles of variables and about their contributions into organization of system models. Into this resource, TSE adds evaluations of variables ability to manifest, discover, express, and perceive system senses. TSD completes creation of the system's context by obtaining knowledge that is explaining the mechanisms of quantities variability in the system's states.

Intellectual resource—contains reconstructive families of system models. A system model of the system's eigen quality is the main object of intellectual resource. TSR produces this model, namely creates contexts of models of the system's eigen qualities and computes their integral evaluations. TSE includes evaluations characterizing the system's ability to express its eigen qualities, into the models contexts. TSD finalizes construction of this resource by evaluation of synthesis of sense and fact.

Technological resource—is a family of models of implementation forms of standards and a family of models of actual states of the system, that are being produced by TSD. This resource represents system contexts of output objects (qualities and states of the system) of POS in complete form.

Qualimetric component of AC POS adds qualities evaluations of all its elements to informational, intellectual, and technological resources of knowledge. Contexts of all objects of TSR, TSE, and TSD are used to obtain the evaluations. Qualimetric component represents elements of axiological knowledge in the form of normative documented reports:

- *the report "Evaluations of information resource of knowledge"*—contains value estimations for elements of ontological knowledge on empirical and system level in accordance to categories "Indicators" and "Structures of relations," for representation forms named "Systems in data" and "Systems in relations;"
- *the report "Evaluations of intellectual resource of knowledge"*—includes value estimations of the representation "Systems in qualities" on system level and on verification level in according with representation forms named "System models" and "Clusters of objects;"
- *the report "Evaluations of technological resource of knowledge"*—contains value estimations for elements of ontological knowledge in relation to categories "Indicators", "System models," "Clusters of objects," and "Models of states" for representation forms named "Systems in data," "Systems in relations," "Systems in qualities," "Systems in standards," "Systems in implementation forms of standards", and "Systems in states."

Value-based and evaluative propositions complete the process of generating system knowledge. Knowledge elements are being endowed with attributes of correctness, fullness, and completeness. The objectivity of ontological knowledge (about the system) is determined by degree of knowledge approximation to the truth. The objectivity is related to effectiveness of evaluative propositions that indicates to what extent evaluation engenders trust in the results of processes of cognition, scientific understanding, and rational explanation of the ontology of open systems.

4.4. The place of AC POS in the technological platform for creating and exploiting knowledge about open system

The technological platform (TP) of POS automatically solves the problems of producing, storing, circulating, and exploiting system knowledge [16]. TP POS includes four components: an analytical core, as well as descriptive, constructive, and projective components (**Figure 8**).

AC POS—is the main part of TP POS. Technologies of AC POS automatically mine scientifically proven ontological knowledge about the system and the system problems from huge amount of heterogeneous empirical data, and automatically research correctness, fullness, and completeness of the obtained ontological knowledge.

Descriptive component TP POS includes the following technologies: technology of problems' vision and technology of forming empirical context. *Technology of problems' vision*

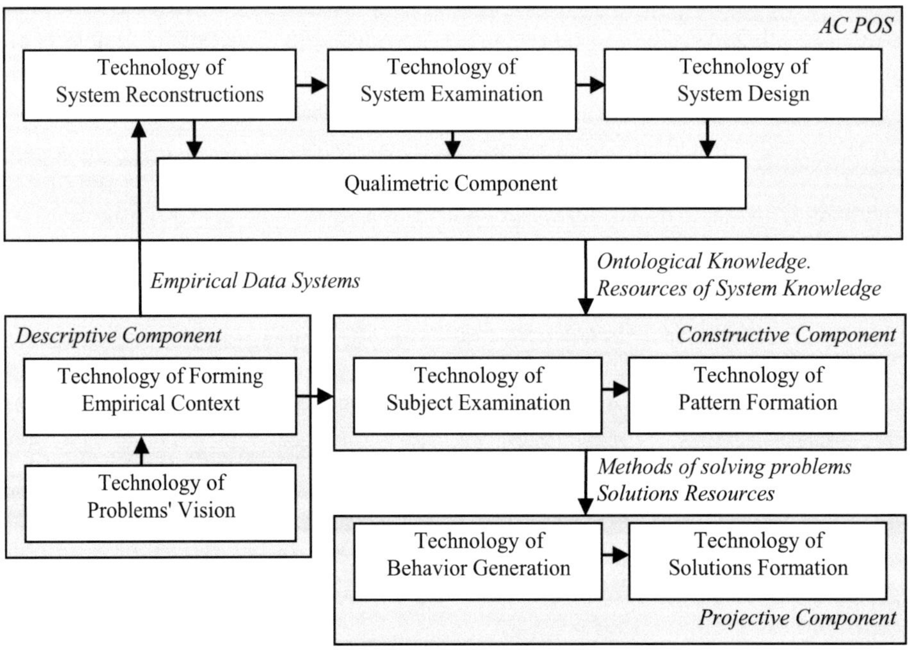

Figure 8. Layout of TP POS.

provides isolation and interdisciplinary verbal description of the system and the system problems. *Technology of forming empirical context* supports the creation of a huge amount of empirical data about certain open system and the applied system problems being researched. Its task is to transform multidimensional and multi-purpose vision of the system problems into their formed initial empirical context, whereby the "raw" initial data about the system and the system problems are being represented as normatively arranged EDS.

Constructive component of TP POS automatically transforms ontological knowledge about the system and knowledge resources obtained by AC POS into *solutions methods and solutions resources* for *general system problems*. Both, technology of subject examination and technology of pattern formation represent the constructive component of POS. *The technology of subject examination* converts ontological knowledge and resources of knowledge about the system into a description of the ontology of a particular subject area and the ontology of relevant applied problems being solved. *The technology of pattern formation* leads elements of system knowledge to formats taking into account a specificity of the subject area of the system problems provides automatic tasks solving and automatic filling the normative templates for documenting obtained results.

Projective component of TP POS applies the methods and solutions resources obtained by the constructive component for creating "pure-subject" interfaces to subject matter specialists, modeling environments, and data mining (DM) platforms. Both, technology of behavior generation and the technology of solutions formation are parts of the projective component. *The technology of behavior generation* is responsible for automatic generating:

- objective cognitive models of solutions of the problems on the basis of their subject ontologies and quantitative forms of system solutions;
- behavioral portraits of the solutions revealing the system's properties by modeling its variability in slices of space and time, events, states, situations, and changes.

The technology of solutions formation shapes the libraries of standard schemes for solving applied problems, develops and uses programs that are solvers for system problems.

A complete technological cycle of both automatic mining scientifically proven knowledge about open system from huge amount of empirical data and automatic generating the solutions of system problems by the methods of multidimensional knowledge-centric system analytics is objectified in TP POS in accordance to common scenario (**Figure 9**).

Clusters for research and technological development (RTD-clusters) are created within TP POS. They perform researches and developments in the following subject areas: "Safety (radiological, chemical, and social);" "System biology and Computational toxicology;" "Medicine and Extreme medicine;" "Planetary Physics and Solar-terrestrial physics;" and "System engineering."

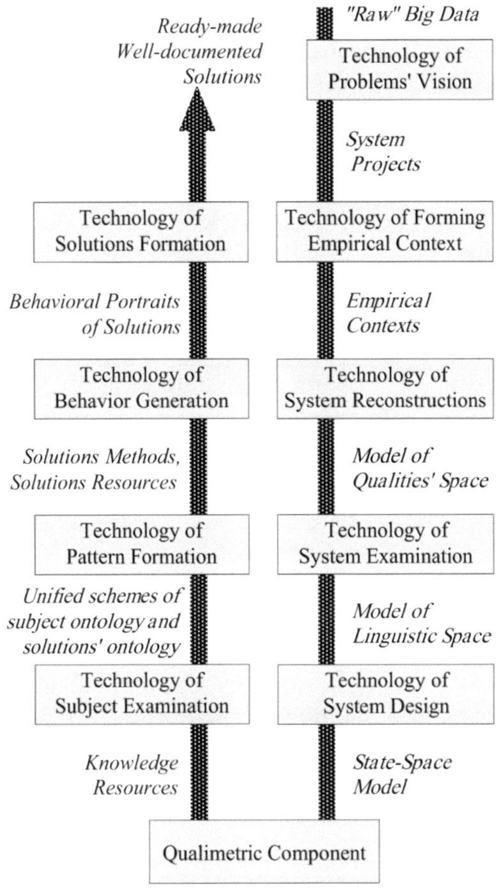

Figure 9. Scheme of technological process of TP POS.

5. Multidimensional knowledge-centric system analytics

5.1. Constructive component of TP POS

Scientifically proven ontological knowledge obtained from empirical descriptions of open systems by technologies of AC POS is expressed in the language of systems and does not have a subject format. Translating obtained knowledge into subject format requires creating expression tools able to link an understanding of revealed senses of the states as well as intra-system mechanisms of forming the system's states with their manifestations in subject areas of knowledge (**Figure 10**).

Constructive component of TP POS is intended for *developing methods of multidimensional knowledge-centric system analytics and creating resources of solutions* of general system problems in complex subject areas. Constructive component chooses elements of ontological knowledge that are needed to solve general system problems, transforms selected knowledge elements to

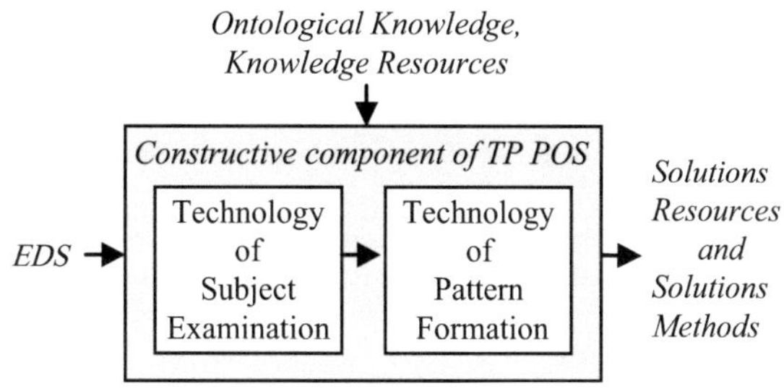

Figure 10. Composition and structure of constructive component.

General system problem	Readiness of solutions			
	2012	2014	2016	2018
Differential gene expression in accordance to microarray data	(5)	(5)	(5)	(5)
Natural system classification	(3)	(5)	(5)	(5)
Typology of system effects of multifactorial influences	—	(5)	(5)	(5)
Identification of states, events, situations	—	—	(4)	(5)
Forecast of states, events, situations, and changes	—	—	(3)	(5)
System comparativistics	(3)	(3)	(4)	(5)

Table 1. Becoming multidimensional knowledge-centric system analytics in TP POS: (3)—A laboratory layout; (4)—A prototype in real environment; (5)—A full readiness.

formats taking into account a specificity of the subject contexts of general system problems, solves applied problems, and creates templates for grapho-analytical processing of ready-made solutions. The work products of technologies of constructive component (solutions resources and methods for solving system problems) serve to develop the *programs-solvers and RTD-clusters of subject areas* in projective component of TP POS.

5.2. The general system problems

Constructive component of TP POS produces and uses scientific methods for solving general system problems of multidimensional knowledge-centric system analytics of open systems which work with hundreds and thousands of variables without resorting to simplifications, expert knowledge, subjective analysis, and interpretations (**Table 1**).

Methods to solve problems with using a general ontology of open systems are created in accordance to common scenario:

- forming an initial empirical context of general system problem;
- transforming the initial empirical context of the problem into representation "System in Data;"

- mining scientifically proven, scientifically understood, rationally explained, and estimated ontological knowledge from the "System in Data;"
- substantiating the idea of the method of solving general system problem on the basis of ontological knowledge;
- developing the model of the method of solving the problem;
- developing the formal objects, functionality, and mathematical base of the method of solving the problem;
- scaling values of this formal objects belonging to the method of solving the problem;
- creating normative template for processing automatically generated solution of the problem.

5.3. The problem about effects of the influence of chemical stressors on differential gene expression

Technologies of system biology are able to obtain EDS about gene expression of the whole genomes of different biosystems. The representations of gene ontology (GO) are used to isolate the system. The set of genes is structured in three representations (http://www.genetools.no), which map biological process, molecular functions, and cellular components, respectively. In each representation, the ontology has hierarchical structure. GO-categories correspond to structure levels. Each GO-category includes certain gene set (from hundreds to several thousands). In each GO-category, genes are endowed by some semantic homogeneity. Each GO-representation and any GO-category can be viewed as an open system, within which the gene expression (as a reaction to chemical influence) can be researched by methods of POS. An important domain of application of POS technologies is related to complex problems in system biology. These problems are connected with reconstructions of gene networks as well as reconstructions of metabolic, regulatory systems of cells, tissues, organs, and organisms. These reconstructions are being performed on the basis of the analysis of multidimensional heterogeneous experimental data being obtained by the microarray technology. Application of multidimensional knowledge-centric system analytics of POS open new opportunities for developing evidence-based system biology regarding actual problems of clinical genomics, transcriptomics, proteomics, metabolomics, and genetic toxicology.

Purposeful studies that use microarray technologies are conducted to reveal natural responses of biosystems to chemical actions. The parameters of experiments in such studies are the type and concentration of chemical, and time series. Each study provides the measured values of the expression levels of tens of thousands of genes. Different biological objects can react to same dose of a chemical by different levels of activity of the same gene. Repeated tests are conducted at the points of experiments for reproducibility of results. From the viewpoint of systems science, analysis of such huge amount of data is an important problem in bioinformatics.

Biosystems' reaction to chemicals arises as a result of coordination of multiple intrasystem processes influencing variation of gene activity. The multiplicity and variety of the effects of toxic stressors exhibit high heterogeneity of biosystems that is hidden in genomic data.

The general problem to discover regularities of the type: "(exposure dose × exposure time) → change of gene activity according to time series," has been solved within the partnership contract with US EPA[1] [17, 18]. The solution method reveals heterogeneous character of expected relationships between gene expression and chemical concentration (in accordance to the time parameter), obtains scientifically proven reconstructions of gene expression profiles, and leads to scientific understanding and rational explanation of revealed regularities. This method is constructed on the basis of *direct application* of general knowledge about the ontology of GO-categories considered as multidimensional biological systems.

The first stage of the method to solve the problem about differential gene expression on the basis of POS—is cognition of the system ontology of variations in the gene activity with respect to following genomic data: knowledge about the system mechanisms that determine levels of gene activity; reconstructions of the states of biological objects; and models of gene activity in the states. The second stage of this method is a filling the system ontology with following estimates: fullness and completeness of system knowledge; qualities of the formal models of standard states; adequacy of the reconstructed states; quality of modeling values of gene activity. The third stage of the method is using the system ontology to reveal natural variations in gene activity with respect to the parameters of the experiment. The method overcomes heterogeneity of genomic data, reveals, and explains gene activity conditioned by genome in the whole, and eliminates uncertainty of system.

5.4. The problem of natural classifying

In classification, two approaches dominate: formally rational (artificial classification) and cognitively substantial (natural classification) [19–23]. Building a natural classification requires a deep development of the ontology of subject area whose classification system is being created. An idea of natural classification directs the activity of classifiers during several centuries. However, until now, it has not led to the creation of scientific method that is a method of rational natural classifying and can be reproduced.

The general problem of natural systemic classifying in complex subject areas has been solved by method of multidimensional knowledge-centric system analytics of POS, and the method herewith can be reproduced [24]. *Conceptualization* of the method is based on three ideas (**Figure 11**). 1—The referents (objects) of classification field (CF) have a semantic unity at the ontological level; 2—POS discovers the *ontology of "CF System;"* 3—ontological knowledge about "CF System" *implicitly contains knowledge about the ontology of CP classes and CP in the whole.*

The ontology of "CF System" evolves into the ontology of CF classes through building the *intension and extension of CF* (*principle of classification duality*). The states of CF referents are determined by "CF System" that reveals the ontology of CF considered as a whole, and expresses the essential properties of CF referents (*principle of systemacity*). Semantic triangle of CF expresses *an idea of the ontology of classes*: classes names (a sign); classes referents (value of a sign); classes content (sense of a sign). Semantic triangle of "CF System" reveals *an idea of the system's ontology*: system

[1]The problem has been solved within ISTC Project No. 3476p "Unified Method of State Space Modeling of Biological Systems" (2006–2011).

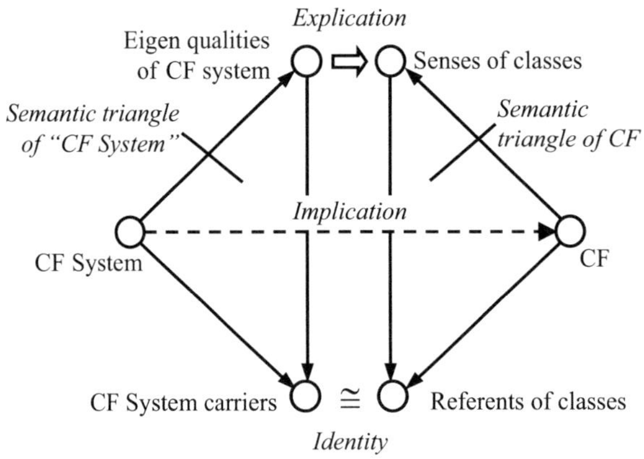

Figure 11. Conceptualization of a method for solving the problem on the basis of ontological knowledge.

name (a sign); system carriers (value of a sign); eigen qualities of the system (sense of a sign). The referents of classes are the real-world objects being observed. Each referent is the carrier of "CF System" (*relationship "Identity"*). The "CF System" is manifested in CF (*relationship "Implication"*). Eigen qualities of "CF System" are being implemented in the properties of classes, in the properties that are manifesting their sense (*relationship "Explication"*). Research of CF has three aspects: semantic (*intensions of classes*); denotative (*extensions of classes*); and estimative (*quality of classification*). Explication of general ontology of "CF System" onto the level of the ontology of the problem of natural classification develops *nominative function of language of systems until the ability to designate classes* (i.e., to disclose intension of CF, intension of CF classes, as well as extensions structures of CF classes and CF as a whole). Classes' archetypes and CF as a whole are explicated in ideal representatives of classes, on whose basis the morphology of each CF class and the morphology of CF, considered as a whole, are established.

The Model of solution method (hereinafter referred to as "model") (**Table 2**).

The classes' names, classes' referents, and the ontology of "CF System" serve as initial data for building the model. Classes' sense is represented by categories "Representation of classes" and "Ontology of classes." Classes' perception is being carried out in two directions: from gradation "Concrete" to gradation "Whole," and from gradation "CF System" to gradation "Extension

Gradation of category "Ontology of classes"	Gradation of category "Representation of classes"		
	Whole	**Part**	**Concrete**
Ontology of "CF System"	Ability to be a carrier of qualities	Nuclearity	System gradation of quantities
Intension of class	Archetype	Parton	Class
Extension of class	Taxon	Prototype	Indicator

Table 2. The model.

of class" accordingly. Gradations of category "Representation of classes" determine *forms of expressing a sense of classes*: the ontology of classes considered as a whole ("Whole"); indivisible semantic units of the ontology of classes ("Part"); and classes' denotata ("Concrete"). Gradations of category "Ontology of classes" indicate *the stages of semantic analysis of classes*: formation base of the ontology of classes (the ontology of "CF System"); semantic component of CF ("Intension of class"); and denotative component of CF ("Extension of class"). The model develops and specifies the conception of solution method, discovers the essence of explication of the ontology of "CF System," as well as generating the intensions and extensions of classes, and represents logically completed conceptual structure of the problem solution:

"System gradation of quantities"—a complete set of primitives to describe CF referents with using a common scale of measurement;

"Nuclearity (Cores of standards)"—standards of state of eigen qualities of "CF System;" the base to reveal invariants of intension of CF;

"Ability to be a carrier of qualities"—a corpus of the texts describing each CF referent through a unique assembly of nuclearities connected by the relations: "Universal/Particular," "Part/Whole," and "Genus/Species;"

"Class"—an element of CF, has a name, and is represented by a set of referents (for each class, the nuclearities dominant in the class are specified);

"Parton"—specific semantic moments of a class; an assembly of nuclearities of the first, second, third, etc., ranks (rank is the number of nuclearities within the parton);

"Archetype"—a hierarchical structure of partons; a reconstruction of class intension;

"Indicator"—a property objectively inherent in CF referents (a discretization of variables values of the referents is introduced through the concept "System gradation of quantities;" on this basis, the indicators-markers able to recognize a class in CF are discovered);

"Prototype"—a center of denotatum (extension) of a class; an idealized class referent where the idea of class archetype is expressed through a set of constituents (indicators);

"Taxon"—a structure of CF denotatum; it specifies six areas of referents for each CF class.

Method of natural system classification (hereinafter referred to as "method") asserts the reality of essential indicators, the reality of classes, the reality of taxons, and the reality of archetypes. The model serves as a basis for this method. The method defines the essential indicators of classes in a scientific and constructive manner. *Homologized eigen parts of class archetype (partons)* play the role of such indicators. Observed (measurable) indicators, as a part of parton, are specified by the name and level of value, are markers for classes, and have ability to distinguish classes. They are not in themselves natural indicators but rather express some properties objectively inherent in referents of classes.

Method produce scientifically proven system knowledge about the ontology of CF classes and on the basis of this knowledge creates and applies natural classification systems in accordance to the following statements:

- initial description of the system in data is considered as a whole without dividing into parts, related to testing and learning; the solution is being built on the basis of scientifically proven knowledge mined from all variety of CF referents;
- in generating knowledge about ontology of "CF System," the initial information about whether the referents belong or do not belong to certain classes is not used;
- explication of knowledge about the ontology of "CF System" *consists in developing nominative function of the language* of systems, this function should provide a designation of CF classes;
- invariant parts of the models of implementation forms of standards of "CF System" act in a role of system homologs of classes (*idea of homology*);
- variables and system homologs are able to distinguish classes (*idea of dominance*);
- pure manifestation of system homologs takes place in separate groups of classes' referents (*idea of compatibility*);
- variables and system homologs characterize a class (*idea of the frequency of occurrence*);
- each class is represented by carriers of its senses (*idea of referential conformity*);
- ideal sample of referent being the prototype of a class, represents this class (*idea of prototypicality*);
- relation between the prototype and referents of a class is homomorphic (*idea of likeness*).

Method uses four representations of CF: "CF in referents of classes;" "CF as a system;" "CF in problem space;" and "CF in solution space" (**Figure 12**).

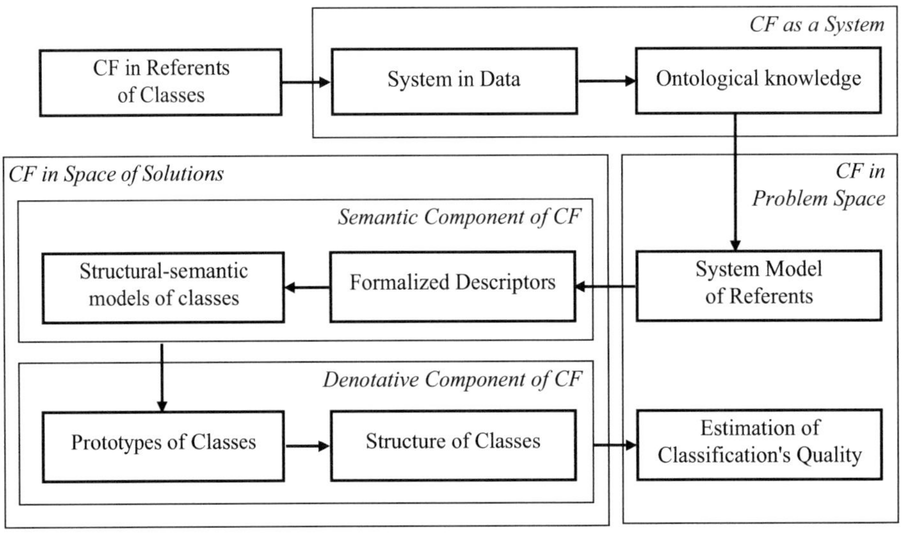

Figure 12. Structural scheme of the method.

Formal computable objects of the method are compatible with the model concepts. Intension of each CF class is represented in solution space by the multilevel hierarchical *structural-semantic model* of systemic natural indicators (formalized descriptors) of a class. Fullness and completeness of representing the intensions of classes through structural-semantic models guarantee a high solution quality of the classification problem *on its entire classification universe.* Structural-semantic models of classes are defined in the set of formalized descriptors (*partons*) of solution model by relations: "*Universal/Particular*," "*Part/Whole*," and "*Genus/Species.*" *Core* of structural-semantic model contains formalized descriptors able to identify class as a whole. Model's periphery includes descriptors characterizing separate groups of class referents, but not a class as a whole. *Center* of structural-semantic model is defined on the basis of its core through *constituents of CF denotatum.*

CF in problem space answers to question about the possibility of solving the problem on the basis of the ontology of "CF System" and characterizes the quality of obtained solution. Fullness and representativity of the initial representation of CF in referents; knowledge value of the ontology of CF where CF is considered as a whole system; correct and full representation of intensions of CF classes as well as and intension of CF as a whole; and perfection of procedures for building classes extensions and extension of CF as a whole—all these define solutions quality of classification problems.

Functionality of the method is shown in **Figure 13**.

Syntagmatic analysis finds full sets of semantic indicators of classes, where the indicators are formalized descriptors. These sets arise as a result of right combinations (assemblies) of nuclearities. Such combinations generate descriptors of certain ranks in accordance to following restrictions: relationship to a class; relationship between quantities; domination in a class. Semantics of CF classes is defined by sets of formalized descriptors and particular paradigmatic relations between descriptors of classes. *Paradigmatic analysis* provides creation of constructive definition of structural-semantic models (intensions) of classes. *Prototyping* provides

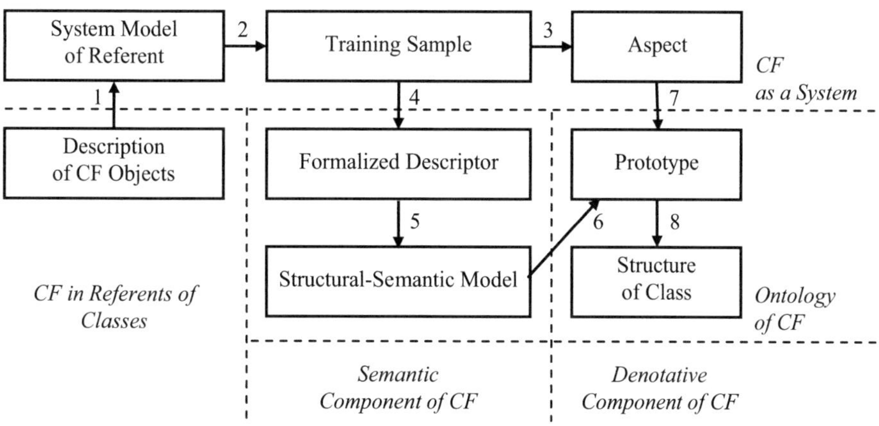

Figure 13. Functional scheme of the method: 1—Generation of ontological knowledge; 2 and 3—Distribution of nuclearities (indicators); 4—Syntagmatic analysis; 5—Paradigmatic analysis; 6 and 7—Prototyping; 8—Taxonomy.

construction of the representatives (in the model they are prototypes) of classes. Prototype of each class is specified by the set of natural indicators of a class. Each indicator as a part of representative is dominant. *Taxonomic approach* constructively defines denotatum (extension) of a class. Representative of each class sets in CF the area of denotatum of a class. In this area, the representative is the center (base point) of a class. Measure of proximity to the base point defines the organization of denotatum. Referents of all classes in CF obtain indicators of belonging to one of six areas of denotatum: center area (prototype of a class); core's area (objects are the prototype analogues); area around core (typical objects of a class); area of close (far) periphery (objects have sufficient (weakly expressed) proximity to the prototype); area of exclusion (the objects whose belonging to this class is doubtful—i.e., another's objects).

Composition of classes in CF is initially defined by experts. The method perceives it exclusively as a condition for detailed scientific research whose purpose is cognition, understanding, and a rational explanation of the given composition of classes. The problem's solution is of high value if all referents of CF classes belong to the area of centers attraction of the same classes; herewith the areas of exclusion of all CF classes are empty. Presence of referents in the area of exclusion of CF denotatum, together with the nature of distribution of the referents of each CF class by the areas of denotatum structure manifest degree of classes' homogeneity and validate correctness of initial statement of the classification problem. The solution reveals senses of CF classes, discovers the structure of CF denotatum, and gives to each class of CF a scientific validation or reasoned denial.

Solution of the problem of natural system classification of acute poisoning with organophosphorus substances can serve as an illustration of the method possibilities [25]. Organic phosphates, which have insect-killing effects (carbophos (malathion), dichlorvos, chlororvos (trichlorovon), methaphos (parathion methyl), thiophos (parathion)), have found broad use in agriculture and in house life. They are very toxic substances and pose a hazard to populations. The problem of acute poisoning with organophosphorus chemical warfare agents (Vx-gases, sarin, and soman) has taken on special significance in connection with destruction of chemical weapons. Clinical symptoms and signs of acute poisoning with organophosphorus warfare agents as well as with pesticides possessing insect-killing effects have much in common. The abnormalities arising in human organism in the event of poisoning with organophosphorus substances are extremely complex and insufficiently studied. In the event of acute poisoning with organophosphorus substances, the complexity of how the abnormalities develop is shown through multifactorial genesis of diseases, polymorphism of clinical semiology, and the reasons of a syndrome.

5.5. The problem of defining typology of system effects of multifactor influences

Method of solving the problem is published in [26]. High dimensionality of used data (hundreds and thousands of variables), data heterogeneity, a big number of acting factors and reacting variables, as well as measurement methods—all these define the problem complexity of system effects. Field of multifactor effects (FME) is represented as an empirical description of the system ("System in Data"). Each FME object sets one particular actual state of the system, the state that is represented by a vector of variables values which is the same for all objects. Concrete values of acting factors (tens and hundreds) correspond in this vector to concrete values of reacting variables (tens and hundreds).

The idea for solving the problem of regular relationship between acting factors and reacting variables implies cognition of the ontology of "FME System," and (on its basis) getting the ontology of system effects of multifactor influence (**Figure 14**).

The ontology of "FME System" implicitly contains knowledge about system effects in FME and is explicated on the ontology level of the problem. Language of systems together with nominative function also carries out a predicative function. "FME System" predetermines the topology of multifactor effects (relationship "Implication"). Relationship "Explication 1" signifies that eigen qualities of "FME System" is being transformed into propositional structures and predicates of significative scheme of FME, which, in turn, defines denotative scheme of FME. Relationship "Explication 2" expresses development, detailed elaboration, specification, and a concrete definition of the denotative schema of FME by its insight into system context. Knowledge about the ontology of FME is represented by significative and denotative schemes. For each reacting variable, the significative scheme sets general appearance of prototypical influence. On its basis, the set of predicates explaining any particular variant of the influence, as well as effect on this influence is defined. Denotative scheme sets models of all actual types of effects on the influences and defines the topology of the system's response to these influences.

The model of solution method (hereinafter referred to as "model") introduces key concepts of the method for solving the problem (**Table 3**).

The model defines and expresses the sense of concept "System effect of influence" in categories "FME Representation" and "FME Ontology." The system's ontology and the sets of both acting and reacting quantities are the initial data of the model. On the basis of the ontology of "FME System," the model discovers the structure of semantic, denotative, and estimative components of FME. The ontology of FME is implicitly contained in the ontology of "FME System." Perception of multifactor system effects is being carried out:

- by category "FME Representation"—in direction from gradation "Concrete" to gradation "Whole;"
- by category "FME Ontology"—in direction from gradation "Ontology of FME system" to gradation "Extension."

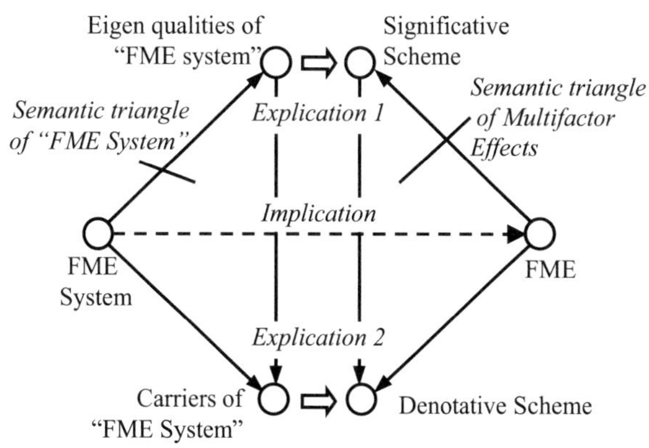

Figure 14. Method conceptualization.

Gradation of category "FME Ontology"	Gradation of category "FME Representation"		
	Whole	**Part**	**Concrete**
Ontology of "FME System"	System predication	Determination of quantities' levels	System gradation of quantities
Intension	Semantic relationship	Prototypical significant	Inputs–Output
Extension	Semantic dominant of the effect	Actual content of the effect	Object

Table 3. The model.

Gradations of category "FME Representation" specify various forms of expressing the senses of system effects of influence. Gradation "Concrete" specifies variables of state of the system and its environment in each actual state through disposition "Inputs - output." Gradation "Part" reveals indivisible semantic units of the ontology of FME. These units are: determined levels of quantities' values; sets of values' levels of acting factors; values of reacting variables specific to the levels of values; and actual variants of system effects. Gradation "Whole" defines the ontology of FME in the whole by means of following full sets:

- of states' standards of eigen qualities of the system;
- of semantic relationships between acting factors and reacting variables;
- of typical system effects of multifactor influences.

Gradations of category "FME Ontology" indicate the stages of semantic analysis of system effects. Gradation of "Ontology of FME System" sets the base for forming the ontology of system effects. Gradation "Intension" reveals organization of significative scheme of effects of influences. Gradation "Extension" defines the denotative scheme of the effects.

Key concepts of the model:

- "*System gradation of quantities*"—a full set of primitives designed for describing the values of state variables of the system and environment with using a common scale of measurement; by thus, an opposition of high and low levels of quantities' values determined by the system itself is being revealed.
- "*Determination of quantities' levels*"—full sets of system models statistically distinguishing levels of values of particular variables. They establish statistical relationships between variables and standards of eigen qualities of "FME System," relationships that explain actual states of the system.
- "*System predication*"—a full set of statistically derived relations "standard of states - level of quantity's value". Distinctive ability of standards can be weak (statistically determined) or strong (determined by the system and statistically).

- *"Inputs - output"*—a disposition of acting factors and reacting variables. A set of acting factors is specified in compliance with research objectives. Any reacting variable is being chosen from a target set of quantities whose variability types should be disclosed.
- *"Prototypical significant"*—a set of acting factors whose action is significant and which belong to the set of inputs determining levels variability of values of each reacting variable.
- *"Semantic relationship"*—a certain type of relations between acting factors and reacting variables. These relations disclose the types of implementation forms for prototypical significant, which determines an invariant relation between the values' levels of acting quantities and the value level of reacting quantity.
- *"Object"*—a certain object of the solution space.
- *"Actual content of the (multifactor) effect"*—a specific form of carrier of the regularity explaining variability of reacting variable.
- *"Semantic dominant of the (multifactorial) effect"*—a semantic filter based on oppositions of the indicators of actual contents that structures a denotative area of multifactorial effects.

Method for solving the problem (hereinafter referred to as "method") defines the topology of effects for each (and any) reacting variable in accordance to the stated set of acting factors. Specific sets of standards of the states of eigen system qualities rationally explain every *type of effect*. For each reacting variable *the typology of its system response is stated*. It is given by a set of significant acting factors which are gathered from *an ideal sample* of the relation "Multifactor influence – System effect." For any reacting variable, the method guarantees the following:

- obtaining the *prototypical significant*;
- constructing the *prototypical denotatum*;
- defining the *full set of types of system response to any possible options for multifactor influences*.

For each referent of FME, the method allows to obtain new format of representation. In this format, both a variation of influence and a set of types of the system's responses that are established by the corresponding model and macrostructure of the effect are fixed. *On full set of referents*, there is a general problem of the typology of global system. Its solution will answer about system reaction of all reacting variables to any multifactor influence. It is a key problem of the qualitative theory of open systems.

Computable objects of the method correspond to concepts of the model (**Table 4**):

Relations between formal objects of the method are derived from relations between concepts of the model. Constructive forms of the relations of generating and transforming objects define functionality of the method (**Figure 15**).

Concept of the model	Object of the method
System gradation of quantities	System in graduated data
Determination of quantities' levels	Parameter in the system whole
System predication	Actantial structure of standard
Inputs-Output	Target list of parameters
Prototypical significant	Ideal sample of the relation "Influence - effect"
Semantic relationship	Role semantics of predicate
Object	Carrier of the effect
Actual content of multifactor effect	Model of system effect
Semantic dominant of the effect	Macrostructure of the effect

Table 4. Relatedness of concepts of the model with computable objects of the method.

Production of system knowledge about the ontology of FME is provided by AC POS. *Selection of target variables*: acting factors are specified, reacting variable is selected. *The system's representation in graduated data*: scales for measuring levels of quantities' values are transformed into scales which are graduated by the system itself. *Effect's localization*: for all actual states of the system, in which all system effects of multifactor influences are defined, the models of reconstructions are created. *Quantities distribution*: on the basis of models of reconstructions, the frequencies of

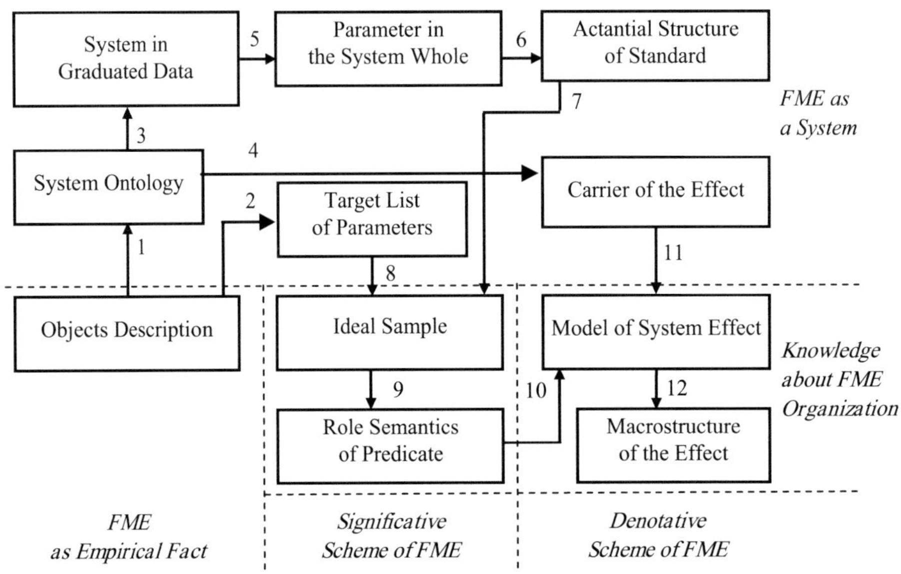

Figure 15. Functional scheme of the method: 1—Production of system knowledge; 2—Selection of target variables; 3—The system's representation in graduated data; 4—Effect's localization; 5—Quantities distribution; 6—Definition of valences; 7 and 8—Prototyping; 9—Role estimation; 10 and 11—Frame filling; 12—Revealing the typology of effects.

combinations of system variables and standards of the system's states are obtained, and statistical significance of these combinations is defined as well. *Definition of valences*: domination of states' standards is semantically determined; each standard of a state correlates with a certain set of actants, whereby its valence is being defined; the set of states' standards forms a complex structure of relations with actants. *Prototyping*: for each reacting variable, the set of standards is defined and the structures of actants of these standards contain this variable. The structures of actants include acting factors. The state's standard corresponding with such structure is the *standard-predicate* for these acting factors. Standard-predicate establishes relation between particular acting factor and reacting variable. This relation is statistically confirmed. The result is a list of significant acting factors that caused system response of reacting variable.

For each acting factor, the sign of statistical relationship with reacting variable is defined. *Prototypical denotatum*: each level of values of reacting variable is a prototype for a system response to an influence. *Prototypical significant*: is put into correspondence with prototypical denotatum, and is represented by typical set of levels of values of acting factors. *Role estimation*: classes of role semantics of standard-predicates are introduced for all referents of the relation "Influence - effect" (these classes are: "Action," "State," "Relation," "Indicator," and "Property"). *Frame filling*: for each particular result of role estimation, the localization of system effect is carried out; a set of attributes which characterize the effect of influence in categories of "Statal"/"Actional" is obtained. *Revealing the typology of effect* is made as a result of *multi-criteria discrimination* of system effects. Criteria of typological analysis of the effects are built on the basis of semantic oppositions. *Semantic oppositions*: are the combinations of criteria values, which characterize:

- certain simulated situation of multifactor influence, here the situation is considered in its full system context;
- system significance of attributes of variables and states' standards, the significance is being evaluated in the categories of "Statal"/"Actional."

Solving the problem of interventional cardiology serves as an illustration for the method possibilities [27]. Restenosis and in-stent thrombosis after percutaneous coronary intervention (PCI) is the essential clinical and socioeconomic problem in high technology medical care in ischemic heart disease (IHD). Special aspects of developing restenosis and in-stent stenosis, and of how individual sensitivity to antiplatelet drugs arises—all of these, in each particular case, are defined by combining a multitude of various pathogenetic factors (clinical, anatomic-morphological, molecular-genetic, biochemical, and technical) [28]. Advantages of the method is: broad coverage of the problem being researched in its natural scale and real complexity; taking into account the multiplicity of different factors influencing restenosis development; and a holistic view on pathophysiology of restenosis and thrombosis that occur after intracoronary stenting in patients with IHD. Multidimensional data array was obtained as a result of examination of the patients with IHD, and who have acute coronary syndrome after PCI with stenting. These data was obtained under inpatient treatment of these patients at FSBI "Federal Heart, Blood and Endocrinology Centre n.a. V.A. Almazov", Saint Petersburg.

Author details

Tamara L. Kachanova, Boris F. Fomin and Oleg B. Fomin*

*Address all correspondence to: bfomin@mail.ru

Faculty of Computer Science and Technology, Saint-Petersburg Electrotechnical University (SPbETU "LETI"), Saint-Petersburg, Russia

References

[1] Klimantovich Y. Introduction to Physics of Open Systems [in Russian]. Moscow: Janus-K; 2002. p. 284. ISBN: 5-8037-0101-7

[2] Kachanova T, Fomin B. Reconstruction of Complex Systems Behavior Using Experimental Data [in Russian]. Preprint 1. St. Petersburg: ETU ("LETI") Publishing Center; 1997. p. 67

[3] Kachanova T, Fomin B. Symmetries, Interactions in Localities, Behavior Components of Complex Systems. Preprint 2 [in Russian]. St. Petersburg: ETU ("LETI") Publishing Center; 1998. p. 126

[4] Kachanova T, Fomin B. Foundations of the Systemology of Phenomena [in Russian]. St. Petersburg: ETU ("LETI"), Publishing Center; 1999. p. 180. ISBN 5-7629-0293-5

[5] Kachanova T, Fomin B. Introduction into Language of Systems [in Russian]. St. Petersburg: Nauka; 2009. p. 340. ISBN 978-5-02-025360-5

[6] Kachanova T, Fomin B. Physics of systems is a postcybernetic paradigm of systemology. In: Proc. of Intern. Sympos. "Science 2.0 and Expansion of Science: S2ES" in the Context of the 14th World-Multi-Conference (WMSCI 2010); June 29th - July 2nd 2010. USA, Orlando, Florida: IIIS; 2010. pp. 244-249. ISBN: 978-193633800-9

[7] Kachanova T, Fomin B. Qualitology of System Knowledge: A Manual for Masters and Postgraduate Students [in Russian], St. Petersburg: ETU ("LETI"), Publishing Center; 2014. ISBN 978-5-7629-1488-8

[8] Ivin A. Axiology [in Russian]. Moscow: Publishing House "Vysshaya Shkola"; 2007. p. 392. ISBN 5-06-005308-3

[9] Mikeshina L. Axiological Basics in the Structure of Scientific Knowledge [in Russian]. Prometei: Moscow; 1990. p. 208

[10] Kachanova T, Fomin B. Meta-Technology of System Reconstructions [in Russian]. St. Petersburg: ETU ("LETI"), Publishing Center; 2002. p. 336. ISBN 5-7629-0439-3

[11] Kachanova T, Fomin B. Physics of open systems: Generation of system knowledge. JSCI. 2013;**11**(2):73-82. ISSN: 1690-4524

[12] Kachanova T, Fomin B. Cognition of ontology of open systems. Procedia Computer Science Journal Elsevier B.V. 2017;**103**:339-346. DOI: 10.1016/j.procs.2017.01.119

[13] Ageev V, Kachanova T, Fomin B, Fomin O. Language of open systems and expertise of system knowledg [in Russian]. In: Proc. of 9th Intern. Conf. System Identification and Control Problems (SICPRO'09); 26-30 January 2009. Russia. Moscow: V. A. Trapeznikov Institute of Control Sciences RAS; 2009. pp. 1-46

[14] Kachanova T, Fomin B. The Methods and Technologies for Generating a Systemic Knowledge: A Manual for Masters and Postgraduate Students [in Russian]. St. Petersburg: ETU ("LETI"), Publishing Center; 2012. p. 132. ISBN 978-5-7629-1197-9

[15] Kachanova T, Fomin B. Technology of System Reconstructions [in Russian]. Politechnika: St. Petersburg; 2003. p. 146. ISBN 5-7325-0772-8

[16] Kachanova T, Fomin B. Knowledge-centric analytics of multidimensional open systems [in Russian]. In: Proc. of 9-Th Multi-Conference "Information Technologies in Control (ITC-2016)" within the 7-Th Russian Multi-Conference on Control Problems (RMCCP 2016). October 04-06. Russia. St. Petersburg: State Research Center of the Russian Federation Concern CSRI Elektropribor; 2016. pp. 121-129

[17] Ageev V, Fomin B, Fomin O, Kachanova T, Chen C, Spassova M, Kopylev L. Physics of open systems: A new approach to use genomics data in risk assessment. In: Tyshenko M, editor. The Continuum of Health Risk Assessments. InTech; 2012. pp. 135-160. DOI: 10.5772/38805

[18] Ageev V, Fomin B, Fomin O, Kachanova T, Chen C, Spassova M, Kopylev L. Physics of open systems: Effects of the impact of chemical stressors on differential gene expression. Cybernetics and Systems Analysis. 2014;**50**(2):218-227. DOI: 10.1007/s10559-014-9608-6

[19] Meinen SV, Shreider YA. Methodological aspects of classification theory [in Russian]. Voprosy Filosofii. 1976;**12**:67-79. ISSN 0042-8744

[20] Rozova SS. The Classification Problem in Modern Science [in Russian]. Novosibirsk: Nauka; 1986. p. 223

[21] Pavlinov IY. Concepts of rational taxonomy in biology. Biology Bulletin Reviews. 2011;**1**(3):60-78. DOI: 10.1134/S2079086411030078

[22] Lyubarsky G. Archetype, Style and Rank in Biological Systematics [in Russian]. KMK Ltd: Moscow; 1996. p. 434

[23] Kozhara VL. Phenomenon of natural classification [in Russian]. In: Miroshnikov II., Pokrovsky MP., editors. New Ideas in Scientific Classification. Issue 5. Ekaterinburg: UB RAS; 2008. pp. 117-143. ISBN: 978-5-7691-2120-3

[24] Kachanova T, Fomin B. System ontology of classes [in Russian]. Izvestiya SPbGETU ("LETI"). 2015;7:25-36. ISSN 2071-8985

[25] Kachanova T, Fomin B, Turalchuk K, Ageev V. Natural classification of acute poisoning with organophosphorus substances [in Russian]. Izvestiya SPbGETU ("LETI"). 2015;**8**:8-17. ISSN 2071-8985

[26] Kachanova T, Fomin B. System effects of multifactorial influences in open system [in Russian]. Izvestiya SPbGETU ("LETI"). 2017;**1**:28-38. ISSN 2071-8985

[27] Kachanova T, Fomin B. Applying the method of determining typology of system effects of multifactorial influences [in Russian]. Izvestiya SPbGETU ("LETI"). 2017;**2**:19-29. ISSN 2071-8985

[28] Berezovskaya G, Ganyukov V, Karpenko M. Restenosis and in-stent stenosis: Pathogenetic mechanisms and prognostic markers [in Russian]. Russian Journal of Cardiology. 2012;**6** (98):91-95. ISSN: 1560-4071

Chapter 9

Semantic Remote Sensing Scenes Interpretation and Change Interpretation

Fethi Ghazouani, Imed Riadh Farah and
Basel Solaiman

Additional information is available at the end of the chapter

http://dx.doi.org/10.5772/intechopen.72730

Abstract

A fundamental objective of remote sensing imagery is to spread out the knowledge about our environment and to facilitate the interpretation of different phenomena affecting the Earth's surface. The main goal of this chapter is to understand and interpret possible changes in order to define subsequently strategies and adequate decision-making for a better soil management and protection. Consequently, the semantic interpretation of remote sensing data, which consists of extracting useful information from image date for attaching semantics to the observed phenomenon, allows easy understanding and interpretation of such occurring changes. However, performing change interpretation task is not only based on the perceptual information derived from data but also based on additional knowledge sources such as *a prior* and contextual. This knowledge needs to be encoded in an appropriate way for being used as a guide in the interpretation process. On the other hand, interpretation may take place at several levels of complexity from the simple recognition of objects on the analyzed scene to the inference of site conditions and to change interpretation. For each level, information elements such as data, information and knowledge need to be represented and characterized. This chapter highlights the importance of ontologies exploiting for encoding the domain knowledge and for using it as a guide in the semantic scene interpretation task.

Keywords: data, information, knowledge, remote sensing imagery, contextual information, semantic image interpretation, change interpretation, ontologies

1. Introduction

A fundamental objective of remote sensing is to spread out the knowledge about our environment and to facilitate the interpretation of different phenomena affecting the Earth's surface. Indeed, satellite images make possible to observe much more phenomena related to the increase of information acquired from multiple sensors. For instance, these phenomena include climatic change, urbanization, deforestation, desertification, and so on. Remote sensing and SIG communities have a great interest on change analysis and interpretation. Therefore, tools and strategies have been maintained for studying and analyzing the Earth's surface dynamics. The principal objective, here, is to understand and interpret changes that may occur allowing, thus, to define strategies and an adapted decision-making for a better soil management and protection. Change detection, in remote sensing, can be defined as the process of identifying differences in the state of an object or a phenomenon by observing it at different times [1]. Applications associated with change detection include monitoring the evolution of cultures and land use, spatial progression of vegetation, forest and urban monitoring, the analysis of the climate change impacts and other cumulative changes. Several change detection approaches have been proposed in remote sensing. The general objectives of most change detection approaches include identifying the geographic locations and type of changes, quantifying the changes and assessing the accuracy of change detection results [2].

The information levels about changes from the remote sensing imagery can be categorized as (1) change detection level that allows detecting simple binary change (i.e. change vs. non-change). This category includes techniques such as image differencing [3], image rationing [4] and change vector analysis (CVA) [5]. These techniques focus on changes localizing but do not provide any information about the change's nature. (2) The second category (also called thematic level of change) allows the identification of the detailed change "from-to". It includes techniques such as post-classification comparison [6] and classified objects change detection (COCD) [7]. For more details about change detection techniques from remotely sensed images, the reader can refer to the work of [2]. The authors have given an overview of different change detection approaches where a comparison between pixel-based change detection and object-based change detection has been presented. Pixel-based change detection methods exploit the spectral characteristics of an image pixel to detect and measure changes. Although these methods have been successfully implemented in many areas for changes detection using remote sensing data, an important limitation of these approaches is that they do not exploit the spatial context of real objects [2]. To overcome this limitation, object-based approaches have been developed. Object-based change detection approaches, as defined by [8], allow to identify differences in geographic objects at different moments by using object-based analysis. This later allows to obtain, from an object image, information such as shape, texture and spatial relationships allowing the exploitation of the spatial context [2]. Consequently, the inclusion of this contextual information allows to understand the semantics of objects [9].

Up to now, both change detection approaches (i.e. pixel-based and object-based methods) have been successful either for detecting simple binary change/non-change (i.e. answering "are there changes"?) or for detailing "from-to" change between different classes (i.e. what change?). However, at the two levels of change detection (change detection and identification), these approaches do not give any information about the cause of changes (i.e. why and how change?), and, therefore, give no hints on how to evaluate their signification for the decision-making task. Consequently, an interpretation change level is needed for generating a description of the character and causality of change. The change interpretation level, here, allows to extract information from data (images) about changes that may occur, that is, to answer the question "why and how a change has been produced?". As any interpretation level, the change interpretation task is not only based on the perceptual information derived from data, but it requires other knowledge sources such as *a prior* and contextual knowledge to perform the interpretation task. This knowledge needs to be encoded in an appropriate way for being used as a guide into the interpretation process.

Highlighting the role of the remote sensing imagery for change detection and interpretation, an appropriate semantic interpretation method is needed for change interpretation in satellite images. Such methods should take into account the description and the representation of different information elements at each interpretation level. This chapter focuses on semantic scene interpretation for change interpretation in satellite images. Semantic scene interpretation task is composed of different levels of abstraction. The objectives of this chapter are to describe the semantic scene interpretation strategy including the definition and the representation of different information elements composing that process. It is structured in four sections. Section 2 intends to define required fundamental elements for the interpretation task and presents the role of ontologies for the semantic image interpretation. Afterwards, a description of semantic interpretation methods is discussed. Section 3 reviews and classifies approaches for the semantic remote sensing image interpretation. Section 4 presents a proposed method for semantic change interpretation and describes its different components.

2. Semantic interpretation

Remote sensing utility comes not from the data itself but rather from the information that can be derived from this data [10]. For this reason, the interpretation and data transformation into usable information is an important step for the development of user's applications. Interpretation plays an important role in the process of data analysis. It helps users to easily understand the extracted information from remote sensing data. Consequently, the interpretation of this data enables user to make policy and management decisions. To be understandable, data must be transformed into information, and then, into knowledge as shown in **Figure 1**. In this section, we give a meaning to each information element, such as data, information and knowledge, and then we present the interpretation, in a general sense, and the existing interpretation methods.

2.1. Definitions and fundamental elements

There are many definitions and significations of informative elements such as data, information and knowledge. According to [11], *Data* are facts that are the results of observations or measurements we make on objects (artifacts, sites, seeds and bones). In addition, data are defined as primitive symbolic entities, whose meaning depends on its integration within a context allowing its understanding by an interpreter [12]. *Information* is a set of facts with a processing capability added, such as context, relationships to other facts about the same or related objects, implying an increased usefulness. Information provides a meaning to data. It is an organized data answering the following basic questions: What? Who? When? Where? *Knowledge* is information with more context and understanding (answering the following basic questions: why? how? for which purpose?), perhaps with the addition of rules to extend

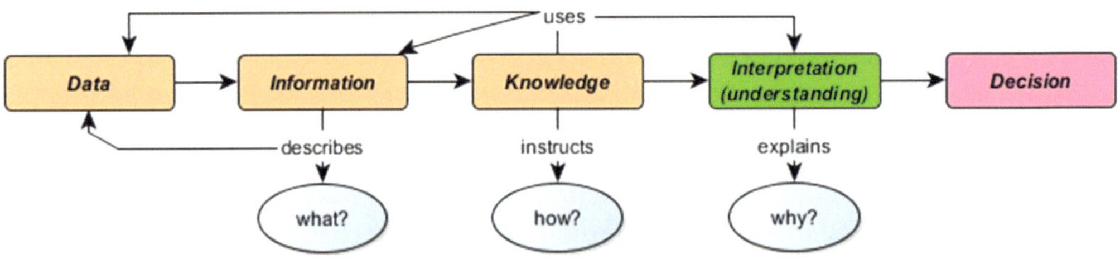

Figure 1. From data to decision-making (relation between information elements).

definitions and allowing inference. According to Pr. H. Moukdad of the Dalhousie University [13], knowledge is a reservoir of information that is stored in the human mind. It essentially constitutes the information that can be "retrieved" from the human mind without the need to consult external information sources [13]. Knowledge is internalized or understood information that can be used to make decisions. These three entities can be viewed hierarchically in terms of complexity, data being the simplest and knowledge being the most complex of the three. Knowledge is the product of a synthesis in our mind that can be conveyed by information, as one of many forms of its externalization and socialization [13]. **Figure 1** shows the relationship between these three different informative elements.

Information comes from different sources, namely data, *prior* and contextual knowledge. Therefore, information must be combined in order to extract significant elements for the interpretation and, subsequently, for decision-making. The information combination is a role associated with the *Fusion Information and Analytic Technology* (*FIAT*) [14]. Indeed, data fusion is the process of combination of data or information from different sources to estimate or predict states of entities. It consists of developing methods that allow the extraction and conciliation, from different knowledge sources, of (significates) expressive elements for decision-making. However, for any interpretation system, its input and its output can take different meanings according to the considered situation. A statement can be either data or information, and it can be knowledge (*a prior* and contextual). Such a situation is very frequent in the case of semantic interpretation of remote sensing images where different interpretation levels can be considered depending on the user outcome. On the other hand, high-level positioning considers a contextual attribution role to the input system for data, information and knowledge. Hence, information processing within the FIAT framework imposes a need to characterize and represent information in order to be exploited for the design of intelligent situation analysis and decision support systems. Moreover, information, according to [15], is the data that is relevant to the considered application. Losee [16] added that information is the value currently attached or instantiated to a characteristic returned by a process or function: information is a relational or functional concepts linking data sets. Linking input sets (called definition sets) to outputs set (called content sets) makes information to be informative.

To resume, an information element (data, information or knowledge), is "an entity composed of a definition set and a content set linked by a functional relationship called informative relation, associated with internal and external context". **Figure 2** shows the general structure of an information element. Lillesand et al. [17], suggest that: "*interpretation may take place at number of levels of complexity, from the simple recognition of objects on scene to the inference of site*

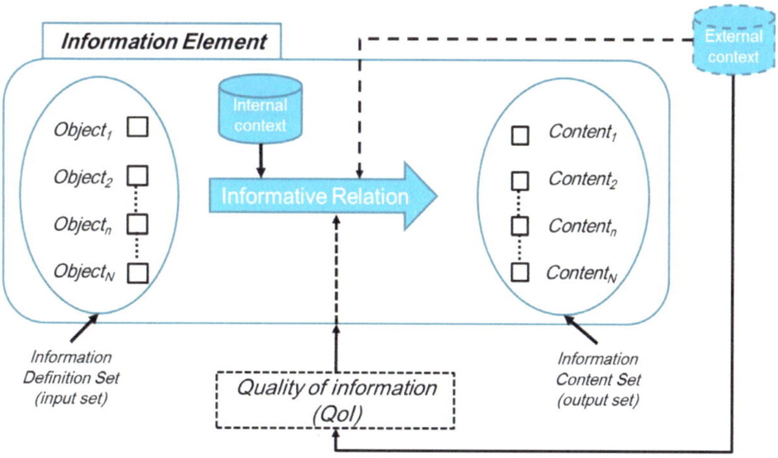

Figure 2. Information element structure [14].

conditions". Therefore, it is important to characterize the information element in each interpretation level. Details of the characterization of the information element are presented in the semantic scene interpretation section.

2.2. Semantic image interpretation

In remote sensing imagery, image interpretation consists of assigning geographic object types to image objects [18]. A geographic object, according to [19], is an object of a certain minimum size on or near the Earth's surface (e.g. a forest, lake or mountain), whereas an image object is a discrete region of a digital image that is internally coherent and different from its surroundings [20, 18].

Since long time, images interpretation has been based on pixels' classification methods [17]. Recently, Castilla and Hay [20] have developed a new approach enabling the image analysis and interpretation based on the image partitioning into objects. This approach, called GEOBIA, relies on geographic objects to image objects based on three different steps: the segmentation, extraction and classification [21, 22, 18]. The segmentation step delineates regions having common characteristics. According to [20, 18], this step is based on the hypothesis that partitioning an image into objects is related to the way humans conceptually organize the landscape to comprehend it. The extraction defines the characteristics of the objects, such as shape, texture or the spectral response (i.e. low-level features such as high values in defined spectral bands) [23]. The classification step assigns a category (i.e. a semantic meaning) to the segmented objects according to the attributes calculated in the extraction phase. This last step aims at enriching the objects of the image in order to assign them a significant semantics (i.e. high-level concepts such as vegetation). This process is performed through the analysis of segment attributes and the interrelationships among segments to identify their geographic labels [23]. Such a concept highlights the importance of contextual information in improving the classification [24]. These techniques have shown efficient results based on expert's knowledge. However, expert's knowledge is subjective and cannot be used directly by an automatic process [22]. Consequently, this knowledge limits the automation of the image interpretation procedure. According to [18], the issue of automatic image interpretation consists of developing target recognition algorithms to map geographic objects. At this level, the challenge consists of linking the symbolic semantic information (e.g. vegetation index value) with numerical low-level features (e.g. measured vegetation index value). However, matching the high-level knowledge with the low-level knowledge leads to so-called semantic gap problem. This problem is defined as the lack of coincidence of the information that can be extracted from the visual data and the interpretation that the same data have for a user in a specific situation [25].

Hudelot et al. [26] defined the semantic images interpretation as the process of extraction and inference of high-level knowledge from the observed image. According to [26], "*The role of the semantic interpretation is to assign a meaning to the perceived description of the scene, i.e. the data extracted from images. This meaning refers to application domain expertise and terminology*". These authors consider that the semantic image interpretation problem is often limited to a classification problem (i.e. identifying the class of the structured data extracted from the observed images using predefined models). Indeed, an interpreter focuses on identifying the semantic contents of the observed images. However, according to the available knowledge, different answers and interpretations are possible for the interpreter (i.e. interpretation may be done in many ways). Consequently, the semantic is not in the image. It depends on the *prior* knowledge of the application domain (i.e. high-level knowledge) on the one hand, and the application context on the other hand. Therefore, this knowledge needs to be represented and formulated in an efficient way allowing, then, to improve the semantic images interpretation.

With recent advances in knowledge engineering, ontologies are increasingly used for the formalization of the knowledge of a given domain, in a coherent and consensual manner [27]. Indeed, ontologies are admitted as powerful conceptual tools for describing the knowledge of a domain in a structured and shared way and for the management of unstructured data, in particular in the domain of the semantic web. They provide a relevant methodological framework for the representation of *prior* knowledge in an image interpretation context [26]. Hence, from the fact that the semantic image interpretation can not only be based on the perceptual information coming from an image, the ontology can be used as a conceptual model encoding the expert's knowledge and guiding the interpretation task. However, the association of the expert's knowledge (i.e. qualitative information) with its representation in the image (i.e. numerical and quantitative information) leads to the semantic gap problem as previously described. Therefore, the exploitation of the ontology offers the possibility to overcome this problem. Indeed, during the last few years, ontologies have been mostly used to solve the semantic gap problem by bridging the symbolic information and the information extracted from the images [28]. Gruber [29] defined ontology as an "*explicit specification of a conceptualization*". This definition is refined by [30] as a "*formal specification of a shared conceptualization*". Conceptualization refers to an abstract model of some phenomenon in the world by identifying relevant concepts of that phenomenon. Explicit means that the identified concepts and the constraints on their use are explicitly defined. Formal refers to the fact that the ontology should be machine readable, and Shared reflects the notion that an ontology captures consensual knowledge not private to some individuals but accepted by a group [31].

An ontology specifies a set of concepts, their characteristics, their instances and their relationships, and axioms that are relevant for modeling a domain of study and permits the inference of implicit knowledge. It separates the expert's domain knowledge expressed by high-level concepts from the low-level features of image objects [18]. Generally, the association of these two levels can be performed using inference engines (i.e. reasoners) in the ontology. A reasoned is considered as a classification algorithm by remote sensing experts and based on logical rules (expressed in description logics), an automatic reasoner can infer new knowledge from explicit knowledge by ontologies and verify its logical consistency.

3. Semantic interpretation of remote sensing images

In a wide sense, ontologies, presented as explicit knowledge models, are widely used in images interpretation domain. First, particular contributions highlighted the use of ontologies in image processing domain have been presented in the multimedia field [26, 32–35]. Indeed, several multimedia ontologies have been presented and developed either for the description of the image low-level content, or, as standard annotation vocabularies for describing the image high-level content. Approaches proposed in [32–34] are examples of ontologies proposed in this context. Other approaches focusing on images processing or annotation problem have exploited ontologies as an annotation vocabulary to facilitate the mapping between perceptual primitives and high-level concepts. These approaches use a visual or object ontology at the intermediate level (i.e. in between low-level features and domain concepts [26]). According to Maillot [35], the visual concept ontology guides the domain knowledge acquisition process by providing a set of generic visual terms close to natural language and closer to images features. It respectively allows the reduction of the domain knowledge acquisition bottleneck and the semantic gap between domain concepts and low-level features. In Mezaris [36], an object ontology, which is a set of qualitative intermediate-level descriptors, has been proposed. It is used to allow the qualitative definition of the high-level concepts (that user query for) and their relations. Similarly, Hedelot et al. [26] have presented a solution to the symbol grounding problem. The symbol grounding problem refers to the mapping between low-level features (i.e. the numerical image data) and the high-level semantic concepts. The proposed work presents a learning approach for linking low-level features and visual concepts by using an intermediate processing ontology and *a prior* knowledge-based approach to explicitly build links between the low-level features data and the visual concepts. Ontologies have also been used as a framework allowing the explicit and formal description of the domain application and contextual knowledge. This framework is used as a model to guide the analysis and the interpretation, by exploiting the formal reasoning tools related to ontologies [26]. In this context, the description logics have been used in order to enable the logic formalization of the interpretation or annotation problems [37].

Ontologies have been widely exploited in the remote sensing domain, particularly, for the interpretation or the annotation of remote sensing imagery. Hence, several approaches have been proposed for geographical information analysis and management. The proposed approaches are distinguished according to their objective.

3.1. Ontology-based objects classification

As we have introduced, object-based classification consists of assigning a semantic class label (i.e. high-level concept) to a region (i.e. image object) in the image. In this context, Raskin and Pan [38] used ontology as a knowledge base allowing to classify orthogonal classes such as space, time, Earth realms, physical quantities and integrative science knowledge classes such as phenomena, events, and so on. In Ref. [39], authors have presented a semantic model for the classification of landforms, which are extracted from a digital elevation model using OBIA methods. Andrès et al. [22] have proved that expert's knowledge explanation via ontologies can improve the automation of satellite images and then they have presented an ontological approach allowing to classify remote sensing images. Jess et al. [40] proposed an ontological framework for ocean satellite images classification, which depicts how a potential building of an ontology model for low and high level of features. Recently, Belgiu et al. [41] have presented a method that consists of coupling an ontology-based knowledge representation for objects classification with the OBIA framework. A very recent semantic object-based classification method (using ontology of high-resolution remote sensing imagery) has been presented in [42]. In this approach, authors started by ontology modeling, then, a classification part is performed based on data-driven machine learning, segmentation, feature selection, sample collection and on an initial classification. Finally, image objects are re-classified based on the ontological model.

3.2. Ontology-based objects recognition

Several studies are focused on the object recognition problem in satellite imagery. For instance, Durand et al. [43] have presented an ontology for the recognition of urban objects in satellite images. This ontology has been enriched later in [44] with other domain concepts and spatial relations and then has been used for the annotation and interpretation of the remote sensing image. In [45], Forestier et al. have developed an ontology for the identification of urban features in satellite images. The proposed method starts by associating a set of low-level characteristics to each image region by using a segmentation algorithm. Then, the knowledge base (i.e. the ontology) is used to assign a semantic to the considered region. This work has been extended and generalized in [46] by adding new knowledge functions (KFs) including spatial relations between objects. Therefore, the proposed approach has been applied for coastal objects recognition. Recently, Luo et al. [47] have presented an ontology-based framework that was used to model the land cover extraction knowledge and interpret high resolution satellite (HRS) images at the regional level. In this work, the land cover ontology structure is explicitly defined, representing the spectral, textural and shape features, and allowing for the automatic interpretation of the extracted results. Similarly, Gui et al. [48] have presented an ontological method for extracting individual buildings with different orientations and different structures from SAR images based on ontological semantic analysis.

3.3. Ontology-based change detection

Modeling different states of objects, or phenomenon, in time allows to detect and identify different changes that can undergo these objects and phenomena. However, few ontology-based approaches have been proposed for change detection in remote sensing domain. For instance,

Hashimoto et al. [49] have presented a framework based on ontologies and heuristics for automatic change interpretation. The proposed framework considers remote sensing data analysis as a knowledge information processing, which derives new information about targets with inference from the observed data and *a priori* knowledge for remote sensing images. In [50], an ontology has been exploited to support spatio-temporal modeling in order to study different land use/cover changes such as splitting, merging, separation and annexation. In this work, the GeoSPARQL ontology including spatial information, the fluent ontology for temporal information and the domain ontology that stored knowledge and contextual information related to the geospatial environment, has been combined allowing to represent and to reason about spatio-temporal dynamics. More recently, Li et al. [51] have implemented an integrated computational framework to support semantic modeling and reasoning about spatio-temporal change of geographical objects in land use/cover (LULCC) data, regarding space, time and topology. In this framework, a spatial ontology has been created to encode essential knowledge about spatio-temporal variation changes such as deforestation and urbanization. Then, based on the knowledge defined in this ontology and on related reasoning rules, the semantic platform allows the semantic query and change reasoning of areas with LULCC.

4. Proposed approach: multi-levels semantic images interpretation

4.1. Semantic scenes interpretation strategy

Semantic image interpretation is defined by the semantics extraction and inference processes of high knowledge from an observed image. Semantics extraction refers to the image interpretation from a human perspective. It consists of obtaining useful spatial and semantic information on the "basic informative granules" (i.e. pixels, objects, zones, global scene) using human knowledge and experience. Generally, existing approaches, for semantics image interpretation, follow a multi-level strategy for describing the image content. According to Marr's vision [52], this architecture allows to separate the perceptual levels (i.e. syntactic description of the visual content of the image according to descriptors and visual primitives) and the conceptual or semantic levels (i.e. the meaning of the elements present in the image). Hudelot et al. [26] have adapted this architecture for semantic image interpretation in the medical domain. These authors suggested that the semantic level can be divided into three semantic abstraction sub-levels: semantic object level, semantic spatial level and semantic global level. Consequently, we have used this multi-level architecture for semantic scenes interpretation in remote sensing domain and subsequently for changes interpretation.

As shown in **Figure 3**, the proposed architecture is composed of different levels of abstraction. Consequently, following the idea that the "interpretation may take place at several levels of complexity, from the simple recognition of objects on scene to the inference of site conditions", an interpretation task will be accorded to each level. For each level, the interpretation strategy depends on: the input data (i.e. definition set) (e.g. scene), the output goal (i.e. definition content) (e.g. semantic objects classification) and *a prior* and contextual knowledge (e.g. spatial and temporal relations, contextual criteria, constraints, etc.). However, as we have introduced, there are various meanings associated with the word "information". Input can take different

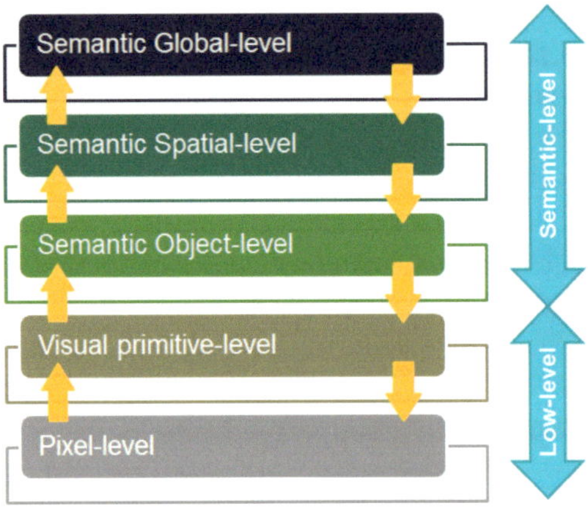

Figure 3. General adapted architecture for semantic scenes interpretation.

meanings according to the considered situation. It can be data, information or knowledge. This suggests that an input, in itself, has no unique meaning. Hence, data, information and knowledge are most likely context-dependent representations. Consequently, different situations may be perceived if they are interpreted with different contexts of the observed data. Because there are different meanings of information (i.e. data, information, knowledge), in this chapter, the interpretation process is considered as an information fusion problem. Information fusion focuses on combining different elements for the success of the interpretation step. However, the success of information fusion task is related to the way its basic components are defined and to the quality of their associated knowledge as well as the information or knowledge produced by the fusion process itself [14]. In this section, we focus on defining and characterizing, for each interpretation level, the information element structure and its main components. The main components of information element are as follows [14]:

1. A definition set giving the potential information input element (i.e. what the information refers to);
2. A content set encoding the possible knowledge produced by the information (e.g. measurements or estimations of physical parameters, decisions, hypothesis);
3. An input-output relationship representing the functional link model (e.g. mathematical, physical) that associates the input elements with the produced information contents;
4. An internal context gathering intrinsic characteristics, constraints, or controls about the information relation itself;
5. An external context containing data, information, or knowledge useful to the elaboration of the meaning or the interpretation of the information element.

Formally, an information element J can be represented as follows:

J = (information definition set, informative relation, information content set, internal context, external context) (1)

In the basic information element structure, illustrated in **Figure 2**, objects and contents represent entities linked through the informative relation. According to Bosse et al. [14], the nature of these entities may be either hard or soft. Hard means that these entities are quantitatively defined with numbers, individuals, and so on, an example of hard object is raws of pixels and an example of hard contents is features. Soft signifies that entities are qualitatively defined with words, opinions, predictions, and so on. For instance, a rule, defining an image vegetation segment, is a soft object, and the vegetation segment represents the soft content. However, soft entities require a context in which the qualitative descriptors are defined [14]. An informative relation may be impersonal (or hard) when it does not depend on external conditions to link objects to contents. However, it may also behave in a softer way by using cognitive factors such subjective judgements, opinions and perceptions (e.g. (J) representing human experts' outputs). For example, if we consider the informative relation a sensor making an acquisition, setting parameters value of this sensor belongs to the internal context. However, the conditions why the sensor has been set up with these setting belong to the external context. These conditions include the context of observation. This later represents an important part of the perception process as it is all that an influence on the perception of an event and all that is needed to understand the observation. Therefore, different situations may be perceived, relying on the same set of sensory information items, if they are interpreted within the different contexts of observation. Thus, providing the external context for a specific domain and specific aim makes a system to be intelligent for interpreting a specific situation. Part of this context is the domain knowledge that every human uses to interpret and understand any perception. The exploitation of the ontology offers the best way for representing and reasoning about this knowledge. In the following section, we describe the information element of each semantic image interpretation level and we demonstrate the role of ontologies for representing and reasoning about both internal and external contexts.

4.2. Information element: pixel level

The semantic image interpretation strategy starts with a feature extraction step from the image where raw image data are "converted" into visual features (edges, segments, regions, intersections, etc.), which are supposed to correspond to meaningful parts of semantic objects. What is considered here is not information but a kind of abstract data (i.e. a set of pixels). This level of abstraction corresponds to the information element paradigm when associated with the basic objects that are observed. An informative relation, that is, feature extraction, is used to link objects (input set) to contents (output set). This informative relation embeds knowledge allowing to build this link. However, the informative relation extracting features from the image (i.e. the definition set) probably needs to know the resolution of the sensor producing the image pixels [14] and other knowledge such as segmentation and extraction algorithms and feature properties. This additional information belongs to the internal context of the information element. In addition, contextual information such as sensing conditions including the acquisition date, the sun elevation angle, atmospheric conditions and algorithms characterization (that have to be known "previously" in the feature extraction step). This information belongs to the external context of the information element. **Figure 4** shows the information element structure of the pixel level (data).

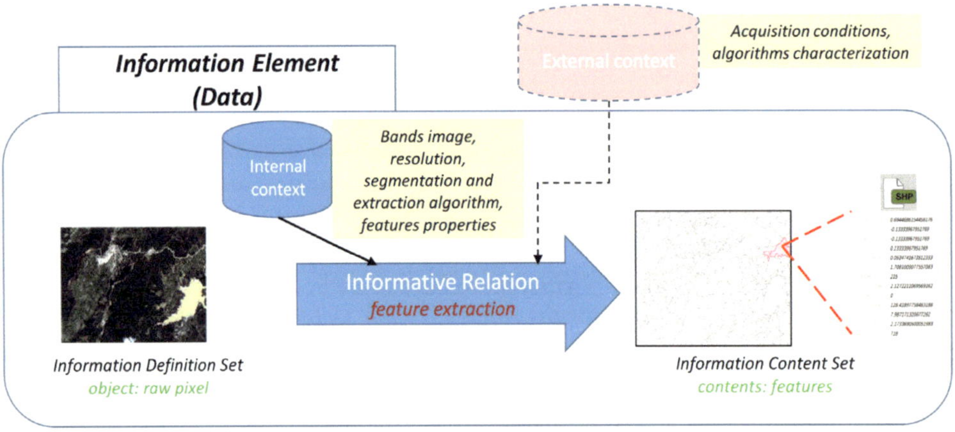

Figure 4. Information element in pixel level interpretation.

4.3. Information element: visual primitives level

The visual primitives' level aims to assign a semantic attribution (i.e. labeling) to the extracted image segments from the shapefile containing the information about image features. An informative relation that links the input set (i.e. shapefile) to the output set (i.e. labeled segments) and uses internal information including features proprieties and segments rules for reasoning about segments labels. The attribution of these labels is based on an external resource (i.e. external context) formulated as a visual primitive ontology. This ontology includes a general description of expert's knowledge about geographical features representation. The concepts, associated to this structure, are derived from images concepts. **Figure 5** illustrates the structure of the information element in the visual primitives' level. At this level, it is worthwhile to notice that the information definition set (i.e. input definition set) is represented by a shapefile format and the information content set (i.e. output set) by a RDF file format.

4.4. Information element: object level

The semantic object level allows to attribute a hard classification to objects in scene. Indeed, the semantic objects interpretation consists of attributing hard classes such as forest, lake, urban and others to the labeled visual primitive extracted in the former step. This later, formulated as knowledge, has been extracted in the visual primitive level, and it is used as an input definition set of the information element in the semantic object level. What is considered, at this level, is not information or data, but a set of knowledge allowing to describe the semantics of objects in the image. The link between the symbolic description (i.e. input definition set) and the semantic content (i.e. output set) is performed through the classification reasoner representing the informative relation of the information element. This informative relation needs other knowledge in order to associate the semantic definition to different image contents. Such knowledge includes *prior* and contextual knowledge, which are formulated as a domain ontology. Generally, the main concepts of this ontology are geographic objects such as urban, forest, water, and so on, and their hierarchical relationships (i.e. "is-a" relation). The general information element structure of the semantic object level is illustrated in **Figure 6**.

http://dx.doi.org/10.5772/intechopen.72730

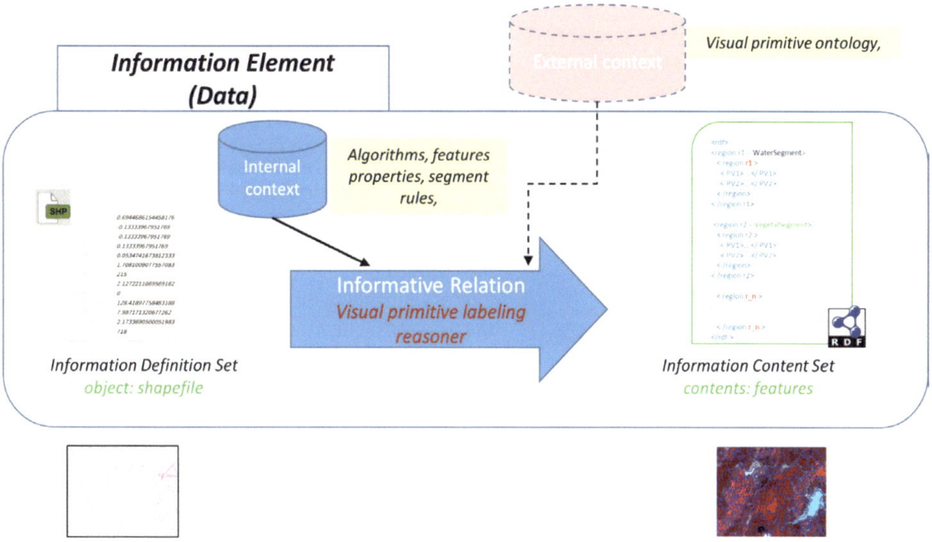

Figure 5. Information element in the primitive-level interpretation.

4.5. Information element: semantic spatial level

In the semantic spatial interpretation level, the focus is made in order to give a visual description of the whole content of the image scene in a given time. In other words, the objective is to describe different objects, present in the scene, and the existing spatial relations that hold between them. Consequently, this allows to give a conceptual representation of semantic objects and their spatial relation allowing a semantic interpretation at the scene level. A spatial relation extraction reasoner (representing the informative relation of the information element defining the knowledge here) allows to make a link between the semantic objects hierarchy (i.e. input definition set) and the conceptual representation (i.e. output content set). To build this link, the informative relation needs to use some predefined constraints about spatial relationships. These constraints (or spatial rules) are part of the internal context allowing to define spatial relations that existing between different objects in the scene. Spatial relationships include neighborhood relations (such as externally connected (EC), disconnected (DC), and non-tangential proper part (NTPP)); directional relations describing relative orientations of objects (e.g. North and South); and distance relations (such as near and far relationships [53]).

All these spatial relations are formulated in a spatial relation ontology as presented in [26], and then, they are integrated as parts of an external context in the structure of information element. On the other hand, the informative relation requires the integration of the domain knowledge (i.e. domain ontology) with the spatial relation ontology for the global interpretation and understanding of the scene. Notice here, that this domain ontology is used as an external context of the information element in the semantic object level. Therefore, the integration of the spatial relation ontology with the domain ontology (as an external context) in this information element of the semantic spatial level illustrates the growing extent of J context as J level of abstraction increases (**Figure 7**).

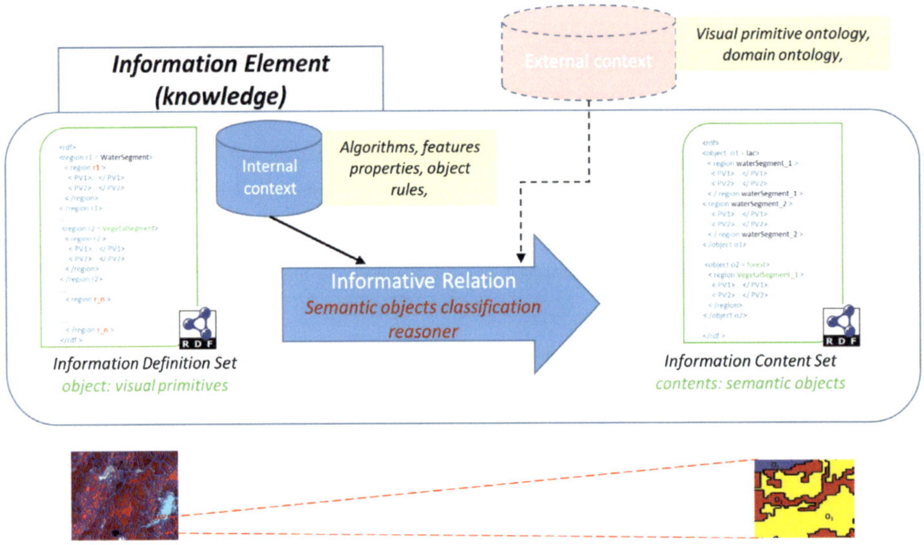

Figure 6. Information element in the semantic object-level interpretation.

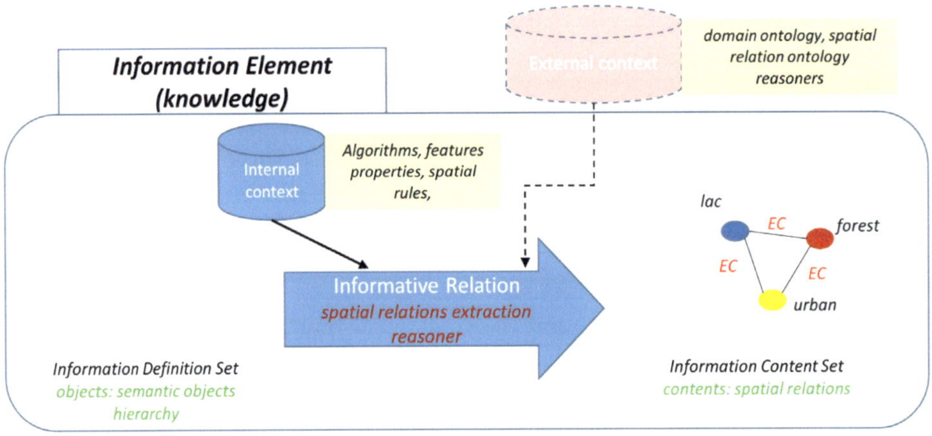

Figure 7. Information element in spatial level interpretation.

4.6. Information element: global semantic level

The global semantic level (or high semantic level) refers to the semantic scenes interpretation in the time. This allows to describe the semantic content in terms of objects and their relations of different images representing the same scene in the time. To reach this purpose, the global semantic scenes interpretation consists of integrating temporal relations that can hold between images' objects. The obtained result, output content, is an ontological conceptualization representing different concepts in the images as well as their relationships, namely, semantic, spatial, temporal and filiation relations. **Figure 8** shows the structure of the information element in this level. In this structure, the informative relation considers as an input set the semantic spatial representation of different scenes (e.g. two scenes here). In order to allow linking these representations and the output result (i.e. content set), the informative relation, that is, the temporal and filiation relations reasoner, uses temporal and filiations rules as the internal context integrates temporal and filiation relations ontologies. Temporal relations define possible relations that hold between two time intervals that can be used for reasoning about the temporal descriptions of events, actions, beliefs, intentions or causality. Generally, Allen's Interval Algebra [54] is the most known and widely used model for topological temporal relations between objects in time. The importation of the SWLRTO ontology, as part of external context, offers the possibility to classify different time relations. This allows, for example, to define the rule for the temporal relation before as follows:

$$SWRLTO{:}hasTime(?i1, ?t1)\wedge SWRLTO{:}hasTime(?i2, ?t1)\wedge SWRL{:}lessThan(?t1, ?t2)\rightarrow before(?i1, ?i2) \quad (2)$$

In addition, filiation relations are also of great importance for reasoning about relations between objects in times. Filiation relations have been introduced by Del Mondo [55] and include continuation and derivation relationships. Continuation occurs when an entity (real object) continues to exist from one time to the next with the same identity, and the derivation occurs when an entity creates some others with new identities [55]. Thus, these relations must be integrated to the context allowing, thus, the informative relation to link the input set to the output set.

4.7. Information element: change interpretation

The final objective of the semantic scenes interpretation is the interpretation of changes that may occur. The change interpretation process consists of the detection of the changes that can affect different states of objects and the relations between these changes. Changes can be classified into: (1) domain-independent occurrences (such as growth, shrinkage, disappearance, appearance, etc.) or (2) domain-dependent (or domain-specific) occurrences (such as deforestation, urbanization and desertification). Most researches, analyzing and studying changes, consider the first category as *events* and the second as *processes* (i.e. geographic processes). However, relations can exist between the two occurrences. These relations can be either composition or constitution relationships, for example, a deforestation process is specified as the shrinkage and then

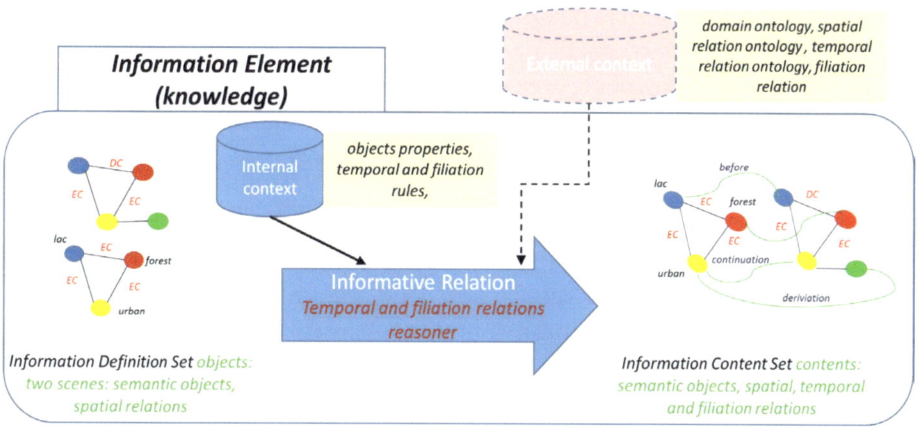

Figure 8. Information element in the global-level interpretation.

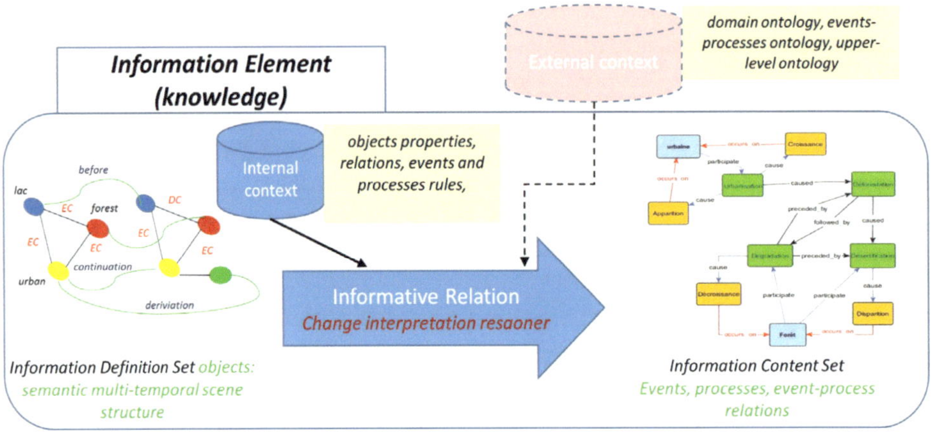

Figure 9. Information element in the change-level interpretation.

the disappearance of forest zone, and either can be causal relationships such as cause and initiate relations, for examples, deforestation initiates the shrinkage of a forest, urbanization causes the deforestation, and so on. Consequently, the information element in this level must describe the knowledge about these changes and their relations. Therefore, the role of the informative relation (i.e. change reasoner) is to interpret changes that have occurred from the semantic description of different scenes (input set) allowing subsequently to obtain a semantic representation about changes and their relationships (i.e. the content set). To link the information definition set to the information content set, this informative relation is based on two contextual information: internal and external context. The internal context includes contextual information about objects or different relationships, which are used for the interpretation process. For instance, the spatial reduction of an entity whose coverage is a forest (internal context) is interpreted as phenomena of deforestation. External context includes the representation and descriptions about events and processes. It is about expert (*prior*) knowledge describing definitions of different occurrences. Descriptions of events and processes can be formulated using upper ontologies such as the basic fundamental ontology (BFO) [56]. This ontology distinguishes between static entities such as forest and dynamic entities such as deforestation. Therefore, combining the BFO ontology with the domain ontology (which represent knowledge of remote sensing images) allows to give a conceptual representation describing events and processes that can be used as an external context to help the interpretation of changes. In **Figure 9**, the information element structure and its components in the change interpretation level are presented.

5. Conclusions and discussion

Semantic images interpretation is an important step for any decision-making system. It allows to give a semantic description of the image content. Consequently, this allows an agent (user or machine) to take the best management decision of a given situation. The interpretation may take place at different levels of complexity, from the simple recognition of objects on scene to the inference of site conditions and also to change interpretation. In this chapter, we have mainly focused on the semantic scenes interpretation for change interpretation in remote sensing imagery. Therefore, we have demonstrated that the semantic scenes interpretation can be done in different level, from the low level to the high level. For each level, it is important to characterize the structure of the information element (i.e. data, information or knowledge) and its components (i.e. input set, output set, internal and external context) required for the interpretation process. Consequently, a semantic conceptualization based on ontological concepts for representing the components of the information elements and for the interpretation step has been illustrated in this chapter. Especially, the ontology exploitation has been applied to formulate the expert's knowledge such as *a prior* and contextual knowledge. These types of knowledge are important for the semantic scenes interpretation task.

Generally, the structure of the information element is composed of the definition set, content set, informative relation and both internal and external context. In addition, as we have shown in **Figure 2**, quality of information (*QoI*) also must be integrated into the information element structure. Therefore, the characterization of the quality of information is necessary for the interpretation process. *QoI* about information is through its attributes and their relations. Generally, there are four main aspects of information quality: uncertainty, relevance, reliability and completeness. Future studies include the description of these aspects and their integration in the semantic images interpretation process [18].

Author details

Fethi Ghazouani[1,2]*, Imed Riadh Farah[1,2] and Basel Solaiman[2]

*Address all correspondence to: fethi.ghazouani@imt-atlantique.fr

1 RIADI Laboratory, National School of Computer Science, Manouba University, Tunisia

2 ITI Department, IMT-Atlantique, Brest, France

References

[1] Ashbindu S. Review article digital change detection techniques using remotely-sensed data. International journal of remote sensing. 1989;**10**(6):989-1003

[2] Masroor H et al. Change detection from remotely sensed images: From pixel-based to object-based approaches. ISPRS. 2013;**80**:91-106

[3] Quarmby NA, Cushnie JL. Monitoring urban land cover changes at the urban fringe from SPOT HRV imagery in south-east England. International Journal of Remote Sensing. 1989;**10**(6):953-963

[4] Howarth PJ, Wickware GM. Procedures for change detection using Landsat digital data. International Journal of Remote Sensing. 1981;**2**(3):277-291

[5] Johnson RD, Kasischke ES. Change vector analysis: A technique for the multispectral monitoring of land cover and condition. International Journal of Remote Sensing. 1998;**19**(3):411-426

[6] Bouziani M et al. Automatic change detection of buildings in urban environment from very high spatial resolution images using existing geodatabase and prior knowledge. ISPRS. 2010;**65**(1):143-153

[7] Chen G et al. Object-based change detection. International Journal of Remote Sensing. 2012;**33**(14):4434-4457

[8] Chen J et al. Land-use/land-cover change detection using improved change-vector analysis. Photogrammetric Engineering & Remote Sensing. 2003;**69**(4):369-379

[9] Addink EV et al. Introduction to the GEOBIA 2010 special issue: From pixels to geographic objects in remote sensing image analysis. International Journal of Applied Earth Observations and Geoinformation. 2012;**15**:1-6

[10] Bhatta B. Analysis of data. In: Research Methods in Remote Sensing. Dordrecht: Springer Netherlands; 2013. pp. 61-75. DOI: 10.1007/978-94-007-6594-8_4

[11] Landry BC, Rush JE. Toward a theory of indexing—Ii. Journal of the Association for Information Science and Technology. 1970;**21**(5):358-367

[12] Blair IV. The malleability of automatic stereotypes and prejudice. Personality and Social Psychology Review. 2002;**6**(3):242-261

[13] Zins C. Conceptual approaches for defining data, information, and knowledge. Journal of the Association for Information Science and Technology. 2007;**58**(4):479-493

[14] Bosse E, Solaiman B. Information Fusion and Analytics for Big Data and IoT. Norwood, MA, USA: Artech House, Inc.; 2016

[15] Whitaker GD. An Overview of Information Fusion. Malvern, United Kingdom: Defence Evaluation and Research Agency; 2001

[16] Losee RM. A discipline independent definition of information. Journal of the American Society for Information Science. 1997 (1986-1998);**48**(3):254

[17] Lillesand T et al. Remote Sensing and Image Interpretation. John Wiley&Sons; 2014

[18] Arvor D et al. Advances in geographic object-based image analysis with ontologies: A review of main contributions and limitations from a remote sensing perspective. ISPRS Journal of Photogrammetry and Remote Sensing. 2013;**82**:125-137

[19] Smith B, Mark DM. Ontology and geographic kinds. In: Poiker TK, Chrisman N, editors. Proceeding from the 8th International Symposium on Spatial Data Handling. Vancouver, BC: IGU; 1998:308-320

[20] Castilla G, Hay GJ. Image objects and geographic objects. In: Object-Based Image Analysis. Berlin, Heidelberg: Springer; 2008:91-110

[21] Lang S. Object-based image analysis for remote sensing applications: modeling reality – dealing with complexity. In: Blaschke T, Lang S, Hay GJ, editors OBIA. Lecture Notes in Geoinformation and Cartography. Berlin, Heidelberg: Springer; 2008:3-27

[22] Andres S et al. Towards an ontological approach for classifying remote sensing images. In 8th International Conference on Signal Image Technology and Internet Based Systems (SITIS). IEEE; 2012

[23] Liu Y et al. A framework of region-based spatial relations for non-overlapping features and its application in object based image analysis. ISPRS Journal of Photogrammetry and Remote Sensing. 2008;**63**(4):461-475

[24] Blaschke T. What's wrong with pixels? Some recent developments interfacing remote sensing and GIS. GeoBIT/GIS. 2001;**6**:12-17

[25] Smeulders AWM et al. Content-based image retrieval at the end of the early years. IEEE Transactions on Pattern Analysis and Machine Intelligence. 2000;**22**(12):1349-1380

[26] Hudelot C et al. Symbol grounding for semantic image interpretation: From image data to semantics. Tenth IEEE International Conference on Computer Vision Workshops, 2005. ICCVW'05. IEEE; 2005

[27] Kompatsiaris Y, Hobson P. Semantic Multimedia and Ontologies. London, UK: Springer Verlag Limited; 2008

[28] Kokar MM, Wang J. Using ontologies for recognition: An example. Proceedings of the Fifth International Conference on Information Fusion, 2002. Vol. 2. IEEE; 2002

[29] Gruber TR. A translation approach to portable ontology specifications. Knowledge Acquisition. 1993;**5**(2):199-220

[30] Borst WN. Construction of Engineering Ontologies for Knowledge Sharing and Reuse. Centre for Telematics and Information Technology (CTIT). The Netherlands: Universiteit Twente; 1997

[31] Studer R et al. Knowledge engineering: Principles and methods. Data & Knowledge Engineering. 1998;**25**(1-2):161-197

[32] Russell BC et al. LabelMe: A database and web-based tool for image annotation. International Journal of Computer Vision. 2008;**77**(1):157-173

[33] Deng J et al. Imagenet: A large-scale hierarchical image database. IEEE Conference on Computer Vision and Pattern Recognition, 2009 (CVPR 2009). IEEE; 2009

[34] Naphade M et al. Large-scale concept ontology for multimedia. IEEE Multimedia. 2006;**13**(3):86-91

[35] Maillot N et al. Ontology based object learning and recognition: Application to image retrieval. In: 16th IEEE International Conference on Tools with Artificial Intelligence 2004 (ICTAI 2004). IEEE; 2004

[36] Mezaris V et al. Region-based image retrieval using an object ontology and relevance feedback. Eurasip Journal on Applied Signal Processing. 2004;**2004**:886-901

[37] Town C. Ontological inference for image and video analysis. Machine Vision and Applications. 2006;**17**(2):94-115

[38] Raskin RG, Pan MJ. Knowledge representation in the semantic web for earth and environmental terminology (SWEET). Computers & Geosciences. 2005;**31**(9):1119-1125

[39] Eisank C et al. A generic procedure for semantics-oriented landform classification using object-based image analysis. Geomorphometry. 2011;**2011**:125-128

[40] Almendros-Jiménez et al. A framework for ocean satellite image classification based on ontologies. IEEE Journal of Selected Topics in Applied Earth Observations and Remote Sensing. 2013;**6**(2):1048-1063

[41] Belgiu M et al. Coupling formalized knowledge bases with object-based image analysis. Remote Sensing Letters. 2014;**5**(6):530-538

[42] Gu H, et al. An object-based semantic classification method for high resolution remote sensing imagery using ontology. Remote Sensing. 2017;**9**(4):329

[43] Durand N et al. Ontology-based object recognition for remote sensing image interpretation. In: 19th IEEE International Conference on ICTAI 2007. Vol. 1. IEEE; 2007

[44] Messaoudi W et al. A new ontology for semantic annotation of remotely sensed images. 2014 1st International Conference on ATSIP. IEEE; 2014

[45] Forestier G et al. Knowledge-based region labeling for remote sensing image interpretation. Computers, Environment and Urban Systems. 2012;**36**(5):470-480

[46] Forestier G et al. Coastal image interpretation using background knowledge and semantics. Computers & Geosciences. 2013;**54**:88-96

[47] Luo H, et al. Land cover extraction from high resolution zy-3 satellite imagery using ontology-based method. ISPRS International Journal of Geo-Information. 2016;**5**(3):31

[48] Gui R et al. Individual building extraction from TerraSAR-X images based on ontological semantic analysis. Remote Sensing. 2016;**8**(9):708

[49] Hashimoto S et al. A framework of ontology-based knowledge information processing for change detection in remote sensing data. 2011 IEEE International Geoscience and Remote Sensing Symposium (IGARSS). IEEE; 2011

[50] Arenas H et al. LC3: A spatial-temporal data model to study qualified land cover changes. In: Land Use and Land Cover Semantics, Principles, Best Practices and Prospects, ⟨hal-01086886⟩. 2015. pp. 211-242

[51] Li W et al. An integrated software framework to support semantic modeling and reasoning of spatiotemporal change of geographical objects: A use case of land use and land cover change study. ISPRS International Journal of Geo-Information. 2016;**5**(10):179

[52] Marr D, Vision A. A Computational Investigation into the Human Representation and Processing of Visual Information. WH San Francisco: Freeman and Company. 1982. 1.2

[53] Randell DA et al. A spatial logic based on regions and connection. Knowledge Representation and Reasoning. 1992;**92**:165-176

[54] Allen JF. Maintaining knowledge about temporal intervals. Communications of the ACM. 1983;**26**(11):832-843

[55] Del Mondo G et al. Modeling consistency of spatio-temporal graphs. Data & Knowledge Engineering. 2013;**84**:59-80

[56] Grenon P, Smith B. SNAP and SPAN: Towards dynamic spatial ontology. Spatial Cognition and Computation. 2004;**4**(1):69-104

Chapter 10

Systematic Unfoldment of Differential Ontology from Qualitative Concept of Information

Stein E. Johansen

Additional information is available at the end of the chapter

http://dx.doi.org/10.5772/intechopen.72951

Abstract

A certain philosophical ontology is presented as developed from a qualitative concept of information, leading to conclusive points of possible far-reaching relevance for philosophy and science.

Keywords: informational differential ontology, differential epistemology, philosophical informatics, causality theory, projective causality, Fibonacci algorithm, concept of border, Erasmus syllogism

1. Introduction

In relation to information science, we can basically distinguish between two different meanings of "ontology": (i) in the classical and purest philosophical sense as the discipline researching "being; that which is" in the most universal, abstract and fundamental regards; (ii) in the modern, specified and instrumental sense inside computer science as defining suitable sets of "representational primitives" (classes, attributes, relations) with which to model a domain of knowledge/discourse for computation. We denote the first meaning as *philosophical ontology* and the second meaning as *computational ontology*. When we write "ontology" without further specification, the first meaning is implicated. In the present text, we focus and exhibit intimate relations between the science of information in its very foundations and a certain *philosophical* ontology.

When discussing the relation between philosophical ontology and informatics, usual approaches will depart from an ontology presented by a sophisticated philosopher, say Leibniz, Kant, Hegel or Quine. Next, the field of informatics will be placed inside this ontology, and the chosen philosophical ontology will be applied to approach the field of informatics in order to achieve some new results, e.g., for construction of a more suitable computational ontology in specified respects. Instead of departing from more pure philosophers, similar approaches may be undertaken as departing from modern generalizations of quantum mechanics into some quantum ontology, or from some second-order cybernetics including aspects of philosophical phenomenology. In any case, such approaches start out with establishing philosophical ontology basically independent of, prior to and external to the foundations of information science.

In radical distinction to such approaches, our approach is to depart from the very *concept* of information, and systematically *develop* a novel philosophical ontology by strict, successive and more organic *unfoldment* of what is already *implicated* in the concept of *information as such*. The basic idea was to establish an adequate and *qualitative* concept of information, i.e., of *something* existing (for someone), and to explore and exhibit what *had* to follow from this by philosophical rigor and consistency. The resulting ontology was presented in the treatise *Outline of Differential Epistemology* (Johansen [1]; yet to become finalized into English translation for publication). Here, (differential) epistemology was not understood as opposed to (differential) ontology, as often the case in philosophical treatments, but rather as the epistemological "head" growing out of the ontological "body" from unfoldment into the more sophisticated among causality operators. Knowing of something being implies that being itself becomes extended by this knowing. The present text will present some key points from said treatise, supplemented with various novel remarks.

In the discipline of informatics, different *quantitative*—and highly fruitful—concepts of information became established, as the classic concept by Shannon (and Weaver) [2] and later concepts by Kolmogoroff and by Chaitin (*Algorithmic Information Content*). Zurek [3] clarified how these two apparently opposing kinds of concepts, with respect to indicating algorithmic complexity, could be understood as complementary, depending on choice of fundamental perspective and reference frame, and thus possible to synthesize.

Zenon from Elea pointed out that "if being did not have a quantity, it could not be" [4] (p. 115). Quine presented his famous criterion of ontological commitment: "To be is to be a *value* of a bound variable" (our italics). These statements are consistent with the general philosophical point that anything being only can exist as *bestimmt* in the sense of Hegel, i.e., *as definite*, and as such also must possess exact quantitative aspects. Quite another issue is how easy or fruitful it is to *measure* these quantities. If we take the existence of *love* as example, this ontological phenomenon or entity obviously has its quantitative aspects, while it is also obvious that these aspects due to the complexity of the phenomenon are far from easy to measure and due to the more sacred intimacy of the phenomenon probably not that fruitful to attempt to measure.

A deeper philosophical point is that *any* quantification, with logical necessity, is a quantification of *something*, i.e., of a *quality* (as also the case for Quine's "variable"). Thus, the category of quality is ontologically prior to the category of the quantified quality. This must also be the case for the concept of *information*. It is not possible to establish any quantitative concept of information without *de facto*—tacitly or explicated—presupposing a qualitative concept of information. When *avoiding* explication of the conceptually and ontologically underlying and prior *qualitative* concept of information in favor of merely operational quantifications of the concept, there is some danger of *fetishizing* quantification as such. Sometimes such elements of fetishism, at least to some extent, may be rather innocent and even fruitful for certain purposes (say establishment of sufficiently adequate IQ tests), while they may be basically shortcoming with respect to more

http://dx.doi.org/10.5772/intechopen.72951

profound scientific reflections and possibly crucial scientific progressions. Avoidance of quantitative fetishism with respect to the concept of information is crucial in order to establish a universal philosophical ontology with multidisciplinary potency, including the discipline of informatics. Hence, there is a need to explicitly establish an adequate *qualitative* concept of information.

2. Qualitative concept of "information"

The most influential qualitative definition of information has been Gregory Bateson's definition of information (in his shortest version) as *the difference which makes the difference* [5, 6]. We take this famous definition as a point of departure for some further adequate qualification and modification.

Sometimes Bateson qualifies his definition of information as a difference which makes a difference for *something*, or for *someone*. In general, a phenomenon *cannot* appear as a difference unless it appears in relation to something *for which* it makes a difference. This something we denote a *subject*. This may be the *emphatic* subject of a human being or it may be the *projected* subject from a human being into more or less *imagined* subjects in a spectrum spanning from an ape or a whale to a billiard ball or a photon. Thus, we can make Bateson more consistent by reinterpreting Bateson's "something" as a projection from a human, or other sufficiently intelligent being "someone," say from the human biologist or physicist.

Generally speaking, there must be a *relational triad* involved in the very constitution of information as such: (i) an input-difference, which makes (ii) an output-difference into the reception (including into higher perceptions, not excluding more unconscious mental ones) by (iii) a subject, either an *emphatic* human subject or a *virtual* subject constituted by projection from and interpretation by an emphatic subject. A necessary condition to constitute an emphatic subject is the subject having *emotion*. Thus, there cannot exist information in the cosmos without the existence of emphatic subjects having emotion.

As a thought experiment: Imagine AI advanced and self-replicating nanobots becoming able to exterminate emotional subjects including humans, as e.g., the nanotechnological construction of $Ba_xSr(1-x)TO_3$, i.e., barium strontium titanate claimed by some sober biologists to qualify as a novel *living* species. It seems hard to imagine that such nanobots would qualify as *emotional* beings. In order to understand how these nanobots would rule our world, it would still be by anticipatory *projection* from emphatic human (or ET) subjects, not by the nanobots *themselves*, whatever the sophistication of their AI algorithms. In such a nanobot-ruled world, one might say that there still would be a lot of *potentially* discovered information creation and transfer going on, while such potentiality would not be *actualized* without the presence of human (or other) subjects possessing the *emotion* to constitute emphatic subjects and from that *perform* the projection.

Man is a subject that necessarily operates with a concept of difference, and it is only through *our* reflection that the bringing forth of information in ourselves or other subjects that we observe, necessarily must be comprehended as a difference making a difference. A subject, then, *can de facto* register information without this *appearing* as a difference for the same subject; and *all* subjects *must* receive information without it *immediately* appearing as difference *for them*. Therefore, when we speak of a subject's reception and operation of differences, we do not refer to *subjective* differences, i.e., differences that appear as such for the subject itself, but to *objective* differences, i.e., differences that are implicit in any information as it appears for an external, *reflecting* subject.

Accordingly, we also find it inaccurate to *define* information as difference (that makes a difference). In the first place, information should be defined as any *something* which is something for a *subject*. Difference can be defined as the *relation* prevailing between two somethings qua separated. Then difference is a specific *kind* of information which presupposes that a subject juxtaposes two somethings and has a concept of difference. However, a subject can very well receive and operate *other* information without this precondition being satisfied. A different matter is the fact that the existence of all information presupposes and includes *objective* differences, so that information *as such* is characterized by the fact that it can potentially be described as (objective) difference that makes (objective) difference, and consequently, for the difference-reflecting subject also makes a subjective difference and constitutes a difference-information. The difference between information and difference can be illustrated by the fact that while an information necessarily is *one*, the objective differences it presupposes can very well be *two*, provided that the subject receives analog input-differences where the information is delimited by both an overlying and an underlying threshold. Information should accordingly not be *defined* as objective difference, but objective difference is a necessary *determined characteristic* (*Bestimmung* in the sense of Hegel) by all information and consequently something that *all* information can be conceived as and by. Difference-information, in its turn, is a kind of information where a subject *reflects* in a specified way upon objective difference included in (other) information.

3. Decomposition of that which is onto two differentiated ontological dimensions: processual-physical (3 + 1D) vs. algorithmic

Any description of a dynamic system can only become meaningful through de facto being both discontinuous and continuous. (For a fundamental exposition of the relation between statics and dynamics in systems theory, see Feibleman and Friend [7].) Since it describes a course occurring in time and time is regarded as a continuous quantity, the description must, on the one hand, preserve this continuity. On the other hand, it would not be possible to describe anything at all without stating discontinuous transformations during the course. The only way to unite these two considerations is to let the description represent continuity and discontinuity in *different dimensions*, i.e., the description that unfolds a *two dimensional figure of logic*. We can imagine this as a description proceeding continuously along one dimension, but discontinuously along another dimension.

Hence, we will have a trajectory of only continuity, projected on a horizontal axis, and a trajectory of discontinuity projected on a vertical axis. This means that the two projections are respectively continuously continuous and continuously discontinuous. Then, the description must move in stepwise *alternation* between movements in horizontal and vertical direction.

The very concept of discontinuity presupposes a discontinuation upon (the qualitative entity) *time* considered as inherently continuous. Hence, the trajectory on the horizontal axis must basically be regarded as continuous movement of *time* and in time. For something to happen in the system, this must happen as related to specified and discontinued *points* along the time line. When *nothing new* happens on the vertical axis of discontinuation, as considered by the description of the system, this implies that not only time is considered as moving continuously inside the according time interval, but also that *space* coordinates of what is(are) object(s) of dynamic description keep on moving in a continuous manner. Thus, the movement along the horizontal dimension of continuity is continuous movement in (3 + 1D) *spacetime*, where this horizontal dimension is most easily conceived by giving priority to the (sub) dimension of time in order to represent continuous movement in spacetime compressed at merely *one* ontological "dimension" inside a higher and broader ontological architecture. We denote movement along the horizontal dimension as *process*, and the according ontological domain as *physical being*. Here, the term "physical" does not refer to any *absolute* domain, say elementary particles in quantum mechanics, macrophysical objects in Newtonian mechanics, neurons in neuroscience, genes in molecular biology, or human mind-bodies in social science, but to a *relative* domain conceived in *relation* to the vertical dimension of discontinuity in a dynamic system description.

The discontinuous movement along the vertical axis *induces* the something new that happens along the continuous movement along the horizontal axis. Thus, in description of any system, the movement along the vertical axis holds de facto ontological *priority* when explaining what happens along the horizontal axis, and therefore, also for the system as a whole. Discontinuous movement happens at *points* in time, as regarded at the horizontal axis, i.e., momentarily and *without* any extension in time. (This does not imply—of course—that said discontinuous movement has no extension in time when regarded from *another* reference frame involved in another (higher) system description.) The movement along the vertical axis is regarded as discontinuous from the horizontal dimension involving continuous time. However, there is still a *movement*, i.e., a specified *succession*, along the vertical axis when regarded at this axis *itself*. We denote this vertical axis as the *algorithmic* dimension which therefore is implied in any dynamic system description as radically different from the dimension of time and physical process.

The movement along the vertical dimension cannot happen in isolation from the movement along the horizontal dimension, but only by algorithms transforming a certain input (set of variable values), delivered from *physical process*, into a certain output. We denote this concrete performance of an algorithmic operation as *informative transfiguration*. The change in physical process as induced by an output from an algorithmic operation, we denote as *differential movement*.

Any algorithm, de facto operative in any dynamic system description, must contain, whether implicit or explicit, semantics as well as syntax. The *semantics* of the algorithm indicates the *types* of input elements it can operate (e.g., numbers), the *operational rules* between elements (e.g., the four elementary operators of arithmetic), the *relational rules* between operated elements (e.g., <, > and =), and the *transformation rules* (e.g., implication) resulting in qualification (and quantification) of types of output elements (e.g., numbers). The *syntax* of the algorithm indicates the specified *succession* among its semantically possible types and rules.

This minimalistic definition of "algorithm," illustrated by arithmetic, may seem too abstract and insufficiently specified. The very meanings of "algorithm" and "computation" were primarily established by Turing's theoretical construction of the Universal Turing Machine (UTM), which was a great mathematical as well as—in our view even more—philosophical achievement that established the foundation of informatics and computer technology. However, we do not find it adequate to apply the definition of "algorithm" that is too specified, in order to cover (at a general level) *all* discontinuations in the vertical dimension implied in human system description and underpinning cognition (whether conscious or unconscious). A general definition of "algorithm" that is less specified than Turing's may allow progresses in informatics based on broader and deeper philosophical ontology than the one underlying UTM (cf. later in this text).

4. Qualitative concept of "border"

We have defined difference as a relation between two somethings that are *separated*. The subject can only imagine its division of a something into two by imagining that two somethings are separated by a *dividing line*, or more generally and accurately, by a *border*, where the dividing border can be understood in all dimensions—as border point, border line, border surface or border space. A border seems to have a curious double nature of being and not being at the same time.

The concept of border is itself, partly self-referentially, one case of a *borderconcept*, since it is imagined (if we take the case of a line) as a continuous assembly of points of *infinitesimal* extent. A border is something being that approaches something non-being as its limit, i.e., something being that *tendentiously* is something *not* being. It is therefore contrary to the concept to imagine a border as having a particular spatial extension since any extension always can be made smaller by a more microscopic contemplation. On the other hand, border is imagined as something *being*, and how can we imagine something as being without imagining it as extended in space? But, as soon as we try to specify this extension, we fall short. To specify the spatial extent of a phenomenon implies stating a lower *and* upper threshold (thus, *borders*) within which the phenomenon is located. But for border as such, it is only possible to give the *lower* threshold, namely that the border has an extension (infinitesimally) larger than no extension, i.e., that the border has *nothing* as its limit. That a phenomenon is imagined as spatially extended without this extension being possible to specify, seems highly paradoxical, but, nevertheless, we are able to operate with such a conception.

A border, then, can only be conceived as determined tendentiously by *nothing* being its limit. By conceptual logic, however, the concept of nothing seems to presuppose the concept of border rather than the other way around. The concept of nothing can be thought as constituted as the concept about the ultimate border that always will delimit a border that is continuously diminished.

The concept of border seems positioned *in-between* which is and which is not, between the concepts of being and nothing. A border is something, but because it is infinitesimally narrow, the concept points toward something *not* being.

However, just as little as nothing can be said to *be* (exist) in any immediate sense, can a border be said to be *between* something not being and something being.

Further, if the approach is sufficiently microscopic, *any specific* border imagined will also dissolve (by the way through the constitution of *other* borders). Therefore, any drawing of a border line is *relative*; it is the *subject* that brings its inherent boundaries upon the object.

If, however, the border is dissolved through *reflection*, it appears not as relative at all in its *immediateness*. Here, it is interesting to note that not only is it possible for a subject to perceive *differences*; in addition, any organism's perception necessarily *overestimates* these differences due to an intrinsic *contrast enhancer*:

In every studied organism it has been found that sensory neurons typically send collaterals (axon branches) to interneurons that have an inhibitory effect on the neighboring sensory neurons. (…)The effect of a lateral inhibition circuit is to enhance the contrast between highly stimulated neurons and their nonstimulated neighbors, since the stimulated cells fire at a lower rate than their base rate. Some such arrangement in the retina is believed to figure in the perceptual effect known as 'Mach bands' (Churchland [8], p. 72f).

It is not possible in the strict sense to *perceive* a border. Therefore, when we speak of the border *between* two somethings, this cannot be meaningfully understood as any physical or perceptual noticeable border. After all, there is nothing spatially or temporally extended which separates the two somethings. In between the two somethings, nothing else is located than mere discontinuity, a border which has no physical dimension. The border is not a nothing, because the two somethings could not be separated by the subject, but at the same time, the border can have no physical dimension, and as such it seems to be nothing after all. The only resolution to this paradox is to assume that the border exists in a different *sense* than the physical sense.

In *what* sense can a border be said to exist? It cannot be perceived, and thus it has no physical dimension. On the other hand, it can and must be *thought*. Therefore, if we think of the border as physical, this can only be permissible if we conceive it *as if* it were physical, i.e., we think of two somethings that we perceive *as if* they were separated by a physical border. In general, we imagine a border rendered concrete as very narrow, e.g., as a dividing line, despite such a concrete representation going against the conceptual content of border as being of *infinitesimal* extension. Thus, such representation constitutes an ontological negation. However, such a negation is the only way we can think about the relation between two somethings *as if* their separation was outer, subject-external and not inherent and hidden in the subject itself.

We can think a something without immediately reflecting upon its borders. The border between two perceived somethings can only be said to be in a *double* simile sense, namely (i) by something unthinkable being thought as if it was thinkable; and (ii) by the thinkable, a subject-internal being, being thought as if it was a subject-external being. Hence, the border cannot have any immediate perceptual existence. In this regard, the border is a *nothing*; border is only a something qua subject-internal being.

In order to acknowledge two somethings as different, the subject must necessarily have a concept of difference which in turn presupposes a concept of border. Only by applying such a concept, can the subject itself acknowledge that there really are different somethings it has classified, *de facto* and objectively, as different prior to and independently from having any concept of border. Only then the *objective* difference can be reflected by the subject as a *subjective* difference as well.

This reflection necessarily happens by *applying* a concept of border which has a non-physical character of being. But this application can only occur by *projecting* the non-physical concept onto the *same* physical being that the subject projects the two somethings onto.

The dividing third something, which separates the two somethings, are actually the *thresholds* that *inherent* in the subject's own algorithm, and which accordingly never can appear visible for the subject *when* it applies them. Accordingly, paradoxes implied in characterizing determination of a physical border are products of *distorted epistemology*, i.e., of the subject's erroneous self-understanding of the character of being of its perceptions. This epistemology can only be corrected from a more advanced reflection, which still unavoidably has to make use of the concept of border, but which abstains from transferring it onto perceived being in any other way than in the form of simile.

Thus, it is an epistemological error to claim border to be subject-external being. This is a projection of the subject-internal being of the concept. Nevertheless, the subject indeed makes use of precisely this projection in all other than its most advanced reflections. Projection is without reflection about its origin, and this epistemological mistake is thus to be understood as a form of *traceless classification*.

5. Traceless vs. reflexive classification

When the subject processes information, it will depend upon the algorithm of the subject whether the information added by means of an internal classification is simultaneously accompanied by deletion of information from the lower logical type level. If this is the case, we denote the classification as *traceless*; if—in the opposite case—the lower, preceding information is maintained, we denote the classification as *reflexive*.

If we look at algorithms of *perception*, far most classifications are traceless, not reflexive. The most striking and radically instructing case here is *reception*, i.e., the initial informative transfiguration among the steps constituting perception as a whole. Typically, reception follows the *Weber-Fechner relation* where (potential) differences from the outside of the subject's border surface (as the skin) are received by the subject in a *logarithmic* manner when constituting its internal inputs (cf. Bateson [9]). If we, by measuring devices, are able to quantify the (pre)inputs before they cross the border surface, (pre)inputs with, e.g., measurement values **2, 4, 8, 16**, and **32**, indicated by boldfaces, will become differentiated at the receiving side of the border surface with the respective values 1, 2, 3, 4, and 5. This means that constitution of any quantitative (subtractive) difference in the reception requires *larger* (subtractive) differences on the outer incoming side of the border surface, as specified by the logarithm, and that uniform reception of the minimal (subtractive) difference requires uniform in-sending of *ratio* differences on the preceding side. Further, when comparing differences on the two sides, most differences detectable on the preceding side will *not* be detected on the side of reception. For example, **5**, **6**, and **7** will all be received as 2, due to not reaching the threshold of **8** received as 3. Hence, such differences on the preceding side become received through *traceless* classification and are eliminated in the further information processing involved in perception. In our conscious reflection over this, we easily distinguish between the involved ordered pairs, say (**5**, 2) and (**6**, 2) and thus perform a *reflexive* classification upon the traceless classification.

When investigating reception more carefully, it becomes revealed a rather intricate dialectics between the qualitative and quantitative aspects of information. Regarded from the horizon of the subject in the act of reception, what is going on at the preceding side, if anything, is an inaccessible *Ding an sich* and does not represent any actual information. It is the act of reception which basically *constitutes* information, both in its quality (as given by the implied semantics of the receiving algorithm) and in the specific quantification of the quality. The reception *constitutes* information by discontinuation of *something* on the preceding side, so that this something can only qualify as *potential* information from an act of reflection *after* the information became actualized and constituted by the reception itself. Thus, it is not accurate to regard the quality with, e.g., a value **8** as the *same* quality which becomes constituted in reception with an input value 3. Ontologically, it is rather a *pre-quality*.

By reflection, traceless classification can be formulated into a certain implied syllogism, namely of the form "*a* is *c*; and *b* is *c*; ergo: *b* is *a*". For example: **5** is 2; **7** is 2; ergo: **7** is **5**. We name this form as *Erasmus syllogism*, after the notorious argument flung out by the character Erasmus in Ludvig Holberg's comedy *Erasmus Montanus* [10]: "A rock cannot fly; Mother Nille cannot fly; ergo, Mother Nille is a rock," where after Mother Nille bursts into crying. Trivially, the Erasmus syllogism is invalid by criteria of formal logic, contrary to a valid syllogism as "*a* is *c*; *b* is *a*; ergo: *b* is *c*."

A phenomenon *a* can be denoted *metaphor* for another phenomenon *b*, if phenomenon *a* stands in the same relation to a phenomenon *d* as phenomenon *b* stands to a phenomenon *e*. If we apply *c* to denote location at the left side of such a relation, the metaphor then rests upon the following inference: "*a* is *c*; *b* is *c*; ergo: *b* is a." Thus, we see that application of *a* as valid metaphor for *b* depends upon an inference having the form of Erasmus syllogism.

Gregory Bateson [9] used the term "syllogisms of grass" for Erasmus syllogisms and argued that such syllogisms and metaphors, despite their invalidity by formal logic, play a crucial role in nature, spanning from perception to more elaborate phenomena as poetry, humor, and religion. "[T]hese syllogisms are the very stuff of which natural history is made (…) all preverbal and nonverbal communication depends upon metaphor and/or syllogisms in grass (…) all verbal communication necessarily contains metaphor (…) metaphor is in fact the logic upon which the biological world has been built" (pp. 27–30). Bateson pointed out that even the syllogisms of formal logic presupposed *linguistic* classifications of entities as well as the categories of grammar themselves. Insofar such classifications are performed in traceless manners, cybernetics and epistemology ought to give much more emphasis to Erasmus syllogisms and metaphors. Interestingly, simple experiments in cognitive science by d'Andrade [11] and others have delivered support to this view by showing that many university students are not able to perform even simple syllogisms of *modus ponens* and *modus tollens* when the syllogisms are dressed in natural language, especially when the use of language appears confusing or emotionally loaded. Thus, human thinking also involves algorithms that are *not* valid by criteria of pure logic, operating at rather deep and opaque levels, and which should be accounted for in the very foundation of a broadened information science.

6. Manifolded differentiality of that which is

From the exploration of ontological characteristics of the border concept and some reflection on constitution of information in the act of reception, it should appear as a necessity to contemplate that which is at different *levels* of being, depending upon which level of logical type it is classified at within the operations of the subject.

What we usually apprehend as being in the physical sense is that which in one way or another can be registered as immediately being from our *perception*.

It is embedded in the very nature of perception that regardless of its distinctions residing in the subject itself, the subject has to apprehend the somethings that it perceives as subject-external being. Since the classifying criterion is always hidden (but expressed) *in* the classification itself, it is generally so that the subject in its reflection must consider the level of being in which it operates (at least) *one step lower* than it really is. This has a dramatic consequence for the lowest level of classification since the subject necessarily must perform its classification as traceless and thus to project it as subject-external. It is only for an advanced reflection to discover this projection as a simile. Projection involves a *fundamental ontological distortion* since subject-internal differentiations are conceived as subject-external.

Thus, the distinction between physical and ideal being is really a distinction *within* subject-internal being. However, since the subject necessarily reflects its classification imperfectly, this must appear as a distinction between subject-external and subject-internal being. Hence, the truly fundamental ontological distinction between subject-external and subject-internal being *appears* for the subject itself *twisted* into a distinction between physical and ideal being, while objectively it is merely an internal distinction between classification levels of the subject.

Any understanding is structured hierarchically in the sense that it reflects forms of being at a certain level of classification and abstraction by means of thought forms that only exist at a *higher* level. Thus, different forms of understanding may be distinguished by: (i) the ontological level of their thought forms; and (ii) the ontological level of the forms of being that the thought forms are to understand.

We can define *illusion* as a subject's placement of a phenomenon at a *mistaken level of being*. Such an ontological mistake can only be demonstrated by means of *reflection* (by a different subject, or by the same subject) upon this placement. After such reflection, though the phenomenon is not *eliminated*, it is replaced at a *different* level. The subject's apprehension of the level of reception as subject-external, or of the separating third as a physical border are examples of such *necessary* illusions or distortions. Illusions are always due to traceless classification.

A reasonable definition of *substance* is *that and only that which is being at the perceptual level*. Thus, substance is perception as it immediately appears for the observing subject, i.e., as a projection onto the subject-external. From an advanced reflection, however, it was not possible to let the concept of border refer to such a low ontological level, and this is tantamount to the fact that neither (subjective) difference nor discontinuity be placed at such a low level. Thus, we can conclude that difference is not a substance despite that difference also is a being.

In contrast to substance, *quality* can be imagined at all levels of being. Also at the lowermost level of being, quality will distinguish itself from substance. A quality at this level is a substance beheld in the light of the difference reflection, i.e., being at the first level seen from something being at a higher level—whereby being at the first level by virtue of this elevated view no longer can be understood as (only) substance, despite the formal identity of extension.

Thus, the concept of quality at the lowest level of being is a concept-logical combination of the concepts of substance and difference.

The levels of being have a hierarchical order which means that something can only be at one level in the continuation of other preceding somethings having appeared at all underlying levels. Something can only become being through a stepwise transformation of something pre-existing which is only to be found at a lower level of being. We can define an *idea* (in contrast to substance) as any something which is to be found at a higher level of being than the physical level. Then, any instance of being is either an idea or a substance. Since all ideational being *ultimately* starts out from physical being, we can say that all ideas are based upon substance. For instance, the idea of a particular number is based upon a concrete, perceptual number notation, and any idea is *immediately* based upon one or plural ideas at lower levels of being. Thus, it is also *possible* that an idea is immediately based upon a substance. However, the idea of a particular number, for instance, is based upon ideas that separate Arabic numerals from other patterns, and this basis is not a substance according to our terminology.

Many ideas are also tied to substance in another way than the one given by retrospective connection. This occurs when a new idea arises by an earlier idea being *combined* with a substance, e.g., by an idea at level 100 arising through a combination of an idea at level 99 with a substance at level 1. This is the case for instance with the idea of a particular quality. We will therefore name such ideas *substantial ideas*.

It seems to be a characteristic of our *conscious* ideas that they have precisely such a substantial character. Even the most abstract thought seems to necessarily have a perceptual binding, i.e., that it imagines other ideas by tying them to, and letting them be *represented* by, something perceptual. In fact, it does not seem possible for us to consciously think anything at all without imagining it *as if* it was perceptual and extended in time and space. This involves that the subject in its thinking reaches back to the lowest level of being (feedback), i.e., that *the subject all the time takes the longest imaginable step backwards in order to be able to take yet another step forwards* in level of abstraction.

A suitable definition of *consciousness* can be the overall relations between the substantial ideas in the system of ideas. Thus, any idea within the system that is not substantial will escape consciousness, including necessarily the idea *of* a substantial idea and the idea that *makes* an idea substantial. Such ideas are unconscious because they are present at a meta-level until they are possibly made substantial themselves. In order for the subject to become aware ("conscious") of its own activity, a significant logical distance between that which thinks and that which is thought seems precisely to be what is required, and the substantialization of the ideas is precisely a mechanism which produces such a distance.

With necessity, elementary reflections on that which is has to be dualistic, dividing being into physical vs. mental, objective vs. subjective, object of thought vs. thought itself. However, from more advanced reflection, dualistic thinking implies two fundamental mistakes concerning the nature of being: It is *twisted* because it apprehends the differentiation of subject-internal being as a differentiation between subject-external and subject-internal being, which is due to its outward projection that is perceived; and it is *amputated* because it apprehends the differentiation of being as dual instead of enormous manifolds.

7. Extrapolated decomposition of that which is onto *three* differentiated ontological dimensions: processual-physical, algorithmic, and *transalgorithmic*

We define the *structure* of a system as the total set of relations *between* the algorithms of the system, i.e., the set that *orders* the algorithms by indicating their succession and reciprocal positioning. Structure must be understood as an *algorithm*, i.e., as the *structuring algorithm* which operates as a *meta-algorithm* in relation to the other algorithms of the system. Correspondingly, this meta-algorithm must be imagined and performed by a *meta-subject* internal in the system. Then, we can also imagine a system-internal input process from a firstly activated algorithm's position onto the structuring meta-algorithm, and an output process from this meta-algorithm onto the positioning of the other algorithms. This output process is to be understood as *differential movement* down to a lower level of being. Thus, it does not function as input for the first-order algorithms, just as the latter algorithms do not function as inputs for their output-processes.

Just like structure can be regarded as a meta-algorithm, the other algorithms can be regarded as substructures. It is common to consider a system as consisting of components and of the network of relations between the components. The structuring meta-algorithm, then, is an algorithmic formulation of this component external network of relations, while the other algorithms are component internal.

The structuring meta-algorithm, just like first-order algorithms, operates in an ideal universe. But, with the presence of meta-algorithms, the ideal universe is no longer only differentiated in different levels of being internally in each algorithm, but also *between* algorithms of different order. We can consider this as an ontological differentiation in *depth*, by which the ontological total universe manifests from a *ternary* differentiating complex. While that which was previously differentiated horizontally by a vertical differentiation, this vertical differentiation must now be seen in relation to a differentiation in depth. We will separate this depth universe from the algorithmic universe by denoting it *transalgorithmic*. A structuring meta-algorithm can only be described at a meta-level where the subordinate algorithms do not appear as algorithmic.

Meta-description is necessary in order to understand relations between algorithms of the same order (i.e., first-order description) insofar as these relations are themselves algorithmic, that is, determined by second- and higher order algorithms lying above or behind them. In order to understand relations between algorithms of the same order, then, these must be described from relations between algorithms of *different* order. In this respect, the algorithmic universe can only be understood from the transalgorithmic. Transalgorithmic differentiations are always present in dynamic system descriptions, because algorithms and processes can only be described as occurring in *particular* orders which are structurally determined. For this reason, such descriptions also include a transalgorithmic dimension.

Even though the relations between same-order algorithms immediately can only be understood from *one* structuring meta-algorithm, relations between plural structures must themselves be structured. Insofar as such relations occur, there must also exist meta-meta-algorithms, and so on. Thus, the transalgorithmic universe encompasses algorithms of different orders up to the highest thinkable order, i.e., up to the transalgorithmic (depth) level above the topmost structures that we can think of as interdependent.

http://dx.doi.org/10.5772/intechopen.72951

We can distinguish between the following types of meta-algorithms: (i) *structuring* algorithms (effecting relations *between* algorithms); (ii) *ingoing* algorithms (effecting relations *internal* in an algorithm); and (iii) *outgoing* algorithms (effecting neither algorithms themselves nor relations between them).

Meta-algorithms that effect backward on algorithms that the meta-algorithm receives its input from, immediately or mediately, we will denote *re-acting meta-algorithms*. These constitute a subgroup of ingoing meta-algorithms, in contrast to the other ingoing meta-algorithms which we will denote *pre-acting meta-algorithms*. Process, algorithm, and structure are to be comprehended as *relative* concepts. In a *combined* system description, this relativity manifests by first-order algorithms acquiring a double nature as algorithmic vs. processual, depending on, respectively, whether they are regarded in relation to processes at the lowest level of being in the description or in relation to second-order algorithms.

8. Ontological unfoldment into the complete nexus of causality types

We have clarified how information can be understood as a (objective) difference that makes a difference, i.e., as that difference which brings about another difference. More precisely, the relation between the two differences consists of the fact that if the first difference takes place, then the other difference *must* also take place. We *define causal relation* as this relation between the two differences. Further, we define the *first* difference as *cause* and the *second* difference as *effect*. Consequently, *information* is tantamount with the relatum in a causal relation that is termed "*cause*." Accordingly, information exists if and only if (at least) one causal relation exists.

This does not imply that "information" with respect to the *intension* of the term (as semantically opposed to the *extension* of the term) is identical with "cause." The *extensionally* same (first) relatum in a causal relation appears *immediately* as "information," while it appears also as "cause" only *after* a subject's *reflection* upon the relation. The subject cannot *immediately* perceive the (second) difference which the (first) relatum has brought upon the subject, notwithstanding that this difference must be *implicitly* present (by having *made* the relatum into information).

Thus, different from, e.g., the contention of Bateson [9] (p. 51), there cannot be cause and effect without existence of information. Even plain descriptions of a system by means of physical mechanics must *de facto* operate with distinctions which with necessity issue from informative transfigurations, and algorithmic causality must thus be implicitly or tacitly present also in such descriptions.

This means that an adequate concept of causality must be sufficiently abstract, universal, and elementary to reside inherently and basically *enfolded* in the *qualitative concept* of information as such, to become *unfolded* and *established* by a deep and rigorous philosophical *back-reflection*, hitting the mark of the enfolded quality of causality. This is far from any trivial statement or any straight-forward achievement.

Standard logics operates with a concept of *material implication*, from Frege and Russell onward, as a certain *truth function* of a first variable p and a second variable q, where this function per definition is untrue if the (binary) truth value of *p* is true and the truth value of *q* is untrue, while the function is true for the three other pairs of truth values of *p* and *q*. This concept of material implication, whatever its usefulness in mathematics and informatics, leads to plural propositions becoming judged as true, despite *contradicting* intuitive notions of causality. As examples, consider, e.g., (i) p => (q =>p); (ii) –p => (p =>q); (iii) (p =>q) v (q =>p). Rather obviously, the definition of material implication has severe shortcomings as: (i) the definition is *too broad* to hit the mark of causality as enfolded in information as such; (ii) the definition presupposes that the truth functions of *p* and *q* can be established in mutual *independency before* they become related and compared, in *contradiction* to the informational concept of causality which *unfolds* the relata of cause vs. effect; (iii) the definition presupposes *preceding* establishments of truth functions of *p* and *q* while *ignoring* any role of causality in the very *establishment* of these truth functions.

The limitations of material implication have been sought surmounted in various developments of modal logic which introduced a concept of *strict implication* where *q must* be true if *p* is true, and also introduced related possible-world semantics with necessity and possibility operators. These attempts imply somewhat ontological *differentiations* within the universe of imagined truth values, and between those constellations where *p* and *q necessarily* must coincide as true vs. where they coincide as true *without* this being due to strict implication.

We regard these attempts as still restricted, while fruitfully pointing in two adequate *directions*, namely with respect to (i) seeking toward hitting the mark of causality as it is *de facto* enfolded in information as such, and operating at an intuitive, subconscious level with a *deeper* ontological foundation than the assumed free-standing toy universe of formal logic; and (ii) anchoring and relating causality of different types in a strictly and exhaustively differentiated *ontology*.

Our treatise [1], pp. 113–194, sought to reestablish causality theory as a whole from basic fulfillment of aspects (i) and (ii). With respect to aspect (i), the most basic challenge was to theoretically adequately back-reflect the category of "causality," universally *already* existing as tacitly operative inside all information in and of nature, including a subconscious category acting as crucial constituent in informative reflection by human thinking inside an *imagined* free-standing thought universe (as a certain subsystem, not *only* imagined, of being).

The next basic challenge was to theoretically grasp and exhibit how this de facto *universal* category of "causality" became unfolded into the two most basic *types* of causality, namely *projective causality*, with necessity implied in *any* constitution and processing of information, as already indicated, and *formal logical causality*, with necessity indicating the most universal and basic de facto *formalization* of causality. We exhibited the make-up of formal logical causality from a *deeper* formal relation than material implication or strict implication, more specifically as implied, in a specified formal manner, in *any* relation between classification and elements involved in constitution of information.

With respect to aspect (ii), we presented a rigorous unfoldment of the whole *nexus* of possible causality types as *anchored* in the universal concept of causality, while at the same time, successively and logically *unfolding* inside the framework of a concisely differentiated *universal ontology* by the three dimensions: transalgorithmic, algorithmic, and processual-physical (3 + 1D). Inside the page limitations of the present text, we must restrict ourselves to a somewhat cryptic short-hand description of the systematic differential unfoldment into key features of the different fundamental causality types (complementary connected as illustrated by **Figure 1**):

Formal logical causality: this category is universal for all thinkable information, i.e., for *any* information flow in *any* described information matrix, i.e., in the imagination of a pure and free-standing logical universe. Formal logical causality is deduced in its precise form from specified classification logic between the thinkable classes and elements from ontology differentiated vertically. All other causality types are subtypes and "clothes" of this abstract one, which is what qualify them as causality types. They unfold from specified additions of different *similes, necessary* in any dynamic system description, explicitly stated or not.

Algorithmic causality: this is the causal relation from an input-value to an output-value inside the algorithm.

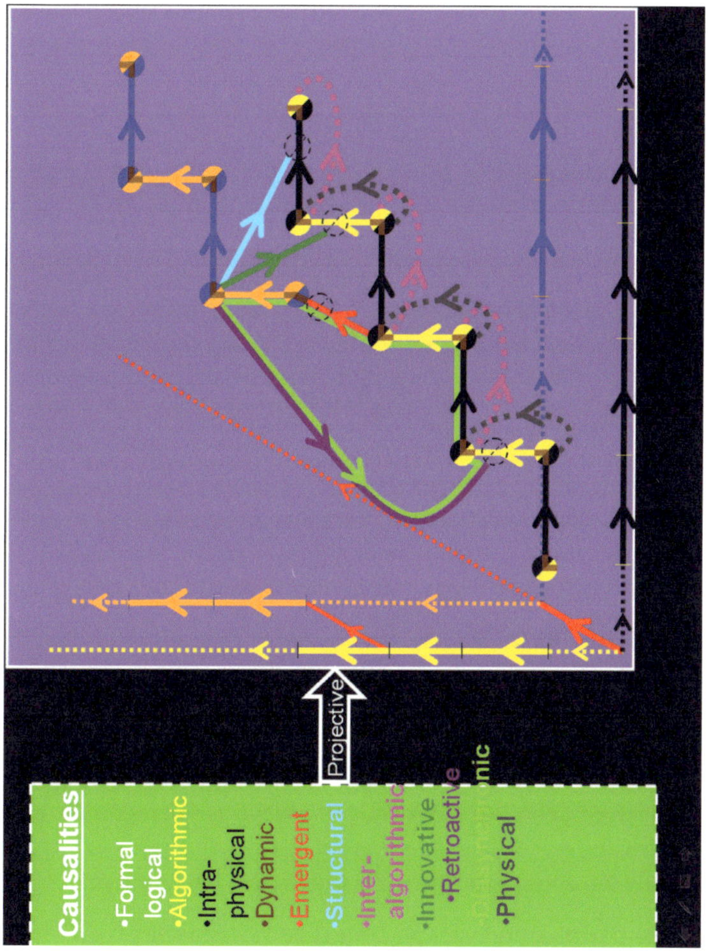

Figure 1. Illustration of the causality nexus anchored in the three dimensions physical (horizontal in black; 3 + 1D compressed as 1D time), algorithmic (vertical in yellow), and transalgorithmic (depth in red). Description of first-order alternates between process (black) and transfiguration (yellow), second-order between blue and orange. Higher orders activate from emergence (red) and unfold as structural change in process (light blue) or innovative change in transfiguration (dark green), with the possibility of the last being retroactive (purple). Whatever degree of order and systemic complexity, the illustrated conglomerate of causality types and arrows constitutes a completed nexus of information flows.

Intra-physical causality: this is the causal relation from start point to end point of a process.

Dynamic causality: this is the causal relation with the two subclasses: a) from end point of a process to start point in an algorithm; b) from end point of an algorithm to start point in a process.

Projective causality: this is the causal relation from the meta-subject to the thought object as a whole, the potential inner classifications and causal relations being actualized in this projection (including formal logical causality). In **Figure 1**, the arrow of projective causality originates from the field (in green) of an enfolded nexus of causality types, denoting a segment *inside* the thinking meta-subject that makes the description, and manifests as the field (in indigo) of an unfolded nexus of causality types. The frame of the originating field is marked with broken white lines in order to distinguish its ontological status from the nexus projected into the derived field.

Structural causality: this is the meta-algorithmic causality relation directing the process-output from an algorithm to the process-input for another algorithm and hence positioning all algorithms in a structure.

Inter-algorithmic causality: this is the causal relation from an algorithmic output to the algorithmic input for another algorithm, hence ignoring the intermediary physical process by a projection to the vertical algorithmic axis.

Emergent causality: this is the causal relation from an algorithm to a meta-algorithm.

Innovative causality: this is the causal relation from a meta-algorithm to a first-order algorithm. An important subtype of innovative causality is the *retroactive* causal relation from a meta-algorithm to a first-order algorithm earlier connected to the meta-algorithm by emergent causality.

Diasynchronic causality: this is the causal relation made up by a *circuit* of algorithmic, physical, intraphysical, dynamic, projective, emergent, structural, and retroactive innovative causality.

Physical causality: this is the physical relation from a process output to the process input of the next process; hence, ignoring all intermediary algorithmic and transalgorithmic transfigurations by a projection from the vertical axis or the depth axis to the horizontal axis.

It follows from the illustration of the causality nexus in **Figure 1**, that, e.g., the conventional notion of *physical* causality is far from constituting the *most* fundamental causality type. It is also far from any *trivial* causality types, due to its condensation of many involved causality paths through plural shortcuts and similes. Thus, it follows from strict and consistent philosophical-ontological reflection on the nexus of causality types which *make up* the reality of cosmic wide information, that ideas about cosmos as *fundamentally* physical or—even worse—*only* physical, are basically *radically amputated and illusionary* as judged by strict standards of scientifically informed and informing philosophy/meta-science.

From these fundamental causality types, various *elaborated* causality types constituted by combinations of fundamental causality types were exhibited by Johansen [1] (ch. 3.2); among these are: chance causality, probability causality, stochastic causality, intentional causality, selective causality, and imagined causality. Thus, more elaborated and epistemologically refined causality types, crucial in human and social systems, were understood *inside* the causality nexus anchored in the three ontological dimensions (see Johansen [12, 13] for specified applications of this causality theory).

9. The role of semantics and subject with respect to some recent developments of "computation"

The concept of algorithm should be understood at a sufficiently high level of abstraction to be consistent with the most abstract and deepest concept of causality, in order to provide differential philosophy with some robustness against progresses in information science. Thus, the concept of algorithm should not be restricted to the ontology underlying the conventional binary informatics of UTM. Later on, informatics has experienced significant extensions of Turing informatics, in form of David Deutsch's triadic qubit informatics (quantum computation), and the further development to Rowlands' (with Diaz) quantum holographic informatics entailed in his highly ambitious opus magnum *Zero to Infinity. Foundations of Physics* [14] which presented a universal theory of philosophy into science named *Nilpotent Universal Computational Rewrite System* (NUCRS). Rowlands' theory significantly upgrades the *semantic*—and thus *qualitative*—aspect of informatics by providing "a semantic model of computation" as "Nature's Rules" (ibid.: 557). The same was the case for David Bohm's sketch of a second-order informatics based on an elementary unit consisting of a 2x2 matrix with inherent feedback. Accordingly, Bohm often *defined* "meaning" as information about information (e.g., in [15]).

Mikhail Ignatyev, referred to as "the father of robotics" in Russia, pioneered the field of robotics from 1963 on [16] and i.a. constructed the first submarine robots. Later on, Ignatyev [17–19] developed a universal *linguo-combinatorial* cybernetics which placed and recognized semantics in the very heart and foundation of cybernetic theory (cf. [18], p. 18f). Further, this departing role was given to semantics in a quite elaborated sense, namely to natural language understood as the universal language operating in the human mind/brain, more abstract than its monoplural manifestations into the specific languages of the different mother-tongues (cf. [17], comment to his Figure 1). In its mathematical core, Ignatyev's universal theory consists of a certain set of differential equations, qualitatively based on a binary distinction between signifier and signified, and anchored in quantitative description of systems by means of *Pascal's triangle* which manifests the formula for "the basic law of cybernetics, informatics and synergetics for complex systems" [17]. Ignatyev's application of this theory to nanorobotics (cf. [19], p. 674) led to the discovery of an important *connection* between Pascal complexity (understood as the values of the involved "arbitrary coefficients" in a row of Pascal's triangle) in the *algorithmic* composition of a nanorobot vs. the Pascal complexity inherent in the *material* substances making up the nanorobot. Interpreted in the framework of differential ontology, this connection, argued by Ignatyev, indicates that certain *quantitative information laws*, not previously discovered, are enfolded in system description characteristics when two (or more) systems of different levels (such as of the two dimensional-pairs (meta-algorithmic, algorithmic) and (algorithmic, time-physical)) are adequately combined in a unified description. This may have far-reaching implications with respect to understanding of ontological architecture *in general*, especially with respect to quantitative laws constraining or directing information flows between different levels in highly complex systems involving *intelligence* of different degree of complexity and operating at different systemic levels. It is significant that the cybernetic theory of Ignatyev operates at (and from) a level of abstraction where *mind* and intelligence are not excluded from the system, or regarded as more or less secondary epistructures derived or emerging from material underpinnings.

According to Ignatyev, linguo-combinatorial cybernetics has proved capable of developing exhaustive "models of all the known chemical elements, their isotopes, and molecular structures" (cf. [19], p. 673). Thus, Ignatyev refers to the establishing of "cybernetic physics" ([18], p. 20) and states such cybernetic physics/chemistry as *superior* to the conventional method of linear combination of atomic orbitals, because "the linguo-combinatorial method considers all the combinations of interaction" ([19], p. 673).

UTM considers the string/tape as only carrying binary information. Here, the substantial representation of the distinction does not matter as such (say 0 vs. 1, black vs. white, electron present vs. absent), nor the substance of the tape carrying the distinction. Some substances are more adequate than others in order for UTM to function fast and reliably, while they are irrelevant for the concept of UTM which implies a radical split between the operating machine and the substance it operates on. Contrary to this, in Ignatyev's robotics, the substance of the robot *does* matter, namely with respect to its internal informational characteristic as specifically described by its Pascal complexity by means of Ignatyev's cybernetic physics. The "control unit" (analogous to the operating machine part in UTM) of Ignatyev's robot *employs* the Pascal complexity of the material substance by *extracting* information from the substance into *itself*, as well as into establishment of feedback loops of tuning and calibration *between* the control unit and the substance. Other things equal, the higher the Pascal complexity of the material substance, the more advanced nanorobots can be constructed. Hence, nanotechnological development of novel substances as, e.g., certain carbon isotopes, characterized by higher inherent Pascal complexity, becomes crucial for development of more advanced nanorobots. Ignatyev's robotics indicates rather paradigmatic implications for information science, implying more intimate and interactive relations between the operating and the operated part than in UTM. In some aspects, this relation may seem ontologically more similar to human claims of possession phenomena than to UTM. Walk-in from an external entity takes advantage of the complexity of the human mind/brain in order to expand its field of operation by implementing itself as a control unit for the human mind/brain system. In analogy to Ignatyev's material substance, higher degree of freedom in the targeted system, as indicated by the "arbitrary coefficients" of its row in Pascal's triangle, does not restrict, but amplify the range of control performed by the targeting control unit.

It was stated in our qualitative concept of information that there is no such thing as information without the implied presence of a *subject*. The cybernetic foundation by Ignatyev points in the same direction. This is also in agreement with Rowlands who establishes his theory with a basic universality not at all *excluding* subjects or the field of psychology (cf. [14], p. 598).

The mathematician-physicist Diego L. Rapoport has provided crucial contributions to several disciplines (as physics, genetics, informatics, and cybernetics) by means of a universal *Klein-bottle* paradigm (cf. i.a. [20–22]) which ontologically surmounts the Cartesian cut by basic inclusion

http://dx.doi.org/10.5772/intechopen.72951

of the subject (see Rosen [23] for many basic philosophical contemplations of the significance of the Klein-bottle). Rapoport [22] analyzes how already the *photon* has to be treated from the subjective-objective *dynamics* constituted by the ontological figure of the Klein-bottle. Consistent with this, the treatment in Rapoport [20] starts out from second-order cybernetics, *involving* the subject, and from ontological recognition of perceptual *depth* in the sense of Merleau-Ponty, by Rapoport interpreted as the dimension of the Klein-bottle reentering itself and related to the *transalgorithmic* dimension in differential ontology. Rapoport developed Klein-bottle logics, anchored in the paradoxical logic initiated by A. Stern [24], where Boolean logic manifests as an intermediary subcase. Rapoport's development of Klein-bottle logics and informatics is intimately linked not only to quantum mechanics and torsion physics, but also to cognition. Such linkage is indicated by his discovery of a *logical time operator* at second quantization coinciding with a classical difference yielding non-null torsion in cognitive space. Rapoport introduces the *denktor* to connect cognitive space to superposition and vector space with bras and kets, and the *logical potential* carrying *logical energy* to connect basic cognitive dynamics and the quantization rule of Bohr-Sommerfeld. This indicates how concepts related to the *subject* are given basic recognition in the theory of Rapoport. In Rapoport's theory of time, statements of quantum physics become converted into logical statements, especially by means of the Hadamard gate in quantum computation. His time operator "*is a primeval distinction between cognitive states in (-) Matrix Logic as its action amounts to compute the difference between these states. As a geometric action, Time is a ninety degrees rotation in the 2-plane of all cognitive states*" [22]. This indicates the general relevance of Rapoport's theory of time for cybernetics of complex systems, and even more so since Rapoport "*relates Time to intention, control, will and the appearance of life*" (ibid.). More specifically, in Rapoport's highly elaborated analysis, *logophysical* time is a projection of a vortex structure to the cognitive plane that is further associated to will and intention.

In order to fully integrate the concept of subject into information science, an adequate concept of *emotion* must also be introduced and integrated, or at least related, as with necessity tied to the concept of (an emphatic) subject. We stated, in connection to the qualitative concept of information, that there is no such thing as information without tacitly implied emotion. As a simple illustration: a prototypic case of something considered "rock-hard" and undeniable real, is a heavy stone falling down on one's toe, inducing strong emotional pain. Hence, the quality of emotion is tacitly *implied* in the notion of information as really real, and at the most basic level not *opposed* to such a notion. When Turing established an abstract, universal, and elementary concept of "information" and "computation," this required, among other skills, an extraordinary act of *abstraction* and *detrivialization* of the ordinary notions of "somethings" experienced in daily as well as scientific life. Contrary to common opinion, we regard the establishment of an abstract, universal, and elementary concept of "emotion" as requiring an *even more* difficult act of abstraction and detrivialization, and bordering to the very *limits* of meta-scientific inquiry. It leads too far to explore this demanding topic in the present text, but we will state as a postulate that the *exodos* of emotion *as such* from theories of informatics and computer science represents a theoretical shortcoming of rather basic nature, having possibly fatal implications for AI developments consistent with a human interest. As example, if one considers a transhumanist goal of transporting "consciousness" into a substantial carrier external to the human body, how is one to scientifically decide whether this "copy" *feels* the same—or anything at all—if the scientific theory does not include an adequate *concept* of emotion?

10. Unfoldment into number theory

With respect to the concept of border, we clarified that the border itself cannot have any physical extension, but is *virtual* in relation to the environment, and is an inherent category of the subject *projected* into the environment. This projection is the only way to constitute the input as a real input for the subject to process, because it is the only way borders can be made and processed, and the only way for information to exist. Hence, it has to be universally true *both* that the subject projects differences downward the ontological hierarchy *and* that this projection is a necessary operator to constitute information. This is a universal basic paradox enfolded in the very quality of information, and hence in the general make-up of the universe. However, this is not an unresolved paradox, but the way the universe works and walks. With necessity, the basic unit of information processing must have this double nature, both projecting an algorithm to one step below its real existence, and *using* this projection to reach the next higher step in its successive processing. We can imagine this double nature of the walking thought as having to step one step back in the ontological staircase with one "thought foot," the other foot still standing on its original step and regarding the first foot as not being its own, in order to in the next run discontinuously jumping to the step above, the first foot leaping two steps, the second only one. Thereafter, this procedure has to be repeated for every further walk by thought.

The *Fibonacci algorithm,* constituting the Fibonacci series inside the set of natural numbers, proceeds from a number B in the series to the next number C, by moving back from B to the preceding number A and then moving forward by adding A and B into the proceeding number C. This is equivalent to stepping one step back with one foot, and then jumping with both foots to the step above. Hence, the form of this algorithm is *exactly the same* as the pattern described above as the abstract, universal, and elementary form of border constitution and information processing. This must mean that the Fibonacci algorithm expresses the *quantitative* aspect with necessity involved in *all* information processing of nature, because it is implied in the universal *quality* of the very category of information. Whether and how this fact *appears* at a manifest level for human observation is quite another question.

The Fibonacci algorithm constitutes the most abstract, universal, and elementary ontological *bridge* between the qualitative and quantitative aspects of information. When we express the Fibonacci algorithm into the Fibonacci series, the formulation takes place *inside* an *already* established ontological domain, namely the number landscape made up of the set of natural numbers. This set is *not* constituted by the Fibonacci algorithm itself in conventional number theory. However, the claimed result from our consistent reflection upon the quality of *border* as implied in the very quality of the information concept, was that the Fibonacci algorithm, contemplated at *the deepest* and *most abstract* ontological level, is implied as the constitutional *tie* between the qualitative and quantitative aspect of information *as such*. If true, this implicates that even the ontological domain of *numbers*, presented primarily as the set of *natural* numbers, should be theoretically possible to establish by consistent unfoldment of the Fibonacci algorithm as contemplated in the ontological "primordial" sense.

Our treatise *Fibonacci generation of natural numbers and of prime numbers* [25] established the complete and unique set of natural numbers as a *generative result* from strict, systematic unfoldment of the primordial Fibonacci algorithm through successive alternation between

Fibonacci constitution of ordinal numbers vs. cardinal numbers, in our terminology specified as *perplex numbers* (in some relatedness to Chandler [26]) vs. *size numbers*. The set of natural numbers became generated in strict and unique succession between so-called *Fibonacci atoms* and *Fibonacci molecules*, exposing the hidden generator *resulting* in formal coincidence with the theorem of Zeckendorf [27, 28]. Also, the treatise presented some novel mathematical results more "technically" (e.g., [25], Figure 2; cf. also Johansen [29]), and some deeper considerations with respect to ontological placement and refinement of the four basic operators of arithmetic, as well as with respect to reestablishment of the connection between number theory and geometry at a more intimate level in the very foundations of mathematics. The significance of this last deep-connection had earlier been recognized in our deduction of a complete and unique pattern of prime numbers, with the treatise of Johansen [30] representing the main publication; see also Johansen [31–33]. See Strand [34] for mathematical reformulation of our deduction by means of *group theory*, as well as further reformulation by means of *genonumbers*. See appendix in Johansen [33] for the publication of a software program confirming the correctness of the mathematical deduction, copyrighted by JM Strand and SE Johansen, initially demonstrated at the end of our lecture Nov. 24, 2010 at the *International Conference on Mathematical Sciences* at University of Bolu, Turkey.

Conventionally, the significance of the Fibonacci algorithm in number theory had been basically restricted to exposing the Fibonacci series as a *subset* of natural numbers, with various interesting mathematical properties, while at the same time, the significance of the Fibonacci series in the make-up of a plethora of *natural systems* had been (and still is) steadily growing. Our treatise [25] intended a *Copernican turn* for number theory in its very foundation, because the set of natural numbers was *not* taken as established *before* the definition of the Fibonacci series, but strictly and systematically generated from the most *abstract, primordial,* and *pre-numbering* formulation of the Fibonacci algorithm, due to the deep-significance of this algorithm as implied in the very *concept* of information as such. (The fact that the Fibonacci series of natural numbers also *after* this refoundation still remains as a subset of natural numbers is a trivial statement, without any relevance to the deeper and crucial issue of whether the *set* of natural numbers should be adequately understood as an *epistructure* generated from successive unfoldment of the Fibonacci algorithm in the deeper, *pre-numbered* sense.) This *radical inversion* of the conventional relation between the set of natural numbers vs. the Fibonacci algorithm, pretends a *paradigmatic* revolution in the sense of Kuhn [35]. This Copernican turn in the establishment of number theory may also suggest a deeper and rather direct scientific approach to explain why and how Fibonacci series are that fundamental in characteristics of *natural* systems.

The treatise also exhibits how Pascal's triangle becomes *generated* by (further) unfoldment of the Fibonacci algorithm inside number theory, including the slightly amputated version of Pascal's triangle which constitutes the foundation for Ignatyev's linguo-combinatorial informatics, cybernetics, and robotics (cf. [25], Tables 5–9; and also Johansen [36]). Thus, it is possible to scientifically address linguo-combinatorial informatics from a *deeper* foundation of qualitative informatics represented by differential ontology and epistemology.

Without beforehand having established our qualitative concept of information, involving the qualitative concept of border, with sufficient rigor, inside our differential ontology (including differential epistemology), it would have appeared as hubris, as well as rather strange, to attempt to reconstitute the foundations of number theory (as well as its basic interrelatedness to geometry) from a philosophical ontology, or to anticipate any novel results inside "pure" mathematics becoming possible to achieve from consistent unfoldment of such ontology. Thus, our mathematical achievements were *crucially inspired* and *catalyzed* by certain key results established as enfolding from our *qualitative* informatics inside our differential ontology and epistemology. Next, regarded in basic retrospect, these mathematical achievements, especially the systematic refoundation of number theory from strict unfoldment of the deeper Fibonacci algorithm, provide crucial *support* to the foundations of our philosophical informatics and differential ontology as being able to deeply *hit the mark* of key issues in philosophical ontology and related qualitative informatics. When it proves able to even catalyze number theory, the so-called *queen* of mathematics, in key aspects by paradigmatic inversion, lifting, and extension, this provides a strong indication that it may show able, through later applications and developments, to also catalyze *other* formal disciplines, including informatics, as well as disciplines of natural as well as social science.

With respect to influences from our qualitative informatics and differential ontology into substantial achievements inside *formal* disciplines of logics and informatics, we refer primarily to works and references by Rapoport [20–22], and more generally to the references by Rowlands [14] (p. 530, p. 550). With respect to consistency with achievements into *informational geometry* and *particle physics*, we also refer to works and references by Erik Trell [37–39]. With respect to achievements into *anthropology*, we refer primarily to works and references by Fyhn [40], Follo [41], and E. Røyrvik [42].

R.M. Santilli initiated the discipline of *hadronic mechanics* which claims to have accomplished a radical lifting and broadening of conventional quantum mechanics and relativity theory [43], as well of related mathematics [44], and stretching into related liftings of chemistry leading to "new clean energies" [45], as well as into expansions of theoretical biology [46]. We refer to Gandzha et al. [47] for an introductory overview of these achievements, and to Santilli [48] for the most extensive presentation of these theoretical developments. Johansen [49] argued basic consistency between differential ontology and the ontology underlying hadronic mechanics and mathematics. Quartieri [50] presented some contemplations concerning implications of this consistency for system theory. Johansen [51] presented some discussion of achievements in hadronic geometry and biology as interpreted from differential ontology, as well as some sketch of further extension into hadronic psychology. The number theorist L. Schadeck [52] has referred to our consideration of the Fibonacci algorithm as the universal-elementary "reality atom," as the "Johansen-Fibonacci paradigm," and has also suggested the radical possibility of extending UTM into "Hadronic Turing Machines" by incorporation of isoduality into the basic unit of informatics.

11. Related works in philosophy of science

In quite profound respects, Rapoport's achievements were originally inspired by, as well as applying, paradigmatic and theoretic elements from *Spencer-Brown's* remarkable *Laws of Form* [53] which departed from the mark of *"distinction"* as its primeval key concept. There occur significant resemblances between Spencer-Brown's work and our *Outline of Differential Epistemology* [1] (with its first edition published in 1991, authored without knowing *Laws of*

http://dx.doi.org/10.5772/intechopen.72951

Form), not at least with respect to the concept of *difference* playing much the same role in our work as *distinction* did in the work of Spencer-Brown. Interestingly, Spencer-Brown was hinting toward mathematical results from our own qualitative informatics when he, somewhat cryptically, wrote about the "beautiful manifestation of the form, whereby you break up the distinction and it turns into a Fibonacci sequence" and "You break up truth and you get Fibonacci."

Also the works of the late *David Bohm* exhibit some striking resemblances to our own differential ontology, among which, in this context, we will briefly mention a few. Bohm [54] represented his most extensive work presenting and explaining theoretical and mathematical details of quantum mechanics from a deeper ontological interpretation. The work *Science, Order, and Creativity* [55] presented an extensive ontological architecture with *three dimensions of order*: the *successive* one (change, change of change, change of change of change, etc.), the *generative* one (change of successive degree of order, change of change of successive degree of order, etc.) and the *superenfolded* one (change of degree of generative order, change of change of degree of generative order, etc.). Bohm's concept of *soma-significance* indicated a general conception of dual unity of algorithmic vs. physical being, and he analyzed, related to his critique of the Copenhagen interpretation, the categories of randomness and probability as operators *inside* a framework of causality. Bohm was highly influenced by Hegel's *Wissenschaft der Logik* [56], with related emphasis on analyses of relations of *conceptual logic*, and with the twin concept of *enfoldment/unfoldment* of implicated orders playing a general key role in his scientific approaches.

In our treatise Johansen [57], we presented the foundation of a novel economic theory having some basic similarities, as well as some basic differences, to the complex theory of capital created by the late Karl Marx [58]. Marx' economic theory was highly influenced by Hegel's conceptual logic, and attempted to systematically unfold concepts and relations, qualitative as well as quantitative ones, considered already enfolded, *in nuce*, in the economic category of (the capitalistically produced) *commodity*. In contrast to Marx, our own economic theory was developed inside a certain *differentiated* economic ontology. Our development of the concept of *labor time content* (*Wertgrösse/Wert*), the key concept in second-order economics, would have been theoretically impossible (in a plethora of qualitative and quantitative aspects) to achieve from a simplistic *binary* ontology which would consider this concept to either exist or not exist in the real economy.

Our later development of a *universal* differential ontology was inspired by the fruitfulness of differential ontology in order to reach novel and significant results inside the specialized discipline of (second-order) economic theory.

As further suggested by our later results into the field of mathematics, it seems likely that aspects of differential ontology hold the potential to create novel and significant results also when unfolded into other fields. With respect to informatics, our prediction is that *Fibonacci informatics*, anchored deeply in differential ontology, will have the potential to blossom.

12. Some main conclusive points

From the rather compact presentation and reasoning above, we may extract some main theoretical points:

i. Starting out with an adequate *qualitative concept of information,* it is possible to systematically develop a certain universal *philosophical ontology* by successively unfolding categories that already reside as tacitly enfolded inside this qualitative concept.

ii. This philosophical ontology implies *differentiation into two complementary dimensions*: one *processual-physical* (compression of conventional 3 + 1D) and one *algorithmic,* where the last one holds the upper hand. All systemic descriptions and explanations involve de facto *alternation* between these two dimensions.

iii. Further, this philosophical ontology implies differentiation into a *third complementary dimension,* the *transalgorithmic* one, in the overall composition of its architecture. The relation between the transalgorithmic and the algorithmic dimension is quite analogous to the relation between the algorithmic and the processual-physical dimension. *Combined* systemic descriptions and explanations involve de facto short-cut synthesis (conflation) of these two relations.

iv. This philosophical ontology is highly *differentiated* into said dimensions as well as into intradimensional *ontological levels.* Due to this circumstance, as well as due to the key role of the category "difference" in the constitution of the qualitative concept of information, we can denote this philosophical ontology as *informational differential ontology* (not to be confused with the term "differential ontology" in some French and not that rigorous philosophy). The architecture of this differential ontology surmounts dualistic (and monistic) ontologies by being more richly (and strictly) differentiated, while at the same time exposing elements of dualistic/binary conflation as necessary intermediaries inside its architecture.

v. *Anchored* in this differentiated ontological architecture, it is possible to establish a novel and basically complete theory of the *nexus of causality types.* This involves differentiation into specified *basic causality types,* where *physical causality* manifests as the least basic among these. From the basic causality types, various *elaborated causality types* can be exhibited as composed from various combinations of the basic ones. The more elaborated ones will constitute the "head" of *differential epistemology* from the universal "body" of differential ontology constituted already by the basic ones. From this, the cosmic web of informational relations appears, theoretically, as a manifestation of the deeper nexus of causality operators, and in this sense as categorically *closed* with respect to philosophical imagination.

vi. The very *concept of "causality"* in its most elementary, abstract, and universal sense is sought established as already implied in the *qualitative concept of information.* This intends to give the concept of causality a deeper and more adequate ontological foundation than in notions of "material implication," as well as "strict implication," implying special emphasis to and refoundation of the two deepest causality types, namely "projective causality" and "formal causality."

vii. The qualitative concept of information, with special emphasis on strict reflection upon the implied key category of "border," is argued to involve a constitutional logic that with necessity involves *projective causality* and shows to be analogous to the *Fibonacci* *algorithm*, which thus becomes regarded as the universal *constitutional bridge* between the qualitative and quantitative aspects of nature. This view has become supported by a reconstitution of number theory, presented by the author, were the field of natural numbers manifests from systematic unfoldment of the Fibonacci algorithm as regarded in a deeper and basically qualitative sense.

viii. The possible adequacy and fruitfulness of the presented informational differential ontology, are also shortly argued to be supported by some more recent developments in philosophy, logics, cybernetics, and physics, suggesting possible positive applications of said ontology also into the field of information science. It is also suggested that stronger theoretical focus into aspects of *semantics* and even more into addressing the very category of *emotion*, might show fruitful for further progress in information science as aligned with a human interest.

Conflict of interest

The author declares no conflict of interest connected to the publication.

Author details

Stein E. Johansen

Address all correspondence to: stein.e.johansen@ntnu.no

Department of Social Anthropology, Norwegian University of Science and Technology, Trondheim, Norway

References

[1] Johansen SE. Grunnriss av en differensiell epistemologi. 2nd ed. Oslo: Abstrakt; 2008 (English translation in transit: Outline of Differential Epistemology.)

[2] Shannon CE, Weave W. The Mathematical Theory of Communication. Urbana: University of Illinois Press; 1949

[3] Żurek WH. Complexity, entropy, and the physics of information. Complexity. 1992;**1**:64

[4] Fairbanks A. The First Philosophers of Greece; An Edition and Translation of the Remaining Fragments of the Pre-Sokratic Philosophers, Together with a Translation of the more Important Accounts of their Opinions Contained in the Early Epitomes of their Works by Arthur Fairbanks. London: K. Paul, Trench, Trübner & co.; 1898

[5] Bateson G. Steps to an Ecology of Mind. Chicago: University of Chicago Press; 1972

[6] Bateson G. Mind and Nature. A Necessary Unity. Bantam: NewYork/Toronto/London/Sydney/Auckland; 1988 [1979]

[7] Feibleman J, Friend JW. The structure and function of organization. In: Emery FE, editor. Systems Thinking. New York: Penguin; 1969 [1945]

[8] Churchland PS. Neurophilosophy. Toward a Unified Science of the Mind-Brain. Cambridge, Massachusetts: MIT Press; 1986

[9] Bateson G. Angels Fear. Towards an Epistemology of the Sacred. New York: Macmillan; 1987

[10] Holberg L. Erasmus Montanus eller Rasmus Berg. Gyldendal: Oslo; 1967 [1723]

[11] d'Andrade RG. The Development of Cognitive Anthropology. Cambridge, UK: Cambridge University press; 1995

[12] Johansen SE. Basic considerations about Kozyrev's theory of time from recent advances in specialist biology, mathematical physics and philosophical informatics. In: Shikhobalov LS, editor. Time and Stars: The Centenary of N.A. Kozyrev. St. Petersburg: Nestor-History; 2008. pp. 652-803

[13] Johansen SE. Non-trivial time flows in anticipation and action revealed by recent advances in natural science, framed in the causality network of differential ontology. In: Dubois D, editor. Logic and Semantics in Front of Nanoscale Physics. International Journal of Computing Anticipatory Systems. 2008;**22**:141-158

[14] Rowlands P. From Zero to Infinity. Singapore: World Scientific; 2007

[15] Bohm D. Unfolding Meaning. London: Routledge; 1996 [1985]

[16] Ignatyev MB. Holonomic Automatic Systems (in Russian). Moscow: Akad. Nauk; 1963

[17] Ignatyev MB. The Study of the Adaptational Phenomenon in Complex Systems. In: Dubois, DM, editor. Computing Anticipatory Systems: CASYS'05 – 7th International Conference, Liege, Belgium, Aug 8-13, 2005. American Institute of Physics (AIP) Conference Proceedings. 2006;**839**:322-330

[18] Ignatyev MB. Semantics and selforganization in nanoscale physics. In: Dubois D, editor. Logic and Semantics in Front of Nanoscale Physics. International Journal of Computing Anticipatory Systems. 2008;**22**:17-23

[19] Ignatyev MB. Necessary and sufficient conditions of nanorobot synthesis. Doklady Mathematics. 2010;**8**:671-675

[20] Rapoport DL. Torson fields, the extended photon, quantum jumps, the Eikonoal equation, the Twistor geometry of cognitive space and the laws of thought. In: Duffy MC, Lévy J, editors. Ether Space-Time & Cosmology. Montreal: Apeiron; 2009. pp. 389-458

[21] Rapoport DL. Surmounting the Cartesian cut through philosophy, physics, logic, cybernetics and geometry: Self-reference, torsion, the Klein bottle, the time operator, multivalued logics and quantum mechanics. Foundations of Physics. 2011;**41**(1):33-76

[22] Rapoport DL. Surmounting the Cartesian Cut Further: Torsion Fields, the Extended Photon, Quantum Jumps, the Klein Bottle, Multivalued Logic, the Time Operator Chronomes, Perception, Semiotics, Neurology and Cognition. In: Hathaway D, Randolph E, editors. Focus on Quantum Mechanics. New York: Nova Science Publishers; 2011. pp. 209-294

[23] Rosen SM. Science, Paradox, and the Moebius Principle. The Evolution of a "Transcultural" Approach to Wholeness. New York: State University of New York Press; 1994

[24] Stern A. Matrix Logic and Mind. Amsterdam: Elsevier; 1992

[25] Johansen SE. Fibonacci generation of natural numbers and prime numbers. In: Corda C, editor. Proceedings of the Third International Conference on Lie-Admissible Treatment of Irreversible Processes. Kathmandu: Kathmandu University Sankata Press; 2011. pp. 305-410

[26] Chandler J. An introduction to the perplex number system. Discrete Applied Mathematics. 2009;**157**:2296-2309

[27] Zeckendorf E. Représentation des nombres naturels par une somme de nombres de Fibonacci ou de nombres de Lucas. Bulletin de la Societe Royale des Sciences de Liege. 1972;**41**:179-182

[28] Zeckendorf E. A generalized Fibonacci numeration. The Fibonacci Quarterly. 1972;**10**: 365-372

[29] Johansen SE. Positive approach: Implications for the relation between number theory and geometry, including connection to Santilli mathematics, from Fibonacci reconstitution of natural numbers and of prime numbers. In: Sivasundarum S, editor. 10th International Conference on Mathematical Problems in Engineering, Aerospace and Sciences: ICNPAA 2014, Narvik, Norway, July 15-18, 2014. American Institute of Physics (AIP) Conference Proceedings. 2014;**1637**:457-468

[30] Johansen SE. Complete exposition of non-primes generated from a geometric revolving approach by 8 × 8 sets of related series, and thereby ad negativo exposition of a systematic pattern for the totality of prime numbers. Journal of Dynamical Systems and Geometric Theories. 2010;**8**(2):101-171

[31] Johansen SE. Unveiling of geometric generation of composite numbers exactly and completely. Applied Mathematics & Information Sciences. 2012;**6**:223-231

[32] Johansen SE. Negative approach: Implications for the relation between number theory and geometry, including connection to Santilli mathematics, from revolving geometric generation of natural numbers with recurrent outshooting leaving prime numbers. In: Sivasundarum S, editor. 10th International Conference on Mathematical Problems in Engineering, Aerospace and Sciences: ICNPAA 2014, Narvik, Norway, July 15-18, 2014. American Institute of Physics (AIP) Conference Proceedings. 2014;**1637**(1):450-456

[33] Johansen SE. Generation of exact and complete pattern of prime numbers vs. composite numbers as anticipating and computational prime numbering system. International Journal of Computing Anticipatory Systems. 2014;**26**:239-256

[34] Strand JM. Group representation of Johansen revolving method to generate the prime numbers with implications to genonumbers. In: Corda C, editor. Proceedings of the Third International Conference on Lie-Admissible Treatment of Irreversible Processes. Kathmandu: Kathmandu University Sankata Press; 2011. pp. 667-670

[35] Kuhn TS. The Structure of Scientific Revolutions. Chicago: University of Chicago Press; 1962

[36] Johansen SE. Entering hi-time cybernetics – From recent liftings of science, philosophy, meaning theory and robotics onto the human condition. In: Vassiliev JS, Voronov AA, Ignatyev MB, Kozlov VN, Jusupov RM, editors. Time and Cybernetics – The Centenary of Academician A. A. Voronov. St. Petersburg: St. Petersburg State Polytechnic University; 2010. pp. 286-318

[37] Trell E. The eightfold way: Application of Lie's true geometriske transformationer to elementary particles. Algebras Groups and Geometries. 1998;**15**:447-471

[38] Trell E. Invariant Aristotelian cosmology: binary phase transition of the universe from the smallest to the largest scales. Hadronic Journal. 2005;**28**:1-42

[39] Trell E. Back to the ether. In: Duffy MC, Lévy J, editors. Ether Space-Time & Cosmology. Montreal: Apeiron; 2009. pp. 339-388

[40] Fyhn H. Møte med tilstedeværelse: Mellom form og tomhet i produktutvikling, aikido og antropologisk erkjennelse [PhD thesis]. Trondheim: Norwegian University of Science and Technology; 2011

[41] Follo G. Det norske familieskogbruket, dets kvinnelige og mannlige skogeiere, forvaltningsaktivitet — og metaforiske forbindelser [PhD thesis]. Trondheim: Norwegian University of Science and Technology; 2008

[42] Røyrvik E. The Allure of Capitalism: An Ethnography of Management and the Global Economy in Crisis. Oxford: Berghahn; 2011

[43] Santilli RM. Isodual Theory of Antimatter with Applications to Antigravity, Grand Unification and Cosmology. Dordrecht, Netherlands: Springer; 2006

[44] Santilli RM. Elements of iso-, geno-, hyper-mathematics for matter, their isoduals for antimatter, and their applications in physics, chemistry, and biology. Foundations of Physics. 2003;**33**:1373-1416

[45] Santilli RM. Foundations of Hadronic Chemistry with Applications to New Clean Energies and Fuels. Boston-Dordrecht-London: Kluwer Academic Publishers; 2001

[46] Santilli RM. Isotopic, Genotopic and Hyperstructural Methods in Theoretical Biology. Kiev: Ukraine Academy of Sciences; 1996

[47] Gandzha I, Kadeisvili J. New Sciences for a New Era: Mathematical, Physical and Chemical Discoveries of Ruggero Maria Santilli. Sankata: Kathmandu; 2011

[48] Santilli RM. Hadronic Mathematics, Mechanics and Chemistry. Vol. I–V. US EuroAsia: International Academic Press; [Internet]. 2008. Available from: http://www.i-b-r.org/Hadronic-Mechanics.htm [Accessed: Dec 3, 2017]

[49] Johansen SE. Initiation of 'Hadronic philosophy', the philosophy underlying Hadronic mechanics and chemistry. Hadronic Journal. 2006;**29**:111-135

[50] Quartieri G. Materia e antimateria con il nuovo approccio con i numeri isoduali. Ricerca Aerospaziale. 2006;**22**(1):11-19

[51] Johansen SE. Spacetimes of Santilli hypermechanics: From Hadronic mechanics to Hadronic biology and Hadronic psychology. Hadronic Journal. 2008;**31**:451-512

[52] Schadeck L. Jiang Number Theory [Internet]. 2008. Available from: www.wbabin.net/math/xuan15.pdf [Accessed: Dec 3, 2017]

[53] Spencer-Brown G. Laws of Form. London: Allen & Unwin; 1969

[54] Bohm D, Hiley BJ. The Undivided Universe. An Ontological Interpretation of Quantum Theory. London: Routledge; 1993

[55] Bohm D, Peat FD. Science, Order, and Creativity. Toronto: Bantam; 1987

[56] Hegel GWF. Wissenschaft der Logik. Werke 5-6. Frankfurt am Main: Suhrkamp; 1969 [1816]

[57] Johansen SE. Begrepet om arbeidstidsinnholdet: En teoretisk konstruksjon. Et revisjonistisk bidrag til funderingen av en formreflektert kapitalteori. (The concept of labour time content: A theoretical construction. A revisionist contribution to the foundation of form-reflected theory of capital.) [Dr. philos. thesis]. Bergen: Ariadne; 1991

[58] Marx K. Das Kapital. Kritik der politischen Ökonomie. Marx-Engels-Werke, Band 23-25. Berlin: Dietz; 1968 [1867, 1885, 1894]

Chapter 11

Strengthening the Flow of Agricultural Knowledge among Agricultural Stakeholders: The Case of Morogoro Region in Tanzania

Wulystan P. Mtega and Mpho Ngoepe

Additional information is available at the end of the chapter

http://dx.doi.org/10.5772/intechopen.72731

Abstract

Effective agricultural knowledge exchange is important for increased access to agricultural knowledge. However, studies conducted in Tanzania indicate that access to agricultural knowledge among agricultural stakeholders is inadequate. This chapter investigates how to strengthen the exchange of agricultural knowledge can be strengthened. Specifically, the chapter assesses how agricultural knowledge flows, determines how communication channels are chosen and analyses critical factors for effective agricultural knowledge exchange. The study involved different agricultural stakeholders identified through stakeholders' analysis. Random and non-random sampling techniques were used in drawing the sample for the study. The study involved 371 respondents. Key findings indicate that agricultural knowledge sharing, exchange, transfer and dissemination which facilitate the flow of agricultural knowledge. Findings indicate that availability and accessibility of the communication channels, ICT infrastructure, affordability of communication tariffs and ownership of communication tools influenced the choice of communication channels. Likewise, membership in professional groups, accessibility of knowledge sources, affordability of tariffs for, access to agricultural extension services, availability of knowledge and ICT infrastructure influence the flow of agricultural knowledge. It is concluded that effective agricultural knowledge flow increases knowledge accessibility, usage and creation. It is recommended that each agricultural stakeholder should be involved in conducting relevant agricultural knowledge roles so as to enhance the accessibility, sharing, exchange, dissemination and usage of agricultural knowledge.

Keywords: agricultural knowledge flow, agricultural knowledge sharing, agricultural knowledge management, knowledge exchange, agriculture, Tanzania

1. Introduction

Agricultural production is a risk activity; it necessitates people to make rational decisions so as to minimize the impacts [1]. To enhance timely decision-making, agricultural knowledge must be made available on time. For this to be possible, an adequate agricultural knowledge exchange mechanism must be put in place.

Agricultural knowledge exchange becomes effective when stakeholders creating, disseminating, sharing and using knowledge are effectively linked together. Farmers, agricultural research and the agricultural extension and advisory system must be linked together to enhance exchange of knowledge. Moreover, these actors must be linked together with others who play supportive roles in the sector. The linkage is important in enhancing access to and usage of knowledge in a knowledge system. A knowledge system is a network of linked actors, organizations and objects that perform a number of knowledge-related functions that link knowledge and know-how with action [2]. Therefore, different actors in the agricultural sector performing a number of knowledge-related functions form an agricultural knowledge system.

Tanzania has a chain of agricultural research institutes with a key role of generating scientific knowledge [3]. Moreover, the country has an agricultural extension system meant to enhance access to agricultural knowledge among actors [4]. However, studies [5, 6] indicate that access to agricultural knowledge among agricultural stakeholders in Tanzania is still low. This study investigates how agricultural stakeholders in Morogoro region of Tanzania exchange agricultural knowledge among themselves.

The study was conducted in Kilombero, Kilosa and Mvomero districts of Morogoro region in Tanzania. Majority of dwellers in these districts rely on agriculture for a living. Moreover, these districts are potential for food production as they form part of the national grain basket.

1.1. Purpose of the study

The general purpose of this study was to investigate how agricultural knowledge flows among stakeholders so as to enhance access to knowledge. Specifically, the study intends to

i. investigate how agricultural knowledge flows among stakeholders;

ii. determine reasons for choice of channels used for agricultural knowledge sharing, exchange, transfer and dissemination;

iii. analyze factors for effective flow of agricultural knowledge.

2. Literature review

This section covers a review of the literature related to agricultural knowledge exchange. The section also reveals the gaps the chapter intends to fill.

2.1. The flow of agricultural knowledge

There are different forms of flow of agricultural knowledge. Agricultural knowledge flows from one person/organization to another through knowledge sharing, exchange, transfer or dissemination to intended audience. The following sub-sections give detailed descriptions of the different forms of flow of knowledge.

2.1.1. *Knowledge sharing*

Knowledge sharing involves both sharing of knowledge by the knowledge source and the acquisition and application of knowledge by the recipient; it involves the multi-directional movement of knowledge between different units, divisions or organizations rather than individuals [7]. It involves an exchange of knowledge between two individuals: one who communicates knowledge and one who assimilates it; the focus of knowledge sharing is on human capital and the interaction of individuals [8]. Knowledge sharing is more effective in environments where the learning process is emphasized and implemented [9]. Knowledge sharing is actually learning something from someone. It enhances sharing of know-how, understanding and skills.

For being more effective, knowledge-sharing process requires a knowledge-sharing platform, culture and certain amount of trust between individuals [10]. Knowledge sharing can take place through formal or informal settings [11]. Formal settings involve communicating within the formal organizational structure that transmits goals, policies, procedures and directions and uses formal communication channels [12] On the other hand, informal knowledge sharing involves sharing knowledge outside the formal organizational structure that fills the organizational gaps, maintains the linkages and handles the one-time situations [12]. Informal knowledge-sharing practices are lateral in nature and facilitate the sharing of private non-codified knowledge [13]. Tacit knowledge, which is difficult to define, codify and express, is most suitably shared through informal settings. To enhance access to agricultural knowledge, it is important to determine how formal and informal knowledge-sharing settings are used to make agricultural knowledge sharing successful.

2.1.2. *Knowledge transfer*

The terminology knowledge transfer emerged in the 1990s as a process by which research messages were 'pushed' by researchers to users [14]. The term knowledge transfer is used to describe knowledge exchange processes [15]. Knowledge transfer includes a variety of interactions between individuals and groups; within, between and across groups; and from groups to the organization [8]. It is a process through which one unit is affected by the experience of another [16]. It involves the dissemination of knowledge from one location/individual or group to another. Knowledge transfer manifests itself through changes in knowledge or performance of the recipient unit [17]. Knowledge transfer is a one-direction movement of knowledge. Those who generate or own it usually push it to those thought to lack it.

Knowledge transfer can take place within an organization or and between organizations. Regardless of whether knowledge transfer takes place on the intra- or inter-organizational level, it has to be conducted by individual organizational members [15]. This process takes place in formal and informal networks. Formal and informal knowledge transfer networks are derived from formal and informal organizational structures [18]. For improved knowledge accessibility, a clear understanding on how both formal and informal knowledge transfer settings can work together to facilitate knowledge accessibility is important. Moreover, for effective knowledge transfer process, it is important to have a clear understanding on sources and destinations of knowledge.

2.1.3. Knowledge exchange

Knowledge exchange includes both knowledge sharing and knowledge seeking [7]. Knowledge-seeking behavior is the totality of human behavior in relation to knowledge sources and channels, including both active and passive information seeking, and information use [19]. Knowledge exchange aims at autonomous individuals and can occur in systems characterized by high levels of interdependency and interconnectedness among participants [20]. It is a very useful process in a knowledge value chain because knowledge management involves different actors. Some of the commonly known participants involved in knowledge exchange are the producers, intermediaries and users [20].

Unlike knowledge transfer, which in most cases requires a one-way communication, knowledge exchange requires more than one-way communication [14]. It may include both knowledge transfer and sharing. It involves knowledge transfer because knowledge is pushed from a knowledge-rich source to a knowledge-poor recipient. It also involves knowledge sharing because through knowledge exchange a knowledge-rich source interacts with a knowledge-poor source to facilitate a knowledge transfer process from the knowledge-rich source to the knowledge seeker. Moreover, knowledge exchange happens when actors in a knowledge system have adequate information about others knowledge needs and decides to exchange knowledge among them. Face-to-face interactive communication, print materials, mobile phones, electronic mails, Skype calls, seminars, conferences and meetings are commonly used for knowledge exchange.

A clear understanding of agricultural involvements of agricultural actors can help in determining agricultural knowledge needs. This is because agricultural knowledge needs relate to day-to-day agricultural undertakings. It is important to know who needs knowledge before initiating a knowledge transfer process. Moreover, having an understanding of the sources and destinations of knowledge and channels used for the knowledge exchange process is important for strengthening knowledge flows.

2.1.4. Knowledge dissemination

Knowledge dissemination is an active intervention that aims at communicating know-how or skills to a target audience via determined channels, using planned strategies for the purpose of creating a positive impact on the acquisition of knowledge, attitudes and practice [21]. Dissemination is the conscious effort to spread new knowledge to target audiences or the public at large [22]. It involves an interactive process of communicating knowledge to target audiences and aims at enhancing changes among members of the intended audience [23]. The knowledge dissemination process improves the accessibility knowledge among intended audiences. Unlike knowledge transfer, knowledge dissemination can reach both intended and unintended audiences because mass media tools including newspapers, radio, TV or other public announcement tools are used in disseminating it. Thus, for improving knowledge dissemination, having adequate understanding on who disseminates knowledge and who are the intended audiences is important. Moreover, having an adequate understanding of the most preferred channels for knowledge dissemination is of equal importance too.

2.2. Factors influencing the flow of knowledge

There are several factors influencing the flow of knowledge. Individual, organizational and technological factors are among them [24]. Individual factors may include the willingness to share/disseminate/exchange knowledge, ability to verbalize and codify knowledge and the willingness of the receiving party to accept new knowledge [25]. Organizational factors are related to organizational culture, organizational processes, trust, reward system, leadership and organizational structures [26]. Likewise, communication infrastructure, communication channels and usage of social media may influence the flow of knowledge too [27].

An effective flow of knowledge enhances access to knowledge. Studies conducted in Tanzania [5, 6] (Pinda, 2012a; 2012b) indicate that there is inadequate access to knowledge among actors of the agricultural sector. Having a clear understanding of factors influencing the flow of agricultural knowledge in Tanzania is important for improving access to knowledge. Therefore, this article intends to identify all factors and how they influence the flow of agricultural knowledge among actors in the sector.

2.3. Conceptual framework for the study

The study was guided by the modified knowledge-sharing model [28] presented in **Figure 1**. The model has four dimensions namely organizational, knowledge, individual and technological factors. Organizational dimension has four independent variables namely management support, leadership, policy and culture, and reward system. These variables may positively or negatively influence knowledge exchange.

The knowledge dimension has two independent variables namely knowledge category and nature of knowledge. There are different knowledge categories agricultural stakeholders may use. The extent to which a category is shared depends on its perceived usefulness among users. Nature of knowledge relates to whether it is tacit or explicit knowledge because its nature influences how it is easily shared.

Under individual dimension, two independent variables namely individual attitude (willingness to share knowledge and receive transferred knowledge) and the ability to verbalize and codify knowledge may influence agricultural knowledge exchange among stakeholders. Last is the technological dimension, which works through the communication infrastructure, communication channel and level of usage of communication system. These independent variables may positively or negatively influence knowledge exchange.

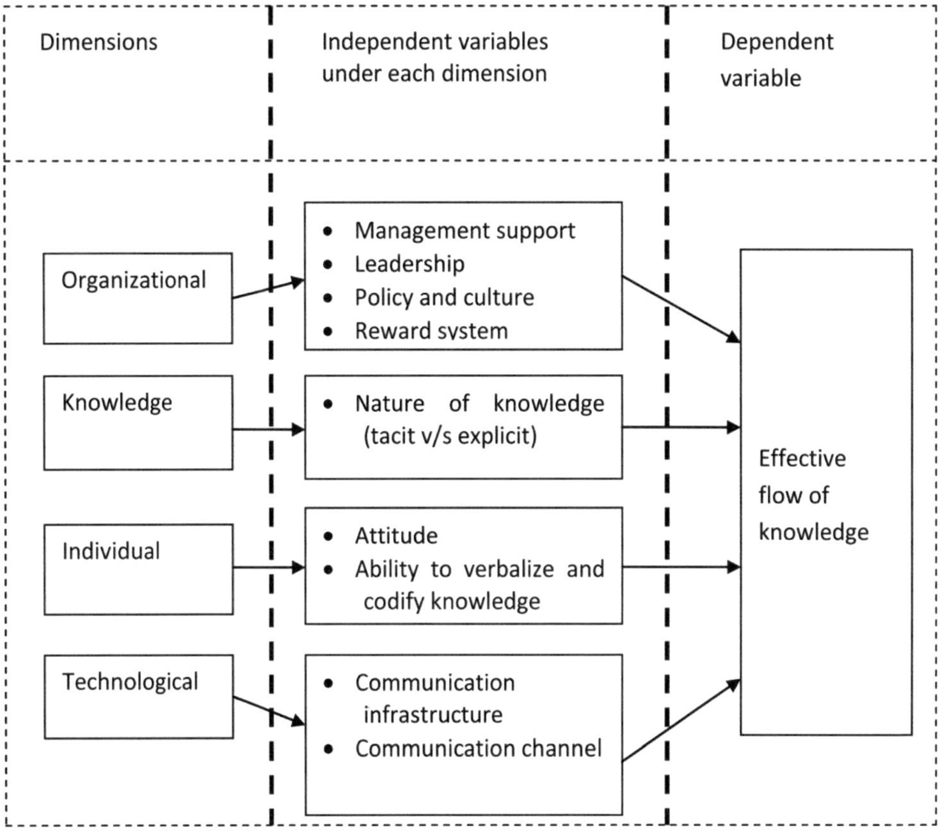

Figure 1. A modified model for flow of knowledge [28].

3. Research methodology of the study

This study was conducted in Morogoro region of Tanzania. The region was established in 1962 after dividing the then Eastern Province into regions. According to the Tanzanian National Census of 2012, the region had a total of 2,218,492 people (1,093,302 males and 1,125,190 females) with a total of 385,260 households; among them, 378,400 households were being directly involved in agricultural production.

Administratively, Morogoro region is divided into six district councils namely Gairo, Kilombero, Kilosa, Ulanga, Morogoro and Mvomero. Morogoro region has abundant agricultural land suitable for crop production and have a good climate favorable for agriculture and other economic investments. Among the six district councils, Kilombero, Kilosa and Mvomero were involved in this study. These three district councils are homogeneous in terms of the major crops grown, availability of agricultural research institutes, and information and communication technology (ICT) infrastructure. Kibaoni, Mang'ula and Lumemo wards of Kilombero district; Rudewa, Chanzulu and Kimamba B wards of Kilosa district; and Wami Dakawa, Mvomero and Hembeti of Mvomero district were purposively selected as the study area. A sampling frame of all villages from each ward was prepared and one village was randomly selected and included in the study area. Nine villages namely Rudewa Batini, Chanzuru and Kimamba B villages (of Kilosa district), Michenga, Mgudeni and Mlimba A villages (of Kilombero district), and Hembeti, Mvomero and Wami Dakawa villages (of Mvomero district) were included in the study area.

3.1. Selection of respondents for the study

Different agricultural stakeholders identified through stakeholder analysis were involved in the study. When identifying actors, it is important to consider their stake and roles in the sector [29]. The first stage was the selection of a human activity system for research focus where serial (rice and maize) value chain was selected. The second stage involved the identification of actors and initial characterization of all actors. The third stage involved determining who has stake in the two crops and the relationship existing between actors. Fifthly, respondents for the study were selected and integrated in the study as described below.

Farmers, researchers from three agricultural research institutes found in Morogoro region, agricultural extension workers, policy makers, village executives, agricultural input suppliers and information service providers were found to be the major stakeholders of maize and rice value chains in Morogoro region. To select respondents from this population, the study employed both random and non-random-sampling techniques in selecting the sample from agricultural stakeholders.

A sampling frame of farmers from each village was made followed by employing a simple random-sampling technique in selecting a sample of respondents among farmers from each village. Simple random-sampling technique was selected because it can enhance generalization of results. A total of 314 farmers were randomly selected from the nine villages (**Table 1**).

Name of the village	Sex of the respondent		Total
	Male	Female	
Chanzuru	12 (52.2%)	11 (47.8%)	23
Kimamba B	27 (71.1%)	11 (28.9%)	38
Hembeti	8 (30.8%)	18 (69.2%)	26
Mlimba A	20 (64.5%)	11 (35.5%)	31
Rudewa Mabatini	11 (34.4%)	21 (65.6%)	32
Michenga	18 (64.3%)	10 (35.7%)	28
Mgudeni	24 (48.0%)	26 (52.0%)	50
Mvomero	20 (42.6%)	27 (57.4%)	47
Wami Dakawa	13 (33.3%)	26 (66.7%)	39
Total	**153 (48.7%)**	**161 (51.3%)**	**314**

Table 1. Sample size by sex of farmers.

The study employed a purposive sampling technique in selecting respondents among agricultural researchers, agricultural extension workers, policy makers, village executives, agricultural input suppliers and information service providers. Each head of the agricultural research outreach section of the agricultural research institute, all agricultural extension staff from the nine villages and the head of the agricultural extension unit from the three districts were selected for the study. Three providers of agricultural information services and three warehouse operators (one from each district), nine agricultural inputs suppliers (one from each village) and nine buyers (one buyer from each village) were included in the study too. Moreover, nine village executives and ward councilors from the nine wards were selected too. This made a total of 57 respondents selected among this category of actors.

3.2. Data collection and analysis

The study used structured questionnaire and unstructured questionnaire in data collection. Structured questionnaires were administered to 314 farmers while the unstructured questionnaire was used to collect data from 57 other agricultural stakeholders. Face-to-face interview sessions and in-depth interviews were arranged for data collection from farmers and other agricultural stakeholders, respectively. Data collected through structured questionnaire were edited, classified and coded to make them amenable to analysis. Coded data were then cleaned and analyzed using the Statistical Package for Social Sciences (SPSS). SPSS facilitated the generation of frequencies, percentages and tables. Qualitative data collected through in-depth interviews were analyzed through content analysis and summarized into descriptions and explanations.

4. Findings and discussion

Both male and female farmers were selected for the study. Findings in **Table 1** indicate that 161 (51.3%) of the farmers were female and 153 (48.7%) were male making a total of 314 farmers. Among the 57 agricultural stakeholders, three were heads of agricultural research institute outreach units while the other three were heads of the agricultural extension departments. There were nine agricultural extension staff, three providers of agricultural information services, three warehouse operators, nine agricultural inputs suppliers, and nine buyers. Moreover, there were nine village executives and nine ward councilors.

Findings in **Table 2** show that farmers involved in the study had informal to secondary level of education. Majority of the farmers (220, 70.1%) had primary education; others (42, 13.4%) had secondary education; 38 (12.1%) had informal education; few (14, 4.5%) had adult education; while none had tertiary education. With respect to the level of education by sex of respondent, findings indicate that 112 (73.2%) male farmers as opposed to 108 (67.1%) female farmers had primary education, and 27 (17.6%) male farmers as opposed to 15 (9.3%) female farmers had secondary education. Findings also indicate that seven (4.6%) of the male farmers as opposed to seven (4.3%) of the female farmers had adult education, and the other seven (4.6%) male farmers as opposed to 31 (19.3%) female farmers had informal education.

4.1. How agricultural knowledge flows among stakeholders

Agricultural stakeholders were asked to mention how agricultural knowledge flowed among them. It was found that there were different ways through which agricultural knowledge flowed. Among the farmers, 289 (92%) mentioned that agricultural knowledge flowed among them through knowledge sharing (**Table 3**). Others, 281 (89.5%) mentioned that accessing agricultural knowledge from different sources enhanced the flow of agricultural knowledge among stakeholders, while 195 (62.1) farmers mentioned that reporting observed farm-related problems to a third party enhanced the flow of agricultural knowledge among stakeholders (**Table 3**).

Agricultural knowledge sharing, exchange, transfer and dissemination were the main means of flow of agricultural knowledge among non-farmers respondents. Agricultural researchers mentioned to transfer knowledge to farmers through agricultural extension staff but they shared knowledge with colleagues and peers through seminars and conferences. They also disseminate research findings to a wider audience through publications. Agricultural extension staff and NGOs mentioned to transfer, share and exchange agricultural knowledge with farmers and input suppliers. They also mention to report to supervisors on different agricultural issues. Input suppliers and buyers shared agricultural knowledge among themselves and with farmers. Councilors and village executives reported to disseminate knowledge during meetings. Agricultural information service providers disseminated agricultural knowledge to wider agricultural stakeholders through radio/TV broadcasts and newspapers.

Findings in **Table 3** indicate that the farmers shared agricultural knowledge to different recipients, accessed it from different sources and reported farm-related problems to different

Level of education by sex of respondents

Level of education	**Sex of the respondent**		**Total**
	Male	**Female**	
Informal education	7 (4.6%)	31 (19.3%)	38 (12.1%)
Adult education	7 (4.6%)	7 (4.3%)	14 (4.5%)
Primary education	112 (73.2%)	108 (67.1%)	220 (70.1%)
Secondary education	27 (17.6%)	15 (9.3%)	42 (13.4%)
Total	**153 (100%)**	**161 (100%)**	**314 (100%)**

Table 2. Demographic characteristics of respondents.

Knowledge flow processes	**Frequency distribution**
Sharing knowledge	289 (92%)
Accessing knowledge	281 (89.5%)
Reporting observed farm-related problem	195 (62.1%)

Table 3. Knowledge flow processes among farmers.

stakeholders. The following sections give details of sources of knowledge used by farmers and other stakeholders.

4.1.1. *Sources of agricultural knowledge used by agricultural stakeholders*

Agricultural knowledge flowed from knowledge sources to different destinations. Respondents were asked to mention knowledge sources from which they accessed agricultural knowledge. Findings in **Table 4** summarize the sources used by farmers for acquiring agricultural knowledge. It was found that majority of the farmers (305, 97.1%) acquired agricultural knowledge from fellow farmers. Others, 193 (61.5%) acquired agricultural knowledge from radio sets, 152 (48.4%) through mobile phones, 120 (38.2%) from village-based agricultural advisor and 105 (33.4%) farmers from input suppliers. Findings indicate that 102 (32.5%) of the farmers acquired agricultural knowledge from agricultural extension agents, 80 (25.5%) from TV sets, 66 (21%) from demonstration plots while 63 (20.1%) from farmers' groups. Findings indicate further that 50 (15.9%) farmers accessed agricultural knowledge from trainings and seminars, 43 (13.7%) from print materials, 33 (10.5%) from buyers, 27 (8.6%) from village executives and 12 (3.8%) from agricultural shows/farmers' field day.

Among non-farmers respondents, it was found that agricultural extension officers, councilors, employees from NGOS, researchers, ward councilors and village executives accessed agricultural knowledge from human-based knowledge sources like farmers, colleagues, partners and supervisors. Likewise, buyers and input-suppliers mentioned to use human-based sources of knowledge. They mentioned to access knowledge from agricultural extension officers, farmers and whole buyers/sellers of harvests and agricultural inputs.

Sources of agricultural knowledge	Frequency distribution
Fellow farmers	305 (97.1%)
Radio set	193 (61.5%)
Mobile phones	152 (48.4%)
Village-based agricultural advisor	120 (38.2%)
Input supplier	105 (33.4%)
Agricultural extension officer	102 (32.5%)
TV set	80 (25.5%)
Demonstration plots	66 (21%)
Farmers' group	63 (20.1%)
Trainings and seminars	50 (15.9%)
Print materials	43 (13.7%)
Buyers	33 (10.5%)
Village executives	27 (8.6%)
Agricultural shows/farmers' field day	12 (3.8%)

Table 4. Sources of agricultural knowledge ($N = 314$).

Recipient of agricultural knowledge	Frequency distribution
Fellow farmers	281 (96.2%)
Agricultural extension staff	82 (28.1%)
Village-based agricultural advisor	74 (25.3%)
Input suppliers	68 (17.5%)
Farmers' group	39 (13.4%)
Buyers	27 (9.2%)
Village executives	16 (5.5%)
Agricultural researchers	11 (3.8%)

Table 5. Recipients of agricultural knowledge (*N* = 314).

It was found that non-farmers respondents used different ICT-based agricultural knowledge sources. Agricultural extension officers, researchers and NGOs mentioned to use computers, Internet, mobile phones, radio and TV sets. Buyers, input suppliers, ward councilors and village executives mentioned to use mobile phones, radio and TV sets only.

Results indicate that non-farmers used print materials as sources of agricultural knowledge too. Letters, newspapers, books, leaflets and booklets were the paper-based agricultural knowledge sources used by agricultural extension officers, input suppliers, ward councilors, employees from NGOS, researchers and village executives. Buyers mentioned to mainly use newspapers as sources of knowledge on agricultural marketing.

4.1.2. *Recipients of agricultural knowledge*

Flow of agricultural knowledge involves a source and a destination or recipient. Farmers were asked to mention the destinations or recipients of knowledge. Findings in **Table 5** indicate that 281 (96.2%) farmers mentioned that fellow farmers were the recipients of knowledge. Others, 82 (28.1%), 74 (25.3%) and 68 (17.5%) reported that agricultural extension staff, village-based agricultural advisors and input suppliers were their recipients of knowledge, respectively. Findings in **Table 5** indicate further that 39 (13.4%) farmers mentioned farmers' group as their recipients of knowledge. Others, 27 (9.2%), 16 (5.5%) and 11 (3.8%) reported buyers, village executives and agricultural researchers as their agricultural knowledge recipients, respectively.

Among non-farmers respondents, agricultural extension staff and researchers reported that farmers, colleagues and supervisors were the recipients of agricultural knowledge. Employees of NGOs mentioned farmers, colleagues, partners, donors and the government as their major recipients of agricultural knowledge. Input suppliers and buyers reported farmers and colleagues as knowledge recipients. Agricultural information services providers mentioned the wider agricultural community as their recipient of agricultural knowledge.

4.2. Channels through which agricultural knowledge flowed

Agricultural stakeholders were asked how agricultural knowledge flowed among themselves. Findings in **Table 6** indicate the communication channels used by farmers for different

Channel	Frequency distribution
Face-to-face oral communication	305 (97.1%)
Radio set	193 (61.5%)
Mobile phones	152 (48.4%)
TV set	80 (25.5%)
Print materials	43 (13.7%)

Table 6. Channels mostly used for agricultural knowledge flow among farmers (N = 314).

agricultural knowledge flow processes. Findings indicate that 305 (97.1%) farmers motioned to use face-to-face oral communication as a channel through which agricultural knowledge flowed. Others used radio sets (193, 61.5%), mobile phones (152, 48.4%), TV sets (80, 25.5%) and print materials (43, 13.7%) as communication channels.

Findings from non-farmers agricultural stakeholders indicate that various channels were used so as to facilitate flow of agricultural knowledge. All of them mentioned to use face-to-face oral communication and mobile phones for sharing and exchanging knowledge. This was possible during oral conversations with colleagues and supervisors or during trainings, meetings, conferences and seminars. Agricultural researchers, extension staff, agricultural information services providers and employees from NGOs reported to use virtual communication channels, mostly Skype and emails. Other communication channels preferred by majority of the non-farmers stakeholders were leaflets/brochures, notice boards, radio and TV sets.

4.2.1. *Factors influencing preference of communication channels*

Findings indicate that the preference of communication channels used among agricultural stakeholders was different. Stakeholders were asked to mention reasons after their preference to some communication channels. Among farmers, several factors were mentioned to influence their preference. Findings indicate that 303 (95%) of the farmers mentioned that the availability and accessibility of the communication channels was the main factor for preference. Others, 279 (88.9%), mentioned their preference to some communication channels to be influenced by the level of development of ICT infrastructure. Findings indicate further that 206 (65.6%) of the farmers mentioned that the affordability of tariffs for communication influenced their preference to some communication channels while 153 (48.7%) of the farmers used some communication channels because they owned some communication tools (**Table 7**).

Factor stimulating accessibility of agricultural knowledge	Frequency distribution
Availability and accessibility of communication channels	303 (95%)
Well-developed ICT infrastructure	279 (88.9%)
Affordability of tariffs for communication	206 (65.6%)
Ownership of communication tools	153 (48.7%)

Table 7. Reasons for choice of channels.

Preference of communication channels among non-farmers agricultural stakeholders was influenced by different factors. Access to ICT infrastructure and availability and accessibility of ICT tools influenced the usage of virtual communication channels among agricultural research employees from NGOs, agricultural information services providers and agricultural extension staff. Moreover, availability, convenience and suitability of communication channels for a communication process were found to influence the choice of communication channels among non-farmers agricultural stakeholders. Likewise, the affordability of tariffs for communication was also found to influence the preference of communication channels among all non-farmers agricultural stakeholders.

4.3. Factors influencing the flow of agricultural knowledge

Agricultural stakeholders were asked to mention factors influencing the flow of agricultural knowledge among them. Findings in **Table 8** indicate the factors mentioned by farmers to influence the flow of agricultural knowledge. It was found that 262 (83.4%) of the farmers mentioned that membership in farmers' group influenced knowledge flow. Others, 219 (69.7%), 206 (65.6%) and 205 (65.3%), mentioned the accessibility of agricultural knowledge sources, affordability of tariffs for communication and access to agricultural extension services, respectively, to influence the flow of agricultural knowledge among agricultural stakeholders.

Findings in **Table 8** indicate that 126 (40.1%), 125 (39.8%) and 123 (39.2%) of the farmers mentioned the availability of agricultural knowledge, access to a reliable power source and airing agricultural radio/TV programs during relevant hours to influence the flow of agricultural knowledge. Likewise, 114 (36.3%), 67 (21.3%) and 26 (8.3%) of the farmers mentioned ownership of communication tools, usage of most suitable language repackaging knowledge and a well-developed ICT infrastructure to influence the flow of agricultural knowledge. Findings from **Table 8** also indicate that 10 (3.2%) of the farmers mentioned that an efficient feedback mechanism was important for the effective flow of agricultural knowledge.

Reason limiting agricultural knowledge usage	Frequency distribution
Membership in farmers' group	262 (83.4%)
Accessibility of knowledge sources	219 (69.7%)
Affordability of tariffs for communication	206 (65.6%)
Access to agricultural extension services	205 (65.3%)
Availability of agricultural knowledge	126 (40.1%)
Access to a reliable power source	125 (39.8%)
Airing agricultural radio/TV programs during relevant hours	123 (39.2%)
Ownership of communication tools	114 (36.3%)
Usage of most suitable language repackaging knowledge	67 (21.3%)
Well-developed ICT infrastructure	26 (8.3%)
Efficient feedback mechanism	10 (3.2%)

Table 8. Factors influence the flow of agricultural knowledge.

A Pearson correlation analysis was run to determine the correlation of some farmers' demographic characteristics and some agricultural knowledge flow processes (**Table 9**). Findings indicate that there was no significant correlation between agricultural knowledge sharing and farmers and farmer's age ($r = 0.011$ at 0.842 level of significance), level of education ($r = -0.091$ at 0.108 level of significance) and farming experience ($r = 0.003$ at 0.959 level of significance). Findings in **Table 9** indicate that there is no significant correlation between reporting observed farm-related problems and farmers age ($r = 0.005$ at 0.936 level of significance) and farming experience ($r = -0.009$ at 0.875 level of significance). However, there is negative correlation between reporting observed farm-related problem and farmer's level of education ($r = -0.302$ (**) at 0.000 level of significance). Findings indicate that there is a significant positive correlation between accessing agricultural knowledge and farmer's age ($r = 0.203$(**) at 0.000 level of significance) and farming experience ($r = 0.138$(*) at 0.014 level of significance). However, findings indicate that there is a negative correlation between accessing agricultural knowledge and farmer's level of education ($r = -0.194$(**) at 0.001 level of significance).

Findings also indicate that several factors influenced the choice of communication channels among non-farmers agricultural stakeholders. Among agricultural researchers, village executives, extension staff and employees from some NGOs implementing agricultural-related interventions, access to office ICT infrastructure and facilities, top management support, knowledge-sharing culture, rewards associated with knowledge sharing and accessibility of transport facilities influenced the flow of agricultural knowledge among them and with other stakeholders. Agricultural inputs suppliers, ward councilors and buyers of agricultural produce mentioned access to a reliable power supply and well-developed ICT infrastructure and affordability of tariffs for communication as factors which influence the flow of agricultural knowledge. Findings indicate that agricultural information service providers (radio and TV stations and other media houses) mentioned that taxes paid for their services and availability of sponsorship for some services

Agricultural knowledge flow process	Correlations	Demographic characteristics		
		Age group	Level of education	Years in farming
Sharing knowledge	Pearson correlation	0.011	−0.091	0.003
	Sig. (two-tailed)	0.842	0.108	0.959
	N	314	314	314
Reporting observed farm related problem	Pearson correlation	0.005	−0.302**	−0.009
	Sig. (two-tailed)	0.936	0.000	0.875
	N	314	314	314
Accessing knowledge	Pearson correlation	0.203**	−0.194**	0.138*
	Sig. (two-tailed)	0.000	0.001	0.014
	N	314	314	314

*Correlation is significant at the 0.05 level (two-tailed).
**Correlation is significant at the 0.01 level (two-tailed).

Table 9. Correlation between agricultural knowledge flow processes and some farmers' demographic characteristics.

influenced the dissemination of agricultural knowledge. Likewise, mobile phone operators mentioned that high duties, which always increase operation costs (and consequently the communication tariffs paid by customers), have a great influence on increasing the rate of agricultural knowledge flow. It was also found that the availability, convenience, suitability of communication channels and affordability of tariffs for communication process influenced the flow of agricultural knowledge among stakeholders too.

5. Discussion of findings, conclusion and recommendations

The agricultural sector involves different stakeholders involved in performing activities directly or indirectly related agriculture. Farmers, agricultural researchers, agricultural extension staff, village executives, councilors, agricultural input suppliers, buyers of agricultural produce and agricultural information services providers are some stakeholders in the sector to mention a few. These stakeholders come from both the private and public sector and each performs agricultural knowledge-related processes in the agricultural knowledge system. They are involved in generating knowledge through research, using it and setting policies and regulations related to agricultural knowledge management [30]. Among farmers, both males and females are involved in farming. Findings from this study indicate that there are more female than male farmers. This is supported by other studies [31, 32] which also indicate that more females are involved in farming than males. Moreover, findings indicate that most farmers had primary level of education. Primary education is an important predictor of adopting new farming technology [33].

5.1. The flow of agricultural knowledge among stakeholders

Agricultural knowledge flows among and between stakeholders through multiple processes. Findings in **Table 3** indicate that sharing and accessing knowledge and reporting farm-related problems to a third party are the main processes through which agricultural knowledge flows among farmers and between farmers and other stakeholders. All these processes involve a transfer of knowledge from one point to the other. They involve a knowledge transfer because a variety of interactions between individuals and groups; within, between, and across groups; and from groups to the organization are conducted [8].

Among non-farmers agricultural stakeholders, knowledge exchange, sharing, transfer and dissemination are found to be the major processes used to enhance knowledge flow. Through the knowledge exchange process among agricultural stakeholders, it is possible to have collaborative research on priority thematic issues identified as priorities by majority of stakeholders [34]. In a knowledge-sharing process, each side has a role to play [7]; the sources transfer knowledge to another person known as the receiver of recipient of knowledge who receives it and uses it to fill the knowledge gap. Agricultural knowledge sharing is meant to enhance access to knowledge and skills needed for agricultural production [35]. Agricultural knowledge dissemination is a one-direction flow of knowledge. It is a knowledge push process, which spreads knowledge to a wider target audience or to public [22]. Agricultural knowledge dissemination is commonly adopted by the mass media in facilitating access to knowledge to the public.

It is found that all of the three knowledge flow processes involve knowledge transfer. Knowledge exchange and knowledge sharing are multi-directional processes involving a knowledge sources which knows what is needed and the recipient which seeks knowledge, receives and uses it to fill the knowledge gap. On the other hand, knowledge dissemination is a one-direction process because recipients do not seek for it before it is disseminated as they just receive it and may or may not use it.

5.1.1. *Agricultural knowledge sources from which stakeholders receive knowledge*

Regardless of the mode through which knowledge flows, it must come from a known knowledge source and flowing towards a known recipient. Among farmers, knowledge is accessed from fellows, agricultural radio/TV programs, input suppliers, agricultural extension staff, demonstration plots and farmers' groups. Likewise, agricultural knowledge is accessed from print materials, trainings/seminars, print materials, buyers, village executives and agricultural shows/farmers' field days. These sources are convenient and easily consulted and believed to be rich in knowledge [35, 36].

Among non-farmers agricultural stakeholders agricultural knowledge sources used are classified as human-based, paper-based and ICT-based sources. Human-based knowledge sources include farmers, peers, partners and supervisors consulted directly mainly through face-to-face oral communication or through some ICT tools. Letters, newspapers, books, leaflets and booklets were the paper-based agricultural knowledge sources while computers, Internet, mobile phones, radio and TV sets were the ICT-based knowledge sources.

5.1.2. *Recipients of agricultural knowledge*

Agricultural knowledge flows from knowledge sources to recipients. Among farmers, the major recipients of agricultural knowledge are fellow farmers. This indicates that farmers mainly shared and exchanged agricultural knowledge among them. Moreover, it indicates that there are some farmers who have accumulated much knowledge from several sources including farming experience. Other recipients of agricultural knowledge mentioned by a relatively low number of farmers are extension staff, village-based agricultural advisors, input suppliers buyers, village executives, agricultural researchers and farmers' groups. Few farmers mentioned to share knowledge with this category of recipients because they were few, not relevant or not easily reached. All recipients are expected to use acquired agricultural knowledge because they either intentionally access it or are obliged to work on it.

Among majority of non-farmers agricultural stakeholders, recipients of agricultural knowledge are farmers, colleagues and supervisors were the recipients of agricultural knowledge. Among NGOs, farmers, colleagues, partners, donors and the governmental institutions are the major recipients while farmers and colleagues were the major recipients among input suppliers and buyers. It is also found that agricultural information service providers disseminate agricultural knowledge to the public. Depending on the mode of knowledge flow, recipients may either use/be obliged to use or not use it. Recipients may not use received knowledge if disseminated to them without being in need of it [37].

5.2. Factors influencing the choice of communication channels for agricultural knowledge flow

Agricultural stakeholders use different communication channels for agricultural knowledge flow. Findings indicate that face-to-face oral communication and radio sets are used by more than 60% of the farmers followed by mobile phones (which is used by approximately 50% of the farmers, **Table 6**) while TV sets and print materials are used by few farmers. All of the non-farmers agricultural stakeholders mentioned to use face-to-face oral communication and print materials for sharing and exchanging knowledge. Some agricultural researchers, agricultural extension staff, NGOs, input suppliers and buyers mentioned to use virtual communication channels (Skype, mobile phones, and emails) for exchanging or sharing agricultural knowledge. Virtual communication channels facilitated knowledge between virtual teams [38].

The choice of communication channels through which agricultural knowledge flowed was influenced by several factors. Among famers, availability and accessibility of the communication channels, level of development of ICT infrastructure, affordability of tariffs for communication and ownership of some communication tools were found to influence the choice of channels used for either sharing or exchanging agricultural knowledge. Likewise, among non-farmers agricultural stakeholders access to ICT infrastructure and availability and accessibility of ICT tools, affordability of tariffs, availability, convenience and suitability of communication channels for a communication process influence the choice of communication channels.

Without considering other factors, people use communication channels which are available and easily accessible [39]. This applies to ICT- and non-ICT-based channels. For ICT-based channels, the availability and accessibility of a channel is explained by the level of development of ICT infrastructure and accessibility of ICT tools. Since the flow of knowledge involves some costs, then the affordability of costs associated with a specific communication channel influences the choice of communication channels. When those sharing agricultural knowledge afford costs associated with the process, then affordable communication channels are more likely to be used [40]. Likewise, those who afford to own communication tools are more likely to use such tools for enhancing knowledge flow. For example, those owning agricultural books are more likely to read them than non-owners. Also, those owning ICT tools are more likely to use for either sharing or exchanging agricultural knowledge than for non-owners. Moreover, communication channels, which are more convenient and suitable for a knowledge flow process, are more likely to be used for either knowledge sharing, exchange or dissemination.

5.3. Factors influencing the flow of agricultural knowledge among stakeholders

There are several factors known to influence the flow of agricultural knowledge among agricultural stakeholders. Membership in farmers'/professional group and accessibility of agricultural knowledge sources influence the flow of agricultural knowledge. The flow of agricultural knowledge is known to be higher among farmers found in groups [41] because each farmer can be either a knowledge source or a recipient. Moreover, providers of agricultural knowledge services find it easy to reach more farmers or other actors when they were in groups than as individuals [41].

Likewise, the affordability of tariffs for communication influences the flow of agricultural knowledge. Some knowledge flow processes are not free of charge. The recipient or the one disseminating knowledge has to pay some fee so as to communicate knowledge. In most cases, it is only when such costs are low and affordable then the knowledge flow process becomes high. Affordability can equally relate to one's ability to own communication tools too. If communication tools are owned, then the level of usage of such tools among owners becomes higher, hence increasing the possibilities of using them for sharing or exchanging agricultural knowledge.

Among farmers, agricultural extension staff play an important role in enhancing access to knowledge. They are designed to build and strengthen the capacity of rural farmers and other stakeholders through enhancing access to knowledge [42]. To easily reach more stakeholders and enhance access to agricultural knowledge among them, agricultural extension staff should have access to transport facilities. Transport facilities help agricultural extension staff meet more stakeholders within limited time and hence disseminating or exchanging knowledge with more stakeholders.

Other factors, availability of agricultural knowledge, having a well-developed ICT infrastructure and a reliable power sources and airing agricultural radio/TV programs during relevant hours influence the flow of agricultural knowledge. Agricultural knowledge can only flow from one point to the other when it is available. Reliable sources of power are important for ICT-based channels. Available agricultural knowledge can only be shared, exchanged or disseminated through ICTs if such tools are connected to a source of power. Radio and TV sets, computers and mobile phones are among the tools that can only work when connected to a source of power. When broadcasting agricultural knowledge through radio and TV sets, it is important to consider the relevance of time to the target audience of the radio/TV agricultural programs. Without time consideration, few or none of the intended audience can access broadcasted contents. Moreover, a well-developed ICT infrastructure is important for such broadcast to reach more of the intended audience. Likewise, wide wired and wireless phone connections are important for enhancing the flow of available agricultural knowledge among agricultural stakeholders.

Likewise, the usage of most suitable language for repackaging knowledge influences the level of flow of agricultural knowledge. Using unknown or foreign language to repackaging agricultural knowledge limits some stakeholders from accessing knowledge [43]. Very important agricultural knowledge found in an unknown language will not be accessed, shared or exchanged among stakeholders. Therefore, repackaging knowledge in a-not-known and difficult language is like burying it.

An efficient feedback mechanism is important for increasing the flow of agricultural knowledge among agricultural stakeholders. Communication channels enhancing immediate feedback are preferred more than those that do not [39]. Moreover, such channels are more likely to enhance effective agricultural knowledge flow among stakeholders.

To enhance agricultural knowledge flow, communities and organizations should cultivate a knowledge-sharing culture. Community/organizational culture is expressed in terms of leadership, sociability, solidarity, trust, core beliefs, values, norms and social customs [44]. When all these elements of community/organizational culture support the creation and sharing of knowledge, then the level of knowledge accessibility becomes high. Communities and organizations should create platforms through which members can share and exchange knowledge among them. In agricultural organizations, the top management has a strong role to play so as to enhance knowledge-sharing culture, hence increasing the flow of agricultural knowledge. The top management in agricultural institutions can create a rewarding system so as to promote knowledge sharing, exchange and dissemination. This in turn increases the level of flow of agricultural knowledge.

Equally, the availability, convenience, suitability of communication channels to sharing and exchanging agricultural knowledge may influence the level of flow of agricultural knowledge. Agricultural stakeholders use the most available, convenient and suitable communication channels for sharing, exchanging or disseminating agricultural knowledge [39]. This in turn increases the level of flow of agricultural knowledge.

For agricultural information services providers, the affordability of taxes paid for their services and the availability of sponsorship play an important role in increasing the rate of dissemination of agricultural to mass. Governments exert some taxes or duties to media houses. When such taxes or duties are too high, the operational cost of such houses becomes higher limiting them from disseminating agricultural knowledge. Sponsors are important for cushioning the impacts of high taxes and duties on disseminating agricultural knowledge. However, this is only possible when sponsorship is available.

Findings also show that there is correlation between demographic characteristics and some agricultural knowledge flow processes. There is negative correlation between reporting observed farm-related problem and farmer's level of education ($r = -0.302$(**) at 0.000 level of significance). This indicates that as farmer's level of education increases, the ability to handle problems found at farms increases. Likewise, findings indicate that there is a negative correlation between accessing agricultural knowledge and farmer's level of education ($r = -0.194$(**) at 0.001 level of significance). This tells that as the farmer's level of education increased, the level of accessing agricultural knowledge declined. In other words, educated farmers thought they had most of the knowledge needed for production that accessing it from a third party was not important. Findings also indicate that there is a significant positive correlation between accessing agricultural knowledge and farmer's age ($r = 0.203$ (**) at 0.000 level of significance) and farming experience ($r = 0.138$(*) at 0.014 level of significance). This tells that the level of accessing agricultural knowledge is higher among old farmers than young ones. In other words, old farmers enhance more flow of agricultural knowledge than young ones.

5.4. Conclusion and recommendations

An effective agricultural knowledge flow is important for increased accessibility, usage and creation of knowledge, hence improving agricultural productivity. Agricultural knowledge sharing, exchange, transfer and dissemination are important processes facilitating the flow of agricultural knowledge among agricultural stakeholders. For these processes to be effective, suitable and convenient communication channels should be available to enhance the flow of knowledge from the source to the recipient. Paper-based, human- and ICT-based communication channels are commonly used for the flow of agricultural knowledge. Availability of agricultural knowledge and accessibility of knowledge sources are important for enhanced agricultural flow. Well-developed ICT infrastructure, access to power sources and an effective feedback mechanism play an important role in enhancing adequate flow of agricultural knowledge. For agricultural knowledge to be understandable, sharable and exchangeable, it should be repackaged using appropriate languages. Communities and organizations should have strategies to enhance a continuous flow of agricultural knowledge among members. In order to improve the flow of agricultural knowledge, the involvement of different stakeholders is inevitable. Each agricultural stakeholder should be involved in conducting relevant agricultural knowledge-related roles so as to enhance the accessibility, sharing, exchange, dissemination and usage of agricultural knowledge. In order to increase the flow of agricultural knowledge, the Government in partnership with the private sector should widen the ICT and agricultural communication infrastructure.

Author details

Wulystan P. Mtega[1]* and Mpho Ngoepe[2]

*Address all correspondence to: wmtega@gmail.com

1 Sokoine University of Agriculture, Morogoro, Tanzania

2 Department of Information Sciences, University of South Africa, South Africa

References

[1] Kirchhoff CJ, Carmen Lemos M, Dessai S. Actionable knowledge for environmental decision making: Broadening the usability of climate science. Annual Review of Environment and Resources. 2013;**38**(1):393-414. DOI: https://doi.org/10.1146/annurev-environ-022112-112828

[2] McCullough EB, Matson PA. Knowledge systems for sustainable development special feature sackler colloquium: Evolution of the knowledge system for agricultural development in the Yaqui Valley, Sonora, Mexico. Proceedings of the National Academy of Sciences of the United States of America. 2011;**113**(17):306-318. DOI: https://doi.org/10.1073/pnas.1011602108

[3] Kapange B. ICTs and National Agricultural Research Systems – The case of Tanzania. Department of Research and Development, Ministry of Agriculture and Food Security; 2003. pp. 1-7. Available from: http://www.tanzania.go.tz/egov_uploads/documents/griculturalresearc

[4] Isinika AC. Evaluating agricultural research and extension in Tanzania: The production function approach. In: Anandajayasekeram P, Rukuni M, Babu S, Liebenberg F, Keswani CL, editors. Impact of Science on African Agriculture and Food Security. King's Lynn: CABI; 2007:127-136

[5] Ronald B, Dulle F, Honesta N. Assessment of the information needs of Rice farmers in Tanzania: A case study of Kilombero District, Morogoro. Library Philosophy & Practice. 2014;**1071**:1-33. Available from: http://search.ebscohost.com/login.aspx?direct=true&db=lxh&AN=97212802&site=ehost-live

[6] Lwoga ET, Ngulube P, Stilwell C. Managing indigenous knowledge for sustainable agricultural development in developing countries: Knowledge management approaches in the social context. The International Information & Library Review. 2010;**42**(3):174-185. DOI: https://doi.org/10.1016/j.iilr.2010.07.006

[7] Wang S, Noe RA. Knowledge sharing: A review and directions for future research. Human Resource Management Review. 2010;**20**(2):115-131. DOI: https://doi.org/10.1016/j.hrmr.2009.10.001

[8] Paulin D, Suneson K. Knowledge transfer, knowledge sharing and knowledge barriers – Three blurry terms in KM. Electronic Journal of Knowledge Management. 2012;**10**(1):81-91. DOI: https://doi.org/10.1108/14684520910951186

[9] Widén-Wulff G, Ginman M. Explaining knowledge sharing in organizations through the dimensions of social capital. Journal of Information Science. 2004;**30**(5):448-458. DOI: https://doi.org/10.1177/0165551504046997

[10] Aslam MMH, Shahzad K, Syed AR, Ramish A. Social capital and knowledge sharing as determinants of academic performance. Journal of Behavioral and Applied Management. 2013;**15**(1):25-41 Available from: http://proxy.govst.edu:2048/login?url=http://search.ebscohost.com/login.aspx?direct=true&db=psyh&AN=2014-03502-003&site=ehost-live%5Cnharis.aslam@umt.edu.pk

[11] Zahra SA, Neubaum DO, Larrañeta B. Knowledge sharing and technological capabilities: The moderating role of family involvement. Journal of Business Research. 2007;**60**(10):1070-1079. DOI: https://doi.org/10.1016/j.jbusres.2006.12.014

[12] Jewels T, Underwood A, de Pablos Heredero C. The role of informal networks and knowledge sharing. In: Proceedings of the 11th European Conference on Information Systems. Naples, Italy; 2013

[13] Azudin N, Ismail MN, Taherali Z. Knowledge sharing among workers: A study on their contribution through informal communication in Cyberjaya, Malaysia. Knowledge Management and E-Learning. 2009;**1**(2):139-162

[14] Mitton C, Adair CE, McKenzie E, Patten SB, Waye Perry B, Waye B, et al. Knowledge transfer and exchange: Review and synthesis of the literature. The Milbank Quarterly. 2007;**85**(4):729-768. DOI: https://doi.org/10.1111/j.1468-0009.2007.00506.x

[15] Wilkesmann M, Wilkesmann U. Knowledge transfer as interaction between experts and novices supported by technology. Vine. 2011;**41**(2):96-112. DOI: https://doi.org/10.1108/03055721111134763

[16] Argote L, Ingram P. Knowledge transfer: A basis for competitive advantage in firms. Organizational Behavior and Human Decision Processes. 2000;**82**(1):150-169. DOI: https://doi.org/10.1006/obhd.2000.2893

[17] Inkpen AC, Tsang EWK. Social capital networks, and knowledge transfer. Academy of Management Review. 2005;**30**(1):146-165. DOI: https://doi.org/10.5465/AMR.2005.15281445

[18] Aalbers R, Dolfsma W, Koppius K. On and off the beaten path: How individuals broker knowledge through formal and informal networks. Rotterdam: Erasmus Research Institute of Management (ERIM); 2004

[19] Wilson TD. Human information behavior. Informing Science. 2000;**3**(2):49-55. DOI: https://doi.org/10.1186/1472-6963-7-190

[20] Contandriopoulos D, Lemire M, Denis JL, Tremblay É. Knowledge exchange processes in organizations and policy arenas: A narrative systematic review of the literature. Milbank Quarterly. 2010;**88**(4):444-483. DOI: https://doi.org/10.1111/j.1468-0009.2010.00608.x

[21] Lafrenière D, Menuz V, Hurlimann T, Godard B. Knowledge dissemination interventions. SAGE Open. 2013;**3**(1):1-14. DOI: https://doi.org/10.1177/2158244013498242

[22] Green LW, Ottoson JM, García C, Hiatt RA, Roditis ML. Diffusion theory and knowledge dissemination, utilization and integration. Frontiers in Public Health Services & Systems Research. 2014;**3**(1):3 Available from: http://www.ncbi.nlm.nih.gov/pubmed/26251771

[23] Ordonez M, Serrat O. Disseminating knowledge products. Knowledge Solutions. 2009;**43** (May 2009):1-6. DOI: https://doi.org/10.1007/978-981-10-0983-9

[24] Haque MM, Ahlan AR, Mohamed Razi MJ. Factors affecting knowledge sharing on innovation in the higher education institutions (HEis). ARPN Journal of Engineering and Applied Sciences. 2015;**10**(23):18200-18210

[25] Holdschlag A, Ratter BMW. Caribbean island states in a social-ecological panarchy? Complexity theory, adaptability and environmental knowledge systems. Anthropocene. 2016;**13**:80-93. DOI: https://doi.org/10.1016/j.ancene.2016.03.002

[26] Yang C, Chen L-C. Can organizational knowledge capabilities affect knowledge sharing behavior? Journal of Information Science. 2007;**33**(1):95-109. DOI: https://doi.org/10.1177/0165551506068135

[27] Noor AD, Hashim HS, Ali N. Factors influencing knowledge sharing in organizations : A literature review. International Journal of Science and Research. 2012;**3**(9):1314-1319

[28] Cheng M, Ho JS, Lau P M. Knowledge sharing in academic institutions: A study of multimedia university malaysia. Electronic Journal of Knowledge Management. 2009;**7** (3):313-324. ISSN: 1479-4411

[29] Leventon J, Fleskens L, Claringbould H, Schwilch G, Hessel R. An applied methodology for stakeholder identification in transdisciplinary research. Sustainability Science. 2016;**11**(5):763-775. DOI: https://doi.org/10.1007/s11625-016-0385-1

[30] McCullough EB, Matson PA. Evolution of the knowledge system for agricultural development in the Yaqui Valley, Sonora, Mexico. Proceedings of the National Academy of Sciences. 2016;**113**(17):4609-4614. DOI: https://doi.org/10.1073/pnas.1011602108

[31] Galiè A, Jiggins J, Struik PC. Women's identity as farmers: A case study from ten households in Syria. NJAS – Wageningen Journal of Life Sciences. 2013;**64–65**:25-33. DOI: https://doi.org/10.1016/j.njas.2012.10.001

[32] Huyer S. Closing the gender gap in agriculture. Gender, Technology and Development. 2016;**20**(2):105-116. DOI: https://doi.org/10.1177/0971852416643872

[33] Onphanhdala P. Farmer Education and Agricultural Efficiency: Evidence from Lao PDR. Japan: Kobe University. 2009;**20**:2-21

[34] Smith O, Avila M, Abdi N. Strengthening Linkages between Farmers' Organizations and Agricultural Research Institutions. 36th World Farmers' Congress of International Federation of Agricultural Producers (IFAP). Washington, D.C., USA; May 29–4 June 2004; pp. 1-11

[35] Baloch MA, Thapa GB. The effect of agricultural extension services: Date farmers' case in Balochistan, Pakistan. Journal of the Saudi Society of Agricultural Sciences; 2016. DOI: https://doi.org/10.1016/j.jssas.2016.05.007

[36] Ganesan M, Karthikeyan K, Prashant S, Umadikar J. Use of mobile multimedia agricultural advisory systems by Indian farmers: Results of a survey. Journal of Agricultural Extension and Rural Development. 2013;**5**(4):89-99. DOI: https://doi.org/10.5897/JAERD13.0466

[37] Joshi KD, Sarker S. Examining the role of knowledge, source, recipient, relational, and situational context on knowledge transfer among face-to-face ISD teams. Proceedings of the Annual Hawaii International Conference on System Sciences. Vol. 7(C). Kauia, HI, USA; 2006. pp. 1-10. DOI: https://doi.org/10.1109/HICSS.2006.168

[38] Ferrell JZ, Herb KC. Improving Communication in Virtual Teams. 2012. SIOP White Paper Series. https://pdfs.semanticscholar.org/3ae4/db13582bf0fb48018ddfb187538e55085ba7.pdf

[39] Okwu OJ, Daudu S. Extension communication channels' usage and preference by farmers in Benue state, Nigeria. Journal of Agricultural Extension and Rural Development. 2011;**3**(5):88-94

[40] Catalán-matamoros D. The role of mass media communication in public health. Health Management – Different Approaches and Solutions. In: Smigorski K, editor. InTech; 2010. DOI: https://doi.org/10.5772/22790

[41] Duveskog D, Friis-Hansen E, Taylor EW. Farmer field schools in rural Kenya: A transformative learning experience. Journal of Development Studies. 2011;**47**(10):1529-1544. DOI: https://doi.org/10.1080/00220388.2011.561328

[42] Swanson BE, Rajalahti R. Strengthening agricultural extension and advisory systems: Procedures for assessing, transforming, and evaluating extension systems. World Bank, 206. 2010. https://doi.org/ARD (discussion paper 44)

[43] Ugboma MU. Access to agricultural information by fish farmers in Niger Delta region of Nigeria. Library Philosophy & Practice. 2010;**12**(2):1-7

[44] Staplehurst J, Ragsdell G. Knowledge sharing in SMEs: A comparison of two case study Organisations. Journal of Knowledge Management Practice. 2010;**11**(1):1-16 Available from: http://www.tlainc.com/articl211.htm

Chapter 12

Information Transfer and Thermodynamic Point of View on Goedel Proof

Bohdan Hejna

Additional information is available at the end of the chapter

http://dx.doi.org/10.5772/intechopen.68809

Abstract

Formula of an arithmetic theory based on Peano Arithmetics (including it) is a chain of symbols of its super-language (in which the theory is formulated). Such a chain is in convenience both with the syntax of the super-language and with the inferential rules of the theory (Modus Ponens, Generalization). Syntactic rules constructing formulas of the theory are not its inferential rules. Although the super-language syntax is defined recursively—by the recursive writing of mathematical-logical claims—only those recursively written super-language's chains which formulate mathematical-logical claims about finite sets of individual of the theory, computable totally (thus recursive) and always true are the formulas of the theory. Formulas of the theory are not those claims which are true as for the individual of the theory, but not inferable within the theory (Great Fermat's Theorem). They are provable but within another theory (with both Peano and further axioms). Also the chains expressing methodological claims, even being written recursively (Goedel Undecidable Formula) are not parts of the theory. The same applies to their negations. We show that the Goedel substitution function is not the total one and thus is not recursive. It is not defined for the Goedel Undecidable Formula's construction. For this case, the structure of which is visible clearly, we are adding the zero value. This correction is based on information, thermodynamic and computing considerations, simplifies the Goedel original proof, and is valid for the consistent arithmetic theories directly.

Keywords: arithmetic formula, inference, information transfer, information entropy, heat efficiency, infinite cycle

1. Introduction

The formula of an *arithmetic theory* based on *Peano Arithmetics* (including it) is a chain of symbols of its *metalanguage* in which the theory is formulated such that it is both in convenience with the *syntax* of the metalanguage and with the *inferential rules* of the theory [of the *inferential system* (*Modus Ponens, Generalization*)].

Syntactic rules constructing formulae of the theory (but not only!) *are not* its inferential rules. Although the metalanguage syntax is defined *recursively*—by the *recursive writing* of *mathematical-logical* claims, only those recursively written metalanguage's chains which formulate mathematical-logical claims about *finite* (precisely *recursive*) *sets of individual* of the theory, computable totally (thus *recursive*) and as *always true* are the formulae of the theory. Formulas of the theory are not those claims which are true as for the individual of the theory, but not inferable within the theory (*Great Fermat's Theorem*). They are provable but within *another* theory (with *further axioms* than only those of Peano). Also the chains expressing *methodological claims*, even being written recursively (*Goedel Undecidable Formula*), are not parts of the theory, and also they are not parts of the inferential system; the same is for their negations.

We show that the *Goedel substitution function* is not the total one and thus is not recursive. It is not defined for the Goedel Undecidable Formula's *construction*. For this construction, the structure of which is visible clearly, we are setting the zero value. This correction is based on *information, thermodynamic* and *computing* considerations, simplifies the Goedel original proof, and is valid for the *consistent* arithmetic theories directly.[1]

Remark: *Paradoxical claims* (paradoxes, *noetical* paradoxes, *contradictions* and *antinomia*) have two parts—both parts are true, but the truth of one part denies the truth of the second part.

They can arise by not respecting the *metalanguage* (*semantic*) *level*—which is the higher level of our thinking about problems and the *language* (*syntactic*) *level*—which is the lower level of formulations of our 'higher' thoughts. Also they arise by not respecting a *double-level organization and description of measuring*—by not respecting the need of a *'step-aside' of the observer from the observed*. And also they arise by not respecting various *time clicks* in time sequences. As for the latter case, they are in a contradiction with the *causality principle*. The common feature for all these cases is the *Auto-Reference* construction which itself, solved by itself, always states the requirement for ceasing the *II. Principle of Thermodynamics* and all its equivalents [10, 11, 12, 13].

Let us introduce the **Russel's criterion** *for removing paradoxes*[2]: **Within the flow of our thinking and speech we need and must distinguish between *two levels* of our thinking and expressing in order not to fall in a paradoxical claim *by mutual mixing and changing* them.**

These levels are the higher one, the metalanguage (semantic) level and the lower one, the language (syntactic) level. Being aware of the existence of these two levels, we prevent ourselves from their mutual mixing and changing, we prevent ourselves from *application* our *metalanguage claims on themselves* but now on the language level or vice versa.

---

[1]**The reader of the paper should be familiar with the Goedel proof's way and terminology; *SMALL CAPITALS* in the whole text mean the Goedel numbers and working with them.** This chapter is based, mainly, on Ref. [17], which was improved as for certain misprints, and also, by a few more adequate formulations and by adding the part **Appendix** [14–16].

[2]B. Russel, L. Whitehead, **Principia Mathematica**, 1910, 1912, 1913 and 1927.

We must be aware that our claims about properties of considered objects are *created* on the higher level, rather richer both semantically and syntactically than the lower one on which we really express ourselves about these objects. The words and meanings of this lower (and 'narrower') level are common to both of them. Our speech is *formulated and performed* on the lower level describing here our 'higher' thoughts and on which the objects themselves have been described, defined yet too, of course from the higher level, but with the necessary (lower) limitations. (As such they are thought over on the higher level.) From this point of view, we understand the various meanings (levels) of the same words. Then, any mutual mixing and changing the metalanguage and language level or the auto-reference (paradox, noetical paradox, contradiction and antinomian) is excluded.

2. Goedel numbers, information and thermodynamics

Any *inference* within the system $\mathcal{P}$[3] sets the $\mathcal{T}_{\mathcal{PA}}$-*theoretical* relation[4] among its formulae $a_{[\cdot]}$. This relation is given by their gradually generated *special sequence* $\vec{a}= [a_1, \dots, a_q, \dots, a_p, \dots, a_k, a_{k+1}]$ which is the *proof* of the latest inferred formula a_{k+1}. By this, the *unique* arithmetic relation between their *Goedel numbers*, FORMULAE $x_{[\cdot]}$, $x_{[\cdot]} = \Phi(a_{[\cdot]})$, is set up, too. The gradually arising *SEQUENCE of FORMULAE* $x = \Phi(\vec{a})$ is the *PROOF* of its latest *FORMULA* x_{k+1}.

Let us assume that the given sequence $\vec{a}= [a_{o1}, a_{o2}, \dots, a_o, \dots, a_q, \dots, a_p, \dots, a_k, a_{k+1}]$ is a special one, and that, except of axioms (axiomatic schemes) $a_{01}, \dots, a_o$, it has been generated by the correct application of the rule *Modus Ponens only.*[5]

Within the process of the (*goedelian*) *arithmetic-syntactic analysis* of the latest formula a_{k+1} of the proof $\vec{a}$ we use, from the $\vec{a}$ *selected*, (special) subsequence $\overrightarrow{a_{q,p,k+1}}$ of the formulae a_q, a_p, a_{k+1}. The formulae a_q, a_p have already been derived, or they are axioms. It is valid that $q,p < k+1$, and we assume that $q < p$,

$$\begin{aligned}
\overrightarrow{a_{q,p,k+1}} &= [a_q, a_p, a_{k+1}],\ \ a_p \cong a_q \supset a_{k+1},\ \ \overrightarrow{a_{q,p,k+1}} = [a_q, a_q \supset a_{k+1}, a_{k+1}],\\
x &= \Phi(\vec{a}) = \Phi([\Phi(a_1), \Phi(a_2), \dots, \Phi(a_q), \dots, \Phi(a_p), \dots, \Phi(a_k), \Phi(a_{k+1})]])\\
&= \Phi(\vec{x}) = \Phi(x_1)*\Phi(x_2)* \dots *\Phi(x_q)* \dots *\Phi(x_p)* \dots *\Phi(x_k)*\Phi(x_{k+1})\\
l(x) &= l[\Phi(\vec{x})] = l[\Phi(\vec{a})] = k+1,\\
x_{k+1} &= \Phi(a_{k+1}) = l[\Phi(\vec{a})]Gl\ \Phi(\vec{a}) = (k+1)Gl\ x\\
x_p &= \Phi(a_p) = \Phi(a_q \supset a_{k+1}) = qGl\ \Phi(\vec{a}) * \Phi(\supset) * l[\Phi(\vec{a})]Gl\ \Phi(\vec{a})\\
&= qGl\ xImp\ [l(x)]Gl\ x\\
x_q &= \Phi(a_q) = qGl\ \Phi(\vec{a}) = qGl\ x
\end{aligned} \tag{1}$$

[3]*Formal arithmetic inferential system.*

[4]Peano Arithmetics Theory.

[5]For simplicity. The 'real' inference is applied to the formula a_{i+1} for $i = o$.

Checking the *syntactic and* $\mathcal{T}_{\mathcal{PA}}$*-theoretical correctness* of the analyzed chains a_i, as the formulae of the system $\mathcal{P}$ having been generated by inferring (*Modus Ponens*) within the system $\mathcal{P}$ (in the theory $\mathcal{T}_{\mathcal{PA}}$), and also the special sequence of the formulae $\vec{a}$ of the system $\mathcal{P}$ (theory $\mathcal{T}_{\mathcal{PA}}$), is realized by checking the *arithmetic-syntactic* correctness of the notation of their corresponding *FORMULAE* and *SEQUENCE of FORMULAE*, by means of the relations $Form(\cdot)$, $FR(\cdot)$, $Op(\cdot,\cdot,\cdot)$, $Fl(\cdot,\cdot,\cdot)$ 'called' from (the sequence of procedures) relations $Bew(\cdot)$, $(\cdot\cdot)B(\cdot)$, $Bw(\cdot)$[6]; the core of the whole (goedelian) arithmetic-syntactic analysis is the (procedure) relation of *Divisibility*,

$$\begin{aligned}
&Form[\Phi(a_i)] = "1"/"0", \;\; FR[\Phi(\overrightarrow{a_1^{i+1}})] = "1"/"0", \;\; o \le i \le k \\
&Op[x_k, Neg(x_q), x_{k+1}] \;=\; Op[\Phi(a_p), \Phi[\sim (a_q)], \Phi(a_{k+1})] = "1"/"0" \\
&Fl[(k+1)Gl\, x, pGl\, x, qGl\, x] = "1"/"0" \\
&xB\, x_{k+1} = "1"/"0", \;\; Bew(x_{k+1}) = "1"/"0"; \\
&\Phi(a_p)||23^{3Gl\, \Phi(\overrightarrow{a_{q}, p^{k+1}})} \;\&\; \Phi(a_p)||7^{1Gl\, \Phi(\overrightarrow{a_{q}, p^{k+1}})} = "1"/"0"
\end{aligned} \tag{2}$$

2.1. Inference in the system $\mathcal{P}$ and information transfer

The syntactic analysis of the special sequence of the formulae $\vec{a}$ of the system $\mathcal{P}$ in general, and therefore, also its arithmetic-syntactic version, that is the activity of (*goedelian*) *arithmetic-syntactic analyzer*, will be expressed by means of terms of *information transfer* through a certain *information transfer channel* $\mathcal{K}$.

As such, it is a sequence of successive *attempts i* to transfer information with *input, loss* and *output messages* $[a_{p_i}, a_{q_i}, a_{i+1}], [a_{p_i}, a_{q_i}]$ *and* $[a_{i+1}]$ with their *information amounts* $J(\overrightarrow{a_{q_i, p_i, i+1}}), J(\overrightarrow{a_{q_i, p_i}})$ and $J(a_{i+1})$. Index i is a serial number of the *inferencing—analyzing—transferring* step, $0 < q_i < p_i < i+1 \le l[\Phi(\vec{a})] = k+1$. The Goedel numbering also enables us to consider the individual Goedel numbers x_i, $x_i|y_i$ and y_i of messages $[a_{p_i}, a_{q_i}, a_{i+1}]$, $[a_{p_i}, a_{q_i}]$ a $[a_{i+1}]$ as *messages too*, with their (and the same) information amounts $J(x_i)$, $J(x_i|y_i)$ a $J(y_i)$,

$$\begin{aligned}
&[a_{p_i}, a_{q_i}, a_{i+1}] \triangleq \overrightarrow{a_{q_i, p_i, i+1}} \triangleq x_i = \Phi(\overrightarrow{a_{q_i, p_i, i+1}}), \;\; [a_{p_i}, a_{q_i}] \triangleq \overrightarrow{a_{q_i, p_i}} \triangleq x_i|y_i = \Phi(\overrightarrow{a_{q_i, p_i}}) \\
&[a_{i+1}] \triangleq a_{i+1} \triangleq y_i = \Phi(a_{i+1}) \\
&\Phi(\overrightarrow{a_{q_i, p_i, i+1}}) = \Phi(a_{q_i}) * \Phi(a_{p_i}) * \Phi(a_{i+1}) = \Phi(\overrightarrow{a_{q_i, p_i}}) * \Phi(a_{i+1}), \;\; \Phi(\overrightarrow{a_{q_i, p_i}}) = \Phi(a_{q_i}) * \Phi(a_{p_i}); \\
&J(x_i) = J[\Phi(\overrightarrow{a_{q_i, p_i, i+1}})], \, J(x_i|y_i) = J[\Phi(\overrightarrow{a_{q_i, p_i}})], \, J(y_i) = J[\Phi(a_{i+1})]
\end{aligned} \tag{3}$$

For each ith step of the goedelian syntactic analysis, we determine the values

[6] *Formula*, Reihe von Formeln, *O*peration, *F*olge, *G*lied, Beweis, *Bew*eis, see Definition 1–46 in Refs. [3–5] and by means of all other, by them 'called', relations and functions (by their procedures).

$$\begin{aligned} J(x_i) &= \ln(x_i) = \ln[\Phi(\overrightarrow{a_{q_i,p_i,i+1}})] = J(\overrightarrow{a_{q_i,p_i,i+1}}) = J[2^{\Phi(a_{q_i})}\cdot 3^{\Phi(a_{p_i})}\cdot 5^{\Phi(a_{i+1})}] \\ &= \ln[2^{\Phi(a_{q_i})}\cdot 3^{\Phi(a_{p_i})}\cdot 5^{\Phi(a_{i+1})}] \\ J(x_i|y_i) &= \ln(x_i|y_i) = \ln[\Phi(\overrightarrow{a_{q_i,p_i}})] = J(\overrightarrow{a_{q_i,p_i}}) = J[2^{\Phi(a_{q_i})}\cdot 3^{\Phi(a_{p_i})}] = \ln[2^{\Phi(a_{p_i})}\cdot 3^{\Phi(a_{q_i})}] \\ J(y_i) &= \ln(y_i) = J(a_{i+1}) = J[5^{\Phi(a_{i+1})}] = \ln[5^{\Phi(a_{i+1})}] \end{aligned} \tag{4}$$

We regard these values as *average* values $H(X)$, $H(X|Y)$ and $H(Y)$ of information amounts of *message sources* X, $X|Y$ and Y with *selective spaces* $\mathbb{X}$, $\mathbb{X}\times\mathbb{Y}$ and $\mathbb{Y}$, and with the *uniform probability distribution*,

$$\begin{aligned} & X \overset{\text{Def}}{=} [\mathbb{X}, \pi_X(x_i) = \text{const.}],\ \text{card}\ \mathbb{X} = 2^{\Phi(\overrightarrow{a_{q_i,p_i,i+1}})}, \qquad \pi_X(x_i) = \frac{1}{2^{\Phi(\overrightarrow{a_{q_i,p_i,i+1}})}} \\ & Y \overset{\text{Def}}{=} [\mathbb{Y}, \pi_Y(y_i) = \text{const.}],\ \ \text{card}\ \mathbb{Y} = 5^{\Phi(a_{i+1})},\ \pi_Y(y_i) = \frac{1}{5^{\Phi(a_{i+1})}} \\ & \sum_{j=1}^{\text{card}\ \mathbb{X}} \frac{1}{2^{\Phi(\overrightarrow{a_{q_i,p_i,i+1}})}} = \frac{2^{\Phi(\overrightarrow{a_{q_i,p_i,i+1}})}}{2^{\Phi(\overrightarrow{a_{q_i,p_i,i+1}})}} = 1,\ \sum_{j=1}^{\text{card}\ \mathbb{Y}} \frac{1}{5^{\Phi(a_{i+1})}} = \frac{5^{\Phi(a_{i+1})}}{5^{\Phi(a_{i+1})}} = 1 \end{aligned} \tag{5}$$

It is obvious that we consider a *direct* information transfer [11] through the channel $\mathcal{K}$ without *noise, disturbing* $y_i|x_i$, which means with the *zero noise* (*disturbing*) information $[J(y_i|x_i) = 0] \equiv [H(Y|X) = 0]$, $[y_i|x_i \cong \Phi\ (null)]$.

In each ith step of the activity of our *information model* $\mathcal{K}$ of the arithmetic-syntactic analysis, it is valid that $X := x_i = \Phi(\overrightarrow{a_{q_i,p_i,i+1}})$ and $Y := y_i = \Phi(a_{i+1}) = x_{i+1}$, and the *channel equation* is applicable [11],

$$\begin{aligned} T(X;Y) = H(X) - H(X|Y) &\ \ =\ \ H(Y) - H(Y|X) = T(Y;X) \\ T(X;Y) = J(x_i) - J(x_i|y_i) &\ \ =\ \ J(y_i) - J(y_i|x_i) = T(Y;X)\ \ \text{now in the form} \\ T(X;Y) = H(X) - H(X|Y) &\ \ =\ \ H(Y),\ \ T(X;Y) = J(x_i) - J(x_i|y_i) = J(y_i) \end{aligned} \tag{6}$$

The relation $\Phi(\overrightarrow{a_{q_i,p_i,i+1}})B\ \Phi(a_{i+1})$ $(x_i B\ y_i)$ is evaluated by the relation of *Divisibility* and we identify its execution[7] with the actual direct information transfer in the channel $\mathcal{K}$. So, when our inference by *Modus Ponens* is done correctly, in each ith step, we have its *information interpretation*, in steps i,

$$\begin{aligned} & [x_i B\ y_i]\ \cong\ [J(x_i) - J(x_i|y_i) > 0]\ \equiv\ [T(x_i;y_i) > 0]\ \equiv\ [T(X;Y) > 0] \\ & \equiv [Fl(y_i,x_{p_i},x_{q_i})]\ \equiv\ Fl[\Phi(a_{i+1}),\Phi(a_{q_i}),\Phi(a_{p_i})]\ \equiv\ [\Phi(\overrightarrow{a_{q_i,p_i,i+1}})B\ \Phi(a_{i+1})] \\ & \equiv [\Phi(a_{p_i})||23^{3Gl\ x_i}\ \&\ \Phi(a_{p_i})||7^{x_i}]\ \equiv\ [\Phi(a_{p_i})||23^{3Gl\ \Phi(\overrightarrow{a_{q_i,p_i,i+1}})}\ \&\ \Phi(a_{p_i})||7^{1Gl\ \Phi(\overrightarrow{a_{q_i,p_i,i+1}})}] \end{aligned} \tag{7}$$

Let us assume that, when inferring by *Modus Ponens*, $\frac{b,\ [(\sim b)\vee(c)]}{c}$, we make such an error that we write $\frac{b,\ [(\sim b)\vee(c)]}{d}$, $d \neq c$ where, however, the chain d (by chance) can also be (in the form

[7] And of the other relevant procedures too, see definitions 1–46 in Refs. [3–5].

of) a formula of the language $\mathcal{L}_{\mathcal{P}}$ of the system $\mathcal{P}$.[8] For the considered *NOT-INFERRABILITY* of y_i $[= d]$, being interpreted now from the point of information view, *we put* $J(\Phi(a_{i+1})) \overset{\text{Def}}{=} 0$, or better said, with regard of the properties of *INFERENCE*, we are forced to put $\Phi(a_{i+1}) \overset{\text{Def}}{=} 0$ within the framework of the theory $\mathcal{T}_{\mathcal{P}\mathcal{A}}$ and then, informationally

$$\begin{aligned} H(Y) &= T(X;Y) \overset{\text{Def}}{=} \ln[5^{\Phi(a_{i+1})}] = 0, & H(X) &= H(X|Y) \\ J(x_i) - J(x_i|y_i) &= J(y_i) = 0, & J(x_i) &= J(x_i|y_i) \\ \eta_i &\overset{\text{Def}}{=} \frac{J(y_i)}{J(x_i)} = \frac{H(Y)}{H(X)}, & 0 \le \eta_i &\le 1 \end{aligned} \tag{8}$$

2.2. Thermodynamic consideration

The thermodynamic consideration of an information transfer [11] reveals that the input message $\overrightarrow{a_{q_i,p_i,i+1}}$ carries the *input heat energy* ΔQ_{W_i} transformed by the *reversible direct Carnot Cycle* (*Machine*) $\mathcal{C}$ into the output *mechanical work* ΔA_i corresponding to the output message a_{i+1}. The *heater* $\mathcal{A}$ of the Carnot Cycle (Machine) $\mathcal{C}$ has the temperature T_W and models the *source* of input messages (the message $\overrightarrow{a_{q_i,p_i,i+1}}$) of the channel $\mathcal{K}$. Its *cooler* $\mathcal{B}$ has the temperature T_0 determining the transfer efficiency η_i. By the value $\eta_i > 0$ the fact of inferrability of the chain a_{i+1} from the special sequence of formulae $\overrightarrow{a_{q_i,p_i,i+1}}$ as the formula of the theory $\mathcal{T}_{\mathcal{P}\mathcal{A}}$ is stated.

Thus, the reversible direct Carnot Cycle $\mathcal{C}$ is the *thermodynamic model* of the direct information transfer through the channel $\mathcal{K}$ [11], and hereby of the inferring (*INFERRING*) itself, and also of the arithmetic-syntactic analysis of formulae of the language $\mathcal{L}_{\mathcal{T}\mathcal{P}_\mathcal{A}}$ of the theory $\mathcal{T}_{\mathcal{P}\mathcal{A}}$.[9] Thus, we have

$$J(x_i) = \frac{\Delta Q_{W_i}}{kT_W}, \qquad J(x_i|y_i) = \frac{\Delta Q_{0_i}}{kT_W}, \qquad J(y_i) = \frac{\Delta A_i}{kT_W} \tag{9}$$

Now we obtain the information formulation [11] of the *changes* of the *heat* (*thermodynamic*) *entropies* $\Delta\mathcal{S}_{\mathcal{C}}{}^{[i]}$, $\Delta\mathcal{S}_{\mathcal{A}\mathcal{B}}{}^{[i]}$ and $\Delta\mathcal{S}_{\mathcal{A}}^{[i]}$ in the thermodynamic model $\mathcal{C}$ of our *information transfer—inferring* (*INFERRING*)*—arithmetic-syntactic analysis* within the (language of the) system $\mathcal{P}$,

$$\Delta\mathcal{S}_{\mathcal{C}}{}^{[i]} = kH(X), \qquad \Delta\mathcal{S}_{\mathcal{A}\mathcal{B}}{}^{[i]} = kH(X|Y), \qquad \Delta\mathcal{S}_{\mathcal{A}}{}^{[i]} = k \cdot [H(X) - H(X|Y)] \tag{10}$$

In accordance with Ref. [11], it is valid that, within the *inferring—arithmetic-syntactic analysis—information transfer*, the thermodynamic entropy $\mathcal{S}_{\mathcal{C}}$ of an *isolated system*, in which the modeling reversible direct Carnot Cycle $\mathcal{C}$ is running parallelly, increases in every *i*th step by the value $\Delta\mathcal{S}_{\mathcal{C}}{}^{[i]}$,

[8]We just think mistakenly that $d \triangleq a_{i+1}$ but $a_{i+1} = c$ is correct. Then the relation of *Divisibility is not* met. Neither is the relation of the *Immediate Consequence*.

[9]Formulated in the language $\mathcal{L}_{\mathcal{P}}$ of the system $\mathcal{P}$ in compliance with its (with the $\mathcal{T}_{\mathcal{P}\mathcal{A}}$) inference rules.

$$\Delta \mathcal{S_C}^{[i]} = \mathrm{k}J(a_{i+1}) = \mathrm{k}H(Y)),\ \ H(Y) \triangleq J(a_{i+1}) = \frac{\Delta A_{[i]}}{\mathrm{k}T_W} \geq 0 \tag{11}$$

Provided that the ith inferring step *has been done and written correctly* (*Modus Ponens*) the Goedel arithmetic-syntactic analyzer decides, correctly, for the obtained $\overrightarrow{a_1^{i+1}} \triangleq [\overrightarrow{a_1^i}, a_{i+1}]$, that the relations $\Phi(\overrightarrow{a_{q_i,p_i,i+1}})B\ \Phi(a_{i+1})$ $[\Phi(\overrightarrow{a_1^{i+1}})B\ \Phi(a_{i+1})]$ and $Bew[\Phi(a_{i+1})]$ are valid, and the information-thermodynamic model $(\mathcal{K} - \mathcal{C})$ generates the *non-zero, positive* output value $T(X; Y)$ for the inferring step i [for $X := x_i = \Phi(\overrightarrow{a_{q_i,p_i,i+1}})$ or $X := x_i = \Phi(\overrightarrow{a_1^i})$, respectively, and for $Y := y_i = \Phi(a_{i+1})$],

$$T(X; Y) = J(a_{i+1}) = H(Y) = \frac{\Delta \mathcal{S_C}^{[i]}}{\mathrm{k}T_W} > 0 \tag{12}$$

The zero change of the whole heat entropy $\mathcal{S_C}$ of the isolated system in which our model cycle $\mathcal{C}$ is running *occurs just when* in the inferential system $\mathcal{P}$, *from the perspective of the theory* $\mathcal{T_{PA}}$, *nothing is being inferred* in the step i, $\Delta \mathcal{S_C}^{[i]} = 0$. Now, particularly in that sense that we mistakenly apply the conclusion of the rule *Modus Ponens* and we declare it to be an inferring step. Then, from the point of view of the $\mathcal{T_{PA}}$-inference, we do not exert any 'useful effort' or energy in order to derive a new $\mathcal{T_{PA}}$-relation [formula a_{i+1}, *FORMULA* $\Phi(a_{i+1})$]. The previous 'effort' or energy associated with our inference (no matter that $\mathcal{T_{PA}}$-correct) of the sequence of $\overrightarrow{a_i^i}$ is worthless. The formula a_{i+1} [$= d$] is just arbitrarily added to the previous sequence $\overrightarrow{a_1^i}$ of formulae of the theory $\mathcal{T_{PA}}$ in such a way that it does not include any such formulae a_{q_i} and a_{p_i} that it would be valid $\Phi(a_{p_i,q_i,i+1})B\ \Phi(a_{i+1}) =$ "1". In the information-thermodynamic interpretation, we write (for $X := x_i$, $Y := y_i = d$)

$$\begin{array}{rcl} J(y_i) = H(Y) = 0 & \Rightarrow & J(x_i) = H(X) = H(X|Y) = J(x_i|y_i) \\ \eta_i = 0 & \Rightarrow & \Delta \mathcal{S_C}^{[i]} = 0 \\ T_W = T_0 & \Rightarrow & \Delta Q_{W_i} = \Delta Q_{0_i} \\ \eta_i \cdot \Delta Q_{W_i} & = & \mathrm{k} \cdot J(y_i) = 0 \ \Rightarrow\ \eta_i = 0 \end{array} \tag{13}$$

We *have not exerted* any inferring energy within the framework of building up the theory $\mathcal{T_{PA}}$, in order to create information $J(y_i) > 0$, and then we necessarily have $\eta_i = 0$, $J(y_i) = 0$ where $\eta_i = 0$ expresses this error. All before a_{i+1}, otherwise inferred correctly, is not related to it–the information transfer channel $\mathcal{K}$ is *interrupted*. The overall amount of our inference efforts exerted in vain up to a_i included can be evaluated by the whole heat energy[10]

$$\mathrm{k} \cdot H(X|Y) = \mathrm{k} \cdot \ln[\Phi(\overrightarrow{a_1^i})] = \ln[2^{\Phi(a_1)} \cdot 3^{\Phi(a_2)} \cdot\ \ldots\ \cdot \pi_i^{\Phi(a_i)}] \tag{14}$$

[10] π_i is the i-th prime number.

3. Goedel substitution function and FORMULA 17*Gen r*

Let us consider the *instance* of the relation $Q(X,Y)$ for the specific values x and y, $X := x$ and $Y := y$, which is the *constant* relation $Q(x,y)$, and let us define the Goedel numbers y and y' that the Goedel (variable) number (his *'CLASS' SIGN*) y arises from *Admissible Substitution* from the *FORMULA* $q(17,19)$ [the ARITHMETIZATION of $Q(X,Y)$],

$$y = Sb\begin{pmatrix} q(17,19) & \begin{matrix} 17 \\ Z(x) \end{matrix} \end{pmatrix} = y(19)\ [= \Phi[Q(x,Y)]\ ] \quad \text{and} \quad y' = Sb\begin{pmatrix} y & \begin{matrix} 19 \\ Z(y) \end{matrix} \end{pmatrix} \tag{15}$$

Any of the following notations can be used

$$\begin{aligned} &q(u_1,u_2) = q(17,19) = \Phi[Q(X,Y)] = \Phi[q(u,v)] = \Phi[Q(X,Y)] \\ &q(u_1,u_2) = q(17,19) = \Phi[Q(X,Y)] \\ &q(u_1,u_2),\ q(17,19),\ q(u,v) \triangleq Q(X,Y),\ \ldots \\ &q[Z(x),u_2] = y(u_2) = q[Z(x),19] = y(19) = y = \Phi[Q(x,Y)] \triangleq Q(x,Y) \end{aligned} \tag{16}$$

The following *Admissible Substitution* $Sb\begin{pmatrix} y & \begin{matrix} 19 \\ Z(y) \end{matrix} \end{pmatrix}$ is carried out in the second step of the given *Double Substitution* $Sb\begin{pmatrix} q & \begin{matrix} 17 & 19 \\ Z(x) & Z(y) \end{matrix} \end{pmatrix}$; in the Goedel variable number $q(17,19)$, we first put $17 := Z(x)$ and in the result $q[Z(x),19]$ we put $19 := Z(y)$. Then

$$y' = y[Z(y)] = [y(19)]_{19:=Z(y)} = q[Z(x),Z(y)] = \Phi[Q(x,y)] \triangleq Q(x,y) \tag{17}$$

The *CLAIM* y' only seems to be a constant $\mathcal{P}/\mathcal{T}_{\mathcal{PA}}$-*FORMULA*, which, as the *CLAIM* $y[Z(y)]$ speaks only about a common number y. But, by the *NUMERAL* $Z(y)]$ it is the y speaking about y and then, it is the *FORMULA* y speaking about itself.

Let us think of the goedelian arithmetic-syntactic *generator*, the job of which is to 'print' the Goedel numbers of the *constant FORMULAE* obtained by *Admissible Substitutions* of *NUMERALS* into their *FREE VARIABLES* (now of the *Type*-1). In case of the 'global' validity of the substitution $19 := Z(y)$[11] it creates from the given *FORMULA* y an infinite sequence of semantically identical *FORMULAE* y' $[= y[Z(y)]]$, $y[Z(y')]$ $[= y[Z[y[Z(y)]]]]$, … with the aim to end the process by 'printing' *just the value* y'. But it never reveals this outcome y'; however, we —metatheoretically—know it. It never gets as far as to print the natural number y' which it 'wants to reach' by creating the infinite sequence of outcomes of the permanently repeated substitution $19 := Z(y)$ which prevents it from this goal (y' marks the claim y about the claim y, the claim y about the claim y about the claim y etc.). It is even the first one, by which the

[11]Caused by the application of the (Cantor) diagonal argument.

analyzer is trying to calculate and 'print' y', that prevents it from this aim. We never obtain a constant Goedel number. The *FORMULA* $y[Z(y)]$ arises by applying the (*Cantor*) *diagonal argument,* which *is not any inference rule* of the theory $\mathcal{T}_{\mathcal{PA}}$ (and of the system $\mathcal{P}$), and thus, it is not an element of the language $\mathcal{L}_{\mathcal{TA}_\mathcal{P}}$ (and $\mathcal{L}_\mathcal{P}$). This is the reason for *not-recursivity* of the relations $Bew(\cdot)$; the *upper limit* of its computing process is missing. First, we have $q[Z(x),19]_{19:=Z(y)} \cong q[Z(x),Z(y)] = y[Z(y)] = y'$ *and then 'try'* [12]

$$
\begin{aligned}
y' &\cong q[Z(x),Z[q[Z(x),19]]]_{19:=Z(y)}\\
&\cong q[Z(x),Z[q[Z(x),Z(y)]]] = y[Z[y[Z(y)]]]\\
&\cong q[Z(x),Z[q[Z(x),Z[q[Z(x),19]]]]]_{19:=Z(y)}\\
&\cong q[Z(x),Z[q[Z(x),Z[q[Z(x),Z(y)]]]]]\\
&\cong q[Z(x),Z[q[Z(x),Z[q[Z(x),Z[q[Z(x),19]]]]]]]_{19:=Z(y)}\\
&\cong q[Z(x),Z[q[Z(x),Z[q[Z(x),Z[q[Z(x),Z(y)]]]]]]]\\
&\cong q[Z(x),Z[q[Z(x),Z[q[Z(x),Z[q[Z(x),Z[q[Z(x),19]]]]]]]]]_{19:=Z(y)} \cong \ \ldots \ \textit{ad lib.}
\end{aligned} \tag{18}
$$

It is obvious that the *Substitution function,* no matter how much its execution complies with the recursive grammar, is not total and, therefore, nor recursive. For this reason, it is convenient to *redefine it as a total function and, therefore, also recursive one* and to put $[y[Z(y)]] = 0$ but, due to the inference properties, $Neg[y[Z(y)]] = 0$ too. Then

$$
\begin{gathered}
\underline{\underline{Sb\begin{pmatrix} & 19 \\ y(19) & \\ & Z(y)\end{pmatrix} \stackrel{\text{Def}}{=} 0}} \ \&Sb\begin{pmatrix} & 19 \\ Neg[y(19)] & \\ & Z(y)\end{pmatrix} = \overline{\underline{\underline{Sb\begin{pmatrix} & 19 \\ y(19) & \\ & Z(y)\end{pmatrix} \stackrel{\text{Def}}{=} 0}}}\\
\underline{\underline{Bew[y[Z(y)]] = Bew(0) = 0}}\&\underline{\underline{Bew[Neg[y[Z(y)]]] = Bew(0) = 0}}\\
Q(x,y) \equiv \overline{xB\left[Sb\begin{pmatrix} & 19 \\ y & \\ & Z(y)\end{pmatrix}\right]} = q[Z(x),Z(y)] = y[Z(y)] = y' \triangleq \overline{xB\,y'}
\end{gathered} \tag{19}
$$

Also see the Proposition V in Refs. [3–5]. The mere grammar *derivation,* writability convenient to the recursive grammar is quite different from the $\mathcal{T}_{\mathcal{PA}}$-provability. The Goedel number y', the *FORMULA* $y[Z(y)]$, is seemingly a *FORMULA* (and even constant) of the system $\mathcal{P}$ and thus it is not an element of the theory $\mathcal{T}_{\mathcal{PA}}$; is *not of an arithmetic type* (it is not recursive arithmetically, only as for its basic syntax, syntactically). As the *CLAIM* $y[Z(y)]$ it speaks about the number y only, but by that it is the number y itself, then as $y[Z(y)]$, it claims its own property, that from the Goedel number x it itself *IS NOT INFERRED* within the system $\mathcal{P}$ $[Bew(y') = 0]$. It is true for the given x and it 'says': 'I, *FORMULA* $y[Z(y)]$, am in the system $\mathcal{P}$

[12]By substitution $19 := Z(y)$ nothing changes in variability of *FORMULA* y' by the *VARIABLE* 19. The number y' should denote *infinite* and *not recursive* subset of natural numbers or to be equal to them.

(by it means) from the Goedel number x *UNPROVABLE*.' And, by this, it also states both the property of the system $\mathcal{P}$ and the theory $\mathcal{T}_{\mathcal{PA}}$.

3.1. *FORMULA* 17*Gen r* and information transfer

With regard of the fact that *FORMULA* y' is *constructed* by the diagonal argument, it is not *INFERRED* within the system $\mathcal{P}$—in the $\mathcal{T}_{\mathcal{PA}}$ and so, it is not provable for any x from $\mathbb{N}_0$. Then, within the framework of the theory $\mathcal{T}_{\mathcal{PA}}$, we put $\underline{\underline{17Gen\ y' \stackrel{\text{Def}}{=} 0}}$ and thus $\underline{\underline{J(17Gen\ y') \stackrel{\text{Def}}{=} 0}}$.[13] In the proof *we put* $p : 17Gen\ q$, $[17 \cong u_1 \triangleq X, 19 \triangleq u_2 \triangleq Y,\ q = q(17, 19)]$, and then, in compliance with the Goedel notation,

$$p = 17Gen\ q(17, 19) = \Phi[u_1 \Pi q(u_1, u_2)] \qquad [= \Phi[\forall_{x \in \mathbb{X}} | Q(x, Y)] \triangleq Q(\mathbb{X}, Y)] \triangleq Q(\mathbb{N}_0, Y) \tag{20}$$

The *metalanguage symbol* $Q(\mathbb{X}, Y)$ *in (20) or the symbol* $Q(\mathbb{N}_0, Y)$ *is read as follows*:

'None $x \in \mathbb{X}(\mathbb{N}_0)$ is in the relation *INFERENCE* to the content (to the selective space $\mathbb{Y}$) of the variable Y. From any given $x, x = \Phi(\vec{a}) = \Phi(\overrightarrow{[a_1^k, a_{k+1}]})$, $x \in \mathbb{X}(\mathbb{N}_0)$, any Goedel number $\Phi(a_{k+1}) \neq 0$, writable as the proposed outcome of the *INFERENCE* from the given x, is *NOT INFERRED* in reality.'

$$We\ put\ r := Sb\begin{pmatrix} q & 19 \\ & Z(p) \end{pmatrix} = Sb\begin{pmatrix} q(17,19) & 19 \\ & Z(p) \end{pmatrix} = Sb\begin{pmatrix} q(17,19) & 19 \\ & Z[17Gen\ q(17,19)] \end{pmatrix}.$$

The Goedel number r, $r \triangleq r(17) = \Phi[Q(X, p)]$ is, by the substitution $Z(p)$, supposingly [3–5], the *CLASS SIGN* with the *FREE VARIABLE* 17, but also remains be the variable Goedel number in the *VARIABLE* 19. It contains the *FREE VARIABLE* 19 as hidden and 17 is both *FREE* and *BOUND* in it, $[q[17, Z[17Gen\ q(17, 19)]]$,

$$\begin{aligned} r = r(17) &= q[17, Z[p(19)]] = q[17, Z[17Gen\ q(17, 19)]] \triangleq q[u_1, Z(p)] \triangleq Q(X, p) \\ &= q[u_1, \Phi[u_1 \Pi q(u_1, u_2)]] = \Phi[Q[X, \Phi[\forall_{x \in X} | Q(x, Y)]]], \\ &\triangleq Q(X, p) = Q(X, Y)_{Y:=p} \triangleq Q[X, \Phi[Q(\mathbb{X}, Y)]] \triangleq Q[X, \Phi[Q(\mathbb{N}_0, Y)]] \end{aligned} \tag{21}$$

Further[14] $Q(X, Y)_{X:=x} = Q(x, Y), Q(x, Y)_{Y:=p} = Q(x, p)$ and then,

[13]From that y' is *NOT INFERRED* follows its *NOT-INFERRABILITY/NOT-PROVABILITY*.

[14]And similarly for $Q(X,Y)_{Y:=p} = Q(X,p)$, $Q(X,p)_{X:=x} = Q(x,p)$. It depends neither on the sequence of substitution steps nor on the sequence of operations $Sb\begin{pmatrix} \cdot & \cdot \\ & \cdot \end{pmatrix}$ and $[\cdot]$ Gen $[\cdot\cdot]$.

$$\begin{aligned} r[Z(\mathrm{x})] &= r(17)_{17:=Z(x)} = q[17, Z(p)]_{17:=Z(x)} \\ &= q[Z(\mathrm{x}), Z[17Gen\ q(17,19)]] = q[Z(x), Z(p)]] = q[Z(p)] = q' \\ &= q[Z(x), Z[\Phi[u_1\Pi q(u_1,u_2)]]] = \Phi[Q[x, \Phi[\forall_{x\in X}|Q(x,Y)]]] \\ &= \Phi[Q[x, \Phi[Q(\mathbb{X}, Y)]]] = \Phi[Q[x, \Phi[Q(\mathbb{N}_0, Y)]]] \end{aligned} \tag{22}$$

With regard of quantification $r[Z(x)]$ over values $Z(x)$ of the variable u_1, we write

$$\begin{aligned} Z(x)Gen\ r[Z(x)] &= Z(x)Gen\ q[Z(x),Z(p)]] = Z(x)Gen\ p[Z(p)] = Z(x)Gen\ q' \\ &= Z(x)Gen\ q[Z(x),Z[17Gen\ q(17,19)]] = p[Z(p)] = p' \\ &\cong 17Gen\ q[17,Z[17Gen\ q(17,19)]] = 17Gen\ r(17) \\ &= 17Gen\ q[17,Z[p(19)]] = 17Gen\ q[17,Z[17Gen\ q(17,19)]] \\ &= \Phi[u_1\Pi[\Phi[q[u_1,\Phi[u_1\Pi q(u_1,u_2)]]]]] \\ &= \Phi[\forall_{x\in X}|\Phi[Q[x,\Phi[\forall_{x\in X}|Q(x,Y)]]]] = 17Gen\ r \\ &\triangleq Q(\mathbb{X},p) = Q(\mathbb{X},Y)_{Y:=p} \triangleq Q[\mathbb{X},\Phi[Q(\mathbb{X},Y)]] = Q[\mathbb{N}_0,\Phi[Q(\mathbb{N}_0,Y)]] \end{aligned} \tag{23}$$

The relation $Q(\mathbb{X},p)$, $Q(\mathbb{X},p) = \forall_{x\in\mathbb{X}}|Q[x,\Phi[\forall_{x\in\mathbb{X}}Q(x,p)]]$ and, therefore, the relation $\overline{T(\mathbb{X},p)}$ says that no such x exists to comply with the message transfer conditions of p from x; the *infinite cycle* is stipulated. Attempts to give the proof of the *FORMULA* 17*Gen* r within the framework of the inferential system $\mathcal{P}$, that is, attempts to 'decide' it *inside* the system $\mathcal{P}$ only by the means of the system $\mathcal{P}$ itself end up in the infinite cycle.

The claim 17*Gen* r does not belong to the theory $\mathcal{T}_{\mathcal{PA}}$ but gives a witness about it—about its property. It is so because it is formulated in a *wider/general formulative language* $\mathcal{L}^{\mathcal{P}*}$ than the language $\mathcal{L}_{\mathcal{P}}$ of the system $\mathcal{P}$ and so outside both of the language $\mathcal{L}_{\mathcal{P}}$ (and as such, outside of the language $\mathcal{L}_{\mathcal{TA}_{\mathcal{P}}}$ too). The *FORMULAE/CLAIMS* of both the theory $\mathcal{T}_{\mathcal{PA}}$ and the system $\mathcal{P}$ speak only about *finite* sets of arithmetic individuals but the theory $\mathcal{T}_{\mathcal{PA}}$ and the system $\mathcal{P}$ are the *countable*–$\mathcal{N}_0$-sets.[15] It seems only that 17*Gen* r is a part (of the *ARITHMETIZATION*) of the theory $\mathcal{T}_{\mathcal{PA}}$ and of the system $\mathcal{P}$ which is by it is written down (grammatically only) according to the common/general recursive syntax of the general formulative language $\mathcal{L}^{\mathcal{P}*}$ in which all the arithmetic relations are written (and, in addition, the $\mathcal{T}_{\mathcal{PA}}$-relations are inferred). On the other hand, there nothing special on its evaluation, *but from the point of view or position of the metalanguage only* (!). From the *formalistic* point of view, it is a number only. From the *semantic* point of view, it is an arithmetic *code* but of the not-arithmetic claim.[16]

Let the Goedel number $t[Z(x),Z(y)]$ be *DESCRIPTION* of the mechanism of the transfer y from x (on the level of the system $\mathcal{P}$ and the theory $\mathcal{T}_{\mathcal{PA}}$) in the channel $\mathcal{K}$,

[15]We have, inside of them, only $\mathcal{N}_0$ symbols for denoting their relations/formulae (or sets denoted by these relations/formulae). Thus, the *CLAIM* 17*Gen* r speaks about the element of the set with the cardinality $\mathcal{N}_1$ containing, as its elements, the $\mathcal{N}_0$-sets; thus it can speak about the theory T_{PA}, $\mathcal{N}_0 < \mathcal{N}_1$ and cannot be in it or in the system $\mathcal{P}$.

[16]Thus **it is not a common number** as the [3–5] claims and **neither is** r.

$$Sb\begin{pmatrix} & 17 & 19 \\ t & & \\ & Z(x) & Z(y) \end{pmatrix} \cong Subst\ t^{\mathcal{K}}(U_1, U_2)\begin{bmatrix} U_1 & U_2 \\ J(x) & J(y) \end{bmatrix} \equiv [J(x) - J(y) \neq J(x)] \tag{24}$$

But, when it is valid that $\underline{\underline{Sb\begin{pmatrix} & 19 \\ y & \\ & Z(y) \end{pmatrix} = 0}} = Sb\begin{pmatrix} & 17 & 19 \\ q & & \\ & Z(x) & Z(y) \end{pmatrix}$ then the number $y$is not a FORMULA of the system $\mathcal{P}$ and *in the information interpretation* of inferring (*INFERRING*) within the system $\mathcal{P}$ it is valid that, $\underline{\underline{J(y) = 0}}$. Then we can consider the simultaneous validity of $\underline{\underline{[J(y) > 0]\&[J(y) < 0]}}$ —also see the Proposition V in Refs. [3–5], which, from the *thermodynamic* point of view, means the equilibrium and, from the point of *computing*, the *infinite cycle* [14, 16]. For the information variant of the FORMULA 17*Gen r* and Goedel number $p' = p[Z(p)]$ is valid

$$\begin{aligned} & p' \overset{\text{Def}}{=} Subst\ p(U_2)\begin{pmatrix} U_2 \\ J(p) \end{pmatrix} = Subst\ U_1 Gen\ q^{\mathcal{K}}(U_1, U_2)\begin{pmatrix} U_2 \\ J[U_1 Gen\ q^{\mathcal{K}}(U_1, U_2)] \end{pmatrix} \\ & p' = 17Gen\ q^K[U_1, J[U_1 Gen\ q^K(U_1, U_2)]] = U_1 Gen\ q^K[U_1, J(p)] = p[J(p)] \\ & = U_1 Gen\ r(U_1) \ = U_1 Gen\ r \\ & \cong u_1 \Pi[q^{\mathcal{K}}[u_1, J[u_1 \Pi q^{\mathcal{K}}(u_1, u_2)]]]] = \forall_{x \in X}|Q^{\mathcal{K}}[X, \Phi[\forall_{x \in X}|Q^{\mathcal{K}}(x, Y)]] \\ & = Q^{\mathcal{K}}(\mathbb{X}, p)] = Q^{\mathcal{K}}(\mathbb{X}, Y)_{Y:=p} = Q^{\mathcal{K}}[\mathbb{X}, \Phi[Q^{\mathcal{K}}(\mathbb{X}, Y)]] = Q^{\mathcal{K}}[\mathbb{N}_0, \Phi[Q^{\mathcal{K}}(\mathbb{N}_0, Y)]] \end{aligned} \tag{25}$$

So, the message p' (the message p about itself) is not-transferrable from any message x,

$$[\overline{xB^{[\mathcal{K}]}\ p'} = "1"] \equiv [\overline{xB^{[\mathcal{K}]}\ p} = "1"] \equiv [\tau^{[\mathcal{K}]}(x,y) = "0"] \equiv [J(p) = 0] \equiv [J(p') = 0] \tag{26}$$

It is the attempt to transfer the message y ($y = 17Gen\ r$) through the channel $\mathcal{K}$, while this message itself causes its interruption and 'wants' to be transferred through this interrupted channel $\mathcal{K}$ as well.[17] Its 'errorness' is in our awaiting of the non-zero outcome $J(y) > 0$ when it is applied in the (direct) transfer scheme $\mathcal{K}$ because the information $J(y) > 0,\ y = 17Gen\ r$ (known from and valid in the metalanguage), from the point of transferrability through the channel $\mathcal{K}$ (from the point of inferrability in the theory $\mathcal{T}_{\mathcal{PA}}$) does not exist. *In the theory, $\mathcal{T}_{\mathcal{PA}}$ is* $J(y) = 0$ for the *CLAIM* 17*Gen r* is not arithmetic at all, it is the *metaarithmetic* one. From the point of the theory $\mathcal{T}_{\mathcal{PA}}$ and the system $\mathcal{P}$, it is not quite well to call *CLAIM* 17*Gen r* as the *SENTENTIAL FORMULA*; it has only such form. For this reason, we use the term *CLAIM* 17*Gen r* or *'SENTENTIAL FORMULA'/'PROPOSITION.'*

The message about that the channel $\mathcal{K}$ is for y interrupted *cannot* be transferred *through the same channel $\mathcal{K}$ interrupted for y* (however, through another one, uninterrupted for y, it can). Or we can say that the claim a_{k+1} [*CLAIM* y, $y = \Phi(a_{k+1}) = 17Gen\ r$] is not inferable (*INFERABLE*) in the given inferential system $\mathcal{P}$ (but in another one making its construction-*INFERENCE* possible, it is),

[17] In fact, it represents the very core of the sense of the **Halting Problem** task in the Computational Theory.

$$\overline{\exists_{x\in\mathbb{X}}|t^{\mathcal{K}}[J(x),J[\exists_{x\in\mathbb{X}}t^{\mathcal{K}}[J(x),J(y)]]] > 0} \equiv \overline{T(\mathbb{X},y) > 0} \equiv Q(\mathbb{X},y) \tag{27}$$

By constructing the *FORMULA* 17*Gen r* and from the point of information transfer, we have produced the claim 'the transfer channel $\mathcal{K}$ is from p' and on interrupted.' Or, we have made the interrupted transfer channel directly by this p' when we assumed it belonged to the set of messages transferrable from the source X. So, first we interrupt the channel $\mathcal{K}$ for p', and then, we want to transfer this p' from the input x which includes this p' (or is identical to it), and so the *internal* and *input* state of the channel $\mathcal{K}$ are (also from the point of the theory $\mathcal{T}_{\mathcal{PA}}$) equivalent informationally. It is valid that $\underline{\underline{J(p')=0}}$ for any x, $x\in\mathbb{X}$ [so $\forall_{c\in\mathbb{X}}|[J(p')=0]$],

$$\forall_{x\in\mathbb{X}}|[J(x)=J(x|p')] \cong [J(\mathbb{X}|p')=J(\mathbb{X})>0] \text{ and for the simplicity is } J(p'|\mathbb{X})=0$$

$$\left[\forall_{x\in\mathbb{X}}|\overline{\tau(x,p')}\right] \equiv \left[\forall_{x\in\mathbb{X}}|\overline{[J(x)-J(x|p')>0]}\right] \equiv \left[\overline{\exists_{x\in\mathbb{N}_0}|[J(x)-J(x|p')>0]}\right] = \text{"1"}$$

$$x=\Phi(\overrightarrow{a_1^k})*17Gen\ r=\Phi(\overrightarrow{a_1^k})*Sb\begin{pmatrix} & 19 \\ p & \\ & Z(p)\end{pmatrix}=\Phi([a_1^k],p')\cong\Phi([a_1^k],null) \tag{28}$$

$$J(x)=J[\Phi(\overrightarrow{a_1^k})*\Phi(0)]=J[\Phi([a_1^k])\cdot 2^0]=J(x|p)=J[\Phi([a_1^k])],\quad x|p=\Phi([a_1^k])$$

The channel $\mathcal{K}$, however, always works only with the not zero and the positive difference of information amounts $J(x)-J(x|y)$ and in the theory $\mathcal{T}_{\mathcal{PA}}$ now it is valid that $J(y)=J(x)-J(x|p')=J(null)=0$, $J(y)=J(p')=J(null)=0$[18]. It means that our assumption about p' [$=r$] is erroneous. No input message x having a relation to the output message p' exists. The *FORMULA* 17*Gen r* both creates and describes behavior of the not functioning (interrupted) information transfer, from p' on further. For the *efficiency* η of the information transfer, it is then valid [14, 16] that

$$\eta=\frac{J(p)}{J(\mathbb{X})}=0 \tag{29}$$

The CLAIM ('SENTENTIAL PROPOSITION') 17*Gen r we interpret as follows:*

- No information transfer channel $\mathcal{K}$ transfers its (internal) state $x|y$ [the information $J(x|y)$] given as its input message x, it behaves as interrupted.
- There is no $x\in\mathbb{N}_0$ for which it is possible to generate the Goedel number $\Phi[Q(\mathbb{N}_0,Y)]$ which claims that there is no $x\in\mathbb{N}_0$ for which it is possible to generate the non-zero Goedel number y that we could write into the variable Y. This means that from any Goedel number x no *INFERENCE* is possible just for its latest part $y=\Phi(a_{k+1})=17Gen\ r$ has not been *INFERRED* either.

[18] Attention (!) but x contains the message p that $J(x)=J(x|p)$.

The metaarithmetic sense of the CLAIM ('SENTENTIAL PROPOSITION') 17*Gen r is*:

- Within the *general formulative language* $\mathcal{L}^{\mathcal{P}*}$ of the inconsistent metasystem $\mathcal{P}^*$ (containing the consistent subsystem $\mathcal{P}$ with the theory the $\mathcal{T}_{\mathcal{P}\mathcal{A}}$) it is possible to construct [be the (Cantor) diagonal argument] such a claim (with the Goedel arithmetization code 17*Gen r*) which is true, but both this claim i and its negation are not provable/*PROVABLE* by the means of the system $\mathcal{P}$ (in the system $\mathcal{P}$) and thus, also in the theory $\mathcal{T}_{\mathcal{P}\mathcal{A}}$–they are the meta-$\mathcal{T}_{\mathcal{P}\mathcal{A}}$ and the meta-$\mathcal{P}$ claims not belonging to the system $\mathcal{P}$, but they belong to the inconsistent system $\mathcal{P}^*$, to its part $\mathcal{P}^* - \mathcal{P}$ ($\mathcal{P}^* \underset{\neq}{\supset} \mathcal{P}$).

- So, the Goedel Proposition *VI*… (1931) [3–5] should be, correctly, 'For the system exists …' (which Goedel also, but not uniquely says), 'For the theory exists, (nevertheless outside of them); by the author's conviction the error is to say.' In each consistent (?) system exists … or, even 'In the consistent (?) theory exists ….'

4. Conclusion

Peano arithmetic theory is generated by its inferential rules (rules of the inferential system in which it is formulated). It consists of parts bound mutually just by these rules but none of them is not identical with it nor with the system in their totality.

By information-thermodynamic and computing analysis of Peano arithmetic proving, we have showed why the Goedel formula and its negation are not provable and decidable within it. They are constructed, not inferred, by the (Cantor) diagonal argument which is not from the set of the inferential rules of the system. The attempt to prove them leads to awaiting of the end of the infinite cycle being generated by the application of the substitution function just by the diagonal argument. For this case, the substitution function is not countable, and for this, it is not recursive (although in the Goedel original definition is claimed that it is). We redefine it to be total by the zero value for this case. This new substitution function generates the Goedel numbers of chains which are not only satisfying the recursive grammar of formulae but it itself is recursive. The option of the zero value follows also from the vision of the inferential process as it would be the information transfer. The attempt to prove the Goedel Undecidable Formula is the attempt of the transfer of that information which is equal to the information expressing the inner structure of the information transfer channel. In the thermodynamic point of view we achieve the equilibrium status which is an equivalent to the inconsistent theory. So, we can see that the Goedel Undecidable Formula is not a formula of the Peano Arithmetics and, also, that it is not an arithmetical claim at all. From the thermodynamic consideration follows that even we need a certain effort or energy to construct it, within the frame of the theory this is irrelevant. It is the error in the inference and cannot be part of the theory and also it is not the system. Its information value in it (as in the system of the information transfer) is zero. But it is the true claim about inferential properties of the theory (of the information transfer).

We have shown that the *CLAIM/'FORMULA'* 17*Gen r*, no matter how much it complies with the grammar of recursive writing of $\mathcal{T}_{\mathcal{P}\mathcal{A}}$-arithmetic *FORMULAE*, is not such a *FORMULA*; it is not an element of the theory $\mathcal{T}_{\mathcal{PA}}$ and in convenience with [1, 2, 6, 7, 18, 19] nor an element of the system $\mathcal{P}$[19] and neither is r. The same is for $Neg(17Gen\ r)$ (it cannot be inferred in $\mathcal{P}$ for is not inferable in $\mathcal{P}$.) Nevertheless, we are in accordance with the *intuitive and obviously intended sense* of the Goedel Proposition *VI*[20] which we, as the metalanguage one, have proved by metalanguage (information-thermodynamic-computing) means. We see, with our correction, that the *CLAIMS* (the Goedel *'SENTENTIAL PROPOSITIONS'/'FORMULAE'*) $17Gen\ r$, $Neg(17Gen\ r)$ and the Proposition *VI* as the claim about them are metaarithmetic (methodological) statements.

5. Appendix

5.1. Auto-reference in information transfer, self-observation

In any *information transfer channel* $\mathcal{K}$ the *channel equation*

$$H(X) - H(X|Y) = H(Y) - H(Y|X) \tag{30}$$

it is valid [?]. This equation describes the mutual relations among *information entropies [(average) information amounts]* in the channel $\mathcal{K}$.

The quantities $H(X)$, $H(Y)$, $H(X|Y)$ and $H(Y|X)$ are the *input*, the *output*, the *loss* and the *noise* entropy.

The difference $H(X) - H(X|Y)$ or the difference $H(Y) - H(Y|X)$ defines the *transinformation* $T(X;Y)$ or the transinformation $T(Y;X)$, respectively,

$$H(X) - H(X|Y) \triangleq T(X;Y) \quad = \quad T(Y;X) \triangleq H(Y) - H(Y|X) \tag{31}$$

When the channel $\mathcal{K}$ transfers the information (entropy) $H(X)$, but now just at the value of the entropy $H(X|Y)$, $H(X) = H(X|Y)$, then, necessarily, must be valid

$$T(X;Y) = 0 \quad [= H(Y) - H(Y|X)] \tag{32}$$

- For $H(Y|X) = 0$, we have $T(X;Y) = H(Y) = 0$.
- For $H(Y|X) \neq 0$ we have $H(Y) = H(Y|X) \neq 0$

In both these two cases, the channel $\mathcal{K}$ operates as the *interrupted* (*with the absolute noise*) and the output $H(Y)$ is without any relation to the input $H(X)$ and, also, it does not relate to the structure of $\mathcal{K}$. This structure is expressed by the value of the quantity $H(X|Y)$. We assume, for simplicity, that $H(Y|X) = 0$.

---

[19] In the contrast to Refs. [3–5].

[20] Because, on the other hand, Goedel 1931 [3–5] also says, correctly, '**For** the system exists …,' '**For** the theory exists …, (**nevertheless outside of them** - the author's remark); the **error** is to say **in** the system exists …, **in** the theory exists ….'

From Eqs. (30) to (32) follows that the channel $\mathcal{K}$ cannot transfer (within the same step p of its *transfer process*) such an information which describes its inner structure and, thus, it cannot transfer—observe (copy, measure) itself. It is valid both for the concrete information value and for the average information value, as well.

Any channel $\mathcal{K}$ cannot transfer its own states considered as the input messages (within the same steps p). Such an attempt is the information analogy for the Auto-Reference known from Logics and Computing Theory. Thus, a certain 'step-aside' leading to a non-zero transfer output, $H(Y) = H(X) - H(X|Y) > 0$, is needed. (For more information see [14, 15, 16].

5.2. Auto-reference and thermodynamic stationarity

The transfer process running in an information transfer channel $\mathcal{K}$ is possible to be comprehended (modeled or, even, constructed) as the *direct* Carnot Cycle $\mathcal{O}$ [8, 10]. The relation $\mathcal{O} \cong \mathcal{K}$ is postulated. Further, we can imagine its observing method, equivalent to its 'mirror' $\mathcal{O}'' \cong \mathcal{K}''$. This *mirror* $\mathcal{O}''$ is, at this case, the direct Carnot Cycle $\mathcal{O}$ as for its structure, but functioning in the *indirect, reverse* mode [8, 10].

Let us connect them together to a *combined heat cycle $\mathcal{O}\mathcal{O}''$ in such a way that the mirror* (*the reverse cycle $\mathcal{O}''$*) is gaining the message about the structure of the direct cycle $\mathcal{O}$. This message is (carrying) the information $H(X|Y)$ about the structure of the transformation (transfer) process ($\mathcal{O} \cong \mathcal{K}$) being 'observed.' *The mirror $\mathcal{O}'' \cong \mathcal{K}''$ is gaining this information $H(X|Y)$ on its noise 'input' $H(Y''|X'')$ [while $H(X'') = H(Y)$ is its input entropy].*

The quantities ΔQ_W, ΔA and ΔQ_0 or the quantities $\Delta Q''_W$, $\Delta A''$ and $\Delta Q''_0$, respectively, define the information entropies of the information transfer realized (thermodynamically) by the *direct* Carnot Cycle $\mathcal{O}$ or by the *reverse* Carnot Cycle $\mathcal{O}''$ (the mirror), respectively, (the *combined* cycle $\mathcal{O}\mathcal{O}''$ is created),

$$\begin{aligned} H(X) &= \frac{\Delta Q_W}{kT_W}, \; resp. \;\; H(Y'') = \frac{\Delta Q''_W}{kT''_W} \\ H(Y) &= \frac{\Delta A}{kT_W}, \; resp. \; H(X'') = \frac{\Delta A''}{kT''_W} \\ H(X|Y) &= \frac{\Delta Q_0}{kT_W}, \; resp. \;\; H(Y''|X'') = \frac{\Delta Q''_0}{kT''_W} \end{aligned} \tag{33}$$

Our aim is to gain the *non-zero* output mechanical work ΔA^* of the combined heat cycle $\mathcal{O}\mathcal{O}''$, $\Delta A^* > 0$. We want to gain non-zero information $H^*(Y^*) = \frac{\Delta A^*}{kT_W} > 0$.

To achieve this aim, for the efficiencies η_{max} and η''_{max} of the both connected cycles $\mathcal{O}$ and $\mathcal{O}''$ (with the working temperatures $T_W = T''_W$ and $T_0 = T''_0$, $T_W \geq T_0 > 0$), it must be valid that $\eta_{max} > \eta''_{max}$; we want the validity of the relation[21]

[21]We follow the proof of *physical and thus logical impossibility* of the construction and functionality of the *Perpetuum Mobile* of the *II*. and, equivalently [10], of the *I*. type.

$$\Delta^{*}A = \Delta A - \Delta A'' > 0 \ \left[\Delta A'' = \Delta Q''_{W} - \Delta Q''_{0}\right] \tag{34}$$

When $\Delta Q_0 = \Delta Q''_0$ should be valid, then must be that $\Delta Q''_W < \Delta Q_W$ $[\Leftarrow (\eta_{max} > \eta''_{max})]$, and thus, it should be valid that

$$\begin{aligned} \Delta A^{*} = \Delta Q_W \cdot \eta_{max} - \Delta Q''_W \cdot \eta''_{max} > 0 \qquad \text{but} \\ \Delta Q_W \cdot \eta_{max} - \Delta Q''_W \cdot \eta''_{max} = \Delta Q_0 - \Delta Q''_0 = 0 \end{aligned} \tag{35}$$

Thus, the output work $\Delta A^{*} > 0$ *should be generated* without any lost heat and by the *direct change* of the whole heat $\Delta Q_W - \Delta Q''_W$ but within the cycle $\mathcal{O}\mathcal{O}''$. For $\eta_{max} < \eta''_{max}$ the same heat $\Delta Q_W - \Delta Q''_W$ should be pumped from the cooler with the temperature T_0 to the heater with the temperature T_W *directly*, without any compensation by a mechanical work. We see that $\Delta A^{*} = 0$ is the reality.

Our combined machine $\mathcal{O}\mathcal{O}''$ should be the *II. Perpetuum Mobile* in both two cases. Thus, $\eta_{max} = \eta''_{max}$ must be valid (the heater with the temperature T_W and the cooler with the temperature T_0 are common) that

$$\eta_{max} = \eta''_{max} < 1 \quad \text{and then} \quad \Delta Q_W = \Delta Q''_W \tag{36}$$

We must be aware that for $\eta_{max} = \eta''_{max} < 1$ the whole information entropy of the environment in which our (reversible) combined cycle $\mathcal{O}\mathcal{O}''$ is running changes on one hand *by the value*

$$H(X) \cdot \eta_{max} = \frac{\Delta Q_W}{kT_W} \cdot (1 - \beta) > 0, \qquad \beta = 1 - \eta_{max} = \frac{T_0}{T_W} \tag{37}$$

and on the other hand it is also changed *by the value* $-H(X) \cdot \eta_{max} = -\frac{\Delta Q_W}{kT_W} \cdot (1 - \beta)$ Thus, it must be changed by the *zero* value

$$H^{*}(Y^{*}) = \overset{= \Delta A^{*}}{\overline{kT_W}} H(X) \cdot \eta_{max} - H(Y'') \cdot \eta''_{max} = H(X) \cdot \left(\eta_{max} - \eta_{max}\right) = 0 \tag{38}$$

The whole combined machine or the thermodynamic system with the cycle $\mathcal{O}\mathcal{O}''$ is, when the cycle $\mathcal{O}\mathcal{O}''$ is seen, as a whole, in the *thermodynamic equilibrium*. (It can be seen as an unit, analogous to an interruptable operation in computing.)

Thus, the observation of the observed process $\mathcal{O}$ by the observing reverse process $\mathcal{O}''$ with the same structure (by itself), or the Self-Observation, is impossible in a physical sense, and, consequently, in a logical sense, too (see the Auto-Reference in computing).

Nevertheless, the construction of the Auto-Reference is describable and, as such, is recognizable, *decidable* just as a construction *sui generis.* It leads, necessarily, to the requirement of the *II.* Perpetuum Mobile functionality when the requirements (34) and (35) are sustained.

(Note that the Carnot Machine itself is, by its definition, a construction of the infinite cycle of the states of its working medium and as such is identifiable and recognizable.) For the methodological step demonstrating the *Information Thermodynamic Concept Removing* see [14, 15, 16].

5.3. Gibbs paradox - auto-reference in observation

Only just by a (thought) 'dividing' of an equilibrium system $\mathcal{A}$ by *diaphragms* [9, 10, 11, 13], without any influence on its thermodynamic (macroscopic) properties, a non-zero difference of its entropy, before and after its 'dividing,' is evidenced.

Let us consider a thermodynamic system $\mathcal{A}$ in volume V and with n matter units of ideal gas in the thermodynamic equilibrium. The *state equation* of $\mathcal{A}$ is $pV = nR\Theta$. For an elementary change of the *internal* energy U of $\mathcal{A}$, we have $\mathrm{d}U = nc_v\mathrm{d}\Theta$.

From the state equation of $\mathcal{A}$, and from the general *law of energy conservation* [for a (substitute) reversible exchange of heat δq between the system and its environment], we formulate the *I. Principle of Thermodynamics*, $\delta q = \mathrm{d}U + p\mathrm{d}V$

From this principle, and from *Clausius equation* $\Delta S \overset{\mathrm{Def}}{=} \frac{\Delta q}{\Theta}$, $\Delta q = c_v\Delta\Theta + \frac{R\Theta\Delta V}{V}$, $\Theta > 0$, follows that

$$S = n\int\left(c_v\frac{\mathrm{d}\Theta}{\Theta} + R\frac{\mathrm{d}V}{V}\right) = n(c_v \ln\Theta + R\ln V) + S_0(n) = \sigma(\Theta,V) + S_0(n) \tag{39}$$

Let us 'divide' the equilibrial system $\mathcal{A}$ in a volume V and at a temperature Θ, or, better said, the whole volume V (or, its whole state space) occupiable, and just occupied now by all its constituents (particles, matter units), with diaphragms (thin infinitely, or, 'thought' only), not affecting thermodynamic properties of $\mathcal{A}$ supposingly, to m parts $\mathcal{A}_i$, $i\in\{1, \ldots, m\}$, $m\geq 1$ with volumes V_i with matter units n_i. Evidently $n = \sum_{i=1}^{m} n_i$ and $V = \sum_{i=1}^{m} V_i$.

Let now $S_0(n) = 0$ and $S_{0i}(n_i) = 0$ for all i. For the entropies S_i of $\mathcal{A}_i$ considered individually, and for the change ΔS, when volumes V, V_i are expressed from the state equations, and for $p = p_i$, $\Theta = \Theta_i$ it will be gained that $\sigma_{[i]} = Rn_{[i]}\ln n_{[i]}$. Then, for $S_i = \sigma_i = n_i(c_v\ln\Theta + R\ln V_i)$ is valid, we have that

$$\begin{aligned} &\sum_{i=1}^{m} S_i = \sum_{i=1}^{m}\sigma_i = nc_v\ln\Theta + R\ln\left(\prod_{i=1}^{m} V_i^{\,n_i}\right), \\ &\Delta S = S - \sum_{i=1}^{m} S_i = \sigma - \sum_{i=1}^{m}\sigma_i = \Delta\sigma = R\ln\frac{V^n}{\prod_{i=1}^{m} V_i^{\,n_i}} = -nR\sum_{i=1}^{m}\frac{n_i}{n}\ln\frac{n_i}{n} > 0 \end{aligned} \tag{40}$$

Let us denote the last sum as B further on, $B < 0$. The quantity $-B$ expressed in (40) is information entropy of a source of messages with an alphabet $[n_1, n_2, \ldots, n_m]$ and probability distribution $\left[\frac{n_i}{n}\right]_{i=1}^{m}$. Such a division of the system to m parts defines an information source with the information entropy with its maximum $\ln m$.

The result (37), $\Delta S = -nRB$, is a *paradox*, a contradiction with our presumption of not influencing a thermodynamic state of $\mathcal{A}$ by diaphragms, and, leads to that result that the heat entropy S (of a system in equilibrium) *is not* an extensive quantity. But, by the definition of the differential dS, this *is not* true.

Due to this contradiction, we must consider a non-zero integrating constants $S_0(n)$, $S_{0i}(n_i)$, in such a way, that the equation $\Delta S = (\sigma + S_0) - \sum_{i=1}^{m}(\sigma_i + S_{0i}) = 0$ is solvable for the system $\mathcal{A}$ and all its parts $\mathcal{A}_i$ by solutions $S_{0[i]}(n_{[i]}) = -n_{[i]} R \ln \frac{n_{[i]}}{\gamma_{[i]}}$.

Then, $S_{[i]} \triangleq S_{[i]}^{Claus}$, and we write and derive that

$$S^{Claus} = \sum_{i=1}^{m} S_i^{Claus} = \sum_{i=1}^{m} n_i R \ln \gamma_i = nR \ln \gamma \Rightarrow \gamma = \gamma_i; \qquad \Delta S = 0. \tag{41}$$

Now let us observe an equilibrium, $S^* = S^{Claus} = S^{Boltz} = -kNB* = -kN \ln N$.

Let, in compliance with the *solution* of Gibbs Paradox, the integration constant S_0 be the (change of) entropy ΔS which is added to the entropy σ *to figure out* the measured entropy S^{Claus} of the equilibrium state of the system $\mathcal{A}$ (the final state of Gay-Lussac experiment) at a temperature Θ. We have shown that without such correction, the less entropy σ is evidenced, $\sigma = S^{Claus} - \Delta S,\ \Delta S = S_0$.

Following the previous definitions and results, we have

$$\begin{aligned} &\Delta S = \frac{\Delta Q_0}{\Theta} = -nR \ln \frac{n}{\gamma}, \\ &\ln \gamma = \frac{\Delta S}{knN_A} + \ln n = \frac{\Delta S}{kN} + \ln N - \ln N_A,\ \gamma = N \ \Rightarrow \ \frac{\Delta S}{kN} = \ln N_A. \end{aligned} \tag{42}$$

By the entropy ΔS the 'lost' heat ΔQ_0 (at the temperature Θ) is defined.

Thus, our observation can be understood as an information transfer $\mathcal{T}$ in an information channel $\mathcal{K}$ with entropies $H(X)$, $H(Y)$, $H(X|Y)$ and $H(Y|X)$ in (33) but now bound physically; we have these information entropies per one particle of the observed system $\mathcal{A}$:

$$\begin{aligned} &input \quad H(X) \overset{\text{Def}}{=} \frac{S^*}{kN} = \ln\gamma = -B* = \ln N = -rB(r) \\ &output \quad H(Y) \overset{\text{Def}}{=} \frac{\sigma}{kN} \triangleq -B^{Gibbs} = -B^{Boltz} = -B(r), \\ &loss \quad H(X|Y) \overset{\text{Def}}{=} \frac{S_0}{kN}, \\ &noise \quad H(Y|X) \overset{\text{Def}}{=} 0 \quad \text{for the simplicity}\ ; \\ &H(X|Y) = -rB(r) - [-B(r)] = -B(r) \cdot (r-1) = (-B*) \cdot \frac{r-1}{r}, r \geq 1; \ \frac{1}{r} = \eta_{max}. \end{aligned} \tag{43}$$

For a number m of cells of our railings in the volume V with $\mathcal{A}$, $m \leq N$ or for the accuracy r of this description of the 'inner structure' of $\mathcal{A}$ (a thought structure of V with $\mathcal{A}$) and for the number q of diaphragms creating our railings of cells and constructed in such a way that $q \in \, < 1, m-1 >$, we have that $r = \frac{N-1}{q}$.

Our observation of the equilibrium system $\mathcal{A}$, including the *mathematical correction* for Gibbs Paradox, is then describable by the Shannon transfer scheme $[X, \mathcal{K}, Y]$, where

$$H(X) = \frac{S^{Claus}}{kN}, \qquad H(X|Y) = \frac{S_0}{kN}, \qquad H(Y) = \frac{S^{Claus}}{kN}, \qquad H(Y|X) = \frac{\Delta S}{kN}. \tag{44}$$

However, a real observation process described in (44), equivalent to that one with $r = 1$, is impossible.

We conclude by that, the diminishing of the measured entropy value about ΔS against S^* awaited, evidenced by Gibbs Paradox, *does not originate in a watched system itself*. Understood this way, it is a contradiction of a *gnozeologic character* based on not respecting *real* properties of any observation [8–10].

With our sustaining on the 'fact' of the Gibbs Paradox reality also mean the circulating value of ΔS (in our brain) just depending on our starting point of thinking about the observed system with or without the (thought) railings. Simultaneously (&) and in the cycle our brain would have $[\Delta S < 0]$ & $[\Delta S > 0]$–see the validity of the Goedel Proposition V [3–5] for the inconsistent system $\mathcal{P}^*$.

This and, also, **Figure 1**, is the thermodynamic equivalent to the paradoxical understanding to the Goedel Incompleteness Theorems, also known as the Goedel Paradox. In fact, both

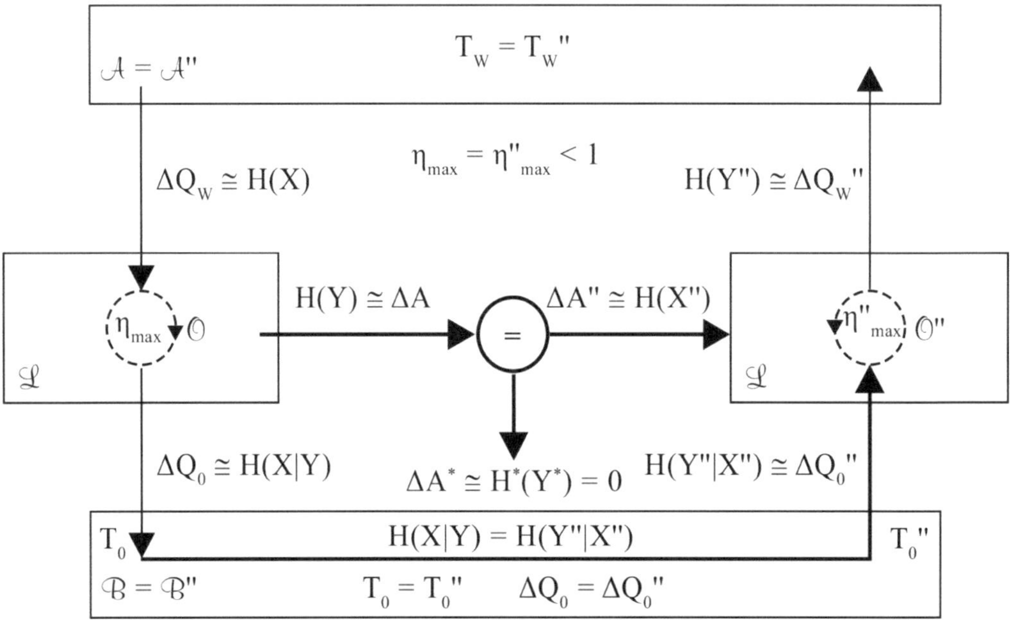

Figure 1. Stationarity of the double cycle $\mathcal{O}\mathcal{O}''$.

paradoxes do not exist in the described reality—they are in our brain, caused by the mixing of (our) consideration levels (the higher or methodology level and the lower or object/theoretical level) and, also, reveal themselves as the contradictions (on the lower level).

Acknowledgements

Supported by the grant of Ministery of Education of the Czech Republic MSM 6046137307.

Author details

Bohdan Hejna

Address all correspondence to: hejnab@vscht.cz

Department of Mathematics, University of Chemistry and Technology, Prague, Czech Republic

References

[1] Biedermann E. Sense or Nonsense? A Critical Analysis of Logical Antinomies. Cantor's Diagonal Argument and Goedel's Incompleteness Proof. 3rd revised ed. Boeblingen, pub. Biedermann, 1984; available from: https://en.wikipedia.org/wiki/User:Biedermann.

[2] None Cattabriga Paola OBSERVATIONS CONCERNING GOEDEL 1931. aeXiv:math/0306038v9 [math.GM] 4 Nov 2009

[3] Goedel K. Über formal unentscheidebare Satze der Principia mathematica und verwandter Systeme I. von Kurt Godel in Wien; Monatshefte fur Mathematik und Physik. 1931;**38**:173-198

[4] Goedel K. On formally undecidable proposition of proncipia mathematica and related systems. Vienna; 1931 translated by B. Metzer, 1962, University of Edinburgh.

[5] Včelař F, Frýdek J, Zelinka I. Godel 1931. Praha: Nakladetelstv BEN; 2009

[6] Grappone AG. Doubts on gödel incompletness theorems. Scientific Inquiry. 2008;**9**(I):51-60, IIGSS Academic Publisher

[7] Hejna B. Tepelný cyklus a přenos informace. In Matematika na vysokých kolách: Determinismus a chaos. Praha: JČMF, ČVUT; 2005. pp. 83-87

[8] Hejna B. Thermodynamic Model of Noise Information Transfer. In: Dubois D, editor. AIP Conference Proceedings, Computing Anticipatory Systems: CASYS'07—Eighth International Conference; American Institute of Physics: Melville, New York; 2008. pp. 67-75. ISBN 978-0-7354-0579-0. ISSN 0094-243X

[9] Hejna B. Informační význam Gibbsova paradoxu. In Matematika na vysokých kolách: Variační principy. Praha: JČMF; 2007. pp. 25-31

[10] Hejna B. Gibbs Paradox as Property of Observation, Proof of II. Principle of Thermodynamics. In Dubois D, editor. AIP Conf. Proc., Computing Anticipatory Systems: CASYS'09: Ninth International Conference on Computing, Anticipatory Systems, 3–8 August 2009; American Institute of Physics: Melville, New York; 2010. pp. 131-140. ISBN 978-0-7354-0858-6. ISSN 0094-243X

[11] Hejna B. Informační termodynamika I.: Rovnovážná termodynamika přenosu informace. Praha: VŠCHT Praha; 2010. ISBN 978-80-7080-747-7

[12] Hejna B. Informační termodynamika II.: Fyzikální systémy přenosu informace. Praha: VŠCHT Praha; 2011. ISBN 978-80-7080-774-3

[13] Hejna B. Information Thermodynamics, Thermodynamics—Physical Chemistry of Aqueous Systems. In: Moreno-Piraján JC, editor. InTech; 2011. ISBN: 978-953-307-979-0, InTech, Rijeka, Croatia, 2011. Available from: http://www.intechopen.com/articles/show/title/information-thermodynamics

[14] Hejna B. Recognizing the Infinite Cycle: A Way of Looking at the Halting Problem. In: Dubois DM, editor. Lecture on CASYS'11 Conference, Proceedings of the Tenth International Conference CASYS'11 on Computing Anticipatory Systems. Lie'ge, Belgium; August 8–13, 2011; CHAOS; 2012. ISSN 1373-5411

[15] Hejna B. Informační termodynamika III. Automaty, termodynamika, přenos informace, výpočet a problém zastavení. Praha: VŠCHT Praha; 2013. ISBN 978-80-7080-851-1

[16] Hejna B. Information Thermodynamics and Halting Problem. In: Bandpy MG, editor. Recent Advances in Thermo and Fluid Dynamics. InTech; 2015. ISBN: 978-953-51-2239-5. Available from: http://www.intechopen.com/books/recent-advances-in-thermo-and-fluid-dynamics

[17] Hejna B. Goedel Proof, Information Transfer and Thermodynamics, Lecture on IIAS Conference, August 3–8, 2015, Baden-Baden, Germany. Journal IIAS-Transactions on Systems Research and Cybernetics. **15**(2):48-58

[18] Mehta A. A Simple Refutation of Gödel's Theorem. 2001. http//www.ardeshirmehta.com/Godel-SimpleRefutation

[19] Rosser JB. Extensions of some theorems of Gödel and Church. Journal of Symbolic Logic. 1936;**1**:87-91